Spatial and Discursive Violence
in the US Southwest

Spatial & Discursive Violence in the US Southwest

ROSAURA
SÁNCHEZ &
BEATRICE PITA

Duke University Press
Durham and London 2021

© 2021 Duke University Press
All rights reserved
Designed by Aimee C. Harrison
Typeset in Whitman and Helvetica Neue Lt Std by
Copperline Book Services

Library of Congress Cataloging-in-Publication Data
Names: Sánchez, Rosaura, author. | Pita, Beatrice, author.
Title: Spatial and discursive violence in the US Southwest /
Rosaura Sánchez and Beatrice Pita.
Description: Durham : Duke University Press, 2021. | Includes
bibliographical references and index.
Identifiers: LCCN 2020021369 (print)
LCCN 2020021370 (ebook)
ISBN 9781478010609 (hardcover)
ISBN 9781478011736 (paperback)
ISBN 9781478021292 (ebook)
Subjects: LCSH: American literature—Mexican American authors—
History and criticism. | Violence in literature. | Indians of North
America—Colonization—Mexican-American Border Region. |
Discourse analysis. | Land settlement—Southwestern States. |
Southwestern States—In literature. | Southwestern States—History.
Classification: LCC PS153.M4 S263 2021 (print) | LCC PS153.M4 (ebook) |
DDC 810.9/979—dc23
LC record available at https://lccn.loc.gov/2020021369
LC ebook record available at https://lccn.loc.gov/202002137

Cover art: Judithe Hernández, *Coyolxauhqui Chicana*, 2008.
22 by 30 inches, pastel on paper.

To Our Parents

A. R. Sánchez
Frances Arteaga Sánchez

Joseph Pita
Beatriz Rodríguez López

Contents

Acknowledgments ix

Introduction 1
Spatial and Discursive Violence in the US Southwest

Chapter 1 26
Spatial Violence and Modalities of Colonialism: Enclosure

Chapter 2 43
Indigenous Spatial Sovereignty and Governmentality:
Rights and Wrongs in Oklahoma

Chapter 3 92
Enclosures in New Mexico: Land of Disenchantment

Chapter 4 148
Texas Narratives of Dispossession: When the Land Became Real Estate

Conclusion 202
Spatial Moorings and Dislocation

Notes 213
Bibliography 241
Index 253

Acknowledgments

All projects have a backstory. This project on enclosures in the US Southwest took a long time to finish as our teaching and mentoring obligations at the University of California at San Diego (UCSD) left little time for research and writing. Life intervenes.

We do very much appreciate the ongoing interaction with colleagues in the UCSD Departments of Literature, Ethnic Studies, History, and Communication for their comments on several of the issues we take up.

Without the writing of all the historians, economists, political scientists, theorists, critics, and novelists cited, our work would not have been possible, and we are most grateful for their scholarship and the opportunity to dialogue with them.

We also much appreciate all the interaction we have had with our graduate students in discussions of these topics in the last few years. We want to give a special thank-you to Barry Masuda of Hawaii, a former graduate student who first introduced us many moons ago to the Midnight Notes Collective and its work on new enclosures. From there we found the works of several other scholars, economists, political scientists, and critics, several of whom had their essays published in thecommoner.org.

Issues of enclosures, social space, gentrification, settler colonialism, and Marxism have been taken up in several graduate seminars and workshops, and we'd like to thank and acknowledge our more recent UCSD students, including Justin Wyble, Caitlin Yamamoto, Randy Williams, Ed Ortiz, Crystal Pérez, Adrian Arancibia, Chris Perreira, Anita Huízar-Hernández, Bernadine Hernández, Leonor McCrory, Melissa Martínez, Bernardo Núñez, Axel Montepeque, Ed Avila, Ryan Heryford, Andrew Escudero, Benjamin Balthaser, Alex Chang, Irene Mata, Martha Gonzales, Ofelia Cuevas, Demian Pritchard, Tania Triana, Yu-Fang Cho, Anna Eng, David Carroll, Irene Villanueva-Smith, Eric Cazdyn, Mari-Paz Balibrea, Mar Alberca, Stacey Trujillo, Norell Martínez, Andrea Zelaya, Jessica Aguilar, Gabriela Cázares, Gabriela Núñez, Alaí Reyes-Santos, Kim Hester-Williams, Jeanelle Horcasitas, Camila Gavin Bravo, Soraya Abuelhiga, Bailee Chandler, Gina di Grazia, Betty Ramírez, Reema Rajbanshi, Luis Cortés, Stephanie Gómez-Menzies, Susana Bustamante, Chris González Reyes, and Brenda Chávez. Our discussions across these many years have been immensely productive.

We acknowledge and appreciate the Duke University Press readers of the manuscript for all their tremendously helpful feedback, comments, and suggestions. We also want to express our gratitude and appreciation to everyone involved in the editorial process, with a very special note of appreciation to Ken Wissoker, Elizabeth Ault, and the Duke University Press staff for all their help in getting the manuscript ready for publication.

Un millón de gracias.

Introduction

SPATIAL AND DISCURSIVE VIOLENCE IN THE US SOUTHWEST

Spatial and Discursive Violence in the US Southwest deals at one level with the imposition of enclosures in the US Southwest during the seventeenth, eighteenth, nineteenth, twentieth, and twenty-first centuries and at another with their discursive configuration in Chicano/a and Native American literature. These processes of enclosure, carried out through colonization and settler colonialism by Spanish, Mexican, and US invaders, led to the dispossession and displacement first of Indigenous populations and later of *Nuevomexicano/a* and *Tejano/a* settlers. The loss of land was accompanied by transformations in relations of production and resulted in concomitant changes in subject formation as well. Invasion and colonization in the Southwest decimated Indigenous populations and led not only to their displacement, destitution, enslavement, and reduction to debt peonage, but also—importantly—to their resistance. Nuevomexicano/a and Tejano/a settlers, originally part of the colonial forces that deprived Indigenous populations of their lands, hunting grounds, and settlements, would in turn, after 1848, find themselves not only despoiled as well, becoming field or ranch workers on lands taken over by US invaders and settlers, but also subject serially to lynchings, massacres, and beatings. This process of dispossession and the various mechanisms of enclosure are central to the narratives that we examine in this work, each set within particular historical circumstances. Assessments of the various and distinct periods and regions discussed are central to our analyses; we start from the premise that the lived experience of those subjected to dispossession, exploitation, violence, and marginalization is often overlooked, as historians prefer to focus on macro events that enabled colonization and invasion. Literature, on the other hand, supplements and complements these accounts as it necessarily centers on characters' perceptions and affect, that is, the experience of enclosure and how it is processed by individuals and their respective collectivities. The narratives produced by Native American and Chicano/a collectivities index these transformations and register how they are perceived, made sense of, and both resisted and assimilated.

Enclosures, of course, have a long history not only in the Southwest and the rest of the United States but also in Latin America and throughout the world. Each particular phase of capitalist development has involved different strategies of enclosure to separate producers from the means of production, principally from the commons. Colonization and privatization are two important strategies and explain why geographical issues and the spatial ideologies that underpin the process of enclosure are fundamental to our understanding of history. In what follows we first address the notion of enclosure as a constituent element of capitalist relations and accumulation in the United States and how the mechanism of privatization is used to carry out spatial violence in the US Southwest.

But this geospatial violence is not specific to this area, nor, for that matter, an issue of bygone days. Recent events in the Amazon region, in Peru, Brazil, and Ecuador, where Indigenous groups continue to rise up to protest land concessions and to claim their right to make use of jungle territories that provide water, timber, and other resources threatened by transnational mining, oil and gas drilling, and logging enterprises are a clear sign that what we are terming enclosures are not a thing of the past; dispossession is an evolving process, not only in the Américas but in Africa and Asia as well. The issue of enclosures, or the separation of workers from their means of subsistence, to paraphrase George Caffentzis,[1] has also been referred to as "accumulation by dispossession," to use David Harvey's coinage.[2] Enclosures then are at the core of the ongoing accumulation of capital, and what makes this concept particularly productive is that it is not limited to land, as dispossession and displacement can take place in multiple domains. In every case, however, enclosures involve appropriation of space, that is, different types of spaces, including territorial, financial, political, and cultural spaces. Enclosure operates, in fact, as the structuring mechanism for both capitalist and imperialist undertakings, and in the United States it goes back to the very beginning of the nation-state.

While the analysis of imperialism in terms of two logics of power, the capitalist and the territorial, allows us to distinguish between neocolonialism and colonialism, in fact the two logics always go together, for, although not entirely capitalist, in the case of Spain, colonialism was never merely political and territorial but economically driven as well, as it enabled the primitive accumulation of capital. The term *primitive accumulation* is generally associated with the first enclosures in sixteenth-century England that gave rise to new social relations with the separation of producers (the serfs) from the commons; these early European enclosures signaled the end of feudal relations and followed both a territorial and economic logic. In the Américas, where enclosures began with the dispossession of the Indigenous populations by Spanish, British, and Portuguese colonizers, colonialism was always likewise both a territorial/military and an economic project, linked as much to the territorial and political expansion of Spain, Britain, and Portugal as to the accumulation of land, gold, and other resources and products.

Massimo De Angelis underscores that enclosures are a fundamental tenet in Marxist economic theory because capital always encloses.[3] As De Angelis, along with Michael Perelman and Caffentzis, has noted, enclosures are often studied as a historical phenomenon, that is, as sites of primitive accumulation.[4] Those who study history as a linear model of development are given to see enclosures as a precapitalist phenomenon that allowed for the accumulation of capital and enabled the transition in Europe from feudalism to capital. But as the Midnight Notes Collective, De Angelis, and even Marx make clear, there are both new and old enclosures, since enclosures are ongoing processes.[5] It is that ongoing and recurrent process of dispossession and privatization that structures our study of Southwest US history and its rendering in cultural forms.

In the transition to capitalism in Europe, common land was enclosed to prevent serfs from using the commons for subsistence. Land tenancy gave rise to "privatization" by "the landed gentry" who used "private" property as the mechanism for accumulating capital, forcibly changing the relations of production. If in Europe these enclosures were first carried out by violence by the lord's forces, by the eighteenth century in England, Marx notes, Parliament handily intervened and "the law itself [became] now the instrument of the theft of the people's land."[6] This shift has clear resonance in the future history of the US Southwest, as we shall see. Words and paper have as much a hand in the process of dispossession as guns and fences.

Land in England was expropriated and privatized, first by force and then through extra-economic means, like legislation. This separation of workers or producers from the means of production (and the redirection of their energies) has been a constant since the very onset of capitalism. In time, this expropriation and the twin processes of privatization and accumulation appear as a constant, even natural, process. In time as well, the privatization of land for new industries; the relocation of communities for roads, freeways, and dams; and the privatization of public services and basic resources, medications, or common space all come to be seen as normal. In more recent times, both economic and extra-economic forces have been brought to bear to produce and maintain this separation and the channeling of productive forces.

No one can be oblivious to the fact that the most egregious "hostile takeover" in the Américas was that of the land of native peoples post-1492. In *Indios, ejército y frontera*, Argentine historian and cultural critic David Viñas brilliantly details how the establishment of positivist liberal states in nineteenth-century Latin America effected the further destruction of the Indian commons, already initiated by European colonial enterprises.[7] As under the mission and *encomienda* systems, the dispossession of Indigenous populations by *hacendados* with the support of newly minted postindependence states was also accompanied by genocide, ethnic cleansing, and the further induction of Indians into forced labor. These processes, and the narratives of settlement (*gobernar es poblar*) by expansion and displacement voiced by the likes of nineteenth-century Argentina's Domingo Sarmiento, were likewise at work in Mexico, especially on the ranchos and haciendas further north, and resonated as well in Texas, New Mexico, and California. North, south, east, and west, enclosures were part of expansion and the juggernaut of modernization, underpinned and fostered by narratives of modernity.

Rationale for Enclosures: A Nation of Laws

Across time and place, enclosures and the reduction or outright loss of the commons were implemented by various means, including invasion and genocide but also coercion, laws, and fraud. Looking at US history, and more specifically at the wholesale dispossession of Indian lands after 1776, reveals that a variety of mechanisms were put in place to enable both the state and individuals to gain control of this ostensibly open territory. Thereafter, various mechanisms were mobilized to dispossess Indigenous populations in the US Southwest region as well as Californios/as, Tejanos/as, Nuevomexicanos/as, Louisiana French landowners, and formerly enslaved people. These included (1) state coercive practices, including wars, treaties, acts and laws, and court decisions; (2) disciplinary actions, including the naming of guardians, designating Native Americans as wards, and establishing reservations (what we might like to call open-air prisons); and (3) governmentality, including the chartering of government agencies that serve to control populations and allow for land takeovers, gentrification—what today goes by the name of redevelopment—and eminent domain, and, last but not least, outright theft and fraud.[8]

In the United States, this dispossession was, we must recall, based in part on exerting military force. Andrew Jackson's forays into the South and his success in forcing Native American tribes to make land cessions are abundantly well known.[9] But, as a rule, force was, more often than not, accompanied by legal measures and state policies that facilitated the use of outright coercion, as in the case of the Removal Act of 1830.[10] Political discourses at times contradicted what was put into effect, as, for example, when official policy (on paper at least) was that Indian lands would be taken only with the landholders' consent and that removal would be voluntary, when in fact native peoples were coerced to abdicate tenancy.[11] Policy statements are often at odds with practices. Moreover, Indians were promised compensation for land taken; yet for many Indian tribes the check is still in the mail. Other means, however, were also employed: fraud, bribery, debt, sale of alcoholic beverages to secure signatures, consumerism, and, foremost among them, the creation of bureaucratic state apparatuses like the Bureau of Indian Affairs, an institution that serves perhaps as the ideal exemplar of what Michel Foucault calls "governmentality."[12] In the dispossession of Mexicans, war, attacks by Texas Rangers and army soldiers as well as vigilantes, and legislation worked in tandem.

What took place in the US Southwest, and the Américas more broadly, was not at all a one-time event or even an anomaly. While speaking about wholly different geographical areas, years ago Samir Amin emphasized the continuous character of primitive accumulation,[13] leading De Angelis to remark further that "the fact that capital encloses is not something that has been sufficiently theorised by critical social and economic theory."[14] Enclosures, the latter notes, are "a continuous characteristic of 'capital logic' once we understand capital not as a totalised system but as a force with totalising drives that exists together with other forces that act as a limit on it."[15] Seen in this way, enclosures are thus constitutive and necessarily an ongoing practice, for capital is, by definition, always looking to "capitalize," to look for what Harvey calls "spatio-temporal fixes" for the overaccumulation of capital that is at one and the same time its goal and its bane.[16] These spatiotemporal fixes are intimately linked to imperialist practices, be they of old or more recent vintage. Today, some would argue that new enclosures are being practiced in a new era of globalization by transnational corporations, the International Monetary Fund, the World Bank, and various nation-states to dislocate peasants from their land and workers from particular industries, in turn giving rise to forced migration and public, as well as private, debt. Thus a variety of new strategies and mechanisms for dispossession are being deployed today. As previously noted, historically military force has been the sine qua non of capitalist development.[17] But it is not always the most cost effective.

In fact, any kind of practice that denies people the right, access, or entitlement to food and the means of subsistence implies dispossession; consequently, the practice of enclosure produces sites of contention and struggle; survival is often the trigger for migration or emigration.[18] As De Angelis notes, current global justice and solidarity movements are organizing precisely in terms of opposition to these new enclosures, for example, by opposing attempts to relocate communities to make space for dams, by resisting the privatization of public services and basic resources like water (as in the case of the 2000 water wars in Cochabamba, Bolivia[19]), by creating commons through occupation of land and buildings (contemporary squatting), by struggling against exclusionary patents (that, for example, make medications prohibitively expensive), and by downloading and sharing music and software. De Angelis further argues that an analytical framework is needed with which to study the "processes of identification, types and modes of enclosures" in the present historical conjuncture and, we would add, a framework that can address what we would like to call the lived "experience" of enclosures—past and present—which is precisely what we often find constructed in literature.[20]

Discursive Legitimation

The fact that this mechanism of enclosure has been actualized at different historical moments and throughout the world requires that dispossession be viewed in relation to the actual means, including coercion, by which the process of enclosure is carried out.[21] In all of these cases, we are talking not only about structuring mechanisms but about the historically specific enabling discourses and practices that allow it. In fact, De Angelis underscores that "if capital encloses it cannot do it without a corresponding discourse."[22] Here he refers to discourses that accompany the establishment of enclosures, that is, the arguments used to gain consensus by convincing populations of the rationality of enclosure based on the logic of capital accumulation, even at the cost of disregarding social needs. Of course discursive violence is itself almost always to some degree spatial, as in racist signs like "No Mexicans or Dogs Allowed" that even as late as the 1960s sought to exclude Mexicans from particular spaces in Texas or in racist comments like "Go back where you came from" voiced recently by the US president to deny people's rightful presence in this country. Here the discourse being marshaled is that of citizenship, the notion of identity and belonging. Race is also a discourse that plays a significant role in dispossession, with respect not only to Indigenous populations but also to Black farmers dispossessed between 1950 and 1969 of six million acres in the Mississippi delta, as noted by the US Commission on Civil Rights with respect to assistance denied to Black farmers by the US Department of Agriculture to enable the takeover of these lands by whites or corporations.[23] One of the points that interests us particularly in De Angelis's formulation is that here a specific subject formation is a necessary corollary of enclosure, as in the case of the transformation of serfs to wage laborers; new norms and regulations to which these subjects must adapt are also instituted. The state, in its supporting role to capital, is central in this as it often seeks the consent of the governed through, as pointed out above, a promotion of discourses of Americanization, fiscal and personal responsibility, debt management, trade liberalization, anti-inflation policies, and the like. Not to be forgotten, especially in speaking of nineteenth-century practices of enclosure, is the whole set of discourses of modernization/modernity that in the United States, Latin America, and elsewhere played out in terms of the opposition of *civilización v. barbarie* and cast those being dispossessed as antithetical to modernity.

The various forms of discursive violence in tandem with material enclosures lead to the despoliation not only of the commons but also of existing communities, for "there is no enclosure of commons without at the same time the destruction and fragmentation of communities."[24] It is this destruction of communities across US history that we would like to engage further in what follows. The fact, however, that the process of enclosing is an "ongoing feature of capitalist regimes" means that the phenomenon is not limited to the United States or to a specific period.[25] Our particular interest in the phenomena of enclosure, both old and new, requires seeing that in distinct historical periods various mechanisms of implementation and conceptual frameworks have served for the actualization of enclosures. Our overriding concern is the configuration of the experience of dispossession in the literary text. With this in mind, how then to approach the literary or cultural text? The text—and we will be talking principally about the novel genre—is a literary actualization with its own generative mechanisms and configurations. The structure of the novel is thus of particular importance, as the organization of the constitutive discourses of this content gives an indication of the historical perspective, that is, of the ideology that undergirds it. The narratives we examine do not—and cannot—provide us with a substantive analysis of the historical contradictions behind enclosure. That is not their raison d'être. Narratives can, however, provide partial analyses; some, especially if they are a pastiche of a particular period, may ignore the complexity and layering of mechanisms and discourses, while others may operate by summoning up amnesia or nostalgia. We consider a variety of elements, including structuring mechanisms, time-spaces, ideology, and other sociopolitical formulations that include race, ethnicity, gender, and class, to see how these are rendered in the texts as they register the aftereffects, as it were, of dispossession.

It makes sense, then, to start by discussing a variety of practices, policies, and discourses reconstructed in fiction that relate particularly to nineteenth- and twentieth-century enclosures in the United States and that have specifically affected Mexican-origin and Indigenous populations; these are discourses that are used either to legitimate and justify enclosures, on the one hand, or to counter and critique the establishment of these enclosures, on the other. Unsurprisingly, perhaps, we find enclosures to be the structuring mechanism of several novels in Chicano/a, Latino/a, Native American, and other literatures in the United States and Latin America. These works do not, of course, use the term *enclosure* or seek to engage deliberately with the concept.[26] Still, we argue, enclosure is the structuring mechanism behind many of these works that have the effect of documenting the experience of being separated from the means of production and in so doing reveal the inner workings of this process as well as the direct and collateral effects on affected communities.

Examining how literary texts deal with the actualization of dispossession and represent it requires that we focus first on the actual, historical events that led to dispossession in what is now US territory. For this, one of our necessary primary sources is the work of historian Paul W. Gates.[27] Time and space are likewise important considerations for us, for without periodization and a focus on regions we cannot begin to see patterns and draw comparisons. A brief discussion of the historical antecedents in England and Spain are to our mind crucial to an understanding of what happened in the Américas, but so are the particular patterns of colonization. The type of economy that developed—be it pastoral, agricultural, or mining—is a key factor, too, in the type of settlement and the particular distribution of lands. The mode of production in the homeland, whether it stressed a capitalist possessive individualism or aristocratic privilege with the personal services of subjected laborers, is also a significant differentiating factor. The next four chapters review how the dispossession of Indigenous populations took place under English, Spanish, and Mexican colonial regimes. As one should expect given the range of variables at work, dispossession took many different forms across time and space, but all were instances of spatial and discursive violence.

Geographical and Political Considerations

This work focuses on enclosures or, more precisely, on the multiple processes of land tenancy, dispossession, and displacement in the Southwest, during several temporalities that beginning in the late sixteenth century brought Spanish colonizers to occupy this space, principally to exploit it, but especially to claim it politically, particularly in view of rival claims by French, British, and Russian powers and later US threats of invasion. Long before the sixteenth century, however, perhaps even as long as 25,000 to 100,000 years ago by some accounts, the Southwest was home to Indigenous populations who used these lands for hunting, cultivation, and residence. Indigenous perspectives and experiences, absent in good measure from most histories of the Southwest (as well as from most Chicano/a literature), would clash with those of gold seekers, soldiers, missionaries, trappers, and settlers who saw these ostensibly open lands as prime for exploitation, appropriation, settlement, and cultivation. For the most part, colonizers saw Indigenous populations dwelling on these lands in one of two ways: either as obstacles to be removed or as a potential labor force to be exploited to gain access to gold, silver, land, crops, and service. The coming of land-hungry US settlers to the Southwest in the nineteenth century continued the dispossession of Indigenous lands begun in the earliest moments of British and Spanish colonization. Not altogether surprising perhaps, the sequential dispossession of Indigenous populations by Spanish, Mexican, and US soldiers and settlers would in turn be followed, after 1848, by the dispossession of Mexican settlers.

It will prove useful to think of the Southwest as a relative space, viewed, conceived, and lived according to the historical moment, the political and economic forces dominant in the area, the geographical location, and the demographic composition of the settlers and Indigenous inhabitants.[28] In the colonial era of New Spain, *la frontera*, the Southwest, was the back of beyond, under Spanish titular control but scantily populated by Spanish settlements, missions, or presidios. In the United States, the frontier designation varied, too, by historical period, at times designating an area west of the original thirteen colonies and later an area west of the Mississippi, the area of the plains, or the Northwest and Southwest. As defined famously by Frederick Jackson Turner, the frontier, for a series of reasons, attracted a continuous westward movement that enabled the United States to engage in a "perennial rebirth" as it expanded into new territory that offered opportunities for growth and "free land."[29] What Turner does not take it upon himself to account for is that this rebirth came at a cost; it was at the expense of Indigenous lives, relocated or exterminated in the process of expansionism. While obvious, clearly this territory was not at all vacant and was in fact taken over by force. Nor could the lands be construed as free. Even today the notions of the frontier and supposedly vacant lands in historical accounts skirt and therefore evade the issue of the United States as a colonizing power in an effort to normalize its expansion westward and distinguish itself from European colonial nations, setting itself apart as exceptional. Gareth Stedman Jones underscores this in saying that the United States' own imperial record is concealed by historians "who speak complacently of the absence of the settler-type colonialism characteristic of European powers [and] conceal the fact that the whole internal history of United States imperialism was one vast process of territorial seizure and occupation."[30] The westward movement cannot be seen as other than a concerted imperialist policy.

Aziz Rana examines the political history of the United States, finding that it has often been couched in terms of republican freedom and a search for liberty and economic independence. But, as he points out, this freedom aspect was accompanied by what he calls the "settler empire," which required the dispossession of Indigenous peoples and the subordination of non-Anglo groups, including Blacks, Mexicans, Chinese, and sometimes Catholic European groups as well as others.[31] As he notes, the mythology of exceptionalism and democratic equality has disregarded "a historical record riddled with ethnic, racial, and sexual exclusion, not to mention real class inequalities and conflicts."[32] A marked contradiction exists between myths of democracy (when in fact matters are decided by the very few, the elected elite sponsored by wealthy stakeholders) and the social and political reality of the vast majority of citizens and residents in this country, down to the present day. There is also a marked dissonance between claims of freedom and equality and the reality of spatial violence of a nation-state in good measure founded on genocide and slavery, that is, predicated, on the one hand, on the extermination and dispossession of Indigenous natives and, on the other, on African slavery. Another significant myth or chimera on which the edifice of American exceptionalism is built is the story of free land for those participating in the westward movement, a myth that some historians, like Lee Benson and Leslie E. Decker, have sought to debunk.[33] Clearly the Southwest cannot be viewed independently of the larger US territory and the land and social policies that affected residents in the nineteenth century and continue to do so today. And clearly, too, US imperialist policies presenting themselves in the twenty-first century can be traced back to the nineteenth century.

As a standpoint from which to depart, we view the Southwest as a territory that can be divided into separate regions and places marked by colonial and imperial differences. And though all the territory was once colonized by Spain, later by Mexico, and then the United States, the type of colonization differed significantly between Texas, New Mexico, and California in terms of established Indigenous populations, the type of colonization that took place (whether military, mission centered, or settler colonialism), the relative distance or proximity to other Spanish colonies or Mexican towns and the political/administrative center, the type of Indigenous land distribution and use, the type of land dispossession implemented, the type of immigration that the region attracted, and, especially, the mode of production and the type of economic development that marked each area. All these differences (geographic, demographic, economic, environmental, and political) served to mark distinctions between how the territory was conceptualized, perceived, and ultimately settled.

The territory that constituted northern Mexico after 1821 was vast; still, the link with Mexico lasted only a historical blink of an eye, that is, for a brief twenty-seven years (1821–48), and in the case of Texas an even shorter period, since Texas claimed independence in 1836, only fifteen years after Mexican independence. In some cases, the link to Spain was in fact stronger, in view, for example, of stipends that the Crown afforded soldiers and officers before 1821; thus, breaking colonial linkages in the process of occupation and deterritorialization, that is, by imagining the territory as no longer Spanish, was thus more difficult in some regions that did not align themselves immediately or positively to Mexican independence or later to the United States. For a different set of reasons, in the absence of strong, long-standing ties to Spain or Mexico, the reterritorialization of East Texas, that is, reimagining itself as an autonomous republic or as a US territory, was a relatively easy process for the Anglo settlers. The very heterogeneity and fluid history of the US Southwest precludes viewing it as a homogeneous region. These southwestern spaces have to be conceived in terms of different temporalities and spatialities and for that reason space and time—in particular in relation to land—need to be seen not as abstractions but as constitutive factors. What is equally clear is that losing the land as private property, in the case of the landed Mexicans, did not necessarily mean a diasporic relocation or losing access to the region. Access and habitation in these lands has, if anything, expanded with the arrival of millions of Mexican immigrant workers since 1848.

We focus primarily, but not strictly, on the representation of land dispossession in the vast territory that is the US Southwest, especially in the work of Chicano/a writers from Texas and New Mexico, viewing these textualizations in relation to historical accounts that address land dispossession. In their configurations of land loss, Chicano/a writers focus primarily on the Mexican loss of land as a defining moment marking the history of Tejanos/as, Nuevomexicanos/as, and Californios/as, for the most part eliding both the Spanish and Mexican dispossession of Indigenous peoples. Admittedly, these writings are in part a response to and refutation of Anglo writings on the notion of vacant lands, Manifest Destiny, and racial superiority. But they likewise evidence discourses bent on claiming Spanish (white rather than mestizo) ancestry and culture and a role in nation building, arguing that marginalized US populations of Spanish/Mexican descent have also contributed to the US national formation. This inclusivist—at times even celebratory, "we, too, are part of the US national narrative"—perspective contrasts sharply with that found in the work of Native American writers Roxanne Dunbar-Ortiz and Mishuana Goeman, who stand out in this regard and reject the multiculturalist narrative of inclusion, making the point that Native Americans are not one more in a succession of ethnic groups seeking inclusion within the US nation.[34]

The texts and writers taken up here are not concerned only with larger issues of space like land, but also with the importance of space in subject formation and with struggles for the control of those discursive spaces. Space, following Neil Smith, can be viewed as both the product of socioeconomic processes and relations and also productive of socioeconomic processes and relations.[35] From that, it follows, and we argue, that the Southwest needs to be seen as both a product of history and productive of history. We will therefore be looking at space in terms of geographical particularity and difference as we consider local, regional, national, and global spaces. The Southwest, inhabited first by Indigenous peoples, then colonized by Spain and Mexico, and later occupied by the United States, was also impacted by more global processes at work in different ways at different times; variables in local responses to colonization likewise reveal marked differences.

The overarching aim of this work, then, is to provide a historico-geographical reading of literary texts dealing with land, dispossession, and settler colonialism in the West and Southwest, focusing particularly on New Mexico and Texas, with discussion of Indigenous dispossession in Oklahoma as well. While Texas and New Mexico are the primary focus of this work, California is necessarily referenced at various times, but not extensively.[36] To lay out the contours and architecture of what follows, we start by exploring not only the concrete establishment of enclosures in the Américas, but also the various modalities of dispossession and colonization that took place in the Southwest between the sixteenth and twentieth centuries. Examining renderings of literary texts in conjunction with historical accounts, we explore issues of dispossession or enclosure in relation to imperialism and colonialism more globally and how these processes carried out or enacted what we are terming spatial and discursive violence in the Américas.

Problematics of Coloniality and Decolonization

Harry Harootunian notes that during the period of the Cold War, Western Marxism progressively distanced itself from economic realms to privilege the cultural, philosophical, and psychological, "especially in the domain of aesthetic production, art and literature, which contributed to valorizing a specific (and provincial) cultural endowment as unique, superior, and universal, regardless of its critical intent."[37] In his critique of cultural Marxism and of postcolonial theorists, Harootunian notes that these critics have often failed to note the coexistence of different temporalities and have failed to account for capital's subsumption of prior modes of production.[38] The confluence or conjuncture of different temporalities, by contrast, figures importantly in the literature that we examine.

This postcolonial move away from political-economic analysis to focus on cultural identities, difference, and what has been called "alternative modernity,"[39] could also be said to characterize current thinking in terms of coloniality as the explicatory historical/cultural paradigm on the ascendant in Latin America. Aníbal Quijano's assessment of colonialism in Latin America in terms of the "coloniality of power" makes a case for highlighting "difference," in this case racial difference, in view of the prevalence of a Eurocentric perspective of knowledge that naturalized colonial relations on the basis of race.[40] It is the colonization of culture that is foregrounded by those proposing the framework of the coloniality of power with an aim toward developing a new concept of modernity based not on the Westernization of non-European societies and cultures but on an alternative epistemic modernity, a "transmodernity" based on transculturalism that is the product of native or domestic epistemologies and modes of production.[41] Like Quijano, Walter Mignolo also sees the imposition of a Eurocentric perspective of knowledge and the blind and blatant ethnocentrism of Western philosophy.[42] Arguing for a consideration of the geopolitics of knowledge and the limits of Western philosophy ("the border where the colonial difference emerges") by stressing the production of a new subjectivity— "decoloniality"—to counter the "coloniality of being," Mignolo argues that the development of an epistemology from a subaltern perspective, from the perspective of colonial difference, is key to decolonization or liberation.[43] In view of the preeminence given to the cultural, it should not surprise us that the reference to the decolonial liberation to come from rejecting imposed Western paradigms speaks largely to an epistemic liberation rather than a material, revolutionary liberation. We would argue that it is not the logic of colonialism or coloniality, as defined by Mignolo, that defines the marginalized of the Américas but the logic of capitalism and dispossession, albeit as part and parcel of one another and mutually constitutive. Culturalist positions such as these privilege culture and tend to overemphasize the global representation of Eurocentric historiography and social science as the key problems, as is obvious in recent trends in Latino/a works stressing decolonization.[44] We argue that a parallel operation underlies the erasure of Indigenous material dispossession while stressing Indigenous cultural contributions.

In contradistinction to this approach, our focus is on cultural representation as a register, but not under a culturalist optic since our overriding concern in this work is what one might term the narrativization of history; put another way, what interests us is the material history of the Southwest, and—more importantly—the capacity of narrative to capture the layering of temporalities and to challenge dominant historical perspectives. To our minds, the coexistence of different temporalities is fundamentally linked to the coexistence of different modes of production attendant to different and contending logics.[45] Under colonialism, a subsumption of earlier forms of production takes place both in the colonial state and in the colonized site—this in view of capital's capacity "to take over what it found at hand and subordinate it to serve the pursuit of surplus value."[46] As noted earlier, formal subsumption or appropriation is what some economists term "accumulation through dispossession," or the establishment of enclosures; this process is naturally central to our work.[47] For example, Spanish colonization necessarily admitted the survival of Indigenous modes of production, especially during the encomienda system, even as Spanish feudal and semifeudal modes and later capitalist modes were being imposed. It is this notion of plural temporalities that will permit us to focus on the various layers of time that characterize all epochs and are especially in evidence in particular practices from different periods of Spanish, Mexican, and US colonialism in the Southwest. Most importantly, we argue that literary and/or cultural representations are productive sites to mine for historical evidence of this type of plural and oftentimes contending temporalities.

For its part, Chicano/a and Latino/a cultural production has of late focused on issues of decolonization, taking as a starting point that we are a colonized people, forgetting in the process—ironically perhaps—the role that our ancestors played as colonizers. Whether the colonizers in what is now the US Southwest were Spaniards, criollos, mestizos, or even Indigenous peoples like the Tlaxcaltecas, they all came from the interior of New Spain (now Mexico), in the name and in the service of the Spanish Crown, and they came north to dispossess the natives of what would become the US Southwest. On the receiving end of subsequent dispossessions, we must acknowledge, too, that we have conveniently developed a selective amnesia for our role in the colonization of the native peoples of the Southwest; our own role in the subjugation and exploitation of Indigenous peoples and, in some cases, the massacre of these natives cannot be skirted, downplayed, or displaced. Spanish colonizers, whatever their race or ethnicity, were in turn replaced by the Mexican state, later to be defeated by US soldiers. The settler colonists sent to the Southwest by Spain were the very same settlers later called Mexicans. Their role as dispossessors continued to be the same, whether under one banner or another. It bears recalling that most people of Mexican origin in the US today are not direct descendants of the initial Spanish or later Mexican colonizers in the Southwest, although New Mexican Hispanos do claim this distinction, choosing to disregard their *mestizaje* with local Indians, as do some Tejanos/as in the lower Rio Grande valley. We are, however—whether we want it or not—descendants of Spanish, mestizo, mulatto, and Indigenous peoples who, by being part of the colonies of New Spain for some three hundred years, were imbricated and implicated in the colonizing enterprise. If truth be told, most of our actual ancestors came to the US Southwest much later than 1848 and primarily after 1900 as immigrants, where they in turn faced xenophobia, racism, exploitation, violence, and classism when they arrived, not altogether unlike what they had experienced in the lands from which they migrated and not unlike what we continue to experience today in the United States.

Our overriding interest, then, lies in examining how history, especially the history of enclosures, is emplotted in literature and how the multilayered temporalities in history are registered and configured. It is in the intersection of these temporalities, an intersection given in dissonance and effected through spatial and discursive violence simultaneously, that contradictions are made visible.[48] A linear view of history inherent in most historical accounts does not—and cannot—capture the complex intersection in dissonance of multiple forces and dimensions. Literature, on the other hand, given its play with structure, voice, and literary strategies and techniques, is perhaps more able to configure multiple temporalities, narrativize the depth of a moment, and explore subject formation under changing spatiotemporal conditions. While no doubt at times guilty of idealizing and attempting to rescue the past as a quasi-utopian space of freedom and enjoyment, literature is nevertheless able to provide a complementary account of the subsumption of precapitalist modes of production by capital and in the process represent the tensions and contradictions of unevenness introduced by this fusion of previous moments along with emerging economic and political configurations.

Historical and Literary Approaches to the Analysis

It becomes necessary, or at least expedient, to lay out some of the tools, concepts, and strategies that we work with in detailing spatial and discursive violence in what follows. Likewise, it is useful to point to continuities in contemporary Chicano/a and Latino/a writing. Dispossession or its enactment through enclosure is not at all a thing of the past. It is still ongoing in the form of displacement, although now in urban areas, a product of urban renewal, gentrification, and eminent domain, and as such it very much continues to be configured in the early twenty-first-century work of Chicano/a and Latino/a fiction writers. Just two examples make the point of the ongoing relevance of these issues. Dispossession is the overriding topic, for example, in *Chavez Ravine*, in which the playwrights and performers of Culture Clash focus on a twentieth-century case of dispossessed Los Angeles barrio dwellers.[49] Dispossession, as we find in this play, can be effected by force or by legislation, or more likely both. Here it is urban planning and eminent domain, for what is purportedly to be a public housing development that led the Los Angeles City Council in the early 1950s to evict and relocate residents from Chavez Ravine, an area of three Chicano/a communities close to downtown Los Angeles: La Loma, Palo Verde, and Bishop. Residents were told that after the public housing units were in place they could return, but the housing project was canceled and the area used instead for the construction of privately held Dodger Stadium. Dispossession and displacement are likewise topics configured in the fine 2007 Helena María Viramontes novel *Their Dogs Came with Them*, which focuses on another Los Angeles instance of dispossession.[50] In this case, the state of California in the 1960s again used eminent domain to buy up land in the East Los Angeles barrio for the construction of a complex freeway system. The East Los Angeles Interchange, consisting of six feeder freeway segments connecting four highways, would displace a good number of Chicano/a residents of East Los Angeles. Displacement also takes place today in urban spaces undergoing gentrification as landlords push low-income tenants out to make room for affluent residents. Smith's analysis of rent gap theory and the impact of gentrification on Puerto Rican renters in Spanish Harlem is likewise captured in Ernesto Quiñonez's novel *Chango's Fire*, where displacement is forced by arson.[51] It goes without saying that the phenomenon of gentrification is taking place broadly, displacing for the most part poor and minority populations.

This work, however, deals primarily, but not exclusively, with configurations of land loss in the nineteenth and early twentieth centuries in Oklahoma, Texas, and New Mexico, focusing on how enclosures and discursive violence figure in cultural production. Land loss has often been seen in relation to the loss of Spanish- or Mexican-era land grants, but that is a rather limited (and limiting) example of the dispossession of peoples in the Southwest. Still, the perspective of historians on land grants—somewhat ironically—is quite useful in highlighting precisely what has been left out by historians and what is possibly better addressed by fiction writers. It will be in these gaps that we find the most intriguing aspects of this reading of history through literature.

In their volume *Land, Water, and Culture: New Perspectives on Hispanic Land Grants*, editors Charles L. Briggs and John R. Van Ness note that a number of studies of Hispanic land grants have been published in recent years from a variety of disciplinary perspectives, but the editors also reflect on the inadequacy of the existing literature on land grants in view of a number of crucial gaps.[52] Some of the lacunae they mention—interestingly—include failure to deal with resistance to Anglo-American domination, the day-to-day activities of land grant residents, the way land grant communities see their history and land/water rights, the physical characteristics of the land, the way land has been used by residents, and the way these factors have affected the settlement of grants: "That is to say, the human ecology has been largely ignored."[53] Briggs and Van Ness further note that many of these studies are written from the perspective of non-Hispano and non–Native American scholars who find it difficult to deal with the notions of community ownership of land, the role of local custom in determining land rights, and the resonance and implications of these land issues beyond a Southwest audience.[54]

For their part, historians like Gerald E. Poyo and Gilberto M. Hinojosa and other contemporary historians also provide a critique of Borderlands historians who fail to "analyze the dynamics of community formation and development" and lament that the few local narratives available "provided only vague references to townspeople and Indians."[55] Others, like Samuel Truett and Elliott Young, suggest a transnational historical approach in a world with border crossers, while still others, like Marvin Mikewell and Alexander Murphy, propose a comparative global approach.[56] A few, like Pekke Hämäläinen and Benjamin H. Johnson, offer historical analyses that consider sex, gender, class, and marriage in their compilation of abridged articles by numerous authors.[57] We agree that this broadening of studies whose scope focuses on the "cultural and socioeconomic underpinnings of Hispanic communities" is necessary.[58] Some Chicano/a historians are understandably especially dissatisfied with a Spanish Borderlands approach that analyzes the Spanish colonial period but does not go beyond it. The Spanish Borderlands notion, as noted by David J. Weber, was derived from Herbert E. Bolton's framework that analyzed the experiences of Spanish colonials in the Southeast and Southwest; some recent historians, however, see no meaningful continuities between the two areas, nor do they see the Borderlands as ending with the Spanish colonial period.[59] Interestingly, Bolton's focus on the Spanish period undoubtedly also influenced early twentieth-century fiction and autobiographical works that sought to stress the Iberian connection. While it is important to note the presence of Spanish colonial settlements in the Southeast long before the British came to the so-called New World, especially in view of the neglect of the Spanish presence in US history, it is also crucial to be conscious of the key differences between colonization in the Southeast and Southwest. Some historians see the Borderlands approach as tied to the US nation-state narrative, with borderlands seen only with respect to the US-Mexico border. Other historians, like José Cuello, see a strong relation between the Southwest and the Mexican colonial north.[60] Taken as a whole, however, historians are increasingly critical of the imperial institutional approach within the Borderlands framework that focuses primarily on missions, presidios, and villas controlled by Crown officials, rather than on social relations, modes of production, and autonomous local interests. Especially absent have been accounts of class and racial relations between settlers and between Spanish settlers and Indigenous tribes, often reduced to comments on raids and conflicts. It is here that more recent scholarship, like that of Southwest historians Raul Ramos and Omar S. Valerio-Jiménez, has taken steps to remediate these lacunae and biases.[61]

These absences and implicit biases within academic historiography and social science scholarship need, however, to be borne in mind as one examines fiction itself. How is land in the Southwest represented in our literature? What is said about social relations, culture, modes of production, and socioeconomic relations between settlers and Indigenous groups? A look at several Tejano/a, Nuevomexicano/a, and Native American texts allows for locating sites of comparison vis-à-vis what historians and sociologists discuss in their scholarship. The question is whether cultural production—and specifically fiction—offers a different perspective, although not necessarily a less biased examination of nineteenth- and early twentieth-century Southwest experiences. While the texts that we consider are quite diverse in their structure, literary strategies, and historical perspective and have been produced in different periods, but primarily in the twentieth century, several limit themselves to a representation of quaint village life, colorful characters, magical events, and the importance of making clear that within these communities there were (often) white, highly intelligent, educated individuals, and that not all were like the Mexican street people to be found in the cities and towns. Ramos puts a finer point on studying social hierarchies within Béxar and the social barriers between military and civilian, elite and poor in Texas. And though some historians write of a "relatively unstratified class and racial structure" and of shifts in attitudes among the Béxar elite, even they admit that when it came to marriage, and therefore to land tenancy and transfer, there was by 1780 a decidedly ethnic racial elite or, more rightfully, a socioeconomic elite operating throughout the area.[62] A dominant elitist and sometimes outright racist positioning is at the core of what we are terming spatial and discursive violence.

Put in broader terms, the question in analyzing Chicano/a literature dealing with nineteenth- and twentieth-century dispossession in the Southwest is, whose story has currency? Whose story is left out? What is said about dispossession? Where and by what means is a discursive violence being enacted?

We have found that the narrative told is primarily that of the landed, whether of Spanish or Mexican origin. By and large—as might be expected—the peons' and servants' stories have not carried weight, much less the story of Indigenous peoples. The narrative more often than not is that of the colonizers, the very same people who dispossessed the Indians. When Anglo settlers and soldiers arrived, the tables were turned and the Spanish/Mexican colonizers became in turn dispossessed, primarily of their land and power. Some of the settler colonists in South Texas, for example, continued to possess the land for a while; they maintained their Spanish language and their culture as the majority population in the lower Rio Grande valley, although English became the dominant official language. Later, macroeconomic factors, that is, changes in the mode of production, led to wholesale land transfer. In New Mexico, as in Texas, legal and economic factors likewise facilitated the eventual loss of land.

For the most part, our Chicano/a literature does not present early settlers, ranchers of Spanish and Mexican origin, as colonizers, as those who deprived Indigenous populations of their lands, killed a good number of them, and reduced a good portion to peonage and slavery, but rather as brave and intrepid settlers, bringing order and modernity to either (1) an empty landscape or (2) a barbaric hinterland. Much is made, on the other hand, of the Spanish origin of these landed ancestors, as if to stress that Nuevomexicanos/as and Tejanos/as, too, are white. The demonstrable truth is that most of the population of Mexican origin in the United States today, as previously noted, can trace their ancestry not to these early colonizers but to subsequent waves of immigrants, primarily mestizo, mulatto, and Indigenous peoples. Attempts at disavowing our role in the colonial enterprise and what might be termed "whitewashing" this history cannot go unacknowledged and are part and parcel of the violent processes carried out on spatial and discursive terrains simultaneously.

It goes without saying that geography plays a prominent role in Chicano/a literature; geography is in many ways destiny, and to recall Harvey, "All geography is historical geography and all history is geographical history."[63] But a caveat is in order: treating these works as part of a homogeneous territory is also highly problematic. As previously noted, many historians have found the Borderlands framework to not be an effective model for analyzing Spanish and Mexican settlements. But if the Borderlands approach has its shortcomings, so, too, does the treatment of the Southwest as one homogeneous region and Chicanos/as as a monolithic grouping. The Southwest, where the majority of people of Mexican origin still reside, is quite diversified, and the particular histories of the areas are quite different. For, as we shall see, colonial settlement in New Mexico, Texas, and California in the seventeenth, eighteenth, and nineteenth centuries varied widely in terms of demographics, class, race, social interaction with Indigenous populations, and proximity to other Spanish/Mexican communities. In fact, the very notion of region would have to be redefined, since in Texas, for example, North Texas and South Texas constituted two distinct and differentiated regions. Shifting territorial boundaries throughout this period also point to the need for a more complex, multiperspectival regional approach that considers and accounts for the multiplicity of temporalities in place in each.

Critical Antidote: Discursive Violence and the Damage Done

Ethnic minority writers in the United States have often felt the need to recount a history that has been neglected, erased, or misrepresented by official discourses and mainstream writers. Often the fictional accountings of the marginalized involve reconstituting memories of the past, whether memories of the writer, of his or her family, or of particular characters. In some cases memory is not only the other side of amnesiac forgetting but should also be seen in contradistinction to nostalgia, as pointed to by Houston A. Baker.[64] Nostalgia as a narrative modality often, if not always, results in a pastiche of a stereotypical past.[65] As Fredric Jameson makes clear, the nostalgic mode is incompatible with genuine historicity, and, in line with Baker, nostalgia conceives of past struggles as a "well-passed aberration."[66] Critical memory, on the other hand, "judges severely, censures righteously, renders hard ethical evaluations of the past that it never defines as well-passed."[67] It is Baker's notion of critical memory that we draw on and adapt in our analysis, while bearing in mind other key notions like those of "cultural memory," "national memory," and "historical memory."[68] In all these cases we have in mind collective memories—or even an intergenerational, almost genetic blood memory as some conceive it—but not always national memory, as in fact several collective memories necessarily coexist within a nation-state, whether within the United States or Mexico, as examples. Likewise, all of these forms of memory involve the effacing or repression of particular memories or traces of memories and, at the same time, the construction, deployment, and manipulation of false memories.[69] How does one then go about a more systematic and revealing analysis of particular effacings, manipulations, distancing, and reformulations of memories? What is the discursive violence being enacted at that level and, more importantly perhaps, to what end? Jameson's notion of strategies of containment provides an access point, for clearly memory is always constituted and contained within particular ideological parameters.[70] Memory, too, is a contested terrain and site of discursive violence that is ironically, not merely in name only, rhetorical.

What we want to stress is that memory and identity are often closely linked to place, and while obvious, there is, as Harvey puts it, a "strong association between place, memory, and identity."[71] Local space is key to the fiction to be analyzed. In several of these texts there is also an overt attempt to construct—or rather reconstruct—a relational memory, a fluid spatial-temporal site subject to numerous influences.[72] But whose memories are being constructed in these various texts? As previously noted, it will be primarily the memory of the elite, the landed colonists, that gets figured. One's social location or relative positioning affects the specific standpoint from which one recalls—or reconstitutes—the past.

The writing of fiction that reconstructs memory, much like historiographic narratives themselves, implies the rewriting or recoding of textualized history, and these rewritings can vary greatly. Weber's examination of perspectives on the Pueblo Revolt of 1680 in what is now New Mexico offers a prime example. In his introduction to a volume that includes essays by five historians of this watershed event, Weber points to several readings. While historians agree, for the most part, on what happened, there is much disagreement as to why. Some posit religion as a primary cause for the uprising; others offer an economic explanation that incorporates additional elements like drought, famine, and Apache raids; still others look to demographic changes and miscegenation.⁷³ These multiple readings within the field of history are, of course, to be found as well when both the object and the optic lens are literary; both readings, however, are necessarily partial in scope and never impartial.

Recent historically revisionist fictions are particularly interesting in this regard. If one takes, for example, the 1999 novel *Shaman Winter* where through the device of a dream sequence Rudolfo Anaya presents how his twentieth-century detective, Sonny Baca, visits 1680, the year of the Pueblo Revolt, one finds that the past here is a simulacrum and accuracy of representation is not an issue. What stands out in Anaya's rendering and representation is the Pueblos' collective decision to rebel, predicated by the Spaniards' flogging and hanging of their medicine men, the prohibition of their rites and prayers to their kachinas and other religious practices, and the destruction of their kivas; although backgrounded, it comes through clearly as well that they were also concerned with the ongoing pestilence, drought, hunger, and wars brought by the Spanish.⁷⁴ While the men visiting the kiva mention the enslavement of their women and children, they do not bring into the picture the odious Spanish colonial encomienda system that underpinned that enslavement. Anaya's focus on religion as the primary cause and concern is in keeping with the rest of the novel, which puts into high relief shamans, kachinas, and the impact of the supernatural on moral and ethical issues of today. That said, Anaya's work stands out for its multiple temporalities and its incorporation of Indigenous concerns and revolts. In that way, it is unique in Chicano/a literature, in which Indigenous history and issues have rarely been configured, unless it is to focus, for example, on Aztec cosmogony. By contrast, as we will see later, the 2009 novel *Forgetting the Alamo, Or, Blood Memory* by Emma Pérez does make it a central point to exercise critical memory and to acknowledge the presence of Indigenous peoples in Texas in 1836, presenting us with another all-too-rare, if brief, instantiation of that often-erased history in our literature.⁷⁵

By and large, however, an overture to realism is the dominant mode of representation in the fictional narratives dealing with enclosures that we will analyze. A suggestive trend in some recent ethnic minority criticism argues for examining ethnic literature in terms of "peripheral realism."⁷⁶ In their work, Jed Esty and Colleen Lye, for example, convincingly point to the importance of theorizing "the referential function of the text," arguing that a peripheral vantage point has much to offer in its recoding of history.⁷⁷ We agree with Esty and Lye that this off-center, eccentric as it were, recoding of sociospatial considerations is crucial for understanding the process of enclosures and for analyzing how they are conceptualized and represented in literature. As spatial-temporal constructions, enclosures require multilayered frameworks that take into account not only the historical moment, the phase of the capitalist mode of production, and the type of enclosure, but also how these enclosures are spatially enacted and imposed. While we draw from a range of frameworks for our analysis of enclosures and literature, the peripheral standpoint suggested by Esty and Lye interests us in particular as we look at what literature includes or leaves out about dispossessions of the past and how it examines earlier periods. We will look to these peripheral representations of nineteenth-century local events for the relevancy of these renderings for regional histories, even when there is—perhaps necessarily—partial distortion involved. In this regard, a brief example is telling: Alejandro Morales's 1983 novel *Reto en el Paraíso* deals in part with spatial violence through a narrative that recounts the dispossession of the historical figure Antonio Coronel.[78] While dispossession of Mexican landowners was in fact widespread throughout the US Southwest after 1848, in this particular case, the Californio Coronel, who supported the Confederacy during the Civil War, who was elected treasurer of the state of California, and who profited personally from the forced sale of Californio lands, cannot be construed as the unmitigated, blameless victim of dispossession through violence as he is represented in Morales's novel. Yet the novel does allow for enunciating a peripheral and translocal vantage point of the many who lost their land in California, even if not in the specific instance recounted. Fiction by definition takes liberties with history, but then again so does historiography. Our analysis thus calls for a review of the historical moments as well as the implementation of a theoretical framework that examines—and takes seriously—how these spatial and sociohistorical issues are configured in literary texts in all their complexity, contradiction, and discursive violence. Space, like time, as we know, is multilayered and variable, and often the site of violence as well. The same follows for literature.

The next four chapters look at the spatial and discursive violence enacted by a variety of both old and new enclosures in the US Southwest and address the range of modalities these enclosures exhibit, including those imposed by force and violence, by means of legislation and treaties, or by court decisions and governmentality as well as through debt and, even more recently, by neoliberal policies, urban renewal, and eminent domain policies.

A short conclusion takes up the overarching issues discussed and the centrality of identity as tied to land—as well as land loss—as an experience, both formative and traumatic. The inscription, as it were, of this relationship to the land and the mechanisms by which land is alienated from its inhabitants is registered in the literature produced in the affected areas and underscores the importance of a nuanced accounting for spatial and discursive violence. We end by discussing the import of contemporary changes and new patterns of the ongoing process of enclosures evident in the current moment and think on how these might lead to the generation of new senses of place identity as we move further into the twenty-first century.

1

Spatial Violence and Modalities of Colonialism

ENCLOSURE

Understanding land policies and practices in the United States and especially in the Southwest in the nineteenth century requires some sense of what came before colonization and what the situation was like in Europe with respect to enclosures and land tenancy. We need to account, if briefly, for past enclosures to understand what came to be in the future, which is our past and present. Before looking at literary examples of how enclosures in the Américas have been figured, it is important to consider as well the type of colonial policies and practices followed in the Américas by the imperial powers of Spain and England. Historians and anthropologists suggest distinguishing between colonialism and settler colonialism, although the latter was part of colonialism, and colonial powers, like Spain, followed varied patterns of colonization at different moments.

The distinctions made by historians and anthropologists on whether to call the European colonization process colonialism or settler colonialism depend in good measure on how colonists dealt with native populations. Did they include or exclude them, and how? In the case of settler colonialism, the land itself was the primary objective; for that reason, incoming settlers sought to displace Indigenous populations, either by forced removal or by extermination, as with British and later US colonization.[1] In the case of colonialism, European colonizers took the land by force but used the labor of natives for the extraction of resources and production, as occurred throughout Latin America. Forced dispossession from the land was often accompanied by extra-economic means, as noted by Marx, and legal discourses were used to justify the spatial violence perpetrated.[2] For example, colonizers as a rule failed to recognize land rights if they were not held privately and if the titles were not recorded in European fashion. Since lands were often held in common, there was no documented native title, no legal evidence that the land was the property of a community. The absence of title was seen as justification for declaring native lands *terra nullius* (land belonging to no one, unoccupied land) and, therefore, "naturally" available to European settlers.[3]

Until relatively recently, US historians did not often focus on or recognize the dispossession of Indians in the United States, other than to call them savages and obstacles to Anglo settlement. Even Paul W. Gates recognizes this discursive violence: "All regarded them as belonging to an inferior cultural group to be used or pushed aside as conditions seemed to warrant."[4] Adolf Berle wants to argue that the United States in the nineteenth century was not involved in imperialist acts: "America in the nineteenth century did expand, but into empty land. It is one thing to conquer a subject people; another to occupy vacant real estate."[5] For Berle, the thousands of Indians in what was to become US territory must have been invisible, much like the Mexicans in the Southwest. The notion of vacant land would thus be a frequently used discourse to justify enclosures, that is, the dispossession of both Indians and Mexicans in the nineteenth century.

Dispossession is thus key to understanding settler colonialism, since the settler plans to reside on the land for life. In effect, the settler often comes to see himself as the authentic native and strives to claim Indigenous status, as noted by Lorenzo Veracini.[6] The very indigeneity of any Indigenous community is called into question, and these community members, ironically, are perceived, portrayed, and treated as "exogenous Others."[7] Today, Palestinians, for example, who have lived on the land for thousands of years, are sometimes represented as non-Indigenous to Palestine in an attempt to justify Israeli dispossession of them and validate Israeli settler colonialism. These "undesirable others" are then removed from the land or transferred and segregated, although there is also the possibility of an assimilatory selective inclusion. Those deemed "unimprovable" are permanently cast out from certain areas, despite being former inhabitants of that land.[8] Here, as took place in the US context, land rights accrue to the "native" newcomers at the expense of the autochthonous peoples.

Perhaps one of the best examples of enclosures that were instituted with colonialism is that offered by Marx regarding Ireland, an island invaded as early as the twelfth century by Anglo-Normans.[9] By the seventeenth century the land had been confiscated by the English conquerors, with the English aristocracy becoming the new landlords, determining the terms and conditions under which the Irish could work and live on the land, with the ensuing system of exploitation of the small tenant farmer reducing the Irish population to appalling poverty.[10] The famine of 1845–47 that came with the failure of the potato crop, even as the export of grain, the basis of the landlord's rent, increased, led to An Gorta Mor, the Great Hunger, with the starvation of at least a million people in Ireland and mass emigration to the United States.[11]

Enclosures on Indian Lands in the Américas

Before 1492, Indigenous populations of the Américas possessed the land, which was held in common and was the source of subsistence. Some Indigenous peoples in the Southwest cultivated the land primarily with corn, squash, and beans, while others used the land primarily for hunting bison, deer, turkeys, and other fowl as well as for fishing and gathering. Most combined modes of production and subsistence. These communal lands were not private property, although Indigenous territorial claims to certain areas were both acknowledged and recognized by other tribes or challenged by invading tribes, with Indigenous groups having to relocate. With colonization, especially by the English and Spanish, Indians across the Américas would lose control of their lands and suffer a cataclysmic decrease in population resulting from violence, disease, and dislocation. How these lands were expropriated, always involving direct or indirect force, was a matter of differing colonial policies that emerged from practices already existing in particular European territories.

Differences in colonial policies are generally linked to European historical events. As Robert Brenner has proposed, "Different class structures, specifically property relations or surplus-extraction relations, once established, tend to impose rather strict limits and possibilities, indeed rather specific long-term patterns, on a society's economic development."[12] We argue that the specific property relations, or what we also call relations of production, in England are what determined the direction that colonization took in the English colonies in the eastern part of what became the United States, just as feudal property relations in Spain and attempts to reproduce the class structure of Castile are what in good measure led to the establishment of some variant of latifundia in Spanish colonial América. While in most of Western Europe by 1500 there emerged "an almost totally free peasant population" so that serfdom was dead by the early sixteenth century,[13] the debasement of the peasantry continued in parts of Spain.[14] Relations of production in the colonizing countries, still in flux as they were, would in fact be fundamental in determining the type of land tenancy and economic structure established in the so-called New World.

Spanish conquerors and later settlers coming to the Américas established the "same seigniorial system, the same latifundist and mortmain organization as in Spain."[15] While in Spain there might have been many peasants hungry for land, early immigrants to the Américas did not come to till the land; they came to seek wealth through mining. In the early part of the sixteenth century there were relatively few Spaniards in the New World, some fifteen thousand. By the middle of the century that figure had grown to some 120,000.[16] The continent's native population, some 12 million according to some estimates (25 million in Mexico alone according to others), was reduced to 9 million in fifty years and in the next century declined even further, with only 1 million in Mexico by 1605.[17] This demographic catastrophe would be a key factor in the importation of Black slaves.

The British began colonizing the east coast of what is now the United States in the seventeenth century, with earlier failed attempts in the late sixteenth century. There were three types of English colonies: charter, royal, and proprietary. In all cases, dispossession of Native populations involved a type of force, whether military or legal, means that have always been explained away as necessary and justifiable. Once under the control of English soldiers, Indian land was acquired by colonists from English charter companies, proprietors, or the king through payment of money; this now-private property was then improved and worked by white indentured poor laborers or convicted felons, prior to the establishment of slavery.[18]

Spanish Enclosures: Space Invaders

Spanish invaders and colonizers arrived in the Américas long before the British. In fact, they explored the northern continental land mass, what came to be called the Spanish Borderlands, as early as 1513 and tried to establish a mission as far north as Virginia as early as 1570 at Ajacan, long before the English explored Virginia and eventually founded Jamestown in 1607. The first colonizers of the East Coast involved in massacring Indigenous populations, subjecting them to servitude and slavery, and dispossessing them of their lands were, in fact, the Spanish. Like the British, the Spanish also considered Indians savages and treated them as inferior beings, questioning whether they were even to be considered human. The later colonization in the Southwest carried out by Spanish and subsequently Mexican soldiers, settlers, and missionaries also led to the decimation and frequent displacement of Indians. Interestingly, this is not a period that Chicano/a historians much deal with or dwell on, as most focus their historical accounts primarily on the US invasion of 1846 and the subsequent colonization and dispossession of Tejanos/as, Nuevomexicanos/as, and Californios/as; it is a formative period nonetheless.

Spain developed various colonizing modalities in its territories in the Américas. David J. Weber notes that at the onset of Spanish colonialism, Spain went in with military force to subdue Indigenous populations.[19] Soldiers were always accompanied by missionaries, who came to Christianize the inhabitants, as the Crown and the Church worked side by side in this colonial venture. Conquered land was considered to be the property of the Crown, and there were no allotments to individuals, a situation that soon brought complaints from the conquerors. As in the Spanish Peninsula, where feudal relations of production and latifundia prevailed and land was owned primarily by the nobility and the Church, in the Américas, Spanish conquerors and colonists took control of the common lands for the Crown under the encomienda system. The land and Indian pueblos were entrusted to an *encomendero* who forced Indian pueblos to continue producing either as before or in new areas, like the mining regions; they were then obliged to pay tribute not to the regional dominant group, the Aztec hierarchy, for example, but to the Spanish encomendero.

The depopulation of Native peoples resulting from their harsh treatment in the fields and mines, the poor diet, and the diseases brought over by the Spanish led to a wholesale decrease in the number of workers on the encomienda. Although the monarchy tried several times to prohibit encomiendas, they continued to exist until the mid-sixteenth century, when they began to be replaced by land allotments to conquerors and explorers. Structurally, by the seventeenth century the encomienda was for the most part a thing of the past, and it would be the privately held hacienda, rancho, or finca, under the control of *latifundistas*, the large landholders, mostly Spanish or criollo (Spaniards born in the Américas) that dominated production in Mexico.[20] By the eighteenth century, however, as Spanish settlers began arriving from Spain, a mixed colonialism ensued: both military and settler colonialism. Under the latter, Indigenous workers became servants for families in towns and/or servants and peons on the ranchos and haciendas.[21]

The inclusion of Jesuit or Franciscan missionaries was an important part of all Spanish colonial expeditions, and in many cases the establishment of missions in existing villages became the principal mechanism for colonizing and Christianizing the Américas, forcibly disciplining and assimilating Indians. In these cases, fewer soldiers were necessary to accompany the missionaries, who through the establishment of missions sought to recruit the Native population from scattered villages into artificial mission communities. Enticing Indians to live in the mission communities was economically important as they were the main producers and workers, but missionization was not always readily accepted. According to Weber, colonial administrators found that while the missionary system of persuasion worked with more sedentary agricultural Indian communities, in the territory where the so-called barbarian groups lived, it was less effective.[22] Among some organized and prosperous Indigenous peoples like the Caddo in East Texas, however, the Hasinai of the Caddo group wanted nothing to do with missions or with the Spanish soldiers who "dishonored women and men alike with their continued assaults."[23] Spanish soldiers and missionaries would be expelled from Caddo lands by 1693.

Missionaries were provided financial and military support by the Crown, especially under the Habsburgs, and though a number of royal edicts against the harsh treatment of Indians by the missionaries were issued, reports began reaching the Crown that missionized Indians in the *reducciones* were rebelling against forced labor, restrictions on mobility, and imposed social norms. More recent historians have tried to view relations of the soldiers and missionaries with Indigenous nations in a more complex way that doesn't focus only on the dispossession, enslavement, and exploitation of Indians. Juliana Barr's study of Indians and Spaniards in Texas, for example, seeks to provide a more favorable account of changing Spanish-Indigenous relations, citing examples like that of the Lipan Apaches, who by the eighteenth century were seeking refuge near the Villa of Béxar from their enemies, the northern nations and Comanches. In time the Spanish would make alliances with the Lipan Apaches, but a bit later Béxar would find it more convenient to ally with the Comanches, the Wichita, Caddo, Taovayan, and other northern Indigenous peoples against the Apaches.[24]

By the late eighteenth century and now under a Bourbon administration, Spanish support for traditional missions began to waver, and new strategies were suggested for the ostensible project of "civilizing" Indians and integrating them into Spanish colonial society, that is, as laborers.[25] Unlike the Habsburgs, who had supported the missionary system, the Bourbons preferred to rely on military officers, whose authority now superseded that of the missionaries. During this supposedly "enlightened" period, military officers in charge of the colonies favored private property, individual liberty, and payment for labor, arguing that missions had largely isolated and failed to civilize the Indians. These critics did not dispense totally with the missions, however, as they "could accomplish much at little cost."[26] Conflicts between soldiers and missionaries were frequent as the former saw that the latter, who were supposed to be trustees holding the lands for Indians until secularization was instituted, in some cases acted as if the lands were theirs by right or title.[27] At the same time all were conscious of the failure of Spanish forces to subjugate or exterminate Indians, particularly the Apaches, in northern Mexico and Texas.[28] Reformers thus saw a need for a new frontier policy. Proposals favoring settler colonialism and private property holdings emerged then for the establishment of Spanish settlements, towns, and markets among Indigenous communities, and it was expected that contact with the Spanish colonists would lead to assimilation.

This third model of colonization, the settler colonial model (which followed, first, military conquest and the encomienda system and, later, the mission system or a hybrid of these), would be implemented in the northeast of New Spain, along the Gulf Coast from Tampico to the edge of Texas at the Nueces River. As relates specifically to the US Southwest, it is important to note the role of the viceroy of New Spain, Revillagigedo, in the early eighteenth century. Influenced by the English model of revenue-producing colonies, the viceroy authorized this new joint public-private undertaking, a *colonia*, a site of colonial settlers, instead of a *provincia* pacified by missionaries, soldiers, or both. Revillagigedo turned to José de Escandón, a wealthy military officer, famous as an Indian fighter as well as a rancher and businessman, to establish the Colonia del Nuevo Santander.[29]

The Franciscans were greatly upset by this new settler colonial model. Moreover, missionaries accompanying the project were now expected to serve the spiritual needs of the settlers as well as the native Indians, acting as parish priests. Most interestingly, Escandón ordered that Indians receive a wage for their labor. Those Indians not interested in staying in the area to work for wages fled or were killed. This conversion to what seemed to be a different, more capitalist mode of labor relations did not in the end prove to be such, as waged laborers fast became indebted peons bound in indentured servitude on Spanish haciendas and ranchos.[30]

After Mexican independence in 1821, municipal common lands and uncultivated Church and latifundia lands were "disentailed," that is, dispossessed and sold, and although dispossessed peasants were hungry for land, most of it would be bought by an emerging class of bourgeois landowners, thereby strengthening latifundia, vast tracts of fertile land stretching for more than 85,000 kilometers.[31] The *hacendados* did not of course work the land themselves; they were by and large absentee landlords. They had tenant farmers or administrators and foremen in charge of production.[32] Dispossession of Indigenous peoples in Latin America continued apace after independence, as noted by David Viñas.[33] These settler land tenancy and Indigenous dispossession trends would be transferred to the northern areas of what is now New Mexico, Texas, and California under both the Spanish and later the Mexican flags.

It goes without saying that the dispossession of Indigenous peoples in the Américas has been continuous since colonial times, even after the wars of independence and on into the twenty-first century.[34] Coercive military action against Indians was used not only in the United States but in Latin America as well to guarantee the elimination or subjection of these populations. This was the case in Guatemala, El Salvador, Mexico, Bolivia, Ecuador, Peru, Chile, Uruguay, Paraguay, and Argentina during the nineteenth century, after independence. Both conservative and liberal governments allied to the landowning families that controlled the oligarchy used military force to remove Indians from their lands. As previously noted, historians often have a hard time acknowledging not only the use of coercion against Indians but the practice of genocide, rape, and marginalization. Viñas critiques the silence of historians, especially but not only in Argentina, who go so far as to ignore the very existence of Indians within the nation-state. The rampant Indophobia that he analyzes leads him to suggest that "ethnocide underlies the origins of contemporary Latin America" during this nineteenth-century period of "capitalismo salvaje."[35] In all these cases, coercion was the means for the enclosure and privatization of the Indian commons that would become the property of the large landholders, all with the approval and blessing of capitalist nations interested in the extraction of natural resources from Latin America. Genocide and the expropriation of Indian lands were so widespread that surviving Indians were reduced to quasi slaves, forced to work in the fields, jungles, and brothels.[36]

Numerous more recent cases of enclosure in Latin America point to continued Indigenous struggles for land, water rights, political rights, and civil/human rights. The Mexican Revolution of 1910 was in part another instance of an Indian/peasant rebellion; in the end it granted some Indians *ejidos* and political rights, although, as Xavier Albó points out, these reforms obviously did not reach the Chiapas region, where tensions between landowners and Indians continue today, and where the EZLN (Ejército Zapatista de Liberación Nacional) movement has recentered the Indigenous question in the national political agenda in twenty-first-century Mexico.[37] Next door in Guatemala, the Maya nations, who had suffered enclosures, genocide, and political repression since colonial times, rose up in arms in the 1980s. The subsequent peace agreement of 1996 may have granted Maya groups a right to their identity and culture, but issues of land and water resources have yet to be resolved. Indigenous dispossession and struggles for land figure centrally in both nineteenth- and twentieth-century Latin American literature, but rarely in US Southwest literature.

In what follows, we focus on US policies that have affected land claims, land allotments, squatting, and homesteading as well as widespread land speculation in the United States, all policies that led to the establishment of enclosures and the dispossession of Indigenous populations and later settlers of Mexican/Spanish origin.

US Land Policies and Indian Removal

Gareth Stedman Jones, as previously noted, points to territorial seizure and the settler-type colonialism characteristic of European powers that was practiced in the United States.[38] This territorialism at home made land and the westward expansion a spatiotemporal fix for nineteenth century capital, to borrow from David Harvey, although of course toward the end of the nineteenth century and during the twentieth century outright territorial imperialism and economic imperialism went abroad, as the United States purchased Alaska, annexed Hawaii, and invaded the Philippines, Cuba, Puerto Rico, the Midway Islands, Guam, and the Northern Mariana Islands.[39] Empire in transit, following Jodi A. Byrd's notion, has been evident as well in US interventions in a long list of Latin American nations during the twentieth century (the Dominican Republic, Cuba, Guatemala, Haiti, Panama, and Nicaragua) and in the establishment of United States–backed military regimes in Latin America, Asia, and the Middle East.[40] It all began, however, with the seizure of Indigenous lands. Whether in the more remote past or more recent times, the seizure of these lands was justified with particular sets of legal discourses and policies.

Notions of purportedly "free" and "public" land are crucial for an understanding of the impulse behind the settler colonialism that would characterize internal US imperialism, as noted by Stedman Jones.[41] The land situation within the Spanish Borderlands and especially in the Southwest after 1848 was, in a fashion, a continuation of land policies established in the original thirteen British colonies of the United States. Land policies varied from colony to colony, as each colony had its own system for granting land, and much as the British tried after 1763 to establish some common policies in all the colonies, each dealt with land disposition in a variety of ways. After independence, issues of boundaries and common property continued. For example, since the Continental Congress was in need of revenue and soldiers who had fought in the revolution had been promised land, Congress in 1780 called for the cession of all western lands (lands beyond original colony limits) to the federal government to be disposed of for the benefit of the country and for settlement.[42] Ceding the lands to the US federal government was said to be of "paramount importance in the growth of national power, in attracting millions of Europeans to settle in new communities of the American West," and for creating transportation systems and funding education[43]—all well and good, except that the land was not "vacant." The official story of US land acquisition is that of a number of congressional land acts, executive orders, and congressional debates on public land, its settlement, and its exploitation for minerals, timber, and water. But alongside and underpinning this history is that of Indian dispossession, warfare against Indians, and massacres of Indians as well as squatting, homesteading, fraud, and abuse of land policies ostensibly on the books. And, of course, the Louisiana Purchase in 1803 and the military invasion of the Southwest in 1846 would expand what was considered public land. The major conflict, as presented in Gates's extensive history on public land policies, is that involving individual settlers and squatters interested in homesteading and, increasingly, speculators, land companies, and capitalist interests.

The problem of who had the right to public lands was a fraught issue from the beginning of British colonization in what would become US territory. There are a number of works on public lands, and for our purposes here we have relied extensively on the comprehensive history of public land development and policies written by Gates for the Public Land Law Review Commission and published in 1968. Public lands were presupposed to be vacant, but of course they were inhabited. In Gates's work the removal of native peoples is just one more item to consider and not the central issue. This foundational dispossession on which the very inception and development of the United States is predicated would take the form of warfare, violence, fraud, treaties, and forced purchase, as we shall see in chapter 2.

As far as the historiographical recounting, or rather skirting, of this process of Native dispossession that allowed for figuring inhabited Indian lands as vacant public lands, not much is said in studies of public land. Gates, as noted by Lawrence B. Lee, focuses on an "incongruous public land system" that, far from spreading democracy in the frontier, led to speculation, abuse, fraud, "rural poverty on a massive scale and the exodus from the land."[44] In his earlier work on California (1958), Gates claimed that "Anglo-Saxon law respecting land titles is exact, clear, and precise and does not allow for the vagueness of the Mexican system in California," but in his later work on US public lands he reconsiders this assessment after thorough research on governmentality, that is, on government policies, actions, and inactions, as he comes to terms with the incongruities in US land laws.[45] It is the political system, the purportedly democratic US land system, that he sees as having failed and malfunctioned. Gates's indictment of federal land policies that, far from supporting the settler and squatter, ended up opening the door to land speculation, land monopoly, and control of timber and mineral resources, fails to recognize that in fact the government succeeded only too well in converting public land, a use value, into a commodity with exchange value that would bring in revenue to a government faced with deficits and would at the same time favor the accumulation of capital by land speculators. Although critical, Gates's analysis of US public land policies, however, does not extend to an indictment of an economic system that fostered capital accumulation through the acquisition of land, nor does he dwell on the initiatory dispossession of Native peoples.

Still, the very scope of Gates's seven-hundred-page history of public lands and federal land policies is extensive and revealing; here he addresses some fundamental issues that relate specifically to what took place in the Southwest and the policies and the economic interests that drove them. Popular historical accounts of settlement by pioneers who were granted land for small farms fail to acknowledge that the early British colonies already saw a good deal of land speculation, an increasing monopoly of landownership, and squatting.[46] Town council members in some cases granted themselves millions of acres; the early eighteenth century was what Gates calls "an era of prodigal grants," running into the hundreds of thousands of acres.[47] Even when small land grants were made, they were often eventually absorbed by larger landholders. By 1775, Gates notes, many small farms had been eliminated. Individuals seeking land often squatted on land granted to others who did not work the land or occupy it. Restitution by owners for improvements made by squatters had to be paid in Virginia and later in other colonies or states as well. Gates indicates that "the recognition of settlers, including squatters' rights, became firmly ingrained in American land law," but however "ingrained," clearly speculators and land companies dominated land acquisition.[48] Newer colonists, finding land already claimed by others in the original colonies, began pushing more and more westward, into "Indian country," a designation on maps that belies the ostensibly vacant character of those lands. In effect, the original settler colonizers established enclosures depriving not only the eastern native Indian population of their lands but even closing off access to land to newer settler arrivals. Enclosures were established anew, pushing would-be settlers as well as freed indentured servants to the frontier, where once again Indians were further dispossessed, displaced, and removed.

Increasingly, especially as the nineteenth century progressed, laws and acts, such as the Homestead Act of 1862, that were meant to support the European squatter and settler, enabling each to acquire 120 acres of public land at $1.25 an acre, were instead used to facilitate acquisition of land in large blocks. The use of dummy entrymen enabled speculators to pretend to follow the law in bidding for land under a variety of programs, land that would later be conveyed to capitalists. Using the Preemption Act of 1841, the Homestead Act of 1862, the Timber Culture Act of 1873, the Swampland Act of 1849–50, and the Desert Land Act of 1877 as well as a variety of scrip (be it veteran, school, or college scrip rights, as well as scrip made available to those losing lands later confirmed, that is, later approved as allotments), capitalist interests were able to maneuver to find ways of having these lands conveyed to them. The role of the government as the tool of capital accumulation in the shape of land could not be clearer. Henry George was right when he called attention to "the blunders governments were making and sanctioning in land policies" and the machinations of monopolists.[49]

The purported ideal of encouraging and incentivizing individual private property through making public land available to a nation of white yeoman farmers for cultivation was proved a fraud as corporations, like the railroads, and speculators gained control of much of the land. In the South, large landholdings for plantations worked by slave labor were the objective. Congressmen and others saw early on that land companies, rather than settlers, were benefiting from public land sales. Andrew Jackson, who himself speculated on lands in the South, especially Creek and Chickasaw lands, once president, expressed concern for protecting settlers against speculators, but in reality his policies and practices accelerated the sale of public lands.[50] Those squatting on public land began to demand right of first refusal preemption rights to buy before auction at $1.25 an acre. Preemption acts would be passed in 1830, 1832, 1838, and 1841.[51]

The numbers are telling: of the 500 million acres granted by the General Land Office between 1862 and 1904, only eighty million went to homesteaders. Most of the land went to speculators, cattlemen, mining concerns, lumber companies, and railroads. Fraudulent claims were all too common, with surrogate agents claiming land whose title would then be turned over to speculators. In addition to the fees to be paid and the occupancy requirements, those requesting homesteads who bought at low prices had to indicate that the land was for cultivation, despite often acting as agents for land speculators who came into thousands of acres, leading Gates to note, "The huge size of larger holdings acquired after the Homestead Act was adopted is almost breathtaking."[52] Breathtaking, indeed, and an acknowledgment of General Land Office corruption.

The Impact of the Louisiana Purchase

US interest in the port city of New Orleans and the navigable Mississippi River dates to the period after 1776 with westward migration. In 1795, the United States signed the Pinckney Treaty with Spain, which granted the United States the right to navigate the Mississippi through Spanish territory and also secured recognition of its southwestern boundary at the thirty-first parallel. France had ceded Louisiana to Spain in 1763 with the Treaty of Fontainebleau, but in 1800 Napoleon, with imperial ambitions of his own in the Américas, induced Spain with the Treaty of San Ildefonso to cede Louisiana—including

New Orleans and the territory to the Rocky Mountains—back to France. The return of these lands to France and the closing of the Mississippi were considered a major threat to the United States, and at that point efforts were initiated to purchase part of the territory. France's defeat in Haiti and events in Europe at the turn of the century led Napoleon to be willing to sell Louisiana. The United States acquired 523,446,400 acres at three cents an acre with the Louisiana Purchase of 1803.[53]

Spain continued to claim Florida, east and west, but in 1810 settlers of west Florida declared their independence from Spain and asked to be annexed to the United States. This President Madison did. Spain, which had encouraged settlers from the United States in previous periods, was unable to maintain control of Florida when the Creek Indians rose up, instigated by the English who resided there. Enter Andrew Jackson, who defeated the Creek and destroyed a number of their villages.[54] In 1818, John Quincy Adams pressed Spain to cede Florida, which it did in 1819. The United States offered to pay its citizens' claims against Spain ($5 million) and to surrender its claims to Texas. Spain also surrendered its own claims to the Oregon Territory. Boundary disputes with Great Britain were resolved both in Canada and in Maine.

With the Louisiana Purchase of 1803, the United States gained millions of acres of public land, but still the country looked to settle Oregon (1835–45). For their part, in Mexican Texas, Stephen F. Austin and other empire builders were establishing settler colonies (1822–36), "and a few Americans were acquiring imperial ranchos in California."[55] Once Louisiana and Florida lands were in the hands of the federal government, individual claims to land granted under the Spanish colonial regimes were examined and either validated or not by the United States. Significantly, many lands acquired through Indian treaties, however, never did become public land.[56] Lands acquired through invasion and war, as in the case of the US Southwest, were subsequently redefined as purchases, and here again individual land grant claims were examined by commissions and either validated or not. Any remaining lands became "public lands."

Private Land Claims and Commissions

Louisiana land claims and the policies and practices instituted by the land commissioners there are especially important in order to make sense of what happened subsequently in the US Southwest. Government commissioners, after reviewing the requirements stipulated by Spanish law to authenticate land grants, found a number of fraudulent, antedated, and unfounded claims in Louisiana. Often the claims were for more land than the Spanish law allowed; often the land had not been cultivated or the dates were wrong. Already then, as would be the case later in California, claimants would complain about "the considerable expense and trouble" involved in proving the validity of their rights to land. Gates is not sympathetic to claims that litigation for land claim validation was exceedingly expensive.[57] Laying blame and finding fault with the Spanish system and the claimants, Gates is likewise quick to dismiss these complaints by indicating that "the land system in all the territory the U.S. acquired from Spain had been very loosely managed."[58] As noted earlier, for Gates, the fault lay with lax Spanish (and later Mexican) administration of land grants, a perspective that had already surfaced in his work on California claims. He would—subsequently—find fraudulent claims and abuse rampant in US land claims as well. Perhaps, one could argue, the fraud widespread in US land cases could also be said to have been caused by the evidently loose management of the US government. It all depended, as was often the case, on who was on the land commission boards.[59] In his work, Gates makes clear that there was much corruption among land office employees.[60]

Canonical US narratives about Anglo settlers in the US Midwest in which land claims are the central issue abound, and the dispossession of Indigenous populations is largely sidestepped or entirely overlooked. One example of the Louisiana experience of Indian land dispossession that additionally includes the aspect of Black-White miscegenation is partly configured in George Washington Cable's *The Grandissimes* (1880), a novel recalling the arrival of French explorers in southern Louisiana around 1682 and the subsequent appropriation of Indian land by the White French creoles.

The Louisiana Purchase went far beyond the present-day state of Louisiana and added some 828,000 square miles to the United States, including lands that now encompass Louisiana, Arkansas, Missouri, Iowa, Oklahoma, Kansas, and Nebraska as well as parts of eight other states. This was the area of the plains or prairie that most often has appeared in US novels and films dealing with the iconic westward-bound crossing of the territory by pioneer wagon trains. The Louisiana territory would attract thousands of homesteaders and squatters to these Indian lands taken over sequentially by the Spanish, French, and later US colonists. A series of land runs took place in 1857, 1889, 1891, 1892, 1893, 1895, and 1901, with tens of thousands of land seekers rushing to the newly ceded territory. The year 1857 would bring one of the largest land rushes in US history.⁶¹ Films and novels on the period as a rule emphasize the trials and tribulations of white settlers in search of land and the pioneer premise as part of US western expansion, leaving out of the narrative frame the dispossessed and displaced Indigenous population.

The sequelae of the Louisiana Purchase were manifold; as noted above, with it came the acquisition of Sioux territory. Despite several treaties (1805–68) of peace and friendship, the United States allowed encroachment on Sioux lands by trappers and settlers, who began moving in, forcing the Sioux to relocate and fight both settlers and soldiers. Originally a farming people, they became increasingly dependent on European goods, including guns, ammunition, utensils, tools, textiles, and so on, ultimately turning entirely to bison hunting.⁶² Constantly displaced and under attack, the Sioux were forced to make further land cessions to the government. In 1890, the US Army would massacre three hundred unarmed and starving Sioux on their way to Pine Ridge, most of them women and children.⁶³ US literature on hardy pioneers crossing the prairie evidences the blind spots or the convenient omission and erasure of previous Indigenous claims to land. In the "westward movement" national narrative of the nineteenth century, *movement* is a choice word as it elides the active and violent dispossession of others as a force of nature, almost—like the movement of the planets and stars—naturalizing it in an attempt to neutralize the spatial violence it entailed.

And yet the westward movement, as historians have come to see, was anything but orderly. Trappers, prospectors, farmers, and herdsmen came, as did land speculators, merchants, millers, artisans, and more, all at different times. Violence, spatial and otherwise, as well as fraud, accompanied the movement west. Turner's notion that the frontier fostered democracy is illusory. Racism, lawlessness, and nondemocratic practices were in fact the norm on the frontier; violence, lynchings of those deemed "foreigners" and of Chinese workers in mining towns, massacres of Indians, violence against Mexicans, and displacement of settlers and squatters alike by land speculators were what in fact characterized the frontier and the pioneer experience rather than democratic practices and the rule of law. The dispossession and the strategies used to appropriate lands faced first by Indigenous populations and later by settlers of Mexican, Spanish, and French descent are not unique if one considers the overall history of land policies of the United States since colonial times. It should not surprise us, then, that given these practices of abuse, fraud, and corruption by both private entities and state policies, by the end of the nineteenth century the vast majority of lands in the United States were in the hands of land companies, land monopolists, and speculators, not at all the fulfillment of the vision of a nation of yeoman citizen farmers.

In the story of enclosures in the United States and the acquisition and disposition of so-called public lands, Indigenous populations have in fact received all too little attention. Their dispossession has been naturalized, and it is the myth of free, vacant, public land that has predominated. This is demonstrably the case as Anglo-European settlers moved ever westward into Native American spaces. But a parallel process of dispossession and settler colonialism also took place in lands that are now the US Southwest. Spatial violence, genocide, and dispossession were very much at the center of the early Spanish and Mexican colonization of the Southwest as well, all with their attendant discursive violence. Despite the long-standing presence and ties to the land and history of the Southwest, descendants of Californios/as, Nuevomexicanos/as, and Tejanos/as need to acknowledge and come to terms with our ancestors' participation in the long story of Indigenous dispossession, a story to be taken up in subsequent chapters.

2

Indigenous Spatial

Sovereignty and Governmentality

RIGHTS AND WRONGS IN OKLAHOMA

Discussions of US public lands are for the most part narrated by historians and novelists from the perspective of white settlers and speculators interested in land acquisition rather than from the perspective of the dispossessed Native Americans, who today are engaged in remapping US history through literature that recognizes their spatial sovereignty and seeks spatial justice.[1] The fact that this territory was not vacant before the settlers arrived seldom, if ever, enters the picture in mainstream narratives, nor does the fact that it was taken over by force and coercion, by state laws and acts (sovereignty), by treating Indians as wards (discipline), and by governmentality (through bureaucratic agencies).[2] The types of mechanisms, means, techniques, and discourses utilized to establish enclosures, thus dispossessing Indians and later Mexicans in the United States, are historically specific and quite telling.

Dispossession in its many forms in what is today the United States has a long history. The violence enacted against native peoples has taken both spatial and discursive forms. Military force was used by British, French, Spanish, and Mexican forces against Indians across four centuries for the acquisition of land, and against tribes trading or allying with rival colonial powers.[3] When the American Revolution broke out (1776–83) many Indian tribes sided with the British; this was met with "punitive-scorched-earth raids into Indian country, North and South" by the colonists.[4] As noted by Dunbar-Ortiz, "U.S. genocidal wars against Indigenous nations continued unabated in the 1790s and were woven into the very fabric of the new nation-state."[5] Displacement, confinement, extermination, and destitution of the Indigenous "other" were not aberrations or anomalies but rather constitutional and have continued throughout the course of US history down to the present, as the confinement and caging of migrants today bears witness.

Along with forced removal and dispossession, a number of treaties would be signed between the US government and Indigenous nations from the country's inception to the present moment. Among the most important of these is the Treaty of Greenville (1795), in which Indians ceded much of Ohio to the United States but were allowed to retain some land that had previously been lost under fraudulent agreements. The Treaty of Greenville, as Anthony F. C. Wallace rightly notes, "contained language that implied that a guardian-and-ward relationship would henceforth obtain between the U.S. and the Indian tribes within its territory."[6] Thus while the rhetoric pointed to the federal government's responsibility to ensure fair and honorable dealings with Indians, in effect the truth was that coercion would be followed by disciplinary measures that made clear that Indian tribes would henceforth be surveilled and constrained.[7]

For these dispossessions a variety of discourses were deployed, whatever seemed most convenient at the time. Thus, as shown by Wallace, by 1830 Secretary of War Lewis Cass as well as Andrew Jackson would argue that the survival of Indians as a race depended on their removal and relocation to territory west of the Mississippi. Cass's assessment of Indian history was based on a developmental analysis and the concept of the "hunter state."[8] Viewing Indians as savages and hunters was inaccurate, as Wallace points out, because eastern Indians depended on horticulture rather than on hunting, with both men and women involved in the planting and harvest.[9] Still, Cass saw no reason to allow "degenerate" Indians to remain on lands that were better suited for agricultural production, that is, for white settlers. But at the same time, Indian removal, he argued, was their only hope. Like Cass, Jackson hypocritically argued that relocation of Indians would "save them from imminent extinction," an end that he considered nonetheless inevitable. He argued for the use of bribes or legislated force to get Indians to cede their lands. Those refusing to leave should be allotted land on the theory that they could soon be induced to sell it and follow their tribesmen west.[10] It cannot be overly stressed that the government, despite evidence to the contrary, argued that Indians did not improve the land, when in fact they did. What becomes abundantly clear is that privatization was seen already then as a means to effect dispossession.

The Indian Removal Act of 1830 stands as the major state act of coercion to remove the Five Civilized Tribes (Cherokee, Chickasaw, Choctaw, Creek, and Seminole) from their lands in the southern United States. Despite heated debate in Congress, the Removal Act was approved in April 1830.[11] It is the best example of sovereignty mechanisms and coercion used to dispossess Indians. The act authorized the president to set aside a territory to which Indians could migrate with the assistance of the government and under its protection. Jackson proposed that the land beyond the Mississippi would be theirs "as long as grass grows or water runs . . . and I never speak with forked tongue."[12] William Penn had used similar words in Pennsylvania. Indians wishing to stay could retain allotments, private parcels of land around their residence; the rest would be sold to settlers and land companies.[13] Immediately after the act passed, harrassment ensued, with mobs of squatters and intruders descending on Indian lands and speculators looking over the lands for purchase. Fraud by speculators led to purchases of land from Indians hired to say they were the owners.[14] When gold was discovered in Georgia in 1829, for example, Cherokee lands were invaded by forty thousand gold seekers; crops were destroyed, houses burned, and livestock seized.[15] Remaining Indians had no tribal rights and were now subject to state laws; they could, however, neither vote, bring suit, nor testify in court. Despite assurances to the contrary, the government did not intervene to protect Indians in the South, and so there was little choice left but to self-relocate. So much for protection under the law.

Interest in these vacated southern lands grew; they were recognized as prime cotton acreage at a time when the Industrial Revolution had transformed transportation and factory production, especially cotton cloth manufacturing, in Great Britain. English factories were producing enormous quantities of cotton goods sold all over the world. The yarn and cloth produced by the British depended on raw cotton from the United States, which at that moment produced two-thirds of all raw cotton worldwide.[16] US industries were also beginning to compete with British cotton mills. Demand for new cotton lands attracted land speculators and settlers who resented the federal government's failure to facilitate their expansion by freeing Native American lands, removing Indians, and turning over the land to the states.[17] As noted by Walter Johnson, expropriated Indian land "provided the foundation of the leading sector of the global economy in the first half of the nineteenth century" with investment capital pouring in from Britain, the Continent, and the northern US states.[18]

Cession and Removal, Diaspora and Genocide

The dismal story of the Trail of Tears is well known. More recent historians are recentering Indian history from the perspective of Indigenous peoples and providing more nuanced and complex accounts of this history.[19] The Five Civilized Tribes, as they were called—already a nomenclature that spoke volumes to the civilization/barbarism presuppositions at work—were forced to emigrate from the South, suffering tremendously in the exodus, mostly because they had to walk in winter weather through unfamiliar country. Provisions were inadequate or not available; shelter and clothing were insufficient; it was, by all measures, a death march. Thousands died along the way. This resulted in changes in the mode of transportation and assistance, but still the trip was arduous, whether by land or water. A life of poverty awaited most in the new Indian Territory, although a few would prosper, establishing farms and ranches, schools and towns. The Five Civilized Tribes would be joined by other displaced tribes in Indian Territory. Wallace estimates that no fewer than sixty tribes were moved to Oklahoma to join the Five Civilized Tribes, including tribes from northern Ohio, Indiana, New York, Michigan, Minnesota, and Wisconsin (Shawnees, Senecas, Ottawas, Miamis, Potawatomis, Chippewas, Wyandots, Menominees, and Winnebagos).[20] Francis Paul Prucha indicates that between 1829 and 1851, eighty-six Indian treaties were signed and ratified, most of them treaties of cession and removal.[21] None went willingly; some Indigenous peoples hid and refused to go; some relocated with their slaves.[22] Conservatively, US treaties with Indian nations deprived Indigenous populations of some two million square miles of land; these treaties were often breached by the government, but, it bears noting, in the process of signing them it recognized Indigenous nations as independent entities, that is, until 1871 when Congress halted formal treaty making.[23]

Reviewing the case of the Senecas in western New York is especially revealing, as the tribe still owned four reserves after selling most of its land in 1797 (Treaty of Big Tree) to the Holland Land Company. Before 1776, the Continental Army had done its best to ravage Seneca settlements that sided with the British, perceived by the Seneca as more tolerable than the "government of extermination-minded settlers."[24] The Ogden Land Company (successor to the Holland Land Company) had retained an option to buy the reserves when the Senecas decided to sell and, eager to buy the valuable land, pushed to remove the Senecas. In view of the Senecas' unwillingness to relinquish their lands, the Ogden Land Company tried the old whisky-and-bribe method to force a few chiefs to sign a treaty in which they agreed to move to Indian Territory. Although the fraud was widely denounced, the Treaty of Buffalo Creek was eventually signed by President Martin Van Buren in 1840.[25] Some Senecas moved, but the majority refused, and those who left eventually returned. Attorneys and others like ethnographer Lewis Henry Morgan would help them file suit against the Ogden Land Company; this lawsuit would eventually end with a compromise by which the land company returned two of the Seneca reserves.[26]

Containment and surveillance of Indigenous tribes, facilitated through the establishment of reservations, were carried out in part by the Bureau of Indian Affairs (BIA)—tellingly at this juncture part of the War Department—created in 1834 by Congress and President Andrew Jackson. Coercion and violence were two edges of the same weapon wielded by discourses that buttressed and validated acts of dispossession. Reservations were intended and served as a type of disciplinary space, a sort of panopticon; Indians on the reservation were contained, watched, and treated as wards by the state. The BIA, now transferred to the Department of the Interior, was one of the primary mechanisms of governmentality used by the state to control Native Americans. Agents were political appointees who managed reservation activities, disbursing annuities, distributing rations, superintending the schools, removing intruders, and policing the reservation space in multiform ways.[27] The bureaucracy of the BIA allowed mismanagement and corruption, as will become more than clear in the case of the Osages. Evidence of corruption led to calls for ending the reservation system and allotting land to individuals; the result of Indigenous dispossession would be achieved by one means or another.

The Dawes Act of 1887: Privatization Policies

In 1887 Congress passed the benchmark Dawes General Allotment Act that destroyed the Indian commons and privatized the land, making it more easily accessible to white settlers, land companies, speculators, and others. The

Dawes Act, as Senator Henry M. Teller noted in 1887, had one aim: "to get at the Indians' land and open it up for resettlement."[28] Legislation was thus one way—a most effective one—to speed up enclosures.

With the Dawes General Allotment Act, dispossession and its attendant privatization were accelerated as all Indians received individual allotments. Indian heads of family were allotted 160 acres, and single persons and orphans over eighteen were given eighty-acre tracts. Allotments were to be held in trust for twenty-five years. Once Indians had an alienable title, after five years, they were expected to sell the land; surplus reservation lands were available to be sold, technically with tribal consent, which was always forthcoming. Only the Five Civilized Tribes expressed opposition to the Dawes Act and were exempted from its provisions.[29]

However, Indian dispossession could not be revealed so blatantly. What Henri Lefebvre calls the "illusion of transparency" served to conceal dispossession.[30] Material gain and the desire for accumulation through dispossession were masked through particular discourses, especially the rhetoric of concern for assimilation.[31] Arguing that private landownership would serve to integrate Indians into general society was a ruse, as Congress knew full well that privatization was being established to dispossess Indians of lands that had previously been—theoretically—reserved for them. Once lands were made private property, Indians rapidly disposed of them as planned. Common land tenancy was to cease to exist, making the reservation land available for purchase, a fact abundantly clear to Native Americans. According to Mishuana Goeman, an estimated ninety million acres of Native held lands in the United States were lost between the Dawes Act of 1887 and 1934, in addition to the untold millions lost before.[32] As a mechanism of wealth transfer, the Dawes Act was highly effective.

In addition to granting full US citizenship, the Dawes Act included an important proviso: the act did not extend to territory occupied by the Cherokees, Creeks, Choctaws, Chickasaws, Seminoles, Osages, Miamis, Peorias, and Sac and Foxes in the Indian Territory, nor to any of the reservations of the Seneca Nation within the state of New York.[33] In 1893, the Dawes Commission would try to extend the allotment act to the Five Civilized Tribes as well, but they proved unwilling to give up their communal lands. In 1898, however, Congress passed the Curtis Act, which by decree brought an end to tribal tenure over land, ending it without the Indians' consent.[34] Tribes that had not agreed to allotment, as directed by the Dawes Commission, now had no choice but to see their land allotted. Cherokees resisted the longest, but in time they, too, were forced to accept allotments. The Curtis Act allowed for the retention of mineral rights, but only the Osages would take advantage of this important proviso.[35] Retention of subsoil rights would be central to the Osage Nation, as presented in Linda Hogan's novel *Mean Spirit*, which we will discuss later in this chapter.

Years later, recognition of the devastation wreaked by the Dawes and Curtis Acts and their failure to promote the much-vaunted assimilation gave rise to the Meriam Report of 1928 and the Indian Reorganization Act of 1934 under the New Deal. The Meriam Report, commissioned by Secretary of the Interior Hubert Work in 1926, focused on the problem of Indian Administration and noted "An overwhelming majority of the Indians are poor, even extremely poor, and they are not adjusted to the economic and social system of the dominant white civilization."[36] The damage had been done already. Native Americans would be faulted, incredibly, for not adjusting well to dispossession and pauperization. The report focused on detrimental policies and legislation that went against the well-being of Native Americans and contributed to problems with Indian education, health, and poverty but at the same time enacted its own reformist discursive violence and governmentality.

Then newly elected President Franklin D. Roosevelt would receive a petition for a repeal of the 1887 Dawes Act in the aftermath of the Meriam Report and in the midst of the Great Depression. As part of his New Deal policies, FDR appointed a new commissioner of Indian affairs, John Collier, who called for a series of reforms that would be the basis for the Indian Reorganization Act of 1934 (the Wheeler-Howard Act) and introduced the Indian New Deal, which called for Indian self-determination and maintenance of Indian cultures, rather than either assimilation or the return of communal Indian land.[37] It was too little, too late.

Tensions between federal and state policies and practices also came into play (as they would later in the civil rights struggles of the 1960s). The Wheeler-Howard Act was opposed by the Oklahoma delegation to Congress, as it saw the law as keeping Indians "in a state of perpetual inferiority and permanently prevent[ing] their assimilation"; a new bill was subsequently proposed excluding Oklahoma Indians from the main provisions of the act.[38] It was meant to "destroy the opportunity for local exploitation of Indian property" and enable unassimilated Indians to return to a system of local self-government and communal land tenure.[39] This act, known as the Oklahoma Indian Welfare Act (1936), eventually did pass but without the provisions that abolished guardianships for restricted Indians and that—importantly—gave the Department of the Interior control over the partition of land and the determination of heirs. Angie Debo finds that the 1936 act enacted some reforms, especially regarding the formation of community organizations and the acquisition of communal lands. One measure that did pass was the supervision by the Department of Agriculture of "agricultural leasing of restricted land belonging to enrolled or unenrolled Five Tribes Indians of one-half or more Indian blood."[40] Another proposal that did not, however, pass, despite the support of the Five Civilized Tribes, was the entrusting of restricted Indian lands to the federal government rather than to state courts. Relevant to our discussion of Hogan's novel *Mean Spirit*, this issue would be especially important to the Osages, as "guardians" in Osage territory would create what Debo terms a "scandalous situation" that would pit the Oklahoma delegation to Congress against the BIA and the Department of the Interior, as the Oklahoma politicians worked to maintain state court control of Indian land and rights.[41] These issues, as we shall see in the next section detailing the situation in Osage territory, would become key to explaining what happened when oil was discovered on Indian lands in Oklahoma.[42] Hogan knows the history of Oklahoma well; her Chickasaw grandparents lived there. She identifies as an Indian woman and comes from a family of pro-Indigenous activists.[43]

Hogan's Novel *Mean Spirit*: Oklahoma Is Not OK

Capital, as Massimo De Angelis notes, encloses, and it encloses continuously, if not always in the same fashion.[44] Hogan's 1990 novel, *Mean Spirit*, not only captures the continuity of enclosures throughout US history but also makes clear that at any moment in history there may be a layering of enclosures, with different types instituted by different means appearing within the same geographic space. Coercion, legislation, and governmentality are the primary means by which enclosures were imposed on Indigenous populations in the United States and elsewhere. With the extraction of natural resources, oil in the particular case of Indian Territory, came corporate capitalism and the further destruction of the individually allotted lands of the Indigenous population.

Mean Spirit focuses on the structuring mechanisms that enabled the repetitive nature and layering of dispossession that destroyed the lives, habitus, and habitats of Indigenous populations. Hogan notes that Indian space has always been at risk of being taken; enclosures are thus an unending process visited on Indians by capital and the state. Memory, especially memory of resistance, is configured as different characters in the novel recall the ongoing

Indigenous struggles against the systems of private property and the state; the characters are also aware of prior attempts to re-create the commons. These examples of counterstrategies of resistance in the novel can be viewed as what Marx calls the reestablishment of the commons based on "co-operation and the possession in common of the land and of the means of production" that he came to see as a "fulcrum for social regeneration" in the future; it is a reason to focus on Indigenous populations of the world who practiced communal landholding in the Américas before the coming of the Europeans.[45] Native peoples would repeatedly try to reproduce communal property holdings in Oklahoma, but to no avail, especially after the passing of the Dawes and Curtis Acts. Capital inevitably interceded to disrupt attempts to re-create the commons; only small communities like the novel's Hill people, established in 1861, were left by the 1920s, as symbols of a utopian society constantly under attack. In her configuration of the destruction of the commons, Hogan examines the role of the state allied to capital and points to efforts to maintain native religions that run counter to hegemonic religions. In addition to providing a critique of capital, the state, and racism, Hogan also highlights the key role and power of women in the Hill settlement who seek to regenerate a commons.[46]

In recalling the various means used for Indigenous dispossession, Hogan's *Mean Spirit* also reviews the particular ideological discourses that have accompanied these enclosures and that have served to justify massacres, violence, robbery, fraud, and racism against Indigenous populations in Oklahoma and elsewhere. Importantly, enclosures, by affecting the populations' relation to production, also create new subjects, in this case wage laborers and consumers, giving rise, too, to the unemployed and lumpen population that we find living in Tar Town in the novel. But the novel does not foreclose on the generation of alternate, contestatory subjects.

Mean Spirit addresses two primary issues. The first is the issue of enclosures, which are discussed (without being so named) in terms of two structuring mechanisms: dispossession and privatization. The other is the recovery of history, and for this we again draw on Houston A. Baker's work in noting the importance of a "critical memory."[47] Hogan's discussion of both issues covers the different strategies used to dispossess Indians and privatize their lands, especially violence and murder, fraud, debt, treaties, governmental accords and practices, acculturation, and consumerism. Crucially important in this chronicling of Indian history is the role of the state in the promotion of enclosures, the relocation of Indians, their extermination, and the destruction of habitat, the denial of their legal and social rights, and the exploitation of their mineral, water, and forest resources.

Hogan's novel is a type of noir narrative, in line perhaps with the contemporary Latin American *novela negra* genre. What characterizes this genre is the new role of the investigator, who may be a detective, a newspaper reporter, a writer, or simply someone with an inquiring mind and who may even know beforehand what the crime is and who the culprits are but who has a difficult time finding them and tying up all the loose ends. More important, the perpetrator is now, more often than not, the system itelf, that is, the state, its agents, and capitalism. In these noir novels, the notion of respect for law and order is seen to be a myth, and people who work for the law are shown to be in cahoots with criminals or even are the criminals themselves. Justice is a discourse that few believe in, and a "nation of laws" works only as a mission statement. The title of Hogan's novel (*Mean Spirit*) refers, in one instance, to a Pentecostal preacher's notion of a land without "mean spirits walking" about, that is, without men with evil intentions, but more to the point, in the second instance, to the government: "Uncle Sam was a cold uncle with a mean soul and a cruel spirit," pointedly referencing the government's authorized massacre of the Sioux at Wounded Knee.[48] The novel thus makes clear that it is the state allied with the interests of capital that allows for the continued historical dispossessions and that furthers genocide, including the cultural extermination of Indians.

Mean Spirit is also akin to Gabriel García Márquez's *Crónica de una muerte anunciada*, a detective narrative that begins with the end, that is, with the murder of the main character.[49] What we, as readers, want to know is why this man was killed and why no one warned him. García Márquez's novel is circular in structure, with an investigator, the narrator-writer, involved after the fact when he returns to his hometown to decipher what has happened. *Mean Spirit* is in a fashion a detective chronicle that records the assassinations of several women and men in Watona. An oil-rich Osage town, Watona is marked by oil derricks, polluted lands, rich Indians with expensive consumption practices, land and oil speculators, a corrupt justice system, and poor Indians, some of whom are forced into a slum—Tar Town—growing at the edge of town, a veritable *cartolandia* (a makeshift shantytown) with people living under cardboard roofs, in sheds, and outdoors. Readers know who the culprits are, but, like the Indians themselves, face the hopelessness of getting any justice.

Hogan's novel is based on historical events, a series of murder cases in Indian Territory in Oklahoma history in the early 1920s.[50] The "Osage Reign of

Terror," as it was called by US newspapers of the period, occurred in Fairfax, Oklahoma, where a cattleman, William K. Hale, for several years a resident in Indian Territory, specifically in the Grayhorse Indian settlement, was accused with his nephew, Ernest Burkhardt, of murdering several Osage Indians, primarily by hiring killers. Hale, who was a prosperous landowning cattleman originally from Texas, owner of a bank and called "King of the Osage Hills," shrewdly had his nephew marry Mollie Kyle, a full-blood Osage with a headright claim to land and oil annuities. Marriage to native women with property—here a headright—becomes a key tactic of enclosure and part of a pattern of overall strategies employed to dispossess people, as is borne out in this and following chapters dealing with New Mexico and Texas.

Mollie and her two sisters (Anna Brown and Rita Smith), as well as their mother, Lizzie, were original Native American allottees. The Hale plan was to eliminate the two sisters and the mother, who had three headrights in their names, paving the way for Mollie to inherit their headrights. Burkhart would then gain control of the mother's and sisters' wealth by eventually killing Mollie and inheriting everything himself. In 1921 Hale and Burkhart hired local men to kill the women by shooting Anna and poisoning Lizzie, followed by placing a nitroglycerin charge in the home of Rita and her husband in 1923, killing both in the explosion, along with a maid. Tying up loose ends, Hale then hired men to kill the killers. The murder of Indian women did not then—as it does not today—attract much attention, but journalists focusing on the "Osage Reign of Terror" spurred the investigation of these deaths by the then newly created US Federal Bureau of Investigation (FBI). Interestingly, the Osages themselves financed part of the costs of prosecuting the killers, as Terry Wilson notes.[51]

According to bureau records, the FBI sent several agents to Fairfax in disguise (one as an insurance salesman, one as a cowboy, another as a medicine man, and a fourth as a doctor); they spent time in the town until they were able to make a case against Hale and those who colluded with him. Given his wealth and power, solving the murders proved difficult, that is, until the nephew confessed to the crimes. The trials—and there were three, for it was difficult to convict the pair since witnesses were paid off or murdered—eventually led to life sentences in 1929 for some, although more than a dozen other murders remained unsolved. In 1925 the federal government passed a slayer statute mandating that no one convicted of murder could inherit the estate of the decedent; it also further stipulated that only "heirs of Indian blood" could inherit from those who were of one-half or more Osage blood.[52]

Although this case is part of the historical background of the early 1920s, the novel does not follow the historical account precisely. It is a fictionalized chronicle of a series of murders in Osage territory, but at the same time it is also a fictional account of the relations between the state/capital and the Indians of Watona, a boomtown like Fairfax, that includes not only Osages but Creeks, Chickasaws, Seminoles, and nonnative people. While the Osages are the majority population, the whites are the dominant group and include the sheriff, doctors, oilmen, oil company executives, government agency officers, and lawyers. The Indigenous population includes full-bloods and half bloods, often of combined Indian background or half white. More broadly, this narrative addresses the numerous murders, the consequences of the oil boom, the establishment of the guardian system, the destruction of habitat, and the presumed government intervention that exhibits a paternalism that actually functions as yet another means of dispossessing Indians and denying them their rights in Indian Territory.

Mean Spirit also attempts to construct a critical memory of the past by doing what the character Michael Horse does throughout the novel: document the events experienced by Indians in Oklahoma. Horse wants to offer "the real story" in opposition to the official story that legal discourse allows: "they have books filled with words, with rules about how the story can and cannot be spoken. There is not room enough, nor time, to search for the real story that lies beneath the rest."[53] Long before Hale's trial, Horse, the chronicler, has been writing down what is going on in Watona: "He was writing for those who would come later, for the next generation and the next, as if the act of writing was itself part of divination and prophecy, an act of deliverance."[54] It was to be a new testament written by Horse, the witness. Through Horse's testimony, the novel makes the readers aware of the strategies of containment that mark dominant discourses about Indians and sets out to counter them through a variety of strategies of its own, redressing the discursive violence that accompanies the murders and dispossession of Horse's people.

Even within Native American literature, the story of Oklahoma has not been fully or critically rendered, and here Hogan was probably thinking of and responding to a version of history offered by John Joseph Mathews in *Sundown*, a novel that deals with male acculturation into white society and with the problems of alcoholism among Indians rather than with dispossession by the state and capital.[55] *Sundown*, first published in 1934, operates rather as a bildungsroman, a narrative of acculturation about a mixed-blood child, Chal, who grows up in Osage territory and loves to ride his horse and dream about being an Indian warrior, hunter, or even a coyote or bird. Sleeping out under the stars and riding hard are his ideas of happiness, and when he goes away to college he finds it difficult to fit in, to be part of the fraternity that he pledges. He does not relate, but he also feels embarrassed by other Indians at the college who do not try to assimilate and who finally leave. An outsider, yet willing to play the game, Chal finally finds a place for himself when war breaks out and he becomes an aviator. After World War I and his father's death, he returns home to a life of idleness, drinking, and fast driving in his roadster until finally, after a two-week drunken binge, nudged by his mother to return to flying, he tells her that he will go to Harvard instead to study law and become an important orator. Mathews's novel, grounded in individualism and written from a decidedly male perspective, is marked by poetic descriptions of nature and focuses on a strictly male-centered world, in which Indian men are enticed by white women, and Indian women, like his mother, are silent partners, lacking voice or agency. The Osage community is seen from the perspective of a nostalgic young man, nostalgic for a world he did not get to live in. For mixed-bloods like Chal and his father, the arrival of white settlers and entrepreneurs is a sign of progress, until oil production diminishes and the town withers. Even the murders of Osage men and women are dismissed in a single paragraph. *Sundown* is not a history of the Osages but rather an individualistic and even nostalgic account of lost cultural customs and the loss of open spaces. The narrative, like the protagonist, is not concerned with enclosures, but with identity and cultural difference.

Hogan, by contrast, is centrally concerned with the repeated instances of Indigenous dispossession. By combining aspects of culture from the Five Civilized Tribes in her representation of a fictional Osage town, Watona, Hogan is able to bring in other Indian histories that interconnect with events in Watona. For example, to stress the importance of women in Indigenous cultures, Hogan re-creates in the novel the role of women in Creek society, with a matrilineal clan system, rather than that of the Osage, which is patrilineal and patriarchal. The novel thus deals with a recovery of history and with enclosures: it centers the loss of the Indian commons and the privatization of land through a variety of means, especially violence and murder. It also addresses issues of acculturation of Indians and how enclosures serve to produce consumers and wage laborers as well as a lumpen shantytown. In all of this, the primary critique is focused on the state, which allows the establishment of enclosures and fails to act to bring the perpetrators of violence to anything resembling justice. In the process, the novel attempts to re-create the lost commons among the Hill Indians, whose runners, like Cria, carry the weight of history on their backs.

Mean Spirit is narrated chronologically in two parts and covers events occurring in Osage territory in Oklahoma during a two-year span (1922–23). Within these divisions are multiple recollections of the nineteenth century (the Trail of Tears, the Ghost Dance, the Wounded Knee Massacre, Crazy Horse) and references to the repeated nature of a variety of types of enclosures imposed on Native Americans in the United States. The narrative takes place almost entirely in the Osage town of Watona (renamed Talbert by the state but still called Watona by Indians) and includes the outskirts, like the Tar Town shantytown; the surrounding forest, rivers, and creeks; the bluffs (the Cave of Sorrow); and the Hill settlement. Watona is a boomtown that with its auction tree, courthouse, two stores, the tribal council building, a speakeasy, picnic grounds, streets, Indian Agency Office, churches, hotel, restaurants, train station, a school, the sheriff's office, and jail figures centrally in the narrative. Portrayed as often bustling, especially on payday when oil royalties and leasing fees are paid to Indians and people come from out of town to sell their wares, Watona also has a carnivalesque atmosphere, with a traveling show, a religious tent service, a Native Indian church service, and other events. The town always smells of oil and smoke and is often rocked by explosions and the sound of gushers struck by the oil workers.

The main characters belong to two households: the Graycloud family (Moses, Belle, Lettie, Louise, her husband Floyd, and their children, Rena and Ben, and Ruth Tate [Moses's sister]), and the Blanket family (Lila, Grace, Sara, and Nola [Grace's daughter]), linked to the Hill settlement and related to Moses Graycloud. The novel shifts from episodes affecting individual members of the Graycloud household to the murder of the two oil-wealthy Blanket sisters (Grace and Sara), with the survivor, Nola, seen to be in peril. Behind these murders and other acts of violence is the aforementioned Hale, the oilman and rancher who controls the town and is in cahoots with Sheriff Jess Gold and others interested in gaining access to Osage lands and oil. The novel makes no secret of who's behind the murders; the intrigue or what interests the reader is whether justice is possible, when in fact the criminal is the state allied to capital, and whether any of the characters will survive. The other main character is Stace Red Hawk, a Sioux Indian who is an FBI agent, sent to Watona with other FBI agents to investigate the violence in the town. Stace, who at first mistakenly feels that a federal agency is the way to help his people, in the end joins the Graycloud family exodus.

Part 1 introduces the characters and tells us about an anomalous set of murders that have taken place in Watona (among them, those of Grace Blanket, Sara Blanket, Walker, and John Thomas as well as those of the deputy sheriff [killed by the sheriff himself], and the owner of the store [also killed by the sheriff]); the jailing of Benoit, falsely accused of having murdered his wife, Sara Blanket, after a bomb is exploded at their house; the marriage of Nola and Will Forrest; the tribal marriage of Lettie and Benoit; the murder of Benoit while in jail; and the auction and bad investments of Nola's money by her guardian. Hale's manipulation of several people to carry out murders, the oil boom, the arrival of the FBI agents, the acculturation and consumerism of the few wealthy Indians who spend their money extravagantly, and the dispossession (robbery) of Indians by the federal agency, their guardians, the oilmen, and those who lease the land are all figured in the narrative. We are also introduced to the Hill settlement, a place in the hills outside Watona to which Indians fled in 1861 to escape and avoid contact and contamination by Western culture and where the commons, traditions, and culture are still upheld. It is a settlement with runners, or watchmen, who protect their own, especially Nola Blanket and later the Grayclouds. Here in the Hill settlement, Nola's grandmother, Lila Blanket, had been the river prophet. Other characters central to the narrative are the hermit Michael Horse, who serves as recorder and witness of history and who keeps the fire of his culture burning; Ona Neck, who sits with the fire when Horse has to go to town; the Baptist preacher Joe Billy and his white wife, Martha; the farmer Jim Josh, who plants his tomatoes in bathtubs; the bad-smelling John Stink; Attorney Forrest; and the local priest.

If the novel's first part focuses on the rash of murders in Watona circa 1922, part 2 focuses on some of the Indians' concerns with maintaining their culture, evident not only in their participation in the native church but also in their contact with Lionel Tell, who comes from Sioux country for a collective sing, and in the portrayal of the call for a return of acculturated Indians to their native culture by relocating to the Hill settlement. This 1923 section also deals with the spirit of freedom and rebellion symbolized by the stallion Redshirt in the midst of additional murders, the attempted murder of Belle, and the murder of Ruth Tate by her husband. Native American concern for the natural environment, the flora and fauna, is revealed in their grief over the destruction of the land, the decimation of eagles to sell their feathers, and the disappearance of bats. Even the once-wealthy Indians are, after a time, dispossessed of everything and end up displaced to the edge of town, to Tar Town—where there are no services, no housing, no food—a shantytown where Ben

Graycloud, for example, ends up after running away from the school in Kansas that he is forced to attend.

Part 2 also reveals the growing disillusionment of the FBI agent Stace with the government, courts, and the FBI, especially when he suspects that his own FBI superior, Ballard, may be involved in what is happening in Watona (because Stace discovers that his boss is reading the mail he sends). The fact that the murders and attempted murders (seventeen in half a year) go on, even after the trials and sentencing of the main villain Hale, leads Stace to suspect the existence of an even larger and more ominous conspiracy and network of criminals, especially when a bomb is placed under the Graycloud house at the end. The novel signals the continuity of violence against Indians, having as an end the establishment of enclosures and the multiple and multiform dispossessions of Indians.

Mean Spirit needs to be seen above all as a recovery of memory with a decoding of historical accounts, especially of the loss of the commons through the establishment of enclosures. It bears witness to spatial violence in different forms: Indian relocation, the state's creation of the reservation, and the creation of new subjects through privatization and renewed dispossession. It is also a narrative recoding—through a composite account—of how the state, that "mean uncle" responsible for much of their grief, has worked to exploit, oppress, and exterminate the Indians of Oklahoma. In what follows, we move to examine how the novel deals specifically with the decoding of the past, what strategies are used by the state and capital to establish enclosures, how actual historical events are recoded in a fictional account, and how narrative reveals the lived experience of those subjected to dispossession, exploitation, and marginalization.

The Commons

A key component in *Mean Spirit* is the reestablishment of a commons in the Hill settlement. While some commodities, like cooking utensils and clothing, have made it to the settlement, the relations of production continue to be precapitalist. Here it is worth remarking that Marx, at the end of his life, came to see that the commons that still existed among Indigenous tribes and other peoples of the world could play a pivotal role in the move away from capitalist relations.[56] What especially impressed Marx, interestingly, was that in the old tribal systems that maintained the commons, it was the gens and not the family that was the important social unit and thus a model for future revolutions and societies.[57] Native American tribes in the United States were communal societies, living collectively and sharing the game hunted as well as the harvest. Agriculture was primarily in the hands of women, with men doing the hunting. It is this communal mode of production that came to be destroyed by the incoming European colonists and settlers. In the end, in Hogan's novel, the commons is shown to be neither compatible with nor possible within modern civilized society. The Hill settlement in *Mean Spirit* has to hide its community, and even the road to the settlement is camouflaged and hidden from outsiders. Indians know full well that historically the commons, that is, the land held in common by Indigenous populations for hunting, gathering, and planting, was always declared vacant land by the state and subject to appropriation by would-be settlers and land speculators. Though this alternative diasporic Hill community is limited to a few acres used for farming with some fishing in nearby rivers and creeks, it succeeds in maintaining Osage culture and traditions.

In Watona, on the other hand, as in the rest of Indian Territory in Oklahoma, enclosures have destroyed the commons that the tribes worked to reestablish on the reservations after having been driven from areas east of the Mississippi and some, like the Osages, from Kansas; new enclosures continue to separate them from the means of production. Recurring enclosures are not only central to Hogan's narrative but part of US history. As noted earlier, the novel chronicles many of these past events as a way of constructing a critical memory, and through this counterhistory it provides what the character Michael Horse calls "an act of deliverance."[58] While historically there are many documented instances of the strategies of Indigenous expropriation between 1492 and the twenty-first century and the forcible removal of Indians from lands that were held in common in the Americas, here the novel recalls the cases via characters who lived through these events.

As noted, these practices date back to the nineteenth century and earlier, and continued well into the middle of the twentieth century and have current twenty-first-century enactments in the antifracking-pipeline struggles of the present. Dennis McAuliffe indicates, for example, that between 1954 and 1962, 13,263 Indians and nearly 1.4 million acres of Indian land were removed from federal protection, making their "richly timbered reservations" available to US timber companies.[59] Although the former Indian owners were compensated, they were effectively dispossessed. In a watershed moment with important consequences, it was during the Nixon administration that this policy was terminated with a restoration of recognition of a few tribes and the passage of the Indian Self-Determination and Education Assistance Act, effective on January 4, 1975. Each Native American tribe now determines membership according to its own criteria. For many tribes, blood quantum is no longer a requirement; some, however, require a one-quarter or more blood quantum.[60]

Foregrounding the Spatial Violence of the State

Historically, various strategies and a whole slew of tactics were used to dispossess Indians, but none, in the end, proved as effective as straightforward acts of physical violence. The early twentieth-century violence in Oklahoma that dispossessed Indigenous peoples is enacted in the Hogan novel as a recoding of previous and still ongoing violence. And violence came in different forms, not necessarily always in the form of warfare. As noted by David E. Wilkins and K. Tsianina Lomawaima, European colonists saw the land as rightfully theirs by dint of "discovery."[61] Whether defined as conquest or couched in Eurocentric and Christian paternalism, discovery was seen to give the white colonists power and privileges over Native peoples. At first, after the arrival of the first British settlers in what is now US territory, Indians seemingly consented to move and share the land with the colonists after being offered goods and trinkets, unaware that they were in fact giving up the land, as noted in Vine Deloria's work.[62] If not willing to make these exchanges, violence, often warfare, was used to force their removal and relocation. The French, on the other hand, preferred a more low-intensity approach, using bartering and persuasion to move Indians, as in the case of the Osages who relocated from the Ohio River valley to Kansas. For their part, the British made Native American tribes war allies against the French and the insurgent US colonies. But on the whole, before and after 1776, irrespective of state regime, violence continued to be the preferred means to force Indian removal.

Early US leaders saw in the Indian a vicious animal that deserved to be exterminated. Washington, for example, cast the Indian in the role of predator, like the wolf.[63] And like the wolf that threatened the farmer's stock, he could—and should—be eliminated if he did not retire on his own. US history is full of accounts of the massacres and military assaults against Indian peoples who retaliated, rebuffed, or refused to tolerate white incursion into their territory. The military expeditions and treaties all led to the further appropriation of Indian lands. Misrepresentation, fraud, and lies at the level of official state discourses were also the discursive forms of violence that facilitated dispossession. Debt, too, was used as a tool of dispossession. Thomas Jefferson himself suggested that "traders might see to it that 'the good and influential individuals run in debt' because once inextricably entangled, they would be willing to pay the debt by 'a cession of lands.'"[64] A variant of this strategy is referenced by Hale in Hogan's novel, when he asks an Indian, Walker, who is indebted to him, to buy an insurance policy making Hale the beneficiary; to cash in, he then has Walker murdered but makes it look like a case of accidental poisoning.

Force, fraud, bribery, and persuasion out of fear were all means that the government used to obtain land cessions from Indians. There was, however, an additional strategy: governmentality, which Hogan's novel details in its portrayal of the interventions of the BIA and the FBI. The creation of the BIA in 1834 would be instrumental in the continued dispossession of Indians. In *Mean Spirit*, BIA agents figure prominently in carrying this objective out. And then, of course, came the 1887 Dawes Act. Allotment, it was said, would detribalize Indians. In a quote that makes telling allusions to a juggernaut-like violence, President Theodore Roosevelt himself noted that in the Northern Plains, allotment "was a mighty pulverizing engine to break up the tribal mass."[65] Indians, though reluctant to make any additional land cessions, had no choice, especially after the Curtis Act of 1898 terminated tribal tenure.[66] Indians knew there was no way to resist dispossession without ensuring their destruction. This fear of imminent confiscation of their property is what leads many families in Hogan's novel to leave Watona and literally head for the hills.

Legitimating Discourses: By Any Means Necessary

State authorities have always made use of a number of discourses to justify enclosures. They not only argued for removal in view of failure to acculturate, despite evidence to the contrary, but also used paternalistic and moralistic discourses that seemingly advocated for Native Americans.[67] Removal and dispossession were said to be in the best interest of Indians, since relocation would ensure—it was argued—the survival of Indian culture. The government has always marshaled discourses of fairness and justice to justify its policies. Already in federal trade and intercourse laws between 1790 and 1834, the United States, in recognizing Indian sovereignty over lands, would argue that these Indigenous nations were capable of land cessions.[68] For "the greater good" of Indians themselves, they would be removed and relocated. But behind the veneer of these moralistic discourses seeking to save Indians, others spoke more directly, like Thomas Jefferson and Andrew Jackson, and indicated outright that Indians were to be driven into submission or extinction.[69] The objective was the removal of Indians so that productive, civilized, and—pointedly—white settlers could improve and develop the land. The particular land use by Indians was deemed inconsequential, even though the Cherokees and the Choctaws operated plantations, had Black slaves, established churches and schools, and, in the case of the Cherokees, had become literate once their language was scripted by Sequoyah.[70] The Indian was thus seen as inferior, as having a primitive mode of production unsuited to modernity.

In establishing enclosures on Indian territory, the state justified land appropriation, land cessions, and relocation by—literally—manufacturing consent, that is, by forcing Indians to "voluntarily" agree to the government's plans. Discourses of these treaties are thus disguised as fair acts that make the state look good, charitable, paternalistic, and concerned for Indian welfare. Behind these moralistic discourses were structuring mechanisms of capital accumulation through privatization. In reality, the government knowingly allowed and promoted squatters and intruders to settle on Indian land; it levied taxes on them, knowing full well that they would have to sell their land in order to pay them, a strategy that would later be used against Californios, Nuevomexicanos, and Tejanos. Indians were granted neither the right to vote nor the right to testify in court or to bring suit against intruders, since they were not citizens. In the South they were prohibited from digging or mining for gold even on their own land, preserving that right for white prospectors who trespassed on their land.[71] Practical in the extreme, the federal government, when it suited its interests, allowed state laws to predominate and dispossess Indians. When the interests of dispossession were better served otherwise, it argued for the primacy of federal policies.

The Removal Act of 1830 is recalled in Hogan's novel by Belle Graycloud, of Chickasaw descent but of mixed blood. Belle is described as a "light-skinned Indian woman."[72] Her grandmother was removed from her Mississippi homeland and forced to go on the Trail of Tears. The Five Civilized Tribes were forced to relocate to what ironically was renamed Indian Territory, where they received around 19.5 million acres. After leaving Georgia, Alabama, and Mississippi, the tribes settled in what is today the eastern part of Oklahoma, a forested area, with the Cherokee and Creek nations in the northern part of this territory, and the Seminole, Chickasaw, and Choctaw nations in the southern part. Most of this land is no longer in Indian hands. Among the Cherokee, Seminole, Chickasaw, Choctaw, and Creek peoples were some who had been farmers in the South, but most were not; they now had land that they were supposed to cultivate but not the capital to make their lands productive beyond subsistence levels.[73] Within Indian Territory, each tribe functioned as a dependent domestic nation, retaining its communal lands, self-government, religious practices, and language. Although each tribe had different land policies, for the most part individuals could occupy and cultivate all the land they wanted; when they ceased to use the land, it reverted to the collective.[74] Nevertheless, Angie Debo indicates that despite this communal mode of land tenancy, some Indians came to monopolize the land, especially mixed-bloods.[75] In the territory, Indians continued to hunt and cultivate gardens, but by the end of the nineteenth century some, like the Creek, went into ranching and, in some cases, leased their lands for grazing to cattlemen, as does Moses Graycloud in the novel. The Five Tribes had different policies on the immigration of non-Indians into their territories; some had slaves and also admitted intermarried whites and freedmen into the community. These multiracial residents produced mixed-race offspring. As Tiya Miles notes, a good number of historical accounts in Afro-Native studies have been published in the last two decades examining the effects of colonialism and slavery in Native community struggles over citizenship and land rights.[76] During the Civil War, some Indians would side with the North and others with the Confederacy. White immigration into Indian territory began well before the Civil War and increased significantly at its end, with thousands of white settlers as well as other Indians moving into the ostensibly reserved territory.

Wounded Knee and US Empire Abroad: 1890–1898

Just as the British applied policies enacted in their internal colonies in Ireland to their external colonies in India, so, too, would the US government soon make use of the paternalistic discourses it deployed to infantilize and enclose Indian nations to justify imperialist actions in the Pacific and the Caribbean. Indian policy, notes Blue Clark, "provided a domestic guide to overseas rule."[77] After 1898, for example, Filipinos were considered both savage and childlike people, another "domestic dependent nation" according to Henry Cabot Lodge, who, like the Apaches of Arizona per Theodore Roosevelt, needed the "wise supervision" that the United States could provide.[78] Mark Twain, too, saw that the United States was beguiling Filipinos "in the name of 'civilization' in much the same fashion that government agents and missionaries had hoodwinked American Indians years before in a sleight of hand policy that had pledged great benefits to the Indians but in reality brought only misery and degradation."[79] Clark fails to mention, however, that state tactics and strategies of dispossession that were first used against Indians and codified in the Removal Act of 1830 would be used in Mexican territories after the 1840s, before being taken to the Pacific and elsewhere, as the United States expanded its territorial sphere of influence in addition to outright physical presence and control.

In effect, the 1887 Dawes Act, in calling for the privatization of Indian lands, also was calling for the definitive elimination of Indian nations, as had already been suggested in the 1830 *Cherokee Nation v. Georgia* US Supreme Court decision.[80] Treaties that had been signed with these "domestic dependent nations" led dispossessed Indians to argue in the courts that Congress had in fact violated previous treaties that it had signed with them.[81] Lone Wolf, a Kiowa band chief from southwestern Oklahoma, for example, protested the allotment of his Kiowa, Comanche, and Plains Apache Reservation lands to individuals and brought suit on the basis of previous treaties signed with the United States, specifically on the basis that a previous treaty required that three-fourths of adult male Indians sign any agreement for land cessions. The Kiowas argued that not only had the signatures for land cessions been fraudulently obtained, but that they did not meet the required number. But the 1903 US Supreme Court ruling in *Lone Wolf v. Hitchcock* held that Indians were "in substantial effect the wards of the government," and that Congress "had plenary authority over the tribal relations" of Indians and could abrogate any treaty rights or amend any treaty whenever it saw fit to do so, "since all these matters, in any event, were solely within the domain of the legislative authority."[82] The federal government had no problem in breaking treaties whenever upholding them no longer served its interest. With this decision, the Supreme Court lay bare that the federal government would always be willing—and able—to rule against Indians if it benefited capital, especially if breaking treaties allowed for the privatization of land and opened up immense tracts of Indian land for development, that is, for land speculation and white settlement. The government's paternalism and treatment of Indians as dependent nations was used to justify what was in fact continuous enclosure by means of manipulation and outright treachery. As Clark notes, "at every turn, the federal government had a substantial hand in precipitating either the action or the reaction to policies designed to coerce the Indian."[83] Many years later, in 1955, the Indian Claims Commission, in recognition of illegal land-taking, awarded the Kiowas, Comanches, and Plains Apaches a remedy of $2 million; lost lands did not even figure in the picture.[84]

The 1887 Dawes Act, as previously noted, imposed privately held land allotments on all reservations, that is, in all areas where land was held communally, except for the area of the Five Civilized Tribes and the Osages, although after the Curtis Act of 1898, tribal governments were also disbanded and tribal tenure of land was terminated.[85] The effect of this allotment policy is evident in the Hogan novel where Indians, like the Grayclouds, possess their allotted 160 acres, use the land for crops, for grazing horses and a few cows, and lease the rest to ranchers for grazing. In some cases their land is leased without their knowledge or approval, as Belle Graycloud discovers. As Stuart Banner notes, it would take several years before the federal government would see allotment policies as a travesty and a failure and begin, with the Indian Reorganization Act of 1934, restoring remaining unsold land to the tribes.[86] By then, of course, the government had succeeded in what it had meant to do all along: privatize the land, dispossess Indians, and make the land available to white settlers and other interests.

In 1901, Congress conferred US citizenship on every Indian in what was by then called Oklahoma Territory.[87] As a result, the Five Civilized Tribes gave up their communal landholding and tribal citizenship in exchange for US citizenship and individual land titles.[88] Private landholding and citizenship were thus tied, married as it were, making evident the close link between capital and the state. In the rest of the country, all Indians would become US citizens by decree after passage in 1924 of the Indian Citizenship Act. Once the land was privatized in Oklahoma and made accessible to the white settler population, the newcomer sector pushed for statehood. In 1907, Oklahoma became a state; in the process Indians became subjects of the state government as well, a situation that would further complicate their rights and recourse for redress, especially once the state named guardians for Indians, as reflected in *Mean Spirit*, when Nola Blanket is assigned a guardian.

The government unremittingly saw fit to break treaties and make changes on Indian reservations throughout the United States whenever it sought to gain access to and make available more Indian land. This double-pronged strategy also continued even while making war on Indians. After the 1864 Sand Creek Massacre of the Cheyenne in Colorado, the Plains Indians, especially the Cheyenne and Lakota, organized against the military and the settlers. The warrior Crazy Horse, who would ultimately be killed by soldiers after surrendering at Camp Robinson, was part of the Battle of Little Big Horn, where General Custer was defeated in 1876, and participated in several other battles against US forces. In Hogan's novel, Crazy Horse is recalled at the sing conducted by the Sioux medicine man Lionel Tall, when he performs the sacred stone ceremony at Ona's house. Other treacheries against the Sioux are also recalled and textualized in the novel. Attempts to open up the territory to white homesteaders by reducing the Sioux to five small reservations in an area in South Dakota where they were expected to farm semiarid land, led to disaster, as the Lakota Sioux began to starve. Faced with destitution and the end of their way of life, they turned to the Paiute prophet Wevokah (also Wovoka) and his Ghost Dance, a religious ceremony or spiritual/messianic revival, a form of resistance, that Indians linked to regaining autonomy and the removal of white settlers from their lands. The dancers wore ghost shirts that they believed made them impervious to bullets, but more importantly, they were also part of a broader movement that rejected US domination and subjection and refused to heed the orders of BIA agents, for example, to send their children off to Indian schools. For this reason, BIA agents outlawed the Ghost Dance, and US troops were deployed to restrict the dancers to the Pine Ridge Reservation. In December 1890, a group of about 350 Sioux on their way to Pine Ridge Reservation were stopped by US troops and forcibly taken to a place near Wounded Knee Creek, where they set up camp. When attempts were made the next day to disarm them and take them to a train bound for Nebraska, soldiers opened fire on the Lakota and killed hundreds, mostly women and children, chasing after those who attempted to flee. The wounded were left to die in an oncoming blizzard, and their bodies were later found frozen in place. This is the massacre scene that Lionel Tall, Stace Red Hawk's friend and mentor, recalls in *Mean Spirit*. The Lakota Lionel Tall had left his wife and young son to travel in 1890 to Canada, where he hoped to spread the word among the Cree about Wevokah and the Ghost Dance. Unable to interest them, as they were primarily concerned with survival and finding food, he returns to Wounded Knee, where he found both his wife and baby frozen dead in the snow, along with many others. This memory is doubly crucial in Hogan's work, as it explains the title of the novel and points quite directly to the role of the state in Native American extermination and dispossession: "Lying in bed that night in Oklahoma, Tall still grieved. He remembered the body of a small girl whose cap had been embroidered and beaded with the American flag. She lay there, one of her blue hands stretched out, as if asking for help. Uncle Sam was a cold uncle with a mean soul and a cruel spirit."[89] Like the frozen child with the embroidered US flag on her cap, several of the Oklahoma Indians, who had moreover served in World War I, used flag-embroidered blankets at Watona events; like the child, they could expect nothing from the "mean spirit" that was primarily interested in dispossessing Indians of their land and decimating a population that both federal and state governments considered a costly obstacle to order and progress. Fear of the army and of yet another removal was so ingrained that when Watona Indians hear rumors from some federal government official that they are to be relocated by the army, they decide to sell their land and leave. Stace Red Hawk runs out into the street to stop the cars overloaded with Indians' belongings to assure them that the rumor is false, but they do not believe him. Historically ingrained fear of forced removal or relocation and massacre is thus again deployed in the 1920s to gain further access to and control of Indian land by means of intimidation and psychological terror, the most effective forms of discursive violence.

While allotment policies and practices led to the effective elimination of Indian communal lands, efforts were soon under way to eliminate any remaining restrictions on the sale and taxation of Indians' individualized property. As Senator Porter McCumber argued, "The states wanted the lands for white settlers and they wanted the lands made taxable."[90] Protectionists feared that Indian dispossession would follow, and for this reason the BIA created categories of restricted and nonrestricted lands and competent and incompetent Indians that only led to further mechanisms of exploitation and oppression, as Hogan's novel demonstrates. Those classified as incompetent were not allowed to sell their land, that is, their allotted 160 acres. If these restrictions were in place on the land, then only 120 of 160 acres could be sold. The Indian Appropriation Act of 1904 removed all restrictions on non-Indian members, that is, whites and black freedmen, who held land within the territory of the Five Civilized Tribes. As the protectionists feared, graft and theft soon followed.

Women and Native Americans, Restricted Status, and Dispossession

As Indians began to lose their land on an ever-wider scale, attempts were made at a congressional level to protect the property of the Five Civilized Tribes' full-bloods by declaring that Indians with high blood quantum should—for their own good—be declared "restricted" or incompetent.[91] The citizenship status that was to come with individual allotment was in fact postponed or undermined by provisions of the Burke Act and the Oklahoma Enabling Act (1906) for those Indians who had the legal status of restricted Indian. In effect, the Burke Act left restricted Indians in a halfway zone between being citizens of the United States and tribal citizens, further constraining their subject status and limiting them as legal actors.[92] These restricted Indians were placed under the jurisdiction of the federal government. BIA personnel were seen as the experts that should determine when an Indian was able and capable of managing his own affairs, that is, when he was legally competent. Then and only then could he or she be declared a citizen. It was finally agreed in 1908 through the Closure Act, also known as the Crime of 1908, that Congress could restrict only until 1931 the sale of forty acres (of the 160 allotted) belonging to mixed-blood Indians and all the land of full-bloods, whom Commissioner Burke called "blanket Indians."[93] Blanket, in fact, is notably in the novel the last name of the assassinated sisters—Grace and Sarah Blanket—who are Osage full-bloods and the children of the river prophet Lila Blanket. Grace's daughter, Nola Blanket, will inherit their headrights and become the wealthiest woman in Watona, a status that places her in a doubly vulnerable situation in the narrative.

Especially in her presentation of Osage women in *Mean Spirit*, Hogan brilliantly figures gender and racial subordination, both disguised as protected classes, to great narrative and critical effect. Women and Native Americans share a restricted status that better allows for their control and dispossession at the hands of guardians. In the person of Nola Blanket, especially, the author signals the discursive maneuvers by which power is exercised and violence enacted: just as women are infantilized under the patriarchal aegis of coverture (*femme couvert*) under the marriage contract, so, too, Native Americans, male and female alike, are infantilized and feminized as blanket Indians (wards of the state) in need of guidance and protection by a wise male father/husband figure, here the US state and its agencies. Contracts, whether in the form of treaties, legislative acts, or marriages, serve in the novel as discursive apparatuses to achieve desired outcomes: policing and constraining those ostensibly in need of oversight and shielding, dispossessing them of their agency, land, or headrights.

After Oklahoma achieved statehood in 1907, it sought to curtail federal control of Indians, but the Burke Act made federal control "conclusive and final."[94] It was the Department of the Interior that determined Indian legal competency, federal decisions that could not be appealed through the courts. Though opposed by those wanting all valuable Indian land to enter the market economy, this federal paternalism and treatment of Indians as if they were children under the supervision of the federal government led to yet another pernicious practice: the establishment of local control over restricted Indigenous land. The 1908 Oklahoma Closure Act permitted the leasing of these restricted surplus properties, while at the same time it placed minors and those declared incompetent under the jurisdiction of Oklahoma probate courts that appointed guardians.[95] In a key scene in *Mean Spirit*, Moses Graycloud, who's been declared competent and has his Certificate of Competency, goes to the council house with other Indians for their quarterly royalties or payment for grazing leases, but receives only a tenth of the money ($200) he's entitled to for leasing his land; when he questions the error, he is informed that as a full-blood Indian he can receive only part of his money. Apparently the Indian Commission (that is, the BIA) had changed the rules, as it always did, arguing now that full-bloods mismanaged their money: "Every Indian in the room had heard this argument and knew it by heart. . . . They knew only that the courts used that argument against them, assuming they were like children and without a nickel's worth of intelligence."[96] Outraged at the injustice and denial of what was rightfully their due, Moses saw there was nothing they could do: "They might be cheated, but they still had life, and until only recently, even that was not guaranteed under the American laws, so they remained trapped, silent, and wary."[97] Here, Horse, "the diviner and translator and keeper of accounts," laments that his people have to "accept still another swindle."[98] This swindle will strain Moses Graycloud's budget, and he knows that he will not be able to both pay his trading post debt and survive until the next disbursement.

The Oklahoma guardianship system led to the further pillaging of Indian land and the plunder of oil annuities, since the appointed guardians handled both; in some cases they sold the ward's land, spent the money, or invested the funds in worthless ventures, as did Nola's guardian, Attorney Forrest in Hogan's novel. By declaring rich Indians with oil on their property incompetent, the guardians, lawyers, politicians, judges, speculators, and others were positioned to profit through their control.[99] The manipulation of these lands and funds by the state-named guardians is an important issue presented in Hogan's novel, underscoring the dispossession of land as well as income derived from their oil.

Mean Spirit is then a narrative composite of a number of historical events and individual Indian cases in Oklahoma. The historical case of Jackson Barnett, called the "world's richest Indian" after oil was discovered on his allotted acreage, is an exemplary case.[100] Property allotted to Barnett, an illiterate Creek Indian, by the Dawes Commission in 1903 was in an area of high-grade crude oil that would make him a millionaire. This land was under federal jurisdiction and also under local jurisdiction according to new Oklahoma state laws. Thus, though a ward of the federal government, he was also a ward of a county court–appointed guardian. Barnett's land was leased first to one oil company and then to another, according to the preference of his guardian; after a compromise was worked out and drilling began, it turned out that the wells drilled on his land were the richest in the Cushing field. The royalties that started to pour in went to the BIA and were used to buy Liberty Bonds or paid out to Barnett's guardian, presumably for Barnett's personal living expenses. The world's "richest Indian" continued living in a shack, receiving only a couple of hundred dollars; he did not manage his own affairs and knew very little of the accruing royalties. In Hogan's novel, the wealthiest Indian in Oklahoma is a woman, Grace Blanket, and it is she who is killed in an attempt to try to gain her headright. In this case the scheme is to kill both Grace and her sister Sara so that her daughter, Nola, can inherit the two headrights; since marriage to wealthy Indian women is moreover seen as the primary strategy for white men to gain control of women's wealth, when Will Forrest marries Nola, he's in line to inherit all her wealth should she die. It is this fearful realization that leads the pregnant Nola to kill her husband and flee to join the Hill people.

    The historical Barnett case showed how disempowered Indians could become, how broadly the BIA defined Indians as incompetent, and the enormous power that the Department of the Interior had over Indian lands and property. In some cases it was the BIA itself, rather than the local guardians, that denied Indians access to their own funds, as noted by Thorne, "based on convictions that income from inheritance or leasing was undeserved or that Indians should be forced to work rather than live on 'unearned' income."[101] In effect, the BIA negotiated and approved leases for grazing, logging, and mineral rights, received the proceeds, and distributed the money as it saw fit. This blocking of access is a key issue taken up in Hogan's novel, not only in the previously cited case of Moses Graycloud, but also in the case of Belle Graycloud's land. One morning, Belle awakes to see a herd grazing on her land without her knowledge or consent. The agency had seen fit to lease her land without bothering to inform her.

    The guardianship arrangements of thousands of Indians in Oklahoma, deemed incompetent by the county courts, offered prime conditions for violence, graft, assassination, and corruption. Guardians used legal strategies to gain control of land;[102] fiduciary obligations notwithstanding, they would not only lease and sell their wards' land but also pocket the money. There were many cases of forgery, embezzlement, criminal conspiracy, kidnapping, swindling, and even the dynamiting of individuals, as related in Hogan's novel.[103] Legal battles between rival guardians profited attorneys.[104] Needless to say, the BIA, the commissioner, and the superintendent as well as the local guardian system were all litigants at one point or another, with suits being brought against different individuals and agents. Another such case is the assassination of Sybil Bolton, a wealthy Osage woman, by her guardian, Woodward, detailed in *Bloodland* (1999), written by Dennis McAuliffe, her grandson. The murders and other criminal acts finally led Congress to call for an investigation of the situation, and in 1928 the Institute of Government Research issued its Meriam Report and established the earlier-referenced Indian New Deal, advocating a return to tribal corporate landholding, tribal self-government, and an affirmation of Indian culture as a way to mitigate the abuse by "authorities."[105]

These reports noted the widespread ignorance, poverty, famine, and disease that existed among the so-called restricted Indians and the graft of their guardians.[106] Enclosures and constraints were now being imposed through varied strategies, some old, some new. In 1933 Congress extended competency restrictions on Osage and Five Civilized Tribes lands to impede the sale of remaining Indian land, but restrictions were in fact lifted on Indians with a blood quantum below 50 percent. The 1934 Indian Reorganization Act acknowledged past wrongs instituted by allotment and called for a return to tribal organization, eliminating in the process the category of incompetency, but communal property was not restored, and the federal trust relationship was maintained, with the federal government managing lease agreements without letting the Indians know "for what purpose, how much the lease yielded, or how long the lease was to run" and without giving them more than a pittance "without accounting or an explanation."[107] To date, the federal government, as noted by Ward Churchill, continues to collaborate with US corporations to exploit Indian lands and their reserves of oil, natural gas, coal, and other mineral deposits.[108] Gross mismanagement of these funds and resources has been a constant, and for that reason the US government continues to be sued.[109]

What Tanis C. Thorne calls a "well-meaning paternalism" to save Indian land had in fact "metamorphosed into an unwieldy and undemocratic bureaucracy."[110] Her assumption that the federal government was acting as an Indian advocate and protector while simultaneously keeping them dependent is a misreading of evidence that she herself presents. In fact, the federal government sought to ensure that Indian lands were made available to white settlers and other interested parties. It kept Indians dependent from the onset, since it removed them from the South and Kansas and ensured what Thorne acknowledges was "legalized robbery."¹¹¹ From the beginning, as Debo makes clear, "the plunder of Indians was so closely joined with pride in the creation of a great new commonwealth that it received little condemnation."¹¹² The government's racist policies and practices of enclosure were calculated to maintain the dominant status quo. Enclosures also led to the migration both piecemeal and en masse of Indian populations, as we find in Hogan's novel, and to unfettered access to Indian land and resources; when Indians did not leave of their own accord, the government relocated them once again. Later, during the Eisenhower administration in the 1950s, the BIA was again using forced assimilation to relocate Native Americans from their communities to distant cities. The 1961 documentary film *The Exiles* is a painful accounting of this alienating experience of dispossession and displacement to urban areas.¹¹³ The film, following the history of the 1956 Relocation Act (Public Law 949), presents Indians removed from the reservation and now in Los Angeles.¹¹⁴ Hogan calls it a "bleak, tragic film" of people "trying to go home."¹¹⁵ Issues of Indian agency, consent, or lack thereof are central to Hogan's novel, where the handicapped status of Indians becomes both the ostensible cause and desired effect of government actions relative to the Indian population: the better to dispossess them.

The Osages: Runners and Chroniclers

Hogan's novel deals centrally with several murder cases in Osage territory in Oklahoma and collects a number of traditions found in Osage culture maintained by the Hill settlement and by some of the Indians in Watona, including the training of runners or watchmen. Louis Burns notes that the Osages were "remarkable walkers" and were known for their speed on foot.¹¹⁶ This pedestrian power, as one might term it, is figured in Hogan's novel where the watchers travel with great speed from the town to the hills, as when, fearing for her well-being, they spirit Nola back to the Hill settlement after she kills her husband. Traditionally, the Osages were ruled by the Little Old Men, or elders. One of the elders' special duties was to serve as chroniclers; they were, Burns says, "the living libraries of Osage history."¹¹⁷ In Hogan's novel, Horse is both chronicler and diviner, helping to forecast weather and locate water as well as recording the history of Indians in Watona. Other examples, like the use of an emetic black drink, Osage funeral practices, their use of peyote in the native church, the survival of the Ghost Dance religious practices, their use of bat medicine, and their concern with keeping the hearth fire burning, symbolic of Osage culture, are also textualized in Hogan's narrative. While much of what has been discussed about the Five Civilized Tribes is key to what happens in Hogan's novel, historically the Osage experience was a bit different and warrants further detail.

Various historians have addressed the complex history of the Osages. Louis F. Burns's *A History of the Osage People*, for example, records the migration, organization, and customs of the Osages before the coming of the European invaders and after, up to the loss of their lands and their removal to Oklahoma. The Osages did not arrive in Oklahoma by a Trail of Tears as did the Cherokee, Choctaw, Chickasaw, Creek, and Seminole Indians. The Osages were originally from east of the Mississippi, probably from around the Ohio River valley. Archaeologists studying artifacts and designs note similarities between mound-building Mississippian people influenced by the Mesoamerican Mayas and Siouan people from the Dakotas. A Siouan society, the Osages separated from the eastern Sioux early on; by the eighteenth century, in contact with French fur traders, they had moved west of the Mississippi. Hunters and warriors, the Osages dominated the area that is now Missouri, Arkansas, eastern Oklahoma, and Kansas and were highly influenced by their neighbors, the Caddoan and Algonquian tribes.[118] From the French, and later the Spanish, the Osages gained access to horses and weapons. By 1802 the French, who regained control of this area, had convinced half the tribe living around the Missouri River valley to move south into villages at Three Forks in what is now Oklahoma.

Contact with European settlers proved deadly to many Osages, who were decimated by a number of epidemics, including smallpox, influenza, cholera, measles, and typhoid fever in the nineteenth century. An additional disease that struck in the 1850s was scrofula, a type of lymphatic tuberculosis. This disease spread among the Osages. One man, called John Stink because scrofula caused a bad body odor, was shunned by his tribe; for this reason he preferred to live alone, like an outcast, with only his dogs. Royalties from his allotment and mineral rights afforded him steak for his dogs, but he continued to live hermit-like outside of town. It is said that one day he suffered a severe scrofula attack, fell unconscious, and was buried when it was assumed that he was dead.[119] When he was later seen walking about, he was considered a ghost. While Terry P. Wilson calls the story apocryphal,[120] still Hogan includes the character John Stink in her account of the murders, and it is his wealth that, like Barnett, makes him a good prospective husband. In *Mean Spirit*, Hale sends his girlfriend China to marry Stink to access his income, but in the end they are unable to marry as Stink has already been declared legally dead.

After the Louisiana Purchase, Osage land was offered to the Five Civilized Tribes, and under pressure from the US government, the Osages ceded what is now Missouri and half the territory that constitutes Arkansas.[121] A second Osage cession of 1,800,000 acres was forced on the tribe in what is now Oklahoma, land that was in turn sold to the Cherokees for $2 million. A third cession would be forced on the Osages in 1825, requiring their removal and further cession of 45,000,000 acres in Kansas and Oklahoma for a stretch of land in what is now Kansas, with a neutral zone fifty miles wide separating them from enemy tribes and with livestock, horses, farming equipment, and "one penny for each six acres."[122] In the meantime, white settlers continued to move into reservation lands, further circumscribing the Osages. When the government decreed the removal of all Indians from Kansas, the Osages were once again relocated. To fathom the scope of the spatial violence enacted, consider that in the seven years between 1864 and 1871 all Indians in Kansas were removed to Oklahoma; the process of sequential enclosures continued.

The Osage Removal Act of 1870, approved by the Osage Council, initiated the migration of about 3,300 Osages to lands they purchased from the Cherokees with proceeds from their Kansas land cessions. The new reservation included some 1,470,000 acres in northern Oklahoma, a forested area with streams, meadows, and game, including buffalo, west of the Arkansas River.[123] Primarily hunters, by 1871 all the Osages had moved to the Osage reservation. By then, however, they were a reduced population of about three thousand, with a majority of full-bloods and a minority of mixed-bloods (primarily the children of white men married to Osage women).[124] The fact that they had purchased their own reservation lands and their fierce resistance to the elimination of tribal government would mark the Osages as a strong nation; they continued to maintain their tribal oranization, seeking the advice of their elders, the Little Old Men, although in time the power of the elders decreased, and by the end of the nineteenth century they followed the pattern of other tribes and established an Osage National Council.[125]

Finding that annuities for lands sold in Kansas were being paid in goods that were not distributed, which had given rise to scarcity and hunger during the severe winter of 1877, the Osages sent a delegation to Washington requesting cash payment instead of goods. After 1879, quarterly payment days were held to distribute annuities from leased land, kept to $70 or $80 per quarter until 1890.[126] These disbursement events and the carnival atmosphere that developed to try to separate Indians from their money or to try to collect on loans made at usurious rates in expectation of annuities are issues discussed in Hogan's novel, as is the sale of bootleg liquor (banned from the reservation) and the resulting alcoholism.[127] *Mean Spirit* illustrates the damage wrought by alcohol in Watona; Graycloud's son-in-law Floyd makes his living in part from bootlegging, and Belle is forced to take drastic action to rehabilitate her alcoholic young grandson. In Hogan's novel, the carnivalesque payment days continue into the 1920s. The incomes that the characters receive in the novel, however, are oil annuities, and there is no mention of land annuities, to which, for example, the full-blood Moses would have been entitled.

The Osages were hunters, never interested in becoming farmers, although women continued to work gardens for subsistence; in time they became involved in leasing their land to cattlemen from Texas.[128] The BIA approved the leasing proposal, and in 1882 the Osage National Council agreed to the first leases, although not all the Osages agreed. In *Mean Spirit*, Hale would lease hundreds of acres for his cattle runs. Although the land was communally owned until 1906, each Indian was allowed to enclose his own fields for cultivation and have a quarter mile of pasturage in each direction from the enclosed fields.[129]

Issues of Identity

The Dawes Act of 1887 was vehemently opposed by the Osages and Five Civilized Tribes, exempting these nations from the General Allotment Act and the measure's forced privatization. But soon white settlers, banking, railroad, and mercantile interests were pressuring Congress for Osage land. The policy of allotment divided the Osages, with full-bloods opposed and mixed-bloods in favor. The issue of who could decide centered on the tribal rolls, with full-bloods insisting that there were fraudulent entries in the rolls. This division among Osages, exploited by outside interests, led the commissioner of the BIA, who wanted to speed up the process of allotment, to move to simply abrogate the Osage National Council. Allotment among the Osages and Five Civilized Tribes was finally enforced in 1906. White settlers, cattlemen, churchmen, and agency workers had by then penetrated the reservation and outnumbered the Osages. Although some Osages employed non-Indian laborers on their lands, there were also numerous white squatters who did not generally consider that Osages rightfully owned their land and therefore saw no problem in trespassing.[130] In a nation of laws, there was no protection under the law for the Osages.

Blood and Oil

When the Osages finally submitted to allotment, they gave up their communal land holdings. Each Indian on the tribal rolls (including 926 full-bloods and 1,304 mixed-bloods or adopted) received 160 acres for each member of the family—and this is a crucial provision—they were also able to stipulate that the tribe's underground mineral resources be retained as a communal holding.[131] In other words, subsoil mineral rights belonged to the tribe rather than to the individuals receiving land allotments. The communal property thus was underground. In his book *The Underground Reservation: Osage Oil*, Wilson reveals the story of the Osage Indian Reservation in Oklahoma and what took place there after the discovery of oil in 1897. Again, what distinguished the Osages from other tribes was their insistence on the collective ownership of underground resources. Oil rights were the property of the tribe, their "underground reservation" so to speak, even after their surface lands were in the hands of the white intruders. Wilson notes that historians like John Joseph Mathews tried to write "a tribal history conceived from a Native American viewpoint, combining documentary and oral research and written with Indians as the primary actors," noting, however, that Mathews concentrates on the Osage cultural legacy and leaves aside for the most part the discovery of oil and much of the twentieth century.[132] For his part, Wilson focuses on relations beween full-blood and mixed-blood Osages, who came to outnumber full-bloods, which brought divisions among the Osages on the reservation, "continually marked by lawlessness and corruption, and occasionally by violence."[133] While blood quantum was (and continues to be) a contentious issue, it is what is behind the determination of annuities that is key.

In Hogan's *Mean Spirit*, subsoil rights are not owned collectively but individually, and problems are not based on whether the individuals are full-bloods or mixed-bloods, since mixture exists within every family. Had the novel followed historical events, as a full-blood Osage, Moses Graycloud would have been entitled to an oil annuity, but since oil is not communal but private property and since there is no oil on his land in the novel, he is entitled only to the grazing fee he receives for leasing out his land. Even this income is reduced when the BIA exercises its stewardship and rules that full-bloods need to be protected and are entitled to only part of their income. Understandably, when oil begins to seep through in Belle Graycloud's creek, it is not a welcome event, and the family does its best to hide the oil. By now, in view of all the violence and murders, the black gold is seen as a curse.

Historically, in addition to land allotted to each Osage individual and to the five towns already established, three 160-acre tracts were also set aside at three towns (Fairfax, Gray Horse, and Pawhuska) as a type of commons, tribal land communally held where Osages could live. But by the middle of the twentieth century, most Osage land was in the hands of non-Indians, and the Osages themselves were impoverished and in debt, their forests destroyed, and their former way of life gone. How it happened is the story of enclosures and the various strategies used by the state and capital to accomplish the disenfranchisement and removal of Indians and the privatization of their land.

Watona in *Mean Spirit* stands in for all the boomtowns full of oil derricks in Oklahoma that came under the control of the companies drilling for black gold. In April 1897, Frank Overless and the Cudahy Oil Company drilled and struck oil at Bartlesville, Oklahoma. In October of the same year, oil was discovered on the Foster lease west of Butler Creek; this would be the first commercial well on the Osage reserve. With the discovery of oil on Osage land, leasing and subleasing of oil areas became fraught as oil companies competed for the right to drill. The Foster brothers would sublease the land and formed the Phoenix Oil Company, later to become the Indian Territory Illuminating Oil Company. Black gold was soon being shipped out by railroad tank cars, and as the volume increased it began to be piped from Tulsa and the Southern Osages to Missouri and from there connected to other lines that reached the East Coast.[134] By 1953, no fewer than 16,962 wells had been drilled, with 6,794 wells producing oil and 216 wells producing gas. The Osages were all millionaires, in theory at least. The real millionaires were the founders of Skelly Oil Company, Sinclair Oil Company, the Phillips Oil Company, the Continental Oil Company (Conoco), and others, including Jean Paul Getty.[135] In time, different methods would be used for production, including water flooding operations, precursors to today's fracking in Sioux Dakota lands. In the novel it is Horse who, while searching for water, strikes oil on Grace Blanket's barren land, which makes her the wealthiest Indian in the territory.

Repeated efforts were made to privatize the subsoil communal domain after the twenty-five-year limit and have the mineral estate pass to the property owner. Opposed to the privatization of the underground reservation, the Osage Council was able to secure three extensions to the Osage Mineral Trust, in 1920, 1929, and 1958. The 1920 extension, however, added a 5 percent gross production tax and a 1 percent roads and bridges tax, to which the Osages finally had to agree after the claims courts ruled against them. A fourth extension in 1963 extended the collective mineral rights in perpetuity.

By 1917, the average Osage family had a yearly income of between $5,000 and $10,000, no mean amount at the time, but this income was often controlled and disbursed by a guardian. In 1921 Congress, responding to evidence of swindles and graft, decided to limit headright payments to $1,000 per quarter for adult Osages and $500 for minors. Despite these Band-Aid attempts at addressing government agents' corruption, oil extraction on Osage lands produced much more money than was ever disbursed; with little or no accountability, surplus funds could be misappropriated with little difficulty. Even the $1,000 maximum per quarter could be garnished for debt payments; debt could also lead to a declaration of incompetence for a competent Indian. Wilson indicates that even after an investigation found that guardians were mishandling funds, and after the Supreme Court had ruled against interpreting 1921 legislation as allowing guardians to manage surplus Indian funds, the situation did not improve. Swindling continued, and the Osages were not protected; moreover, no one was ever jailed for malfeasance. It was a situation profitable for both guardians and attorneys.[136] The fraud taking place was acknowledged and rationalized as an unavoidable outcome of progress; as one attorney noted, "any man with good judgement would know that this is a white man's country and progress and civilization depends upon . . . white civilization."[137] The fraud and outright theft as well as the machinations having to do with competency and restrictions on the basis of blood quantum are taken up and criticized in Hogan's novel as strategies used by individuals and local governments in conjunction with the federal government, with the final aim being to dispossess Indians of their agency, rights, and lands, in the case of the Osages, lands that they had purchased.

Marriage, Merger, Murder: Skewed by Gender

The Osage wealth attracted not only swindlers, graft, corruption, merchants charging exorbitant prices, usury, and all types of irregularities but also men who wanted to marry Osage women in order to share and possibly later inherit their headrights and thus the oil royalties attendant to that birthright. Marriage, as noted previously, was yet another strategy deployed for dispossession. In 1925 the federal government moved to protect the Osages by requiring that all debts contracted by restricted Indians be invalidated unless approved by the secretary of the interior, that is, the BIA. When four years later it moved to pay off the debts by using surplus Osage funds, purported creditors lined up at the trough, and multiple invoices were submitted, of course. Historians likewise record a number of cases in which supposed guardians of Native American interests personally profited from both marriages and debts. None is as famous—or rather infamous—as the Osage Reign of Terror in Fairfax, Oklahoma, which is at the heart of Hogan's novel. But there are other cases, like that of Sybil Beekman, an Osage woman whose murder was made to look like suicide. In the previously mentioned work *Bloodland*, Dennis McAuliffe describes his search for details on the murder of his grandmother and how he came to the conclusion that her assassination was ordered by her own guardian, who was also, as it happens, her stepfather—yet another in a series of instances of appropriation of headrights and oil royalties, and an example of the violence brought to bear to achieve dispossession.[138] Indigeneity combined with womanhood prove to be particularly dangerous conditions.

In time, royalties diminished, especially during the Depression, and by 1938 the $1,000 maximum was eliminated. What was, however, not dismantled was the guardian system. Putting Indians under tutelage continued to be a key element in land and wealth transference out of Native American hands. Some homesteads were sold in the 1920s to pay tribal owners' delinquent taxes; it was not until 1938 that Congress exempted tribal homesteads from taxation, that is, until the year 1984.[139] By 1935, no less than a third of the allotted lands had passed out of tribal Osage hands.[140] Wilson's history and assessment of the underground reservation is especially interesting as he prefers to lay the blame for this dispossession not on the federal government but on settlers, ranchers, and corporations. Rather than looking at how the state functioned to assist corporations, settlers, and ranchers in alienating Native American land and oil rights, Wilson curiously prefers to see analyses "blaming institutions for the destitution of Native Americans" as an outcome of the anti–Vietnam War era.[141] But clearly the federal and local governments permitted, authored, and validated the wrongdoing against the Osages, just as they had so many times before in US history. Counter to such readings, Hogan's novel, with an alternate version of events, points to the link betweeen capital and the state. In *Mean Spirit* we see that the state—in all its forms and with all its actors and proxies—is behind all the dispossession and violence against Native Americans.

Taken collectively, the sensational murders of the 1920s, the attempts of white men to control their Indian wives' headrights, that is, their petroleum royalties, and the consumerism of the newly rich Indians are all examples of the impact of capitalism and enclosures on the Osages and are all richly configured in Hogan's *Mean Spirit*. It explores both the old and new strategies used to dispossess Indians and deny them their lands and rights. Nor does the presence of a Native American FBI agent in the novel curb the violence against Indians or bring justice, as seen in Stace Red Hawk's underlying—and well-grounded—suspicion that his own boss, Ballard, and the agency are involved in some way in the travesties being perpetrated against Native Americans.

The repeatedly enacted strategies of enclosure lead to the spatial violence of dispossession, forced sales, destruction of habitat, loss of resources (water, land, oil), the creation of shantytowns, the forced leasing of land, acculturation and consumerism, the loss of leasing fees and annuities, the loss of life, and finally migration. While exodus, as noted by Callinicos, can possibly be constructed as a form of resistance, it is so only under certain conditions of struggle.[142] In *Mean Spirit* the Graycloud family has to flee, accompanied by Stace Red Hawk, who is no longer willing to serve the FBI and the state. Their exodus is not to a utopian promised land; however, it does point to another world that is possible in their search for the survival of both their immediate present and—importantly—the collectivity's past, after their house has exploded and burned to the ground: "No one spoke. But they were alive. They carried generations along with them, into the prairie and through it, to places where no road had been cut before them. They traveled past houses that were like caves of light in the black world. The night was on fire with their pasts and they were alive."[143]

Enclosures in Other Hogan Novels

Mean Spirit is not Hogan's only work dealing with Indigenous enclosures. Three of her other novels also address them, highlighting various strategies used to dispossess Indigenous populations of their lands. While enclosures are the structuring mechanisms, dispossession is not discussed outright in those terms; the discourses of enclosure are the subtexts of the narratives, subtexts that become evident in a reading of historical layering and the literary rewriting of this underlying or structuring narrative. Given the novelistic format, this actualization, this narrative rendering of dispossession and its discontents, variously experienced by characters, is framed in terms of particular novelistic formal constraints and ideologically configured in relation to particular discourses and strategies of containment. The fact that Hogan provides a fictional rendering of historical events allows for a layering or overlapping of several issues and temporalities that are particular to one or another Indian nation.

Hogan's 1998 novel *Power* offers a good example of the layering of an ecopoetics and historical moments. It, too, is an allegory of spatial and discursive violence. The novel focuses on a fictitious Indigenous tribe, the Taiga people of Florida, a Creek/Seminole-related group that, unlike the modern Florida Seminoles (involved in business with casinos, hotels, and a variety of tourist, cattle, and citrus enterprises on reservations in three areas), has been reduced in number, living on a small acreage that includes a wild animal reserve and a settlement site above Kili Swamp, where the elders maintain the culture and traditions. Like the Seminoles, the Taiga in the novel are members of the Panther Clan, and they share myths and traditions with their Seminole cousins. The misfortune of the Taiga is traceable "clear back to when the first white men wandered lost in the swamps and grasses and forests," but the Taiga learned to survive by hiding from soldiers and moving about the swamps silently.[144] Like some Seminoles, the Taiga refused to be relocated to Arkansas and Oklahoma during the nineteenth century. The Taiga elders, moreover, rejected modern, that is, capitalist, ideologies, although by the twentieth century there is perforce some consumption of commodities. A few Taiga, on the other hand, move into the white world and acculturate, like the main character's mother, who tries to pass for white. The Taiga carry with them layers of history: life under Spanish conquest and later British and US invasions. As in *Mean Spirit*, in *Power* enclosures have been serially imposed by force, massacres, treaties, legislation, and corruption that have decimated the community, until now only about thirty remain who continue to identify as Taiga. Enclosures here are viewed from the perspective of the dispossessed, the Panther People, who are concerned not only with loss of land but also with the dwindling of the wildlife the land sustains. The land, the forests, the bodies of water, and the wildlife, as the novel notes, have been destroyed by sugarcane plantations, cattle, highways and streets, and towns full of white houses with red roofs. Settlement has destroyed the Taigas' way of life until now only the small reservation exists. The elders see it all, "the drained swamps, the rushing cars, the near destruction of their world, all of it mixed in right next to the old, dark-leafed world they cling to as if it will save them, and maybe it will."[145] Hunting and sports (figured in the text with the image of swamp buggies) have invaded the Taiga reservation, illegal though they may be. Ecological disasters and despoliation are thus also seen as accompanying the processes of enclosure in the novel.

Of course, discourses of progress are used to justify encroachment on Taiga land and to explain away acculturation. Only in memory is there a chance to counter the notion that there is no alternative, because the Taiga recall and seek a different world, to be attained, however, through cultural struggle that often appears as the last remaining strategy left to the dispossessed, as we shall see later in critical writings dealing with New Mexico literature, but in these Indigenous texts the maintenance of culture always involves safeguarding a specific separate space. Spatial and discursive violence always go together, so, too, spatial and discursive resistance.

Like *Power*, Hogan's 1995 novel *Solar Storms* focuses on both old and new enclosures, on what De Angelis terms an *ex novo* separation of the producers from the means of production.[146] Once capital develops, it produces and constrains the conditions of its own existence and reproduction. In this particular case, natural resource depletion operates as a type of enclosure imposed in the past by European explorers, colonists, hunters, trappers, settlers who dispossessed Indigenous populations and destroyed the natural habitat of animals and plants, and in the Québec of the 1970s, the space and time of the novel, by the state through its direct appropriation of Indian lands and resources. In 1971, the state-run electric company Hydro-Québec, a mixed public/private corporation, identified the water resources in the James Bay area in Québec for enclosure in order to establish a major hydroelectric project. It began by building the James Bay Road for transporting materials and later scheduled the damming of several rivers in northern Québec, diverting waterways and flooding territory claimed by Cree and Inuit Indian people.[147] Initially planned as a major infrastructure undertaking for an independent Francophone Québec, the James Bay Project became controversial not only in Canada but internationally in view of plans to sell electricity to the states of New York and Vermont.

The project that began in 1973 with the building of dams along the La Grande River to generate electric power stations had already displaced the Cree and Inuit, who accused the Canadian government of violating previous treaties in expropriating their land, initiating protests that led to several lawsuits and a court injunction against Hydro-Québec in November of that year. The injunction was soon overturned, and legal battles followed until in 1975 the James Bay and Northern Québec Agreement was signed between Indian tribes and the utility, leaving the Cree with some land and the payment of $225 million over twenty years by the Canadian and Québec governments to the Cree Regional Authority and the Makivik Corporation on behalf of the Inuit. With this agreement, the tribes surrendered 981,610 square kilometers of the James Bay/Ungava territory, with each group, the Cree (5,543 square kilometers) and the Inuit (8,151 square kilometers), left with particular lands recognized as Indigenous for their exclusive use and benefit.[148] The Cree have argued since then that Hydro-Québec is not keeping its part of the bargain, especially regarding the performance of environmental impact assessments. Additional consequences have followed the enclosure and transformation of these Indigenous lands. The hydroelectric power project brought outsiders from the south to the area and a number of new problems, including alcoholism, drug abuse, prostitution, and family violence as well as the pollution of rivers, the poisoning of fish, the flooding of areas used by a variety of native animals, and, of course, consumerism.

During the 1980s and 1990s the second part of the James Bay Project continued despite legal battles. With the building of new dams, the utility company's generating capacity increased dramatically, to some 15,000 megawatts, making it able to export electricity to US states, especially New York.[149] The North American Free Trade Agreement also became involved, which did not allow the United States to discriminate against Canadian electricity, however environmentally unsound its production might be within Canada. Environmental groups in the United States, on the other hand, protested the puchase of imported Canadian electric power, especially after the well-publicized 1990 canoe protest that carried Grand Chief Matthew Coon Come from Hudson Bay to the Hudson River in Albany, New York, provoked pressure on the Quebec government and led ultimately to the suspension of the multibillion-dollar power purchasing agreement with Québec. As a result, the third phase, the Great Whale River project, was suspended indefinitely. Additional projects, however, like the Rupert River diversion are still planned today.[150] Throughout the current struggle, Canadian Indians' right to self-determination has not been recognized; what has been recognized are their rights to local government, their own school boards, and their own hunting, fishing, and trapping, limited as these increasingly are. Nomadic hunters by tradition, the 5,000 Cree of James Bay and the 3,500 Inuit to the north require large tracts of land for their subsistence, but, as has happened time and time again, with their land and livelihood gone, they have become dependent on government subsidies as traditional forms of subsistence are no longer available, that is, since their hunting grounds have been flooded. This hydro-development venture is not unique to Canada; similar projects have displaced people throughout the world, creating at the same time environmental hazards including mercury poisoning, decomposition of vegetation with the release of greenhouse gases, seismic hazards, destruction of habitat, and loss of species, including, in Canada, the loss of caribous (10,000 died trying to cross the Caniapiscau River), beluga whales, migratory birds, freshwater fish, seals, and so on. Enclosures, De Angelis notes, involve a corresponding teleological developmental discourse. In this case, the discourse of those promoting this enclosure again justify it on the basis of progress (new schools, a clinic), the modernization of a backward area, the introduction of work opportunities, and the production of pollution-free electricity. What is not mentioned is the accumulation of capital for the Hydro-Québec corporation and a political entity (Québec) interested in autonomy. These promises of benefits, as the *Solar Storms* character Auntie knows, are only that, promises that will never be delivered.[151]

It is this displacement of the Cree and Inuit and the destruction of their way of life, their means of subsistence, and their identity, along with their struggles to keep the Hydro-Québec company from diverting the waters; flooding their streams, lakeshores, and forests; ruining fish and animal habitat; and destroying vegetation and crops that the population depends on for subsistence, that the novel *Solar Storms* configures. But Hogan's work also represents Indian struggles to resist this dispossession and habitat destruction. In *Solar Storms*, the project is first revealed when two young men reach a fishing village called Adam's Rib and tell of government plans to build dams; already, without warning, agreement, or compensation, it has begun to flood the land, displacing Native populations, both animal and human, and affecting the habitat, especially of healing plants, thus ending a traditional way of life. Eventually, the villagers are warned, the impact will reach Adam's Rib. And while Indians do not attain the right to self-determination, still, the struggle itself is seen as important and necessary, even while both dividing the community and uniting it.

Tracing the impact of enclosures and the destruction of the environment is one focus of the work, but Hogan's novel is also concerned with memory, with remembering the past, the earlier enclosures imposed by French and British settlement, the repeated relocation of the Cree and Inuit to more remote northern areas, with the arrival, each time, of white settlers, loggers, trappers, churchmen, traders, and, later, capitalist interests that desire to exploit yet another natural resource. It is the impact of these earlier enclosures that affects a central character Hannah, a dark-skinned young woman with flaming red hair, whose mother was a descendant of Indians residing on Elk Island, some thirty miles east of Adam's Rib. When settlers took over their island and deforested it, they deprived Indians of their means of subsistence, and consequently they began to starve. When incoming settlers put out deer meat poisoned with cyanide to kill predatory wolves, starving Indians ate that meat. Many of them died. Symbolic of the effects of this enclosure are the two women, Loretta and her daughter Hannah. Both are said to retain the almond smell of cyanide on their skin and clothing, and both are damaged irreparably, weak and dangerous at the same time, sadistic and cruel, even while seemingly defenseless and abused by men. Recalling Loretta, Agnes explains, "the curse on that poor girl's life came from watching the desperate people of her tribe die."[152] Hannah is said to have no conscience and to be incapable of loving another person. Her cruelty is evident in her abuse of her own daughter, Angel, whose face is scarred from her mother's bite marks and the use of a clothes hanger to torture her. Agnes and Bush attempt to protect Angel when she is born, after Hannah leaves her out in the snow to die, keeping her with them when Hannah leaves; but at the age of five, family court rules that Hannah is entitled to her daughter. She takes Angel south to Oklahoma and continues to abuse her; the state then removes the child, has her undergo several surgeries "to put her face back together," and then sends her into foster care.[153] Each time, Angel runs away from the foster home and is subsequently sent to another. In time she learns that she has a sister, who is also damaged and self-destructive. When she is seventeen, Angel attempts to connect again with family in Adam's Rib. Angel's trip north, with bus fare underwritten by her grandmother Agnes, is an attempt to recover her past, to reconstruct her memory, by re-membering her dismembered past, putting back together, reintegrating her past with her present, learning about the cause of her scars, and reconnecting with her Indian roots. State agencies, whether Indian schools or foster homes, are figured as continuing the work of dispossession initiated by the dispossession of land.

In the process of establishing new enclosures, De Angelis remarks, new subjects born of and normalized to the capitalist market need to be created. We find this, especially in Hogan's *Mean Spirit* but also in *Solar Storms*, where by 1973 Indigenous groups are consumers of all the appliances, utensils, tools, food products, and popular culture artifacts (radios, music, etc.) available. Although their means of communication with the outside world, especially to publicize their habitat damage, are limited, once they are surrounded by troops, police, construction workers, and massive machinery, they discover that their limitations can be made to work both ways. The small mail plane, the railroad, and the new road built into their remote area are their only connection with the outside world; for that reason, the Indians decide to block access to Adam's Rib and other villages by setting up obstacles of all sizes on the road, closing off the villages so that workers and machinery cannot get in. Enclosures thus produce not only consumers but also protesters against the state and the hydroelectric corporation, resisters who in this case can retaliate by enclosing the village to protect it, dispossessing the invaders of access, much as in *Mean Spirit* the Hill People attempt to hide their community as a safe haven from toxic external forces.

Despite the ongoing struggle and marshaling of strategies of resistance, in *Solar Storms* the problem is not resolved. What the text offers is a figuration of Native people's efforts to organize against yet another instance of enclosure, their internal divisions, their dying traditions and practices, their dying Indigenous languages, all the while underscoring the interest and need of the characters to establish links to their roots and reinforce their identity. In the case of enclosures of the past, both Indigenous tribes and nature faced the destructive and dispossessing power of trappers, hunters, and settlers. As in the case of the Taiga in *Power*, the outsiders in *Solar Storms* are sportsmen, who hunt for fun, fish for fun, and use the land to play golf. The comparison is made clear when Angel notes that the builders of dams arrived to negotiate with the leaders at Two-Town Post: "To the builders of dams we were dark outsiders whose lives had no relevance to them. They ignored our existence until we resisted their dams, or interrupted their economy, or spoiled their sport. We'd already seen the results of the orange-caped hunters who had no need for meat."[154]

Losing One's Self

Solar Storms provides the story of two types of enclosure—past and present—framed around a gendered narrative of the recovery of an Indigenous past and identity. It is the narrative of multiple displacements, of alienation at both the material and psychological levels. The key problem is survival in the face of genocide and destruction of one's identity and way of life. The damage is done, however; fragmentation and dysfunction permeate both individual lives and that of the collectivity, as the novel shows through the toxic relationships that ensue and that the characters are at pains to repair.

Both *Power* and *Solar Storms* pose the problem of enclosure within narratives concerned with the aftereffects of dispossession vis-à-vis efforts toward the preservation of Indian culture, highlighting the strong role of women in this endeavor. The separation of Indians from their means of subsistence is also a separation from their way of life, their culture, and this separation or dispossession—this loss of self with toxic family consequences—continues despite remoteness or the establishment of reservations, as we see in *Mean Spirit*. The loss of wholeness of identity—individual and collective—cuts across all these lands in Hogan's novels, Florida, Oklahoma, and Canada, and just as the lands are enclosed and partitioned, so, too, are the people; just as the land is fragmented and torn asunder, so, too, are the people shown to be suffering the short- and long-term effects of both physical/material and discursive/psychological violence in their loss of integrity or selfhood.

In Hogan's *People of the Whale*, the locale shifts to the Pacific Northwest, but the processes manifest parallels.[155] Here again, as in the previous novels, events around historical Indians are not directly configured in the text; instead, in the narrated account, fictional tribes are stand-ins for historical peoples. In this particular case, the whale-hunting Makah/Nootka Indians of the Pacific Northwest, living between Washington State and Vancouver, are symbolically represented by the A'atsika people in the novel. The A'atsikas are said to have hunted whales in the open ocean from canoes. Culture and continuance of a particular way of life are again of primary concern, but what will separate the people from their means of production is another form of removal, of physical displacement from their land, this time in the shape of imperialism that takes A'atsika youths away from their fishing village to fight as US troops in Vietnam. Years later, as the narrative moves forward, what threatens A'atsika culture is capitalism and consumer markets, seen in the desire of young A'atsikas to hunt whales for profit, not for their own needs as called for by tribal tradition, but to market the whale meat to Japan, where it is an expensive delicacy. Notions of tradition, tribal rights, and ecological sustainability also go by the wayside when the A'atsikas now advocate to end an international moratorium on whale killing.

Displacement, enclosure, culture, memory, the role of elders and that of strong women are shared benchmarks found across Hogan's novels. Other contemporary novelists likewise focus on dispossession and especially on the role of culture in attempts to restore Indigenous commons, memory, and identity, as in the case of Leslie Marmon Silko, a Laguna Pueblo writer.

Enclosures in Silko's Work

Particularly in Silko's widely read *Almanac of the Dead*, enclosure underlies narratives of the deterritorialization of the Américas north and south by sequential colonial powers and capitalists' interests leading to the dispossession of Native peoples and the destruction of their culture.[156] Central to the novel are narratives that find means to counter exploitation, oppression, and dispossession through organized efforts coming from the south to reterritorialize the Américas and in the process unite Indigenous peoples in the United States with Chicanos, leftists, Asians, and Blacks to take back the land. Silko's novel *Ceremony*, on the other hand, focuses on the impact of World War II on a young man, Tayo, drafted and separated from his Navajo community, his culture, his access to the means of production, and therefore his role as a family provider.[157] The contradiction born of fighting for the very same US government that dispossessed Indians is brought into sharp relief upon Tayo's capture by the Japanese, the ensuing long march as a POW, the death of his cousin Rocky, the sight of Japanese lined up to be killed (soldiers he couldn't shoot because they looked just like his uncle Josiah), the prison camp, the hospital, and his return home suffering from PTSD. But Tayo has a family and a reservation to return to, even if not his own home; it is a place where his war-scarred peers are wracked by alcoholism and a deep desire to enact violence, even if the "destroyers"—this time not enemies from abroad but from within his US homeland—"took almost everything," even if they fenced the land and stole their cattle, even if they took the uranium from their land to build deadly weapons.[158] It will be a renewed conciousness of clan and land gained through Navajo ceremony that will in the end save Tayo from the "witchery" of capital and the state bent on death and destruction; life and the potential for regeneration, the novel posits, are the antidote and prescription for physical and cultural survival.[159]

In Silko's *Gardens in the Dunes*, the mechanisms of enclosure in the Southwest as sites of both loss and resistance are perhaps best configured, linked to issues of dispossession not only in the Américas but throughout the world.[160] South of Needles, California, near the Arizona border, are the sand dunes where the last of the Sand Lizard people (four women, including Indigo, Sister Salt, their mother, and their grandmother) find refuge in the late nineteenth century from those who have taken their land, kidnapped Indians to serve as servants, or removed them to the reservation at Parker. The fictional Sand Lizard people, much like the historical Kumeyaay Indians of what is now the San Diego area, are displaced from their ancestral homelands with the argument—again—that they lacked valid title to the lands that they and their ancestors had lived on.[161]

The history of the remnants of the Kumeyaay people can be extrapolated in part from the autobiographical/testimonial narrative of Delfina Cuero published in 1970. This narrative can be fruitfully read next to Silko's tracing of the avatars of the Kumeyaay in the fictional Sand Lizard people.[162] Like the Kumeyaay Delfina Cuero, in *Gardens in the Dunes*, the four Sand Lizard survivors' greatest fear is—understandably—ending up on a reservation.[163] In the early twentieth-century Southwest, the Sand Lizards, two women and two young girls, prefer staying in their underground sand dune shelter near a spring. But while the women are able to grow vegetables (the grandmother stores the seeds to plant in the oasis) and gather food and hunt rabbits for subsistence, other needs require walking to Needles to seek employment and get supplies; this temporary migration is also necessary when nothing grows or what grows is eaten by other travelers. In Needles, they build a lean-to and work, washing clothes or selling their woven baskets to tourists riding the train; the women also participate in a Ghost Dance and get to see Wevokah before being attacked by soldiers and the Indian Reservation police. After the girls escape to the dunes and after their grandmother's death, they seek news of their mother, last seen at the Ghost Dance. The two sisters, however, are caught by the Indian reservation police and soldiers, who split them up, sending Sister Salt to the Parker reservation and Indigo to the Sherman Institute in Riverside, California, from which the latter runs away. Once at Parker, Sister Salt is sent to a "school" run by the Colorado River Indian Agency, where her "training" is doing laundry for government employees and later for survey crews planning construction of the Colorado River Aqueduct. As Sister Salt explains, "This was no school, this was a prison."[164]

Indigo, too, sees the institute as a prison, and she decides to run away. Her escape leads her to the home of Hattie and Edward, newlyweds from the northeast living in Riverside, California. Edward is involved in a special type of enclosure: the acquisition of rare or valuable botanical products, whether exotic orchids from Brazil or *Citrus medica* cuttings from Corsica, as an agent of US companies interested in the appropriation of these plants for propagation and commercialization. We see this dispossession of flora and destruction of habitat occurring today in Chiapas, in the Amazon, and elsewhere. The orchid expedition turned out to be a failure, and he and Hattie decide to move to Riverside, where they find Indigo hiding after her escape and decide to take her with them to Europe for the summer. The trip to Europe will allow Edward to procure citrus cuttings in which the US Bureau of Plant Industry is interested. Later, however, when permits are rescinded, Edward decides to push ahead on his own, interestingly making use of his wife and the "native" Indian child to serve as tourist cover. Once in Corsica, customs officers board their ship and find that Edward is hiding proscribed plant cuttings. Edward's intended dispossession of the plant wealth of other countries ends when back in New Mexico he falls for a meteorite ruse, invests his wife's money, and loses it all. Hattie responds by choosing to leave Edward and goes with Indigo to Needles to find Sister Salt, who has left the Parker reservation and by then has a baby.

Returning to the arid desert of the Southwest, the disillusioned and now-widowed scholar Hattie is subsequently beaten, raped, and left for dead near an Indian reservation. The rapist is a white man hired to drive Hattie to Indigo and Sister Salt's encampment. During her convalescence in Needles, Hattie realizes that the white townspeople will do nothing to punish her white assailant; it is a town that prefers to blame Indians. As she recovers at the encampment where Indigo and her sister and friends await Wevokah, Hattie's family appears to reclaim her and take her home; although she resists, having decided to cast her lot with the native women, she reunites briefly with her family in town. That same night she slips away and gains some degree of revenge and satisfaction when she burns down the wagon stables and half the town of Needles. Hattie's allegiances have shifted as a result of her gender positionality.

We see in the work of Silko and Hogan alike a combination of structuring mechanisms—enclosures and culture—figuring prominently. The historical and material dispossession is a fait accompli, it seems, and all that's left is calling on and reinforcing a critical historical memory. Narrating the brutal dispossession of a people to inscribe it in memory also serves as a harsh caveat to others who may suffer similar dispossessions. Like Native American critics (including Roxanne Dunbar-Ortiz, Nick Estes, Mishuana Goeman) who are today analyzing settler colonialism and the impact of various forms of US imperialism on Native nations and their lands, Hogan and Silko, too, seek to recover and nurture a critical memory and provide a cognitive mapping of what is too often repressed or disguised in US history regarding the genocide of Indigenous populations by colonists, settlers, soldiers, state agencies, and the state itself.

Occupation Hand in Hand with Despoliation

Dispossession of Native Americans continues today in manifold ways, as evident most blatantly in the Dakota Access Pipeline, which was moved downstream toward the Standing Rock Sioux Reservation and away from its initial proposed location upstream, near majority-white Bismarck, North Dakota. The Standing Rock Sioux are aware of the implications of fracking for their water supply and livelihood. Other reservation lands throughout the United States continue to be despoiled. Water on the Pine Ridge Reservation has been found to be contaminanted by arsenic, lead, and various forms of carcinogenic radiation as enclosures continue under different guises.[165]

According to the Worldwide Institute, 317 reservations in the United States are "threatened by environmental hazards, ranging from toxic wastes to clear-cuts" in forested areas.[166] The Oglala Sioux are also waging a battle against the Crow Butte Resources uranium mining operation thirty miles southwest of the reservation border, which is polluting their water. Near the Akwesasne reservation in New York, Onondaga Lake has likewise been polluted. An estimated 165,000 pounds of mercury were deposited between 1956 and 1970 because of the Honeywell Corporation's chlor-alkali process, according to the New York State Department of Environmental Conservation. Uranium mines also pollute Navajo crops and water supplies in Arizona as well as in Wyoming, where the Wind River Reservation lands are contaminated by carcinogens and radioactive materials. Whether through the use of dioxin-laden herbicide, uranium mining, or oil and gas field runoff, Native American reservations continue to face dispossession, in these cases, by being deprived of a supply of water necessary for life.

Spatial violence continues to assume many forms today through a variety of practices that dispossess Indigenous communities and pollute their soil and water. Writings like those of Hogan and Silko speak strongly to this continued material and discursive violence in an organic way that is compelling and that makes us more conscious of the degree to which enclosures, whether in the shape of military incursions, settler colonialism, uranium mining, or oil fracking, have been a constant, in fact, the constant and constitutive nature of US history.

Enclosures in New Mexico

LAND OF DISENCHANTMENT

Chapter 2 deals with spatial and discursive violence against Native Americans who were dispossessed across the United States, with a focus on Oklahoma. Indians in New Mexico did not, of course, fare much better, whether under Spanish and Mexican settler colonialism, or subsequently under the US flag. During Spanish and Mexican colonialism, Indians in New Mexico would be subject to servitude, dispossession, slavery, cultural deracination, and genocide. Like the native Pueblo people, Mexican settlers would later also find themselves dispossessed under US settler colonialism. Representation of spatial violence and different modalities of enclosure in Chicano/a works dealing with New Mexico has been for the most part limited to the dispossession of Mexican landowners after 1846, without much if any recall of Mexican and Spanish dispossession of the Indians.

Enclosing Indigenous lands in New Mexico was the basis for Spanish/Mexican colonialism and later—literally—the grounds for capitalist production. Indigenous populations of New Mexico stand out for having risen up in concerted rebellion against colonization and dispossession on numerous occasions. Most noteworthy perhaps is the date in 1680 when Pueblo Indians drove Spanish soldiers, missionaries, and settlers out of New Mexico. Spanish colonizers and their troops would return, of course, and what David J. Weber calls the "cycle of exploitation, contention, and rebellion" would continue.[1] Across time and most often against overwhelming odds, Native Americans of New Mexico reacted against the invader, even if this fact is skirted or minimized in some historical and literary accounts.

Fredric Jameson, along with Massimiliano Tomba, proposes that human history involves a multiplicity of temporalities and suggests that it is through narrative that we best grasp and see these temporalities, this deep history. Jameson posits as well that consciousness of history always involves emplotment and interpretation, that is, a taking of sides.[2] In what follows, we focus on the emplotment of temporalities in New Mexico history and literature, as evidenced in a number of texts and documents dealing first with Spanish and Mexican settler colonialism and then with US settler colonialism after 1848, examining in the process the interpretation of history, that is, the emplotted consciousness of history these texts provide, especially the emplotment of enclosures, that is, of spatial and discursive violence.

New Mexico is intriguing as an example of a heterogeneous colonial project. In part, it followed the example of early colonialism in Mexico, bringing soldiers and missionaries to the far-off New Mexican territory in search of mineral wealth; finding none, their interest shifted to the land and the project of Christianizing the Indians. In the process of appropriating the land, subjecting Indians to forced labor, and coercing them to abandon their religious and cultural practices, they decimated the population. Here, too, we find early settler colonialism, as families accompanied soldiers and established themselves in scattered communities outside the villas, exploiting Indian labor and buying Indian slaves from the Indians themselves.

We need first to bear in mind key periods of New Mexican history: (1) the territory of New Mexico inhabited by a number of Indigenous tribes or pueblos before colonization, (2) the territory under Spanish colonialism (1598–1821), (3) the colonial province as Mexican territory (1821–46), (4) the territory as a US colony (1846/1850–1912), and (5) the territory admitted to the Union as a state in 1912. Each period is marked by enclosures of a different order, with the last two presenting continuing Native American dispossession, along with that of Hispano/a landowners. As is often the case, in each succeeding period the past temporalities intrude, giving each period a particular specificity.

The long and complex history of New Mexico has been taken up by a number of historians. What interests us especially is what has been said by historians and fiction writers alike about the settlement of Indigenous lands and land dispossession. Cultural critics, for the most part, have not focused on enclosures related to the dispossession of Indians, although the loss of Nuevomexicano/a lands often comes up as a recurrent theme, as does the maintenance of cultural traditions. Much is made in these works about the resistance value of both representing and safeguarding this cultural history, although for the most part they refer to elite Nuevomexicano/a culture, the culture of rich landowners who had peons, slaves, and sharecroppers on their lands. Perhaps only in the collection of the mid-twentieth-century Federal Writers' Project (of the WPA) do we find descriptions of village life, work, and the development of tools and instruments of labor of the peons and small-farming settlers as well as a number of folktales.[3] Contradictions abound in all the texts, as is perhaps necessarily the case when a people are invaded, defeated, and colonized.

Pre-1598 New Mexico

Weber estimates that before the arrival of the Spanish colonizers, over 35,000 Pueblo Indians inhabited the area that later came to be known as New Mexico.[4] Roxanne Dunbar-Ortiz, on the other hand, reports that there were ninety-two villages in the northern Rio Grande area with an estimated population of 100,000 when Francisco Vázquez de Coronado's army of some 300 soldiers plus Indian, mulatto, mestizo, and Black servants invaded in 1540.[5] On the basis of archaeological evidence, historians hold that precolonial Pueblo settlements relied on hydraulic agriculture, using intensive irrigation farming to cultivate corn, beans, and squash along the Rio Grande by 1500. More western Indian groups, however, practiced dry farming. Descendants of earlier Mogollon, Anasazi, and Hohokam civilizations in the Southwest, they lived in autonomous villages, in adobe homes that were several stories high, and spoke different languages. Albert H. Schroeder provides a map that includes dozens of pueblos, or towns, of Northern Tiwas, Southern Tiwas, Tewas, Towas, Tanoas, Keres, and Tompiros groups residing in central New Mexico, with Hopis and Zuñis a bit farther west.[6] Land in these villages was communally possessed; family units organized production and contributed their surplus to those in need.[7] The Pueblos were in contact—and sometimes in conflict—with Apaches and Navajos, especially in times of scarcity and drought. By 1700, however, there were only about seventeen thousand Pueblo Indians, a decline that Weber attributes to European diseases, forced labor, violence, and "migration" away from Spanish settlements.[8]

Arrival of Spanish Explorers, Settlers, and Conquerors

Enclosures in New Mexico were first instituted by force, with the dispossession of Indigenous populations by Spanish soldiers, missionaries, and settlers, as part of Spain's imperial project in the Américas. Spanish explorers first came into contact with the Pueblos of the northern Rio Grande in the early sixteenth century (1540s). Nuevomexicano writer Eusebio Chacón in several remarkable essays published in the newspaper *Las Dos Repúblicas* in 1896 provides an overview of the exploration and settlement of New Mexico.[9] After hearing about the eight-year trek across the Southwest (1528–36) of Cabeza de Vaca and three other survivors (Dorantes, Estevanico, and Alonso) of the shipwrecked Narváez expedition, the viceroy of Nueva España became intensely interested in exploring Dorantes's claims of a city of gold in the north and sent a small expedition north from Culiacán, led by a missionary, Friar Niza, and Estevanico to check out these reports. Estevanico was killed by Zuñi Indians, and Niza returned, reporting having seen the sought-after golden city of Cibola from a distance.[10]

In 1540, a larger expedition led by Coronado marched north from New Spain with more than 1,300 men, including 300 Spaniards, 6 Franciscans, and some 1,000 Indigenous soldiers and servants, to what is now New Mexico, west to the Grand Canyon and Colorado River, and farther north and east to Kansas in search of the equally fabulous city of Quivira. In his historical review, Chacón recounts violence against Indians and the Spanish invasion of several Indigenous communities for food and lodging as well as the harsh winter faced by the soldiers, Coronado's long trek to the Arkansas River in search of the nonexistent Quivira, and the return to Mexico City in 1542 of a broken Coronado with his remaining troops. Acknowledging that the conquerors came in search of gold and of the fabulous Gran Quivira and lamenting the hard fate that awaited them, like other narratives about New Mexico's colonial past, Chacón's essay is told from the perspective of Spanish scouts, conquerors, and colonists. What none of Chacón's texts addresses is the impact of this invasion and settler colonialism on Indigenous populations in New Mexico, other than to mention the extortion of food from them. In fact, what is remarkable is the degree to which the Indigenous perspective is largely left out of most Nuevomexicano/a literary narrativization of New Mexico's past, with a few exceptions.

New expeditions would follow. In 1580, three friars and a handful of soldiers returned north to explore the region and found large Pueblo settlements, seeing in them potential laborers and, of course, converts. In 1582, another expedition, headed by Antonio de Espejo and a friar, returned and gave the viceroy an encouraging report that led the Crown to authorize "pacification and settlement" of La Nueva México, implicitly acknowledging that the latter depended on the former.[11] Several individuals applied for the position of governor and captain general of New Mexico. Juan de Oñate, a criollo from a wealthy silver-mining family, was chosen as *adelantado* to head the New Mexico exploration and settlement, underwriting the costs himself.[12]

In 1598, Oñate took possession of New Mexico and established the first Spanish colony in the Southwest.[13] And like other settler colonists, these soldiers, missionaries, and settlers proceeded to oppress, exploit, and reduce native Pueblos to slavery and servitude. Victor Westphall says that after discovering that there was none of the coveted gold, the main reason for colonizing the area was to establish both missions to Christianize the Indians and settlements to support the missionaries.[14] While that might have been part of the colonizing mission, clearly the colonizers and soldier-settlers who came hoped to improve their own socioeconomic standing, as is clear from Oñate's request to the Crown for colonial settlement of New Mexico. Colonization was thus an investment for the head of the colonizing venture, who hoped to increase his wealth by mining minerals, gain the title of hidalgo for himself, and likewise benefit his accompanying soldier-settlers.[15] Privately underwritten but sanctioned by the Crown, the colonization project was first and foremost an economic undertaking. James Brooks finds that the colonial encounter in the Southwest was driven by two powerful impulses, inclusion and exclusion. Following that logic, inclusion in the New Mexican instance would mean subordination and exploitation of Indigenous populations.[16]

Once in New Mexico, colonizers tried to win over native peoples with promises of protection from enemies and with the introduction of new crops, livestock, and trade. Weber records that the soldier-settlers who arrived in 1598 faced a tough winter, with nothing to eat save what was extorted from Indians: corn, beans, and squash. Frustrated and disillusioned, the soldiers resorted to torture, murder, and rape.[17] Facing this fate, Indians of Acoma retaliated by killing eleven Spanish soldiers. Using the Requerimiento, which obligated conquered Indians to pledge allegiance to the king and accept Christianity or face violence, Oñate ordered the decimation of the Acoma Pueblo and sent a group of seventy-two soldiers to avenge the fallen soldiers. They were able to gain the top of the Acoma mesa where the pueblo was situated, kill five hundred men and three hundred women and children, and destroy the pueblo, taking some five hundred women and children captive. Some eighty men were made prisoners and condemned to servitude as well as to the mutilation of a hand or foot.[18] Christian pacification, indeed.

The Acoma massacre is described in the 1610 epic poem *Historia de la Nueva México*, by Gaspar Pérez de Villagrá.[19] Seeking to produce a historical account in verse comparable to Alonso de Ercillas's now-classic *La Araucana* (1569–90) on the conquest of Chile, Pérez de Villagrá, a Mexico-born criollo who accompanied Oñate in his conquest and colonization of New Mexico in 1598, provides us with the first historical chronicle and account of violence—spatial, discursive, and otherwise—within what is now US territory.[20] While the literary quality of Pérez de Villagrá's work is deemed disappointing by critics, his first-person chronicle of events in Acoma in 1599 has great historical value. As befits the epic genre, in Villagrá's account, the enemy, the Indians of Acoma, are presented as heroic, valiant warriors, worthy opponents of the Spanish soldiers who henceforth vanquished and then massacred them, taking hundreds of prisoners as well. It is the genre's constraints that allow for a different representation of the Indian other. This foundational moment, the genocidal barbarity of the Acoma massacre, seldom, however, figures in later Nuevomexicano/a narratives of the past.

Throughout the period of Spanish colonization, soldier-colonists used brutality, massacres, mutilation, and slavery against Indigenous peoples who resisted subjugation and dispossession, including the Pueblos, Apaches, and Navajos. Family separation is a long-standing practice in conquest and colonialism; soldiers and missionaries participated in the exploitation and enslavement of Indians, distributing the young among settlers; many captured Indians—young and old—were sent south and sold in Mexico.[21] Reports of abuse along with soldier desertion led to Oñate's replacement as governor in 1606. Begun as a semi-independent enterprise led by an adelantado, the New Mexico colony was deemed a failure, and the Crown considered abandoning it, but Franciscans argued against this and urged the king not to abandon the now-baptized Indians in the isolated New Mexico colony, hundreds of miles distant from other settlements of New Spain. The king decided to transform it into a Crown colony, to be governed by officials named by the viceroy in Mexico.[22]

Three years after Oñate's departure, in 1609, the colony of Santa Fe was founded, and in 1629 new Franciscan friars arrived to establish missions and root out Indigenous religious practices; thirty-five encomiendas were established, with Pueblo Indians (men, women, and children) serving as semifeudal workers forced to till the land in order to pay tribute to the encomendero in kind. For the missionaries, Indians not only worked the soil but raised the stock, prepared the food, constructed the mission buildings, and carried out all the necessary labor. Indian-cultivated lands were to be respected, according to several Spanish decrees, but of course all encomiendas were by definition enclosures of Indigenous lands.[23] Dissension between the governor and the Franciscans, the imposition of Christianity, the depopulation of Indian villages with many dying from disease and others fleeing to distant villages, the imposition of passes to travel between villages, and the hard labor to which the Indians were subjected, along with the extreme punishment imposed on those who rebelled in any way, led to a number of Indian uprisings in 1632, 1639–40, 1644, 1647, 1650, and 1667, and to a unified offensive by the Pueblos in alliance with the Apache, Navajo, and Hopi, in the successful Pueblo Revolt of 1680. This rebellion, with concerted attacks on Spanish settlements, led to the freeing of Indian servants, slaves, and prisoners. More than four hundred Spanish colonists and twenty-one priests were killed.[24] Surviving Spanish settlers were forced to leave New Mexico and resettle in what would later be El Paso, Texas. The Spanish, however, would be back.

The isolation of the New Mexico colony meant it was cut off from other colonies and could not expect assistance. Recolonizing was again attempted and accomplished in 1692, with eight hundred soldiers and settlers, plus seventeen friars and servants, brought in to reestablish the villa at Santa Fe and to establish a presidio in 1693 as a base from which to subdue the Pueblos by raiding their villages, burning their crops, and taking hostage the women and children. Faced with this reality, many Pueblos fled into exile, a diaspora that led many of them to live among the Apaches, Navajos, and Hopis. In his edited volume on the Pueblo Revolt, Weber includes essays by five historians with varying explanations for the causes of the 1680 revolt.[25] Multiple historical interpretations of the particulars notwithstanding, the sheer brutality of the destruction of the Pueblo civilization and its oppression and exploitation eloquently explain the causes for the rebellion.

What might be termed the post-1692 reconquest of New Mexico did effect some changes in colonial patterns, giving rise to other modalities under which colonialism was practiced. For one, the events of 1680 put an end to the encomienda model, and after 1692, when the recolonizing mission was instituted, the primary settlement procedures depended on land grants made by the governor to settlers, not to encomenderos or religious orders. Since these colonial-era land grants were subsequently questioned or invalidated by the US Court of Private Land Claims and are the subject of a number of Nuevomexicano/a texts, a brief review of the types of grants allowed by Spanish and later Mexican law is in order. As David Maciel and Erlinda Gonzales-Berry note, "No single conflict proved as significant and detrimental to Nuevomexicanos as that related to land ownership. Land was the most abundant and valuable commodity in the northern reaches of the Spanish empire."[26]

Land, however, was not a commodity when the Spanish colonialists first came to Nuevomexico, as Spanish settlers did not pay for their land. The land was a grant, a *merced*, of Indian lands the Crown claimed by royal fiat, meant to entice settlers to go to an area distant from central Mexico. The grants were not private property; all land was royal land, and the king retained ultimate title.[27] Royal grants, or *mercedes*, allowed for the use of the land; they were usufruct concessions that induced settlers to participate in colonization.[28] Settlers were, however, expected to pay taxes. Grants were supposedly made by the king or viceroy, but in effect local officials (governors and *alcaldes mayores*) issued most of the grants. After 1754 grants required confirmation before *audiencias*, but in view of the cost of presentation to the territorial assemblies, Victor Westphall comments that this requirement was seldom met.[29] For his part, Marc Simmons identifies three categories of land grants: communal land grants made to individuals wanting to found a new community; private land grants made to farmers, ranchers, and others to develop rural property; and—notably—Pueblo Indian grants, guaranteeing full possession to Indians of all the lands they occupied or used. In addition to these land grants, or mercedes, in the villas or towns, lots were also distributed to *vecinos* (neighbors), and on the fringes of the municipality there were commons, or *ejidos*, and pasturelands.

Private grants were made to those able to develop agricultural and pastoral lands after petitioning the governor for "vacant" lands, that is, areas not claimed by another settler and therefore considered Crown lands. Once approved, the petitioner was granted possession of the land through a written document; the grantee was to remain on the land for at least four years to receive a fee-simple title. Large grants could also be subdivided so that newcomers could work the land and provide the grant owner a share of the product, along much the same line that serfs did in Spain.[30]

Minifundios, that is, small landholdings for self-sufficiency, became the rule, although there were a few large landowners, especially ranchers in the lower Rio Grande valley. Community grants were also given to the *genízaros*, converted Indians detached from their Indigenous communities, and to settlers of the lower *castas*, which were envisioned as a buffer between Spanish settlements and Indian villages.[31] Land was allotted for cultivation, houses, and stables. Ranchos and farms, however, were often established without grants, by squatters claiming vacant lands. Use of the land conferred a right to the land.[32] After US invasion, this form of land tenancy became an issue as it was not recognized by US land commissioners as a valid, that is, legal, right and title to the land. Settlements were scattered throughout New Mexico, but in the late eighteenth century efforts were made to consolidate settlements around villages.[33] Colonists also herded sheep on lands acquired in partnership with wealthy stockmen who contracted to have a flock cared for by a *partidario* who kept some of the stock as his own; if the partidario lost the allotted stock to a disaster or Indian raid, he became indebted to the owner, the *patrón*, whether a churchman or rancher. Indentured work and debt peonage were thus common in New Mexico during both the Spanish and Mexican periods, which is evident from recent research, just as it was on Mexican ranches and haciendas. While men made up most of the debt peons, women and children were also forced to work to pay off what was in effect a perpetual family debt, one that would continue beyond 1848.[34] These peons were primarily Indigenous or mestizo workers.

Debt Peonage and Slavery

In the highly telling twentieth-century Federal Writers' Project collection cited earlier, several testimonies recall indebted peonage in Las Placitas, a village near the Sandías.[35] A case in point: those indebted to José Leandro Perea were forced to make the annual trek over the Santa Fe Trail to Kansas to sell Perea's wool. Many died along the way. Peons in debt bondage were also forced to buy their goods at the Perea store, further increasing their debt: "It was the law that the *peones* must buy what they needed from the *patrón*'s store."[36] Moreover, "it was the privilege and custom of the rich dons to see to it that such obligations grew rather than diminished."[37] Those peons who decided to desert, forgoing payment, were hunted down and flogged. Those unwilling to promise never to do it again were hanged; their sons inherited the debt.[38] That not even in death was the debt discharged speaks to the "special relationship" between peon and patrón.[39] The narrative of Mateo and Raquel in the WPA collection tells how the peon José María, in bondage to Perea, received a lashing for failing to show up for work on a day when he chose to work on his own plot. The *mayoral* tried to force José María to declare that he would never be absent again, and when he refused, he was beaten again and sent to guard the sheep up in the Jemez Mountains. Once there, he deserted. A warrant was issued for his arrest; it was a crime for a peon indebted to his patrón to flee. José María was captured, dragged back to Bernalillo, and hanged. In 1836, his son, Mateo, was then ordered to take his father's place in bondage for life. The son would inherit the debt and die frozen in the mountains looking after Perea's sheep. It would not be until 1867 that bondage was legally abolished, but even then the patrón could force labor from those in debt.[40]

Interestingly, court cases have registered what has often been omitted or denied elsewhere in historiography or literature. In *Mariana Jaramillo v. José de la Cruz Romero*, argued before the New Mexico Supreme Court in 1857, for example, the court noted that peons are "a class of servants in New Mexico, bound to personal service for the payment of debts due their masters."[41] Ruling that the peon system maintains "similar relations between master and servants as are found to be established between the master and his slave in different states of the union," the court further noted that both men and women could be in debt peonage.[42] Here the court ruled in favor of Mariana, finding that no proof of her indebtedness was presented except for the claims of her master, constituting a violation of Mariana's rights. This post-1848 case indicates that a peonage system instituted during the Spanish and Mexican periods was still ongoing in 1857. The "peculiar institution" of peonage was finally abolished in 1867, but even then "documented" debts had to be repaid.[43] After 1867, some peons continued working for their former patrónes, but most sought work elsewhere, on the railroad or as miners; a few returned to their Pueblo families, and some continued to work their own small plots.[44]

It should be noted that in addition to debt peonage, its near cousin, slavery, also characterized relations of production in New Mexico, and as noted by William S. Kiser, Indian slavery has only recently attracted the attention of historians.[45] While Spanish/Mexican settlers came to New Mexico to occupy and work the land, the actual labor was often done by Indian workers or slaves bought from Comanches or other nomadic Indian tribes who sold their captives. Dora Ortiz Vásquez's stories in *Enchanted Temple of Taos* reveal historians' silence on this topic; she tells the story of Rosario, a Navajo slave girl who worked as a maid for Padre Martínez. Separated from her child when she was purchased by Martínez while her little girl was bought by another Nuevomexicano/a family, Rosario was unhappy. Noticing her unhappiness and with an eye to "family reunification," Martínez decided to buy Rosario's child from the family that had taken her.[46] This story is one of the few available by a Nuevomexicano/a author that speaks directly to the issue of Indian slavery within the Hispano/a community. The narrative is especially noteworthy because it allows for decoding a variety of temporalities, including pre- and postinvasion Taos, times of peonage and slavery, juxtaposing the realm of the marvelous (like the appearance of Christ to a shepherd boy) and the historical.

The slave trade was of course practiced not only by Indian traders like the Comanches and Navajos, who kidnapped and trafficked their Indian and Nuevomexicano/a captives to colonists and other tribes, but by the Spanish as well, who sold captives to other Nuevomexicanos/as or farther south in New Spain. In the WPA testimonies, we encounter another description of patrón José Leandro Perea from Bernalillo, who not only had peons in bondage but Navajo slaves as household servants.[47] In his work *New Mexico Past and Future*, Thomas E. Chávez offers a brief but telling sketch of María Rosa Villalpando, a married Nuevomexicana woman with a child. Both were kidnapped by the Comanches in 1760, along with fifty-five other women and children, many of whom were returned or bought back by the Nuevomexicanos/as. Held by a Comanche, Villalpando was traded to the Pawnees in the north, had another child, and was only ransomed ten years later by a French trader, Jean Sale dit Lajoie, who married her and with whom she had two more children.[48] Humans, not only as labor but as property, also had their transfer circuits. What is surprising is to find recent historians suggesting that slavery in New Mexico was unlike that of African slaves in the US South, as Indian slaves were integrated into the host community.[49] This notion of a happy, interdependent family is echoed by Cleofas M. Jaramillo in her narratives, as we shall see.

While the land, during the various tenancy regimes under which it was held, was primarily worked by Indian peons and Indian slaves, some Nuevomexicano/a criollo and mestizo settlers worked the land as well. Westphall indicates that more than 113 private and community grants, totaling 7,294,190 acres, were recorded during the 128 years that land grants were made by Spain, with many, especially in the case of squatters, unrecorded (more than six thousand).[50] These private and communal grants would be the subject of much litigation in the nineteenth and twentieth centuries after the US invasion and the coming of the cattlemen. Although the New Mexico colony attracted few Spanish settlers, it was, in fact, the most populous Mexican province in the Southwest in 1846.

What stands out most, however, in post-1846 Nuevomexicano/a texts is the general praise of Spanish colonizers, as in the case of Cleofas M. Jaramillo. Her autobiographical sketch, *Romance of a Little Village Girl*, makes it a point to recall that her ancestors, the Spanish conquerors and colonizers, were explorers, adventurers, pioneers, and in effect martyrs, forced to endure the Pueblo Revolt of 1680.[51] The colonizers, she says, came to conquer hostile Indian tribes, savages. For Jaramillo, the Spanish colonists were ambitious, talented, cultured people interested in the arts and education, bringing civilization to the territory. Jaramillo's idealization of her ancestors and the preservation of Spanish cultural traditions are what in good measure characterize her *Romance of a Little Village Girl*. Bent on exalting a heroic Spanish past, Jaramillo sees the colonizers as entitled to the land of the Indigenous populations residing in New Mexico by dint of discovery and development. At no point does she even suggest that Indians were dispossessed and subjected to slavery and servitude. Many other Nuevomexicano/a narratives share this idealization of the Spanish colonizers.

Land Grants under Mexican Rule

New Mexico's period under Mexican rule was relatively short: 1821–46. Mexican independence in 1821 did not substantially change social relations in New Mexico, and social stratification continued as before under a different flag. Visitors to New Mexico during the Mexican period noted the sharp class differences between the *ricos*, who owned haciendas, and the *pobres*, the poor class, a social stratification that in part led to the bloody insurrection of 1837 over questions of taxes and militia service and pointed to the animosity between classes.[52] Mexican independence and the growth of the economy in northern Mexico would, if anything, "strengthen the institution of debt peonage," notes Weber.[53] Indians taken captive during military campaigns were in turn enslaved and often sold to ricos whose human stock and labor pool grew. Debt peonage and slavery were in fact another form of enclosure, dispossessing the laborers of their labor power for the benefit of the landowners. We can see how in this way land grants to now-Mexican Nuevomexicanos/as were not the only enclosures at work in the ongoing processes of dispossession.

Weber notes that social stratification in the Southwest was not race based, as black men, like Pío Pico, could rise in stature to become governor of the territory.[54] Whether discussing California or New Mexico under the Mexican regime, Weber clearly disregards local conditions and the complex relation between race and class. It is evident that race was an important factor not only in Nuevomexicano/a writers' overwhelming stress on the whiteness of their ancestors but in the elite's rejection of the 1837 Indigenous/mestizo insurrection leaders.[55] Gender also played a key role in status in New Mexico, for men were the property owners, although in California a number of women requested and received land grants in their own name. In New Mexico, most of the landed ricos were men, except for Gertrudis Barceló, who owned gambling establishments. Under Spanish and French law, women were able to maintain property separate from that of their husbands if they had acquired it prior to their marriage. Still, even though widowed women, for example, exerted a degree of agency, there is no avoiding the fact that they were subservient to men, a practice noted even in what Weber describes as the feeding of men by the women, who then ate separately.[56] Women's roles and place in Nuevomexicano/a society, although they outnumbered men on the Spanish/Mexican frontier, remain understudied aspects of the area's history.

Rebellion in Nuevo México: Centralists versus Federalists

Issues of federalism versus centralism arose in Mexico after independence, when President Santa Anna proposed a centralist constitution in 1836, replacing the federalist 1824 constitution.[57] In New Mexico, opposition to Mexican centralism was led by lower-class Nuevomexicanos/as, Pueblo Indians, and genízaros/as, not by the elite.[58] The rebellion of 1837 against the newly appointed Mexican governor, Albino Pérez, and against increased taxation broke out in Santa Cruz de la Cañada, near Chimayó. Pérez was caught and beheaded, as were three local ricos. The uprising is attributed to a growing sense of the territory as a distinct homeland, strengthened by the appearance of the first Spanish-language paper, printed in Taos by a priest named Martínez.[59] But clearly elite Nuevomexicanos/as did not agree with the rebels, nor was the notion of a Nuevomexicano/a homeland necessarily key to what underpinned the Chimayó rebels' class- and race-based uprising against outsiders as well as powerful locals.

The insurgents named a new governor, José González, who was a Taos and Pawnee buffalo hunter with an Indian mother and a genízaro father. The racism and classism of Nuevomexicano ricos made them unhappy with the notion of an *indio* governor; with the help of former governor Manuel Armijo and later acting governor Mariano Chávez, the ricos from Rio Abajo organized against the rebels under the Plan de Tomé. Weber sees the conflict as a class war, pitting New Mexico oligarchs against the lower classes, seen as a mob by the ricos, with Armijo and his allies ultimately taking control of Santa Fe and crushing the lower-class revolt.[60] The ricos, once again in power, did nothing to address the underlying economic problems, privilege, taxation, and exploitation that had led to the rebellion. The elite had little understanding and even less sympathy for the grievances of Nuevomexicano/a pobres.

The Nuevomexicano/a elite had no quarrel with the centralist constitution of 1836 but did dislike having outsiders from the far-off Mexican capital named as governors, which also occurred in Alta California. Governors sent from Mexico were seen as incompetent and arbitrary, and the local elite preferred to govern themselves. In November 1845, Armijo became governor again. Suspecting that Mexico might sell the territory to the United States, a group of citizens drew up a plan calling for the establishment of the República Mexicana del Norte, separate from both Mexico and the United States. Weber comments that New Mexicans were not aware that a purchase offer had been rejected by Mexico, nor in fact that war had broken out between the United States and Mexico, until reports reached Santa Fe that US troops under Brigadier General Stephen W. Kearny were approaching New Mexico, leading Armijo to flee. Sporadic guerrilla activity against the invaders would, however, break out.[61]

Writing from the perspective of the invaders can lead an author to draw curious conclusions from events. Weber, for example, tries to justify some Nuevomexicanos/as' support for the US invasion as follows: "The neglect that frontiersmen perceived from Mexico contrasted with the warm interest that foreigners, especially Americans, demonstrated toward the region."[62] What lay beneath this "warm interest" was a desire to appropriate lands and resources. While recognizing the invasion as an act of imperialism, Weber falls back on a most Turnerian conclusion: "The United States not only benefited from this imperialistic expansion, but many historians are convinced that the very process of settling new lands had a salubrious effect on American character and institutions."[63] Much as Weber tries to give the US invasion a positive spin, clearly this act of US imperialism would lead to the colonization of the Nuevomexicanos/as and their dispossession. The motif of invasion and its sequelae figure prominently in several twentieth- and twenty-first-century Nuevomexicano/a texts, as does the centrality of land grants.

Governor Armijo's Bountiful Grants

In 1841, as Malcolm Ebright notes, Governor Armijo granted lands to Guadalupe Miranda and Charles Beaubien in an area east of the Sangre de Cristo mountains, a grant that would later become part of the Maxwell land grant of no fewer than two million acres in northeastern New Mexico and southeastern Colorado. This grant far exceeded the number of acres allowed by the Mexican government under the Mexican Colonization Law of 1824, which limited the amount of land one person could receive to 48,000 acres.[64] The Sangre de Cristo grant was for 998,780 acres and the Beaubien-Miranda grant for 1,714,764 acres.[65] After the US invasion, Spanish/Mexican land grants were routinely scrutinized and questioned by US authorities, and yet, interestingly, these two enormous and illegal grants were "among the first to be confirmed by the United States; their combined acreage (2,713,545) exceeds the entire acreage of New Mexico grants confirmed by the Court of Private Land Claims, thus calling into question the entire process of land grant adjudication."[66] Millions of acres were granted during the Mexican period, many to American, that is, US petitioners.[67] Through the sale of granted and confirmed land, the future governor of New Mexico, Charles Bent, for example, acquired a quarter interest in the Beaubien-Miranda grant—a half-million acres more or less.[68] Enough said.

Nuevomexicanos/as like Padre Martínez soon came to protest Armijo's massive grants, arguing that the Beaubien-Miranda grant impinged on the communal lands of the Taos Pueblo and included a foreigner as co-owner (Charles Bent).[69] These grants would be rescinded and later reawarded under new administrations.[70] They both could and would award them, since some among the landholding Nuevomexicano/a elite would ally and mesh their interests with the US newcomers. In terms of land distribution practices, however, it is true that under the short Mexican rule a larger acreage was generally granted than under Spain.[71] As in the United States, Indigenous lands in the Mexican territories and states not held by settlers were declared public lands, and the territorial government was able to grant these lands to supporters and to those providing the administration with much-needed loans.[72] There were, however, more than six thousand smallholding squatter claims in New Mexico, not conveyed by a formal grant.[73] As Westphall notes, "Local custom—by common consent—allowed for the acquisition of land by using it."[74]

Settler colonialism was as much a Mexican as a Spanish practice. These settlers, however, considered themselves Hispanos/as rather than Mexicans.

For their part, Pueblo Indians were able in some measure to retain some of their lands, and genízaros, deracinated Indians who were separated from their communities, also held land grants on the frontier of the Hispano/a settlements.[75] Dunbar-Ortiz reports that there were some seventy thousand Mexicans in New Mexico at the time—although the number is disputed by other historians—with only about a thousand white settlers; Pueblo Indians were considered Mexican citizens as well.[76] Being considered Mexican citizens did not, however, put an end to encroachment and enclosure of Indian lands.[77] In fact, the opposite proved true during the period following Mexican independence; dispossession of Indigenous lands grew exponentially. Land became a primitive mode of capital accumulation, and already by the early nineteenth century it was being bought and sold as a commodity. With the US invasion and the invalidation of land titles, lands declared public became an even riper field for speculation, homesteading, and the creation of national reserves. As noted by Andrés Reséndez, market and commercial interaction with the United States had come to dominate the New Mexico economy as early as 1843.[78]

Invasion in Historiography and Literature: The Case of New Mexico

The response of Nuevomexicanos/as to the US invasion has been much discussed by New Mexican historians, literary critics, and fiction writers in terms of accommodation versus resistance. The texts that we examine focus primarily on cultural resistance and do not, for the most part, address the moments of armed resistance, practices that, as we have seen, played a key part in New Mexican history as early as the seventeenth century.

Countering the oft-held notion that Nuevomexicanos/as were by and large reduced to accommodation as a form of cultural resistance, Carlos Herrera provides repeated examples of armed resistance.[79] In 1846, Brigadier General Kearny invaded New Mexico and set up a US military government before moving on with his forces to California. Kearny decreed that any resistance to the invasion would be considered "traitorous." Herrera understands Governor Armijo's lack of resistance to Kearny's troops as accommodation but also as an instance of resistance, a contradictory notion on its face, to be sure.[80] We know that Armijo had previously, in 1841, repelled a group of Texans penetrating the territory, but this time, Herrera argues, Armijo opted for the more prudent course and retreated to Chihuahua, leaving his subaltern Juan Bautista Vigil in charge. Vigil immediately pledged loyalty to the United States before being replaced by Charles Bent, a West Virginia–born trader-trapper appointed by Kearny. Herrera reads Vigil's accommodation as a way "to ensure that New Mexican culture would be preserved," while admitting that Vigil's own business interests may have colored his decisions.[81] Although much is made of the preservation of New Mexican culture, its maintenance cannot be attributed to the convenient and even opportunistic accommodation of political figures. Rather, culture survives if the people survive, even if their culture is subsequently subordinated vis-à-vis an emergent culture.

But accommodation to regime change, now the United States, was not acceptable to all Nuevomexicanos/as. A group in Santa Fe began to plan an uprising, but when discovered by Vigil, now serving as Bent's secretary, members of the group were arrested. Rebellion, however, did in fact break out in January 1847 in Taos. A band of Nuevomexicanos and Indians under Pablo Montoya killed Governor Bent and several other US soldiers. Termed a massacre by US supporters, the revolt led to US army troops under Commander Sterling Price coming to subdue the rebel forces. Price then shelled Taos for two days until the New Mexicans surrendered. Herrera estimates that around two hundred Nuevomexicanos died in these battles. The leaders were tried, convicted of treason—not insurrection—and hanged, despite the fact that these Mexican citizens did not see themselves as part of the United States; insurrection in the face of invasion is not treason, strictly speaking, as the invaded owed no loyalty to the United States. As Lewis H. Garrard noted in his chronicle of a trip to New Mexico and Colorado with a group of trappers at the time, it was preposterous to accuse the citizens of another nation of treason:[82]

> "It certainly did appear to be a great assumption on the part of the Americans to conquer a country and then arraign the revolting inhabitants for treason." And he adds: "Treason, indeed! What did the poor devil know about his new allegiance?"
>
> After the judgment, he leaves the courtroom:
>
> "I left the room sick at heart. Justice! Out upon the word, when its distorted meaning is the warrant for murdering those who defend to the last their country and their homes."[83]

Other skirmishes followed with raids against the invaders. As noted by Herrera, the two rebellions (Taos and Mora) "were part of a larger New Mexican movement to reject U.S. occupation of their homeland," adding that they were triggered by "resentment of abusive acts performed by U.S. troops and an overwhelming desire to resist conquest."[84] Historians, more often than fiction writers, comment on the armed resistance of rebels that attacked the invaders in Taos, Arroyo Hondo, and Mora. The insurgents would be defeated by US troops. Like the Spanish who discursively used the Requerimiento to justify the domination and massacre of Indians in the Américas, in New Mexico, it was an attitude of "we invade and defeat you and accuse you of treason if you protest and resist." Faced with invasion of their land and defeat of their attempts at resistance along with the loss of property rights under the new US regime, understandably, hundreds of Nuevomexicanos/as chose to relocate south to Mexico after the signing of the Treaty of Guadalupe Hidalgo in 1848.[85] Mexico offered land, and many chose self-repatriation, moving to the area of La Mesilla, then part of Mexico; ironically, after the Gadsden Purchase in 1853, this land, too, would become part of the United States.

Literary Representations of the US Invasion

More so than other regions of the US Southwest, New Mexico has a long tradition of writers, from colonial times to the post-1848 period, notably including several women. Most of the twentieth-century texts dealing with the nineteenth-century Southwest follow a particular format: sketches of local color, with a focus on landscape, traditions, festivities, food preparation, and historical romances. Nash Candelaria's work *Not by the Sword* (1982) follows this pattern.[86] Setting aside the larger political and economic struggles, the novel focuses on one family's loss and the importance of having an heir to carry on the family legacy and retain what little is left of the hacienda. Family loyalty, especially allegiance to the local patrón, is the dominant motif. Although Westphall indicates that there were no haciendas north of the present Mexican border, court cases, WPA narratives, and Candelaria's *Not by the Sword* suggest otherwise and tell of hacienda-like relations and a patrón system, which in the novel, for example, leads to the lynching of an innocent old Indian accused of stealing.[87]

Following a format similar to that of Jovita González and Eve Raleigh's 1930s novel *Caballero*,[88] Candelaria's text offers the US invasion of New Mexico as a historical backdrop to a narrative of the Rafa family and its fragmentation. Internal family division is symbolized by the Rafa twins, Carlos and Tercero, Carlos being the privileged firstborn, heir apparent, and, much like González's character Álvaro in *Caballero*, a rebellious young man given to recklessness, womanizing, gambling, and arrogance. Carlos's participation in the failed armed resistance against the US invaders and his death leave Tercero, who joined the priesthood as was expected of him, facing the loss of land and the end of the old Hispano/o way of life. The twins symbolically represent the two instruments of Spanish colonization, the missionary and the soldier, both there to extend the empire and to colonize. A pattern of twins every two generations suggests destiny, with history repeating itself: "As if, over the decades, people did not change but were reborn to live out their destiny."[89] The twins also represent the two reactions to post-1846 invasion and conquest: armed resistance and accommodation, foregrounding Hispano/a land loss and family fragmentation but speaking little about previous dispossessions.

To its credit, Candelaria's novel brings together various temporalities in contradiction as it reviews a semifeudal past that is overthrown by a capitalist invading force. Episodes recount the childhood and youth of the aging patriarch, the purchase by an ancestor of a Navajo slave who becomes the patriarch's grandmother, and the narrative's present, which is 1846, detailing the life of the Rafa twins. After the US invasion, the authoritarian patriarch, Don Francisco, like the territory of New Mexico, is reduced to loss and debt, and after Carlos's death, the family is dependent on Tercero, who must resign from his clerical duties to care for his parents, eventually marrying to carry on the family line.

Nuevomexicanos/as are presented as fervently Catholic traditionalists, very much taken with their Spanish ancestry and *hidalguía* (nobility). Faced with imminent invasion, marginalization, and displacement, the Hispanos/as see themselves as the true owners of the land, having been there "always," as Tercero's grandfather says. The fact that they have not always been there, that they were descendants of Spanish invaders themselves, settler colonists who took the land from the Indians, is not considered by the grandfather and is explained away by Tercero in terms of "universal" power hierarchies: "Very simply, the hierarchy has to do with conquest and possession. The Spanish came and took the land from the Indians. Their weapons were the sword, the gun, and the horse—driven by a fierce will to possess. Therefore the Spanish were at the peak of the hierarchy—conquerors. While the Indians were at the bottom."[90] Might seemingly makes right. In this way, the novel reveals the inherent racism and colonialist perspective of the Nuevomexicano/a landowners. Indians are represented for the most part as a menace, as savages, and even as a plague to be overcome: "The Indians were like a disease that lived off the bodies of the settlers, flaring in feverish attacks, then subsiding to a tenuous state of tolerance that was neither sickness nor health."[91]

After Mexico obtained its independence in 1821, as we saw previously,

Nuevomexicanos/as reacted against the appointment of a Mexican as governor. Although Maciel and Gonzales-Berry argue that "Nuevomexicanos certainly perceived themselves as an integral part of the Mexican nation," it is evident that after only twenty-plus years and especially given the distance between the Nuevomexicano/a settlements and those in Chihuahua, Mexican national identity could not have been strong, as shown in the Chimayó rebellion of 1837.[92] In Candelaria's novel, however, the Nuevomexicanos/as identify as Mexican. National identity is not in question; some reject being forced to be part of the United States, despite Kearny's statement, "We come amongst you as friends. Not as enemies; as protectors—not as conquerors. We come among you for your benefit, not for your injury."[93] Such words have been echoed many times in US interventions around the world.

The difficult choice between resistance and accommodation to conquest reappears in several Nuevomexicano/a narratives. Candelaria's novel suggests that some felt that without weapons and money there was little they could do against the well-armed US troops; these men prefer to surrender when word reaches them that Kearny is on his way. Likewise in Rudolfo Anaya's *Shaman Winter* (1999), the villagers of Las Vegas, after hearing that Kearny's troops are advancing on New Mexico, listen to Don José Aragón, who warns that Kearny is bringing two divisions, with thousands of infantrymen and artillery, making resistance futile: "To resist will mean our young men will die."[94] Novelists confront the issue by explaining that there was no way to resist, and yet some Nuevomexicanos/as in fact did resist and led the insurrections at Taos and Mora. These rebels are not presented favorably in the narratives, however; they are hotheads like Carlos. Don Francisco, Tercero's father, sees them as foolish rabble-rousers who have nothing to gain and everything to lose.[95] Candelaria's novel thus reads the invasion as generally favorably received. It is a version of history that favors the United States, even if wary of the onslaught of "Americanos": "Already the American army had been welcomed wherever it had appeared. . . . Yet things had stayed much the same. Even the peons—the poorest and least educated—saw the coming of the Yankee as a welcome change. The Americanos would bring money. There would be more trade. Perhaps they would even conquer the Apaches and Navajos and Comanches, something that the Mexican government could never do."[96]

Not all welcome the invasion, however; plotters against it who meet in Santa Fe will be betrayed and arrested; some fear losing not only land and power but their culture as well. Candelaria's novel and other Nuevomexicano/a works continue to return to the contentious historical moment of reaction to US invasion, the various positions taken, and the roles played by clergymen. Candelaria presents Padre Martínez as fearing that New Mexico has been conquered by infidels and that their faith and religious practices are in danger. By contrast, Fray Angélico Chávez indicates that the priest admired the US system of religious liberty and separation of church and state.[97] M. E. Vigil also underscores that Martínez "viewed the occupation in more pragmatic terms as a *fait accompli*."[98] All these writers converge in stressing the import of intellectuals like Martínez, whose positions had political influence. Fray Angélico Chávez recognizes Martínez as a Nuevomexicano intellectual who published the first book in New Mexico (an orthography text), schooled women, printed schoolbooks, and tutored those who wanted to go to Durango, as he did, to become priests. He also wrote for the *Gazette*, using the pen name José Santisteban.[99] While Bishop Lamy condemned the Penitentes, a lay Catholic brotherhood, Martínez befriended them and disregarded the bishop's prohibition of native-made *santos*. Called a hothead by his critics, Martínez was considered the instigator of every uprising, including the Taos revolt against the US invaders.[100]

Cleofas Jaramillo's *Romance of a Little Village Girl* also recalls the moment of invasion and the arrival of Kearny and his troops and offers an interesting take on the Nuevomexicano/a dynamics of accommodation. Governor Armijo by this time had left the capital and gone to El Paso. Vigil's almost immediate surrender, Jaramillo says, was not supported by New Mexicans nor Pueblo Indians, who both resented their treatment by the US soldiers and feared losing their lands. In response, dissenters began plotting an uprising, and in January 1847 an insurrection broke out in Taos. In Jaramillo's version, she narrates that Charles Bent, "elected first governor of the territory," was killed in the Taos rebellion. As historian Herrera points out, Bent, in fact, was not elected; after taking New Mexico, Kearny appointed Bent governor; the latter was, however, related by marriage to Jaramillo's family.[101] Jaramillo does not go further into the US invasion, preferring to note that another Jaramillo daughter married another newcomer, Carson, and that these US immigrants who settled in Taos and married into prominent Spanish families brought "a new era of prosperity" to the area.[102]

Jaramillo portrays the Anglo immigrants who came after the US invasion as "adventurers, trappers, wide-eyed gamblers and towering gold-seekers."[103] As time went by, after 1848, she writes, the sons of Spanish families were sent to eastern schools and upon their return were unwilling to work the land. As a consequence, "the fortunes of the Dons soon passed out into the hands of the strangers, for minimum sums."[104] For Jaramillo, it was an unwillingness to work the land on the part of New Mexico's Hispanos/as that led to their dispossession and not, for example, the questionable adjudication of the Court of Private Land Claims.[105] But not all Hispano/o landowners lost their land, nor was the land worked by the landowners themselves but in large measure by peons. She recalls that her father continued to be involved in "sheep raising, farming and mercantile [business]."[106] They also had a store. She recalls that her mother had three or more servants to help with the housework, and her father had peons. Her parents, she makes it a point to note, "were not the haughty kind of Dons; they never made their servants feel that they were inferior. There was no need, for our servants knew their place and kept it."[107] Jaramillo paints—unquestioningly and uncritically—a highly stratified society both before the US invasion and after. It is worth remarking that the notion that there was no peonage in New Mexico is negated in Jaramillo's narratives recalling the past; she demonstrates nostalgia for this oppressive social hierarchy, where servants "knew their place," at the same time that she critiques Hispanos/as' lack of entrepreneurship and Anglo work ethic.

Negotiating New Mexico's Status as a US Colony

New Mexico would remain a territory, that is, a colony of the United States, until 1912, a full sixty-four years after the signing of the Treaty of Guadalupe Hidalgo that made it part of the United States. Historian Juan Gómez-Quiñones points out that Nuevomexicanos/as would continue to be politically prominent in the territory through the late nineteenth century, holding elected and appointed office at several levels.[108] A circle of some twenty Nuevomexicano/a families controlled these positions through the so-called patrón system.[109] Since the governor, secretary, district judge, attorneys, surveyor general, and US marshal would all be appointed by the US president, which also occurred later in Puerto Rico, retaining political leverage at both national and territorial levels was important. Congressional reasons for not readily admitting the territory as a state were at least partly rooted in racism, regarding both Native Americans and mestizos. Having just passed through a period in which Congress had been unwilling to grant New Mexico statehood on the basis of its "mongrel" population that was unfit for citizenship and self-government, the Nuevomexicano/a elite defended itself, not through an antiracist political stance but by claiming whiteness and calling themselves Hispanic or Spano-Americans.[110] This accommodation was not an act of resistance; it was a call for selective assimilation predicated on the basis of their whiteness. Spatial dispossession resulting from US invasion is tethered to discursive reaction that reenacts violence by—again—delegitimizing and erasing those not belonging to the Nuevomexicano/a elite.

Many of the nineteenth- and twentieth-century Nuevomexicano/a writers stress their Spanish ancestry, their whiteness, whether Jaramillo or Eusebio Chacón. Although Chacón was appointed official translator and interpreter for the US Court of Private Land Claims in 1891 and served for four years, his essays do not deal with the fact that few New Mexican land grants were approved by the court, much less with what the US takeover of their territory meant for non-Hispano/a New Mexicans.[111] What he does do is defend the "Spanish American" population of New Mexico, for example, against an article published in the *Review* of Las Vegas that portrays and ridicules Hispanos/as as "dirty, ignorant, and inferior people, a mixture between Indians and Iberians whose lack of an evangelical light always holds us back."[112] The article's author, a "sectarian missionary woman," is taken to task for not knowing much about Spanish and Mexican people, much less anything about Indians. Chacón identifies as a Spanish American: "No other blood runs in my veins than the one brought over by don Juan de Oñate and later by the renowned ancestors bearing my name."[113] New Mexico, says Chacón, is a place where "the purity of physical features of the conquerors have been preserved."[114] He does acknowledge that "some mixture has occurred, only slightly and rarely," although in any event, "if it were true that we were a mixed race, there is nothing disgraceful or degrading about this," arguing that Romans also mixed with Goths, as did other European peoples.[115] What is at stake in Chacón's refutation is that the writer of the article "has only come in contact with the lowest element of our community."[116] The discursive violence of the class and racial attitudes of the Hispano-American elite is evident in Chacón's writing as well as in others' work, including that of Cabeza de Baca and Jaramillo; they are more keen on highlighting their "racial purity" than on pointing to the blatant racism inherent in the "missionary woman's" assessment of New Mexicans.

Dispossession under US Rule

Dispossession and displacement of New Mexican Hispano/a colonists and Pueblo Indians from their lands by Anglos after 1848 would primarily come through the actions of the surveyor general, the Court of Private Land Claims, and the Supreme Court, as well as through the manipulation of court decisions by New Mexican ricos and wealthy whites. Claimants were at a severe disadvantage before these governmental agencies, as the burden of proof fell on them rather than on those who fraudulently profited from the rejection of claims.[117] Denial of these claims points to the bias of the US government that more often than not disregarded Spanish/Mexican custom and land usage and ignored multiple claimants of communal grants by focusing on the principal settler (often already bought out by speculators), as if he were the sole claimant. Communal claims were generally dismissed; only private land claims were found to be legitimate. The use value of land was not recognized, only its exchange value. Land loss also came in the form of the land-grabbing practice of opportunistic lawyers who demanded a portion of land for their claimants' representation and then brought a partition suit, insisting on division of the grant and forcing a sale, as dictated by court procedures.[118] As Ebright makes clear, Hispano/a brokers or middlemen often facilitated the acquisition of the lands by speculators.[119] In some cases it was a Nuevomexicano, like M. S. Otero, a wealthy sheep rancher, cattleman, and businessman, who put up the money to have the Tejón grant approved by Congress, keeping the entire grant for himself after taking the other Tejón residents to court. The people of Tejón were dispossessed of all but their huts, even if in time the Oteros, too, would lose the land to their lawyers.[120] The US government was especially interested in not authorizing communal land claims as, once rejected, they came to belong to the government as "public lands."[121] Only 24 percent of land claims in New Mexico were confirmed.[122] Mirroring the processes that took place in California, where, however, more than 73 percent of the claims were confirmed, the dispossession of the Hispanos/as took various forms in addition to the legal dispossession by the courts and surveyor general, including "forfeiture through back taxes, credit foreclosures, lawyers [sic] fees, outright purchase, swindle, [and] appropriation of *ejido* (common land) into the public domain."[123] The travesties of land grant adjudication in New Mexico have never been acknowledged by the US government; the aftereffects of this dispossession are, however, narrated in New Mexican literature.

Article 10 of the 1848 Treaty of Guadalupe Hidalgo, which would have validated all grants that were valid under Mexican law, was deleted from the treaty by the US Senate prior to ratification (although under the Protocol of Querétaro, legitimate titles valid under Mexican law were to be deemed legitimate by the United States, provided they had been made before the cutoff date of May 13, 1846).[124] The State Department, however, rejected the protocol as it saw the United States as having a legitimate right to all the land acquired, having paid $15 million for this real estate deal.[125] After invading Mexico all the way to Mexico City and appropriating more than a third of Mexican territory, the United States found discursive means by which to whitewash its imperialist act by compensating Mexico with that sum.

As noted in chapter 2, determining the validity of claims had two major precedents: the 1803 Louisiana treaty and the 1819 Florida treaty. In New Mexico, land validation claims did not go well, especially in comparison with California.[126] Ebright presents several reasons for these differences in validation, but the most salient are (1) the fact that there was fraud or manipulation of land laws to wrest land grant property from Hispanos/as, and (2) the fact that claims adjudication was unfair and favorable to the speculator rather than to the settlers living on the land grants.[127]

The two main strategies used by speculators to obtain land in post-1848 New Mexico were the tactical purchase of the principal settler's interest in a community grant and the partition suit. The first is of special interest here, as it applies to the Tierra Amarilla grant, a communal grant whose principal was Manuel Martínez. As noted by Ebright, the fact that the grant documents only mentioned Martínez, the *poblador principal*, led the US surveyor general, who was averse to communal claims, to confirm the claim only to his heir and not to the settlers living on the land.[128] As soon as it was confirmed, the heir, Martínez's son Francisco, sold it to the land speculator–attorney Thomas Benton Catron, the leader of the Santa Fe Ring, who then resold it, in the process dispossessing the settlers of their commonly held land. The heirs of these settlers have gone to court many times to try to regain their Tierra Amarilla lands, but to this day have not been successful.[129]

The same Tierra Amarilla grant figures prominently in Jaramillo's autobiographical sketch, *Romance of a Little Village Girl*. Jaramillo is especially proud of her great-grandfather, Don Manuel Martínez, who petitioned Mexico in 1835 for land for himself, his sons, and some neighbors. She says, "The Government heard his petition and gave the Martínez family the Tierra Amarilla grant of over three hundred thousand acres, the richest grant in water, timber and grazing land in the northern part of New Mexico."[130] Jaramillo does not mention, however, that Tierra Amarilla was a community grant, that the neighbors were grantees of the land as well, and that her ancestor's heir ascribed to himself the whole of the community land. This claim to being the descendant of a major land grant holder of northern New Mexico is crucial to Jaramillo, more important than the fact that this ancestor misconstrued himself as sole grantee. Nuevomexicano/a collusion and duplicity in the dispossession of community lands is thus misrepresented by some twentieth-century Nuevomexicano/a writers intent, on the one hand, on underscoring their Hispano/a bona fides and, on the other, on obscuring their role in the dispossession of others' lands, whether claimed by Native Americans or other Nuevomexicanos/as.

The US government had a vested interest in rejecting claims for common lands, because, if rejected, as previously noted, they became public lands, government lands. Take the case of San Miguel del Bado: here inhabitants sought confirmation of their grant for several villages, and the Court of Private Land Claims confirmed the entire grant. The government then appealed to the Supreme Court, which reversed the claims court decision, holding that common lands belonging to the governments of Spain and Mexico now rightfully passed on to the US government. Only occupied lands were confirmed, not common lands.[131] The ruling also stipulated that every step of the claim had to be met: grant recorded in archives, approved by the deputation, within the specified period, and so on. Rejection was justified by forgery of the document, insufficient proof of grant, failure to notify owners of adjoining lands, failure to settle the land within four years, continuous possession thereafter, and so on. Ebright does point to one exception, the *Chaves* court decision, which allowed a community grant made to the town of Cubero in Valencia County in 1833 to stand. While the claimants had no documents, they were able to show that they had been in continuous possession of the land since 1833.[132] Fraud and embarrassment over validations like the two-million-acre Maxwell grant referenced earlier led to the establishment of a five-judge Court of Private Land Claims in 1891 by President Benjamin Harrison.[133] Ironically, this new act made it even harder to validate claims as the nineteenth century came to a close.

Under Spanish and Mexican law, the governor could make grants, but so could other officials like the lieutenant governor, alcaldes, *ayuntamientos*, and prefects. It was the custom to consider these grants valid. In some cases, the governor revoked grants made by lesser officials. The Court of Private Land Claims rejected all grants not specifically made by the governor.[134] In one case, a copy of a grant that was made out by an alcalde was presented, but because it was not made by an *escribano* (notary) (none were available), it was rejected: "The claims court rejection of the Embudo grant because of the supposed lack of authority of *alcaldes* to make certified copies was outrageous," the upshot being that Court of Private Land Claims readings of Mexican and Spanish laws were biased and highly selective.[135]

Maciel and Gonzales-Berry's work on rejected land claims indicates that the lack of funds to meet expenses in establishing titles and boundaries, failure to pay taxes, and the taking of land for forest reserves led to the dispossession of Nuevomexicanos/as of millions of acres.[136] Delays in surveying as well as fraud and manipulation of land laws further enabled their land loss. Both see that different attitudes and land-use practices exacerbated the conflict between Nuevomexicanos/as and Anglos: "Nuevomexicanos emphasized use and occupancy rather than ownership. In addition, there was an established tradition of communal land for the common good and the collective use of an entire community. Such practices were alien to Euro-Americans."[137] In fact, all these Euro-Americans were immigrants or descendants of colonists from countries that had historically undergone a shift from feudalism to capitalism, where the commons was a familiar practice, but by 1846 the dominant mode was capitalism, with private individual holdings. As had earlier occurred in Europe, communal lands were to be privatized, as we saw in Oklahoma in chapter 2 and as occurred swiftly in post-1848 New Mexico.

The loss of land tenancy rights in New Mexico thus came with invasion and the imposition, with the support of the US government, of capitalist relations of production that valued not the legacy or use value of the land but title and the land's exchange and market value. Silvia Rodriguez indicates that by the early 1900s, at least 80 percent of the grant lands claimed by Hispano/a subsistence farmers in New Mexico had been lost.[138] The dispossessed Hispanos/as of New Mexico were proletarianized and, in part, urbanized, but most, while displaced from their grants, nevertheless stayed in the area, and many continued to work the land, as indicated in the WPA testimonios. Some migrated to California; others willingly chose to relocate to Mexico after being offered land in La Mesilla on the Mexican side of the new border that, through the Gadsden Purchase of 1853, became part of New Mexico. Ranching, timber, mining, and railroad booms and busts faded away and were replaced by tourism booms and the government's installation of research labs at Los Alamos and Sandía, so that today New Mexico's economy depends primarily on its oil and gas production, federal and military spending, and tourism.[139] Although there has been a demographic shift, with an increase in Anglo migration, today the population of New Mexico (about two million) continues to be predominantly of Mexican/Spanish (49.1 percent) and Native American (10.9 percent) origin.[140]

Armed Resistance to Dispossession: The Gorras Blancas

By the mid-1880s, according to Gómez-Quiñones, "economic conditions for the Mexicans in Nuevo Mexico had deteriorated considerably," and Nuevomexicanos/as were losing both communal and private lands, through both legal and illegal means.[141] Conflicts over land grants and the institution of enclosures through the fencing of common lands provoked armed resistance.

At the end of the nineteenth century, aside from the Indigenous peoples, the Nuevomexicano/a population of Mexican and Spanish origin was still the majority population in New Mexico. Anselmo Arellano estimates that close to 80 percent of New Mexico's total population was made up of "native Hispanos."[142] The largest and most populous county was San Miguel County, with Las Vegas, the county seat, larger than even Santa Fe and Albuquerque. In 1890 the Gorras Blancas (White Caps) rose up there to protest "bossism" and the establishment of large landed estates by incoming Anglo and Mexican businessmen and speculators who began fencing the common lands claimed within the purchased grant.[143] Community land grantees and their descendants found themselves likewise dispossessed when only the primary holder was recognized as titular landowner. Conflicts also increased as land grabbers who secured land titles stretched the boundaries beyond the stipulated areas and began fencing their lands, depriving Nuevomexicanos/as of the public commons and access to grass, wood, and water. So, too, were the Gorras Blancas a reaction to the dispossession by both elites and incoming squatters on what were considered ancestral lands.

The Gorras Blancas came into existence in response to this process of enclosure.[144] They rode at night in their white caps, cutting fences, destroying crops, and burning barns, houses, outbuildings, railroad bridges, and sawmills. Like the seventeenth-century Digger Movement in England, the Gorras Blancas represented the dispossessed and the small landholders deprived of the commons. San Miguel County Nuevomexicanos/as first organized raids after Anglos and ricos began erecting barbed wire fences to enclose common land. Six of the region's major grants were community grants, among them the Las Vegas grant, an area of 1,100,000 acres, where "most of the controversial fencing occurred and it was from these grants that most of the night-riding Las Gorras Blancas came."[145] As noted by Robert J. Rosenbaum and Robert W. Larson, the Gorras Blancas struck at least seventy-eight times between April 1889 and September 1890, being "unique in nineteenth century New Mexico. They were also remarkably successful. By the end of the summer of 1890 no fences enclosed the common lands in the San Miguel country and none were being constructed."[146]

There was a great deal of popular support for the Gorras Blancas from Hispanos/as, políticos, and Hispano businessmen. Some Anglo homesteaders, small ranchers, and railroad workers also opposed enclosure by large land and cattle companies: "Their opposition, however, stemmed more from the conviction that the land in question was public domain and therefore available for preemption, rather than from sympathy for the plight of *los hombres pobres* or an understanding of, or belief in the integrity of community land grants."[147] Posting *proclamaciones*, nailed to buildings by the Gorras Blancas, was an effective tactic. It was in Las Vegas that the Spanish-language newspaper *La voz del pueblo* was published, and it, too, supported the Gorras Blancas. In fact, the majority of people in Las Vegas County supported the Gorras Blancas.[148]

It is telling that the chief justice of the territorial court, James O'Brien, saw the "outrages" of the Gorras Blancas as the "protests of a simple pastoral people against the establishment of large landed Estates, or baronial feudalism."[149] Historians have seen the Gorras Blancas as rising up to protest the establishment by incoming Anglos of large landed estates, theft by land grabbers, cronyism, and abuse by local tyrants, while at the same time proclaiming their right to resist.[150] Weber includes in his anthology a copy of the Gorras Blancas' platform and the speech offered by the publisher of *La voz del pueblo*, Felix Martínez, critical of both the fence cutters and the land grabbers but especially of the land thieves: "The fence-cutters in their lawlessness must be suppressed, but the land thief in his evil-doing must also be put down and put down to stay."[151] When several members of the Gorras Blancas were brought to trial, they were found not guilty when witnesses against them did not appear in court. Eventually their members would include more than a thousand Nuevomexicanos/as.

Despite the approval of the Las Vegas grant in 1895, with the final survey coming in 1900 and the naming of an Anglo-controlled land grant board of Las Vegas by the legislature and judiciary, Anglos pressed for New Mexico holdings to be open to homesteading and speculation; here, as elsewhere, the Hispanos/as lost out: "For all intents and purposes, the Las Vegas grant was in the hands of land speculators by 1902 and its common lands were disposed of in the name of progress."[152] New enclosures and new dispossessions continued. Something similar happened to the San Miguel del Bado grant, also a community grant. In 1897 only lands actually occupied with houses and garden plots were validated, with again "the balance of the grant being declared public domain."[153] This case established an important precedent: "the court could remove all unoccupied land (that is, land held in common) from its community grant confirmations."[154] Few politicians were interested in defending the rights of the poor landowners; among the few was Governor Edmund G. Ross, who in 1887 vetoed a bill that allowed land speculators to claim a land grant and left it up to the community landholders to contest the claim. The bill, Ross concluded, was a "cunningly devised scheme of robbery as directed mainly to the eviction of the occupants of this class of land grants."[155]

Some thirty years later, in 1927, matters had not improved; the Gorras Blancas were still active and attacked fencing around the Preston Beck grant, adjacent to the village of Antonchico, "an assault that was met by machine gun fire."[156] They also destroyed timber to be used for railroad ties in view of the railroad's violation of the people's water rights, depressed wages, and the raising of freight rates.[157] As Arellano notes, "As an organized group, the Gorras Blancas were probably the most secretive and closely-knit organization of men ever to exist in the territory of New Mexico. Their protest against the encroachment on and theft of their lands began in 1889, and by the end of 1890, their notoriety had spread throughout the territory and reached the eastern states."[158]

They were supported not only by *La voz del pueblo* but also by the Knights of Labor organized in New Mexico in conjunction with other Knights of Labor in the Midwest, although the national president of the Knights of Labor, Terence Powderly, was ambivalent in his support of New Mexican members and their agenda.[159] By "emphasizing the anti-monopoly and anti-land-grabbing positions of the union as a national organization, Juan José Herrera, the Knights of Labor organizer, was able to link the protests of the angry Mexicanos living on the threatened grants in San Miguel to common labor issues of the day."[160] Given the turmoil, including actions against powerful railroad interests, New Mexico's governor would visit the area, but the idea of focusing solely on repressing Gorras Blancas activity and not on land thieves was not well received locally. The editors of *La voz del pueblo*, for example, "felt that the governor should also try, by proclamations and other means within his power, to suppress the ruthless appropriation of people's lands, whether grants or government property, and also to guarantee their rights and privileges to wood, water, and grazing grounds."[161] Resentment over Nuevomexicano/a land loss was still very much an issue.

The collaboration between the Knights of Labor and the Gorras Blancas to seek redress for enclosures would in time lead Democratic Party leaders and disaffected Republicans to create a political party, El Partido del Pueblo Unido, or the United People's Party, in New Mexico, even before New Mexico became a state in 1912.[162] Their demands would unite the population and lead to their victory in the 1890 November elections. Out of this election came pressure for Congress to create the US Court of Private Land Claims "for the purpose of determining and adjusting land claims in the territories that were acquired from Mexico."[163] Still, subsequent court decisions generally went against the Nuevomexicanos/as, given what Ebright calls "the adversarial climate of the Court of Private Land Claims and the judicial climate of the Supreme Court."[164] After 1897, the claims court rejected the common land claims of every communal grant and in the specific case of the San Miguel del Bado community grant, only 5,207 acres out of 315,300 acres were confirmed.[165]

Not all the Nuevomexicano/a elites supported the Gorras Blancas, just as not all were against the Santa Fe Ring, the emergent dominant political machine in the territory. Eusebio Chacón published his two *nouvelles*, titled *El hijo de la tempestad* and *Tras la tormenta la calma*, in 1892, during a period of intensive political action by Nuevomexicanos, especially in San Miguel County, where the Spanish-language newspaper *La voz del pueblo* gave a platform for Nuevomexicano/a opposition to the dispossession of residents of the Las Vegas land grant who were being fenced out of their communal lands. Chacón, while not directly referencing the Gorras Blancas, writes a fantastic/romantic narrative, *El hijo de la tempestad*, about a bandit. As the title notes, he is figuratively the son of a storm, having been born during a storm and abandoned by his father when his mother died after giving birth. *El hijo de la tempestad* is a Gothic *costumbrista* tale of a child born and raised in a cave by a gypsy woman and a monkey, who is actually the devil. The child is claimed by the devil as his instrument to bring misfortune to humanity. The boy grows up to be the head of a group of bandits that steal, kidnap, and rape women; they murder, raid, and pillage villagers near the caves where he and his men dwell with the gypsy and her monkey/devil consort.

In *El hijo de la tempestad* a group of soldiers confronts the bandits who have taken several villagers prisoner; the bandits take to their swords but are defeated and killed. Once the gypsy also dies, she is said to be in hell, sweeping the dwelling of the devil, the place to be occupied by "ciertos politicastros que traen a la patria muy revuelta."[166] Whether the disparaging reference to "politicastros" refers to El Partido del Pueblo Unido, which supported the Gorras Blancas and the Knights of Labor, is not explicit but probable. The text is clear in lamenting the political unrest that afflicts the land, discursively solving the problem by banishing the rabble-rousers to hell.

Other Nuevomexicanos/as who likewise did not support the Gorras Blancas include Manuel Cabeza de Baca, the uncle of writer Fabiola Cabeza de Baca, who would form a counterorganization to the Gorras Blancas, Los Caballeros de Ley y Orden, allied with the Republican Party, and publish another newspaper, *El sol de mayo*.[167] In it he published a narrative expressly critical of the Gorras Blancas; he also wrote about a local bandit, Vicente Silva, a text mentioned by Fabiola Cabeza de Baca. For some elite Nuevomexicanos/as who engaged in fencing the common lands, the Gorras Blancas were dismissed as mere bandits. Families were divided on the issue; while Manuel Cabeza de Baca advocated against the Gorras Blancas, another family member, Ezequiel Cabeza de Baca, was a writer and associate editor for *La voz del pueblo* and an organizer of El Partido del Pueblo Unido that supported them.[168] Here, as earlier, with the contentious but seminal figure of Padre Martínez, New Mexican writers capture and textualize the conflicting ideological positions that held sway in the period.

Candelaria's third novel, *Inheritance of Strangers* (1985), begins to deal allegorically with land loss, giving its reading of the place of the Gorras Blancas in New Mexican history. Continuing the saga of the Rafa family of *Not by the Sword*, Tercero, having left the priesthood and married, with children and grandchildren, faces land dispossession. The novel recounts how Tercero and other landowners see the need to have a lawyer represent their land claims as a group; but lawyers take advantage of the situation and—as so often happened in reality—press for the sale of land to pay for their services. Tercero highlights the danger of land loss in a legal system that does not consider occupancy and use but only legal documents. The period is the late nineteenth century, and the Rafas, like other Nuevomexicano/a landowners, have lost a good part of their land but still retain enough to cultivate and make a living for their families. Tercero, or Don José Antonio as he is now known, in the meantime has become a trusted political ally of the Democrats. Charting the disenfranchisement of Nuevomexicanos/as, the novel shows that while they are the majority population they are nevertheless the underclass, no longer deciding anything.

Inheritance of Strangers picks up in the year 1890 when the local Nuevomexicanos/as, including Francisco, Tercero's son, decide to reject the handpicked Democratic candidate for sheriff, Plácido Durán, and organize themselves as the Hombres de Libertad, riding at night (like the Gorras Blancas) with white hoods to attempt to scare Durán into giving up his candidacy. The plot backfires when Francisco is left near death after a severe beating at the hands of ruffians led by Benito Durán, Plácido's brother; Francisco's son, Leonardo, goes out to seek revenge and is instead shot to death by Durán. In Candelaria's novel, the Hombres de Libertad (unlike the Gorras Blancas) are not portrayed as fighting against land grabbers but rather are denigrated for being shock troops for contending political parties vying for power. This distorted version of El Partido del Pueblo Unido and the Gorras Blancas figures the revolt as solely a political conflict between the Democratic Party, controlled by the well-to-do Anglos, and the poorer Nuevomexicanos/as, who reject the candidate favored by the Anglos. Historically, El Partido del Pueblo Unido won the 1890 elections. Moreover, the purpose of the Gorras Blancas in cutting fences was "to suppress the ruthless appropriation of people's land, whether grants or government property, and also to guarantee their rights and privileges to wood, water and grazing ground."[169] This campaign rooted in land issues disappears from Candelaria's accounting, as does the generalized public support and success of the Partido del Pueblo Unido in the 1890 elections.[170] The sociohistorical context is at best secondary and distorted, if not dismissed, in the novel as a petty internecine political conflict at the local level and not as an example of an important instance of collective struggle against wholesale Nuevomexicano/a dispossession.

History and nostalgia are likewise central to the work of Fabiola Cabeza de Baca, who also looks back on the late nineteenth century. In her novel *We Fed Them Cactus* (1954), she recalls the period of the Gorras Blancas without mentioning them specifically.[171] Cabeza de Baca briefly references the conflicts of sheep versus cattle that arose across the Southwest in this period, narrating the arrival of cattle companies and their attempts to displace the New Mexican sheepmen by building fences: "The New Mexicans were ready to fight for the land which traditionally had been theirs, and out of this grew up an organization of influential New Mexicans for protection against the usurpers. These citizens banded together and, by cutting down a few fences, discouraged fence building by those who had no titles for the land."[172] While identifying the newcomers as usurpers and recalling this act of resistance, Cabeza de Baca makes it a point not to associate them with the Gorras Blancas, saying that they called the organization *"Caballeros de Labor*, Gentlemen of Labor," but she does not link these "Caballeros" or Knights of Labor to the Gorras Blancas, as Rosenbaum and Larson do, labeling the Gorras Blancas "marauders" and bandits who "wore white hoods over their heads when they were out pillaging and came to be known as Los [sic] Gorras Blancas, the White Caps," further noting that the Gorras Blancas called themselves "*El Partido del Pueblo*, the People's Party: It became a secret society."[173] In Cabeza de Baca's version, it was the respectable Hispanos/as that had to organize against these marauders: "the good citizens formed a new party which they called *El Partido de la Unión*, the Union Party, composed of members of both major political parties," and this new party (possibly her uncle Manuel Cabeza de Baca's Los Caballeros de Ley y Orden) stood in opposition to the "marauders" of the Partido del Pueblo.[174] Since her uncle was a founder of the opposing party, her negative representations of the Gorras Blancas are perhaps colored by his position. What is clear is that Nuevomexicano/a writers of the period are very much invested in portraying themselves as standing in opposition to perceived lawlessness. Strikingly absent, in good measure, too, in these literary representations is any mention of the initial dispossession of Indigenous lands in the region. It falls to more recent fiction writers and historians to take up the issue of Native American dispossession.

Again, in the work of Cabeza de Baca and other Nuevomexicano/a writers there is a concerted attempt to delink from any kind of armed insurrection against enclosures and the spatial violence being perpetrated against Nuevomexicano/a landholders. We know that resistance to the expropriation of land grants in New Mexico continued throughout the twentieth century. The legacy of the Gorras Blancas lived on in the Rio Arriba country to the northwest. There a new group, La Mano Negra, is said to have emerged in the late 1920s to mid-1930s. Like the Gorras Blancas, they continued to resist Anglo encroachments and the oppression of Nuevomexicanos/as by cutting fences as well as "barn and haystack burning, cattle maiming, firing shots to warn intruders and arranging ambushes."[175]

Rosenbaum and Larson point out that "it is in light of this legacy of long-term skirmishing [what we might term low-intensity resistance] that the June 5th, 1967, courthouse raid at Tierra Amarilla must be viewed."[176] This tradition of guerrilla resistance, as exemplified by the Gorras Blancas and La Mano Negra, is seen as an antecedent to the courthouse raid at Tierra Amarilla by Reies López Tijerina and La Alianza Federal de las Mercedes (the Federal Land Grant Alliance), a militant organization formed in the 1960s that demanded a return of the land grants (mercedes) taken from the Hispano/a villagers.[177] As Rosenbaum and Larson write, "Tijerina could get people to attack the courthouse because they knew how to do it and doing it made sense to them," adding that Tijerina's attack on the courthouse "was a fundamental, normal, basic, and understandable part of Mexicano life."[178] This time the raid was symbolic. "No one was under the illusion that raiding the courthouse at Tierra Amarilla . . . was going to bring about a return of lands once held in common on the Tierra Amarilla grant. The raid was part of a larger strategy involving political action, action which antedates, significantly enough, the organization of Tijerina's Alianza."[179]

Moreover, Tijerina and his Alianza movement have to be acknowledged as crucial aspects of the Chicano/a movement's broader denunciation of US land usurpation throughout the Southwest in the late 1960s and 1970s.[180] Sergio Elizondo, in his novel *Muerte en una estrella*, for example, recalls Tijerina's participation in the United Farmworkers' March from the Rio Grande valley to Austin in 1966, connecting a series of struggles: land, labor, and legal.[181] Tijerina's subsequent incarceration brought an end to his leadership and, in time, to the Alianza movement. Nevertheless, the Alianza's call for redress against enclosures and expropriation of Hispano/a lands attracted a good deal of attention at the time and sparked a renewed interest in land issues that went back to the nineteenth century. This action further linked them to contemporary Chicano/a farmworker and civil rights struggles.

Political Showdown in Lincoln County

Of course, not all the land conflicts in New Mexico were over land grants; some were over economic and political power, as reflected in Candelaria's novel, but land inevitably figured in as well. What has come to be known as the 1878 Lincoln County War, the topic of several Western films (*The Left Handed Gun*, 1958; *Chisum*, 1970; and *Young Guns*, 1988), is described by Maciel and Gonzales-Berry as a range conflict fought "to determine political control and the ownership of land in the region."[182] Although in the actual Lincoln County conflict Nuevomexicanos/as figured prominently, they are left at the margins in these films, as noted, too, by Rosenbaum and Larson.[183] As these historians indicate, Lincoln County held lands and water supplies not granted by either Spain or Mexico that Nuevomexicanos/as traditionally used for grazing, but these would soon be invaded by Anglo settlers, including "discharged soldiers, Texas cattlemen, active Army men, and Indian agents."[184] The competition for economic and political control of the land would lead to local warfare. Prior to the intra-Anglo war that involved men like Billy the Kid,

John Chisum, Alexander McSween, and Pat Garrett, the area had already seen racist conflicts between Nuevomexicanos/as and Anglos over land and water rights. Again, it was in part a battle of cattlemen versus sheepherders, a conflict between private landowners versus communal landownership: "It was a struggle for both possession of resources and the ways they were to be used."[185] While the Nuevomexicanos/as were able to control the water resources and land in early skirmishes, they soon lost out to Anglos and newcomers from Texas and elsewhere.

Otero and El Chivito, a.k.a. Billy the Kid

Central to at least the popular culture version if not the historical account of the Lincoln County War is the legendary figure of William Henry Bonney or McCarty or Antrim (1859–81), better known as Billy the Kid. In 1936, Miguel Antonio Otero Jr. (1859–1944), a former territorial governor of New Mexico, would capitalize on the sensationalist portrayals of Billy the Kid and write a counternarrative of his own: *The Real Billy the Kid*. Otero would also write three autobiographical volumes about his life on the frontier and his years (1897–1906) as governor of New Mexico Territory, appointed by President William McKinley. Otero's grandparents were immigrants from Spain who came to New Mexico, where Otero's father was born.[186] Otero's father, Miguel Otero Sr. (1829–82), studied at St. Louis University and at Pingree College in Fishkill, New York, obtained a law degree at St. Louis University, and served as New Mexico's territorial delegate to Congress (1855–61). He married a woman from South Carolina and lived with his family in St. Louis, in Washington, DC, in Colorado, and in New Mexico. The family, says Vigil, was "decidedly pro-American rather than pro-Mexican in nationalistic sympathies and would generally be more identified with Anglo-American culture and values than most Hispanics."[187] Vigil further notes that Otero Sr., in addition to being a wealthy, educated businessman, banker, teacher, merchant, and railroad executive, was also a large landowner, owning, with his brother, some one million acres of land in the Bartolomé Baca land grant in Valencia and Bernalillo Counties.[188]

The elder Otero is a telling figure of the New Mexico Territory period, especially in his role as a power broker. In 1859, as a delegate to Congress, he gave a speech before the House of Representatives on Indian depredations in New Mexico. He was also in favor of extending slavery to the territory.[189] Otero Sr. was also seen as unfriendly to Hispanos/as, for he had attacked the delegate José Manuel Gallegos in Congress, calling him a member of the Mexican Party and himself a member of the "American Party" in a move to replace Gallegos.[190] In his work on Padre Martínez, Fray Angélico Chávez recalls the negative opinion and false charges made by Otero Sr. in Congress against the native clergy; in this case, notes Fray Angélico, Otero was merely reproducing "the standard lies contained in American publications of the times," to the delight, for example, of Bishop Lamy.[191] What is clear is that in the positioning of loyalties that was at stake in New Mexico politics of the period, Martínez and Gallegos stood in opposition to the "American Party" that Otero had organized.[192] Neither Otero Sr. nor Otero Jr. were advocates for the Nuevomexicanos/as; they clearly saw themselves and aligned themselves as white Americans. The past has much to teach us, as there remain Oteros in our present as well.

Miguel Antonio Otero Jr. was born in St. Louis and lived for many years outside New Mexico. The family returned to New Mexico when he was a child but then lived in Missouri and Colorado as well while his father was involved with merchandising and railroad businesses. The Oteros returned to New Mexico at the end of the nineteenth century, at a time when thousands of Anglo and foreign businessmen, railroad managers, mine operators, financiers, and homesteaders were coming to the territory.[193] With the coming of cattlemen, cattle would compete with sheep for grazing land, giving rise to the conflicts epitomized in the Gorras Blancas insurrection. It is during this period that Otero Sr. founded and ran the large merchandising firm of Otero, Sellar and Company and the San Miguel State Bank in Las Vegas.[194] As the son of a wealthy man, Otero Jr. would be sent back east to study, where he earned a degree from the University of Notre Dame. Like his father, he married an Anglo woman, the daughter of a former chief justice of the Supreme Court of Minnesota, who knew little about Nuevomexicanos/as—but then, neither did Otero Jr., whose mother also was an Anglo. While he might not have known much about Nuevomexicano/a culture or local customs, he did like to socialize and join hunting parties in New Mexico. He looked like an Anglo, with blue eyes. It is when the younger Otero became involved in New Mexico politics, becoming an active member of the Republican Party of San Miguel County and holding various public service positions, that he discovered his Nuevomexicano/a identity—that is, when he needed the Nuevomexicano/a vote to win elections. In fact, Cynthia Secor-Welsh, in her introduction to Otero's *My Life on the Frontier, 1864–1882*, remarks that he was considered by some as "agringado" (like his father), as he chose to settle in East Las Vegas rather than Hispanic-dominated West Las Vegas.¹⁹⁵ Otero did not "greatly or overtly favor Hispanos," adds Gómez-Quiñones.¹⁹⁶ He was also critical of the Native Americans of New Mexico, and of the Penitentes, whom he considered "some of the most desperate . . . and lowest and meanest of the natives," and he also rejected the activities of the Gorras Blancas. As Secor-Welsh further notes, "Yet even as Otero disapproved of his fellow Hispanics, he had to seek their political support to succeed in county politics."¹⁹⁷ In a country and state where Hispanos/as were considered inferior, Otero emphasized his Anglo traits and connections, but when it was convenient, he referenced his Hispano/a background. Secor-Welsh indicates that he always referred to the Hispanos/as as "them" or as "this class of people," and "rarely hinted that he was partially of Hispanic origin." One Nuevomexicano, Lucero, found him unfriendly to "native Spanish-Americans."¹⁹⁸

Displacement of the Nuevomexicano/a elite from the circles of privilege and power with the annexation of New Mexico by the United States led to the new political power nexus of the time, the Santa Fe Ring, a political machine under the leadership of Thomas B. Catron and Stephen Elkins, who dominated territorial politics from 1872 to 1896. Gómez-Quiñones describes Catron as a major opponent of "assertive Mexican Democrats or Republicans." After the 1860s, he notes, Catron was "the major Anglo political figure in New Mexico, one who enjoyed cooperative relations with some Mexicans."¹⁹⁹ Secor-Welsh writes that Otero Jr. had been Catron's political apprentice as late as 1896, but Otero fashioned himself as independent and not beholden to the Anglo political machine.²⁰⁰ In his second volume of *My Life on the Frontier*, Otero calls the Santa Fe Ring "one of the most corrupt, unscrupulous, and daring organizations ever connected with its history."²⁰¹ In truth, however, Otero operated with Catron's direct legal or political support. A chance meeting with William McKinley at the Republican National Convention of 1892, where he was a delegate, led to Otero's appointment as governor in 1897, although he was not one of the names proposed to the president and although he lacked the support of either party, Republicans or Democrats. Perhaps this explains why upon his appointment Otero made a speech to Hispanos/as calling himself "the first native born Governor of New Mexico," clearly seeking to identify with Nuevomexicanos/as for political purposes, even though he was not native born (he was born in Missouri) and his views and interests aligned him with the new Anglo power centers in New Mexico.²⁰²

Putting the Mexican Back into the Wild West: Vaqueros/Cowboys

More intriguing perhaps than Otero's particular personal positioning and political history is what Chicanos/as have made of him a hundred years later. In his introduction to Otero's work on Billy the Kid, John-Michael Rivera stresses Otero's interest in incorporating Hispanos/as into Wild West narratives that typically focus on Anglo-Americans.[203] Otero is described as an "elite Nuevomexicano," which is only partially true; yes, Otero was part of the elite, but he was neither born nor brought up in New Mexico and did not always identify with the Hispano/a community. While Rivera is right in contrasting two versions of the history of Billy the Kid, that of Pat Garrett and Ash Upton and that of Otero, the one provided by Otero is told not so much from a Nuevomexicano perspective (despite briefly including the comments of Salazar, Jaramillo, Chávez, Silva, and others who stress that Billy was well liked within the Nuevomexicano/a community) as from a markedly anti–Santa Fe Ring perspective. In Otero's telling of Billy the Kid's history, the number of Anglo witnesses is far greater than that of Nuevomexicanos/as, and their views are more extensively included. There is also precious little about Nuevomexicanos/as in the text except to say that some rode alongside Billy the Kid and his mostly Anglo circle at several moments, or invited him to eat with them, or hid him in their homes.

In his autobiography, Otero self-servingly brags about having met Wild Bill Hickok, Kit Carson, Billy the Kid, Doc Holliday, Buffalo Bill, Pat Garrett, and many other famous nineteenth-century Western figures, including the infamous General Custer. It is after his political career is over that Otero decides to write his autobiography in three volumes and a book on Billy the Kid. His intent—more than putting the Mexican back in the Wild West—was to counter Pat Garrett and Ash Upton's version of the life and death of Billy the Kid, since Garrett was in the pay of the Santa Fe Ring and allied to the corrupt Lincoln County administration (controlled by the Murphy, Dolan, and Riley clans). Otero's version upends the outlaw/lawman dichotomy, presenting Pat Garrett as the murderer of an unarmed man, Billy the Kid. Foreshadowing today's law enforcement justification for police violence, the lawman Garrett portrays himself heroically by claiming that Billy was armed when in fact he was not. There is no love lost for Garrett and less so for Catron in Otero's rendering of the story. Garrett is presented as a thief, coward, and mercenary who is said to have gotten what he deserved in 1908 when he was shot and killed.[204]

It is in fact Catron and the Santa Fe Ring that Otero seeks to denounce, although Otero himself was a rival capitalist, a banker, a merchant, and an ex-politician. In his foreword to Otero's *My Nine Years as Governor*, Ray John de Aragón sees the Santa Fe Ring as "a shifty group of land grabbers and speculators who were stealing Spanish and Indian land grants throughout New Mexico." Otero, he goes on to say, had "inherited a ranch of nearly a million acres from his father and the Ring was trying to lay claim to a portion of it by expanding the boundaries of an old Spanish land grant they had swindled."[205] In his second volume of *My Life on the Frontier*, Otero mentions mining and land interests held in New Mexico by the Otero family. The backstory for the Otero claims is revealing. In 1846, two Mexican citizens working the Nuestra Señora de los Dolores Mine signed over all interest in the mining property to Antonio José Otero and Juan Antonio Otero, both brothers of Miguel Antonio Otero Sr.—importantly—to cover unpaid debts. Otero goes on to note that right before the US-Mexican war, Governor Armijo had granted José Serafín Ramírez land adjacent to the mine. When the two Otero brothers died, the Catron-led Santa Fe Ring bought Ramírez's land grant and extended the boundaries to include the Otero mine. When one of the sons of Juan Antonio Otero discovered the deed to the mine among his father's papers, the Oteros moved to reclaim the mine. When his father died, Miguel Antonio Otero Jr. took over the fight. It involved a takeover by force and a shootout. In the end, the Otero mining property was lost to lawyers and others.

The million-acre Otero family land claim refers to the Bartolomé Baca land grant and figures prominently in Otero's narrative. In 1829, 1834, and 1841, these lands were given to Baca, who had been a governor and captain general of the province of New Mexico from 1823 to 1825. Subsequently, in 1845, Governor Armijo made a grant to Antonio Sandoval of nearly half a million acres located precisely in the center of the Bartolomé Baca grant. In 1874, Manuel Antonio Otero and his brother Miguel Antonio Otero Sr. bought the Baca grant from his heirs in Mexico City. Meanwhile, in 1881 Sandoval, for his part, sold his grant to G. Nolan and J. P. Whitney, and the battle was on. In 1903, the US Court of Private Land Claims adjudged that Baca had abandoned his grant when he returned to Mexico. This battle over land would lead to the death of Manuel Otero, who was shot by Whitney, the man who had bought the Sandoval grant.[206] Episodes such as these point to the legal and physical disputes over land that would develop after 1848, increasingly involving Anglo interests.

Although he makes no mention of the Otero land holdings, Gómez-Quiñones sees Catron and his associates as using political offices "to secure contracts, concessions, and property." He further states that Catron and Vigil "both became immense landowners who often manipulated laws, deeds, and tax debts, and in several instances, both appropriated entire land grants."[207] What is clear is that wealthy Nuevomexicanos, like Vigil and Otero, were as much involved in land speculation and the dispossession of other Hispano/a grantees as Anglos as early as the 1820s. Even priests, like Father Hayes, were involved. As Ebright makes clear, "Land grant speculation was not the exclusive province of the Anglo, however. Many Anglo speculators worked through Hispanic middlemen in acquiring land grants."[208]

Rivera presents the Oteros as exemplars of a powerful New Mexico political family that lost its land and power to the Santa Fe Ring and the Republicans, but in fact both Oteros had been Catron allies at some point. Rivera's reference to Otero's loss of numerous land holdings and two silver mines is not clear, since the Baca claim and the Nuestra Señora de los Dolores Mine are the only two properties mentioned by Otero himself in his autobiography's second volume.[209] Rivera adds, "The Lincoln County War symbolized not only the passing of the old west, but more importantly for the Oteros, the passing of the prominence of Hispanic Culture in New Mexico."[210] Speculators and powerful brokers themselves, the Oteros—despite Rivera's assertions—would continue to thrive after 1878. The Lincoln County War took place between 1876 and 1878, and elite Nuevomexicanos like Miguel Otero Sr. and Elfego Baca continued to profit from their association and backing by the Santa Fe Ring. In fact, a number of Nuevomexicanos/as opposed to Catron would be assassinated during the 1890s, a testimony to the ring's power, and Otero Jr. would be appointed governor in 1898 and served for eight years. Gómez-Quiñones suggests that "though he worked with Catron, Otero also somewhat cut him down politically."[211] What is ironic is what historian and mayor of Santa Fe Ralph E. Twitchell (cited in Vigil) says about Otero as governor: "During his incumbency, under his leadership and with the patronage of his office, the Republican Party organized a political machine so powerful that even the appointment of a notary public was considered in some localities a great favor and mark of political recognition."[212] Otero Jr. in effect became a power broker in New Mexico politics, like Catron himself. His power had little or nothing to do with the maintenance of Nuevomexicano/a culture, and more to do with power positioning in a moment of political and economic transition.

Rivera also reads Otero's work on Billy the Kid as representing the "two most dominant oppositional historical views of New Mexico history: the Anglo-American version and the Hispanic version."[213] There is in fact very little about Nuevomexicanos/as or Nuevomexicano/a culture in the Otero text, unless brief mentions of Nuevomexicanos/as eating with Billy or hiding Billy in their huts or ranchos constitutes providing a cultural history. Moreover, describing Otero as an "elite Nuevomexicano" intent on countering those who would destroy "the land and traditions that Otero once knew as Hispanic Nuevo Mexico" is a stretch.[214] Otero was more of an outsider, as noted by Gómez-Quiñones, whose interest was in securing political and economic power and not in upholding or rescuing native Nuevomexicano/a traditions or people.[215] Unlike someone like Rafael Chacón, Otero did not grow up with Nuevomexicano/a songs, ways of life, and cultural practices.[216]

Otero's goal in his book on Billy the Kid is fundamentally to contest versions of events written by cronies of the rival Santa Fe Ring, "the most lawless machine in that territory's history."[217] What Otero's narrative does show is that Billy was a likable sort, agreeable to Nuevomexicanos/as and others who worked with him, but that he was also an outlaw, a cattle thief, and a murderer. The historical truth is that William H. Bonney, Billy the Kid, El Chivito, was all these things, but that the man who killed him, Sheriff Pat Garrett, was worse and lied about his cowardly killing of Billy the Kid. Thomas E. Chávez, in his work *New Mexico Past and Future*, on the other hand, follows the conventional Anglo praise of Pat Garrett when he says, "Pat Garrett eventually hunted down and killed the Kid after the latter had escaped from jail, killing two lawmen in the process. Garrett, one of the West's honest lawmen, was killed while bringing in a Santa Fe Ring gunman who had been charged for murder."[218] In the process of providing an alternate perspective—although not necessarily a Nuevomexicano/a perspective—on Billy the Kid, Otero gives readers a lively narrative with horse chases and gun battles and a good bit of male bonding. Otero's more favorable reading of the Kid has in fact become the dominant view in film.

Chicano/a historians' and cultural critics' stress on Nuevomexicano/a cultural heritage is abundantly clear, an interest that they feel is shared by earlier writers. Maciel and Gonzales-Berry certainly think so: "Thus a coalescing of cultural expression and sociopolitical concerns flourished, in what, from today's standpoint, can assuredly be viewed as a self-conscious struggle for cultural hegemony."[219] This emphasis allows for presenting what took place in New Mexico in a more favorable light, rather than focusing on the dispossession, racism, and discrimination to which first Indigenous peoples and subsequently Nuevomexicanos/as were subjected, even at the hands of other Nuevomexicanos/as. Special pride is taken in the cultural maintenance of traditions: "Yet, more than in any other part not only of the Southwest but of the entire nation, Nuevomexicanos were able to preserve their autochthonous traditions, social networks, language, and political involvement. In many instances, Nuevomexicanos were more than a match for Anglo-American colonialism."[220] Ultimately the majority of Nuevomexicanos/as were no match for Anglos when it came to land rights and political power. Those that accommodated, however, fared better. Even a recognition of accommodation is often taken as cultural resistance. But can accommodation be read as resistance?

Hispanos/as and Statehood

Nuevomexicanos/as' insistence on being called Hispanos/as has at times led to their being criticized by Chicanos/as from other states for assuming positions that entail an elitist whitening of the population, an identification that seeks to negate the mestizaje that defines a good portion of the population of Mexican origin, while at the same time—importantly—obscuring or skirting the underlying wholesale dispossession of Native Americans. What writers like John Nieto-Phillips argue is that the need to counter congressional insults that Nuevomexicanos/as were undeserving of statehood because they were a "mongrel race," Spanish-speaking, Catholic, semipagan, illiterate, backward, aggressive, violent, uncivilized, and lower class undesirables in the US body politic, led to a response on the part of the elite and political leaders to highlight their Spanish, European origins.[221] Like Eusebio Chacón, who stressed the purity of his Spanish blood, others took up the Spanish American identity and eliminated any reference to Mexico, despite the name of the state: New Mexico. The fact that New Mexico Territory was under Mexican control for only twenty-five years would reinforce this non-Mexican identity, but what was being referenced when US congressmen referred to them as Mexicans was not so much nationality as their racial identification, a nonwhite status that Congress deemed made them backward and incapable of self-government.[222] If empowerment and validation required identifying as Spanish Americans during the statehood struggle from 1850 to 1910, continuing to identify as Spanish or Hispano/a later on was seen by other Chicanos/as as a questionably elitist and racist attempt to present themselves as white. Here, too, accommodating to the racial definition of what makes an American was not a form of resistance; it was a yielding to and collusion with the racist norm. After being a US colony for over fifty years (since 1850), in 1912 New Mexico was finally admitted into the union as a state.

Literary Representations of Enclosure

If nineteenth-century fiction by Nuevomexicanos/as was in good measure characterized by picturesque sketches of manners in the costumbrista tradition, so, too, were early twentieth-century narratives, but with an important shift. The newer literature was written in English and had an English-speaking Anglo reader in mind. Those writing in the nineteenth century, like Eusebio Chacón, wrote in Spanish and dealt with traditions and local culture, and the intended addressees were Nuevomexicano/a readers. Chacón's second narrative, *The Calm after the Storm*, like most costumbrista tales, presents the story of a love triangle. One of the suitors is a scoundrel and the other a righteous man who has the girl's best interests in mind. The story has a didactic message and stresses the high moral standards of Hispano/a society; twentieth-century sketches, on the other hand, would either imitate or contest Anglo sketches about New Mexico's life, landscape, and customs.

Genaro M. Padilla's work, for example, rightfully notes that late nineteenth- and early twentieth-century writings by Anglos on New Mexico created a romantic fantasy about Nuevomexicanos/as and Indians that reified their social history, dehumanized them, and fetishized them.[223] With stress on Spanish heritage and origins also came an interest in promoting "an idealized, biracial (Spanish and Indian) image of New Mexico's society and history. This Spanish colonial image served to attract Anglo-American immigrants and tourists to the territory and rendered a new and romantic understanding of Nuevomexicanos' 'Spanish American' identity, history and culture."[224] Citing Ramón Gutiérrez, Gabriel Meléndez states that references to pre-Columbian Indigenous myths "were not a concession to the cultural legacy of Indian people as we might think upon them today; rather, as Gutiérrez explains, these 'must also be placed in the larger cultural movement begun in the 1880s to turn the harsh realities of New Mexico into a "Land of Enchantment" for investors, tourists, health seekers, alienated literati and artists to explore in the west.'"[225] It was, according to Gutiérrez, the Atchison, Topeka and Santa Fe Railroad that "tried to create a lost world and return to primitivism."[226] Much like the restored missions in Old California, in New Mexico an exotic pastiche would be created for Anglo consumption, one that Nuevomexicanos/as would both contest and contribute to in their writings.

Historians, on the other hand, offer a more detailed and critical assessment of the process and effects of land dispossession in New Mexico from

1598 to the late twentieth century than do fiction writers, who tend to offer nostalgic accounts of the past and to accommodate to dominant cultural perspectives on Nuevomexicanos/as; historical assessments based on the "fantasy heritage" associated with Bolton and his Spanish Borderlands analysis also predominate.[227] While resentment over land loss undoubtedly figures in the fiction, as does armed resistance by villagers, narrators in stories and novels have preferred to focus on traditions, folklore, and moralizing didactic stories. Those involved in armed resistance or seeking redress for historical wrongs are generally portrayed as bandits or outlaws who are to be corralled in a nation under the rule of law.

Fray Angélico Chávez's Didactic Tales

Nuevomexicanos/as who have focused on nineteenth- or early twentieth-century New Mexico include Fray Angélico Chávez, whose short stories offer didactic sketches of village life with magical or supernatural elements of saints, angels, and spirits appearing, all with an edifying bent.[228] Although Padilla finds Chavez's work to be contestatory and even subversive, we instead view his stories as rather conservative—in both senses of the word—tales of a nostalgic accommodation, either to religious beliefs or to village norms. There is, for example, a degree of internal critique, as in the story "The Penitente Thief," in which the practicing Penitents are shown to be not only sinners but murderers and thieves. Other stories deal with family issues and attitudes toward mestizos, and a few mention issues of land dispossession.[229] While some social critique is offered, such as the less-than-positive portrayal of French priests (calling up the historical figures of Lamy and Machebeuf, perhaps) who disdain the unsophisticated village folk, captured in "The Lean Years," there is little in the way of historical context for particular social issues or the violence of land dispossession. "The Lean Years," for example, has as its backdrop the loss of a community land grant with the arrival of the railroad at Las Vegas, but there is little historical contextualization. What the story emphasizes is the exemplary personal behavior of José Vera, who continues his loving attention to his wife, Soledad, after an accident leaves her paralyzed and leads to her early death.

As noted by Padilla, the motif of "the romance of the Southwest" generated by Anglo writers, artists, and tourists who traveled to New Mexico at the turn of the century would establish the discursive parameters for writing about the fast-vanishing Nuevomexicano/a culture.[230] Nuevomexicano/a writing about the past would be constrained by this established genre and follow in the pattern of romantic sketches, in both the Anglo and Latin American traditions. Padilla brilliantly signals the contradictions: "When in the act of remembering they confront the unpleasant reminders of their own conquest and subordination, they often retreat into whispers of discomfort, confused historiography, muted social criticism, or silence."[231] What is not remembered—and therefore erased—is not only their conquest but the Hispanos/as' dispossession, exploitation, and enslavement of Pueblo Indians. In the work of Cabeza de Baca and Jaramillo, moreover, it is not conquest that is an unpleasant reminder, but rather the loss of upper-class status and the loss of land that precipitated downward mobility for some and pauperization for many. That said, in constituting themselves as "Spano" and white, it is undeniable that resentment over the loss of land grants after the US invasion figures prominently in Nuevomexicano/a literature, but the deeper historical context is often elided and the particulars are misrepresented, as in the case of casting the land issue as private holdings rather than communal land grants, although in the end both would often be lost.

Selective Memory Coupled with Nostalgia

In *We Fed Them Cactus* (1954), Cabeza de Baca, through a series of sketches, offers a nostalgic account of Nuevomexicano/a traditions and practices, including the buffalo hunt, the rodeo, fiestas, evening gatherings to hear and tell stories about the past, the environment, religious festivities, the herb remedies of the *curandera*, Indian raids, trade with the Comanches, bandits, mustangs, and the coming of the homesteaders, the Americanos. The narrator, the daughter of a rico landowner, seeks to remedy the distortions of historical accounts with respect to her ancestors, the white, landed, blue-eyed descendants of the early Spanish colonists. While pointing out that some of the grantees did manage to keep their lands, Cabeza de Baca recalls their overall loss of land with the coming of the homesteaders. She also notes that the owners of the grants lost their lands because they were unable to pay for the surveying required by the government and as a consequence, "most of the land became public domain."[232] Of course, it was not merely the surveying costs that undoubtedly were a factor, but more often the result of court decisions and enclosures that intentionally led to dispossession.

Cabeza de Baca focuses on the life stories of Nuevomexicanos/as on the Llano Estacado, the Staked Plain, in northeastern New Mexico, an area that extends to the panhandle of Texas. The narrator's family resided in Llano Estacado, where the patrón had overseers and herders. Here the herders were indebted peons, as she describes the relationship: "If a man became indebted to a rico, he was in bond slavery to repay. Those in debt had a deep feeling of honesty, and they did not bother to question whether the system was right or wrong. Entire families often served a *patrón* for generations to meet their obligations."[233] The text does not question debt peonage nor racialized social stratification. Cabeza de Baca recalls hearing a story about Billy the Kid from a servant in her great-aunt's home: "Her grandfather had been a bond slave in my grandmother's home and her whole family had to serve out the bondage. Once they were free, they still worked for the family in some capacity or other."[234] Although not a detailed commentary about inherited debt bondage and servitude in New Mexico, her work does—importantly—acknowledge them in passing, as she takes pains to praise the servants' honesty and willingness to serve, idealizing what were in essence master-slave relations.

History in the novel is narrativized from an elite perspective, for Cabeza de Baca's narrator underscores her "aristocratic rearing," "ladylike life," and her family connections.[235] Her father was a white, blue-eyed man who owned the Spear Bar Ranch, with cattle and sheep. One of her ancestors, Don Luis María Cabeza de Baca, she states, in 1821 was granted a tract of land called Las Vegas Grandes, consisting of half a million acres. Her rendering of the past is that Don Luis María's heirs held title to the Las Vegas land grant, and when "the citizens of Las Vegas petitioned that they be given title to the grant, and after reaching an agreement with the heirs of Don Luis María, the land was turned over to the petitioners."[236] As noted earlier with respect to Jaramillo, what Cabeza de Baca does not indicate is that the Las Vegas grant was in fact a communal grant and not a private grant and thus was never the personal, individual property of Don Luis María Cabeza de Baca, as argued.[237] Claiming that one's ancestors privately owned thousands of acres is thus a way to claim being of a higher class, whether the claim is true or not.

This class perspective is constantly emphasized in her narrative. Cabeza de Baca makes it clear that her narrator's colonial ancestors, those that settled on the Llano, were members of the wealthy landowning class and lived "in splendor with many servants and slaves. Their *haciendas* were similar to the Southern plantations."[238] Wealthy Nuevomexicanos/as were not like "the people of the streets," that is, the lower orders. They were white, often with red or sandy hair and blue eyes, like those of her father. These early settlers, she insists, "were of the landed gentry, in whose veins ran the noble blood of ancestors who left the mother country, Spain, for the new world."[239] This oft-repeated emphasis on being of European extraction is typical of many Nuevomexicano/a writers. Their wealth is expressed in the beauty of the hills, forests, canyons, valleys, springs, lakes, and great stretches of prairie for their sheep and cattle to forage. Work was done largely by sheepherders, cowboys, and peons, but in Cabeza de Baca's father's case, supervised by the landowner. Many of the "Hispano families" would end up losing their lands after the US invasion, and those who managed to retain their lands and even acquire more would face drought and the Dust Bowl, created, she complains, by squatters or homesteaders who plowed the barren land, leaving the Hispanos/as unable to feed their stock in 1918 and later again in the decade of the 1930s, as happened with her father. Suffering repeated losses, Cabeza de Baca portrays the father figure as diminished and beaten: "The land which he loved had sucked the last bit of strength which so long had kept him enduring failures and sometimes successes but never of one tenor."[240] She ends her piece by noting that though he is gone, "the land which he loved is there" and green again.[241]

We Fed Them Cactus is notable for its multivoiced narration. Through a variety of narrators, including ranch hands, servants, neighbors, villagers, and family members, Cabeza de Baca captures the habitus of the rural elite but also the class structure that configures and conditions the narrative. A good worker is said to be characterized by "honesty and loyalty towards his patrón."[242] Workers are described several times as being "as much a part of the family as the children of the patrón,"[243] and she is most insistent on the lack of a class structure: "There may have been class distinctions in the larger towns but the families in the Llano had none; the *empleados* and their families were as much a part of the family of the *patron* as his own children. It was a very democratic way of life."[244] This idealized assessment of the past is, of course, countered by her comments about indentured servants, whose whole families have to serve out the debt bondage. This idealization is also taken up, as noted earlier, in Brooks's *Captives and Cousins*, which stresses the notions of kinship developed between servants/slaves and Nuevomexicano/a families.

By contrast, Indigenous populations of the region appear, however, only in a negative light. For Cabeza de Baca, Spanish settlers came to colonize "an almost savage country";[245] Indians, like the Comanches, are presented as thieves who rustled cattle and horses and are even said to have kidnapped children. However, once the Indians were rounded up and put on reservations, the text goes on to say, the land became safe for sheepmen. The class and caste oppression of Indians, peons, and genízaros is thus in good measure bypassed in

Cabeza de Baca's portrayal, as is the dispossession and enslavement of Indigenous peoples.

Cabeza de Baca's texts allow that not all the Nuevomexicanos/as, however, were large landowners; she briefly mentions tenant farmers and those who participated in partidario contracts, a sharecropping of sorts, but with livestock. She also mentions communal grants (like that of Antonchico) but does not explore the topic further nor indicate that her own family's Las Vegas grant was also initially a communal grant. Rather than noting that fencing and elimination of the commons impinged on Hispanos/as' livelihood, as protested by the Gorras Blancas, Cabeza de Baca remarks that fencing the land did away with the cattle rustling. Acknowledging that the lack of definite property boundary markers and the lack of official titles led to the loss of land, she goes on to say, "much of the land was lost even after it was taken up by the courts. The history of the New Mexican land grants would fill volumes, but it is not a part of this story."[246] Skirting a topic that might not please her Anglo readers is an ideological maneuver that might be geared to attract readers more interested in reading about a romantic, idyllic past. For this reason, perhaps, the loss of land through court action, foreclosures, failure to pay taxes, and as fees for surveyors and lawyers is never taken up in detail, but these measures are mentioned in passing. Cabeza de Baca does recognize the consequences, however; with the disappearance of their holdings, she says, the Hispanos/as disappeared from some areas, leaving only topographical markers, like the names of towns, canyons, mountains, and so on; some Hispanos/as, she notes, took advantage of the Homestead Act of 1862 and were able to take up 160 acres of land, remaining in the area; this suggests, however, that some lost their homesteads "because of ignorance of the homestead laws."[247] Nuevomexicanos/as in Cabeza de Baca's reading of New Mexican history are in part to blame, but here again she demurs and deflects, saying that "all this belongs to a subject too vast to discuss in this history of the Llano."[248] In this way, she recognizes that a variety of factors led to change in New Mexico, but she retreats from discussing the new capitalist mode and relations of production that brought with them the privatization of lands, the railroad, the building of highways, urbanization, and migration primarily of settlers or, as they are termed, "nesters" from other US states. She is particularly concerned, however, at the narrative's end with the drought of 1918, after all an act of God, not of man, that led to her father having to sell his cattle and eventually the land he loved.

Nostalgia notwithstanding, land loss or dispossession is at bottom the driving mechanism of Cabeza de Baca's work because it spells the end of the elite status of a number of wealthy Nuevomexicanos/as, who after the US invasion lost their property and therefore wealth. The narrative takes great pains, however, to insist that loss of land and status does not erase the cultural capital of the Nuevomexicanos/as, who pride themselves on their ways, traditions, and the European roots that distinguish them and mark them as white. That this land was previously occupied by Indians is not taken as a relevant consideration; that the population was/is largely mestizo is ignored; that the Hispano/a and Mexicano/a past included indebted servitude and slavery is also not an issue, as we are assured that all lived happily within the large haciendas. It is the experience of the elite of this past, viewed nostalgically, that is the dominant narrative in *We Fed Them Cactus*.

In 1949 Cabeza de Baca would write a second book, *The Good Life: New Mexico Traditions and Food*, which again presents readers with an idealized small farm family, the Turrietas, and their way of life. This family is part of an isolated village that still retains land and traditions from the earliest period of Spanish colonization. In her introduction, Cabeza de Baca says this is not only a cookbook but a repository of folklore. The book describes the subsistence economy and self-sufficiency of the family, highlighting the recipes offered by Señá Martina, the old medicine woman, who knows all about herbs, can remedy any ailment, and cooks the tastiest sweetbreads. Señá Martina is said to have been a slave in the García family but had not wanted her freedom, "yet she had always been free."[249] She is represented as the stereotypical "happy slave" of Southern literature who in old age continues to earn her keep by helping out neighbors with her remedies and cooking. Especially close to Señá Martina's heart is Doña Paula Turrieta, the main character and matriarch whose family has maintained a small farm and whose harvests of wheat, peas, squash, beans, and so on, and tending of pigs and goats provide for their livelihood. The text includes a good number of recipes for Anglo cooks eager to try these exotic Nuevomexicano/a recipes. Here Cabeza de Baca offers an idealized sketch of early twentieth-century villagers, whose daily life is presented as a quaint anachronism, a time capsule of sorts, where little has changed since the Spanish colonial period. This book, like Cabeza de Baca's *We Fed Them Cactus*, seems addressed to an Anglo readership, a factor that perhaps constrains its renderings of both past and present.

Cleofas Jaramillo: Revisionist History

In his fine essay on Jaramillo, whose 1941 *Shadows of the Past* (*Sombras del Pasado*) also provides a series of sketches of Hispano/a and Indigenous customs in New Mexico, Padilla argues that the author "unwittingly" participated in Anglos' fetishizing of Mexican American and Native American people by "constructing a version of culture that dehistoricized social relations, substituting a romanticized culture."[250] Padilla's assessment of Jaramillo's work is convincing, and what is more, as we have seen here, could be extended to much of New Mexican literature dealing with the late nineteenth and early twentieth centuries. Jaramillo's sketches or *cuadros de costumbres* make evident that the narrator decries the changes that have taken place in the territory, lamenting that old Hispano/a customs have vanished, replaced by modern songs, dances, clothing, and music. Change came also with the railroad, the *carroferril*. This social and cultural change is countered here as in Cabeza de Baca, through nostalgic sketches of the past. At work, too, is a desire to provide an authentic Nuevomexicano/a version of traditions and recipes to counter derisive, if not racist, Anglocentric versions of her native culture.[251]

In an attempt, then, to forestall what is on the horizon, Anglo appropriation of a vanishing Nuevomexicano/a culture, Jaramillo recalls life in her childhood, providing picturesque descriptions of the landscape around the valley of Arroyo Hondo. Her nostalgic descriptions of rivers, hills, mountains, rocks, and "sleepy adobe villages" abound, recalling, too, that in the past the people lived in constant fear of bandits and hostile Indian tribes.[252] Striking in Jaramillo's work, however, is how the land is tied to memory. She recalls the trade caravans made up of white covered wagons that went from the northern part of New Mexico all the way to Chihuahua. She also offers sketches of social types: strong women like Doña Mariana (La Fuerte), who was kidnapped by Indians and rescued, along with sketches of domestic life, with regard to the preparation of food, sugarcane syrup, wine, soap, candles, needlework, wool carding, knitting, the gathering of the cereal seeds at the end of harvest, sketches of religious celebrations, wakes and mourning practices, the worship of saints, and the celebrations of the Penitentes as well as the practice of witchcraft and the problem of priests who were not always celibate. Additional sketches describe games, sports, horse racing and gambling, and card games, all threads of a cultural tapestry now a mere shadow of its past.

The historical context is the story of the Jaramillo family. Padilla argues that these sketches operate as an affirmation of subjectivity, a countering of "cultural effacement," but in a way, what they do is provide an elite representation of the past, mostly devoid of historical context. Absent critical memory and historical grounding, the Jaramillo text, like the mouthwatering recipes included, can be consumed without causing indigestion. Even when documenting land loss, what is important to her is to make clear that the Jaramillo family was wealthy and white. Wealth and the purity of blood go together in her narrative. In noting the importance of blood purity among the elite, she explains that "a great deal of intermarriage between first and second cousins occurred in order to keep the Spanish blood from mixing," since "there were so few pure Spanish families in the small villages."[253] Racial mixing is rendered as negative, an impurity, whereas racial purity is a type of cultural capital that can be possessed and preserved. The Jaramillos' material wealth, too, is explained in terms of their ownership of vast acreages. Yet as we have previously seen, Jaramillo presents the Tierra Amarilla grant of over 300,000 acres as a cession to her ancestors, the Martínez family, and not as a communal grant. Her family, she tellingly says, brought "civilization to wilderness" by "means of bloody battles and peaceful laws."[254] That these lands were Indigenous lands, taken by bloody force, is not posed as a problem since she claims Hispanos/as brought civilization to a savage and lawless area. Again, spatial and discursive violence go hand in hand.

Certain aspects of village life are suggested rather than detailed. The existence of a company store on her father's land, for example, is revealed as she describes how the goods were displayed within the store. The implications of debt peonage, with workers forced to buy goods from the company store, is alluded to but not discussed. What she does describe at length are Indigenous feasts (like the Feast of San Gerónimo). Her sketches also recall post-1848 moments dealing with the Gorras Blancas, casting the insurrection as a conflict with recent homesteaders rather than as a reaction to dispossession by Hispano/a farmers who depended on communal land use. Elite families send their sons back east to study, while at the same time Hispano men are chastised for their lack of industry, which impedes social mobility and leaves them unable to compete with the incoming Anglos. There is both nostalgia and blame in Jaramillo's lament that there was now a new notion of time: "The Land of Poco Tiempo has become the land of haste and hurry."[255] Time and space are fused in a narrative of tandem losses of land and an idealized culture.

In *Romance of a Little Village Girl* (1955), Jaramillo also sets out to describe ethnographically a series of Nuevomexicano/a traditions, feast days, the Penitentes' ceremonies, celebrations, weddings, food served on those special occasions, and her family's works of charity as well as the games played. In her chapter "Penitente Ceremonies of Holy Week," she recalls going home from school to Arroyo Hondo for Easter vacation and participating in the religious ceremonies enacted by the Penitentes: "The penitente brotherhood took charge of the religious ceremonies, inasmuch as there was no resident priest in the town in my time."[256] The same point is made by fellow Nuevomexicano writer Sabine R. Ulibarrí in his 1977 novel *Mi abuela fumaba puros*, where he describes the Penitentes procession, the self-flagellation, and their chanting.[257] He also recalls that in villages that had no priest and no government official, the Penitentes were the repositories of memory and tradition; they were the ones who knew how to read and write, had manuscripts and books, and taught people the prayers, rites, and traditions that the Hispanos/as wished to conserve. These were isolated villages, as Ulibarrí notes, "abandoned first by Spain, later Santa Fe and Mexico, and finally by the United States."[258] And it was the Penitentes, he says, who "filled the administrative, religious, and cultural vacuum."[259] If cultural identity and cultural memory were necessary for political resistance, then the Penitentes clearly played a key role. In this regard, Ulibarrí and Jaramillo share a perspective regarding the Penitentes, recognizing them as cultural repositories, a view markedly different from the rejection of the tradition voiced by outsider Bishop Lamy, for example, who viewed them as suspect and unorthodox.

Reinscribing the fact that elite Nuevomexicano/a families intermarried, Jaramillo recalls in *Romance of a Little Village Girl* her own romance with her cousin, Senator Venceslao Jaramillo, their marriage, trips, the birth of their daughter, his illness, and his death. Loss of land and personal loss are joined when Jaramillo is unable to meet the mortgage payment and loses a ranch and later her teenage daughter to an intruder who breaks into her home and kills her. Her sorrow lasts for many years, but writing her memories and a cookbook serve as therapy for her grief. She further states outright that hers is a response to a book by an author who fails to distinguish between the Spanish and Mexican or Indian people, "wasting time and a God-given talent writing about the lower things in life."[260] Both the race card and class bias are prominent in her work. Jaramillo writes to make sure that the elite of Spanish origin of New Mexico are not confused and conflated with the "underprivileged class who, on account of their poverty, lack a moral education and modern facilities for better living."[261] Earlier times are recalled with nostalgia; those were times of abundance, with many house servants and peons. Everyone was happy in those days, she says. She takes great pains to make clear that she belongs to the elite class of Nuevomexicanos/as, going out of her way to claim that class differences did not then divide people, given, as previously noted, that in her parents' home, everyone knew his or her place.

Despite acknowledging land loss as responsible for diminished social and economic status, a good many of these Nuevomexicano/a texts focus on the preservation of cultural traditions; cultural capital prevails as the salvageable and significant value, once more tangible land, water rights, and political power have been lost. Accompanying this focus on cultural capital is the notion of accommodation as a form of resistance, which marks many of the twentieth-century Nuevomexicano/a texts that look back on the late nineteenth century.[262] One thing is clear: accommodation cannot be taken as resistance; it may be necessary, it may be inevitable, even unavoidable, but it cannot be construed as resistance. Moreover, as noted by Rodriguez, the "crystallization of land as a symbol of Hispano cultural survival" is highlighted in these narratives, as further expropriation of different types has accelerated.[263] Loss of land is equivalent to loss of culture, and once it is lost, writers either elect or are forced into a strategy of nostalgia and the recovery of land in memory. Jaramillo's title *Shadows of the Past* speaks to this process of both material (land) and immaterial (cultural) alienation.

Water Rights: Sites of Old and New Enclosures

As Nuevomexicanos/as knew all too well and their writings confirm, land cannot be considered separately from water rights, and as noted by De Angelis, dispossession of water rights is yet another form of enclosure.[264] Sylvia Rodriguez notes that "control over land and water remains the primary bone of contention in the relations among Indian, Hispano, and Anglo populations in northern New Mexico."[265] Rodriguez discusses water rights conflicts in the area of Taos, a topic taken up as well in the recent fiction of New Mexican novelist Rudolfo Anaya. In his works, struggles over water rights concern the area from the Río Grande to Albuquerque, north to the Jemez Mountains, Santa Fe, Taos, Santo Domingo, and Córdova and extend from the Indigenous past into the twenty-first century. Water is the new focus of dispossession and enclosure. In Anaya's *Alburquerque* (1992), a wealthy businessman, Frank Dominic, wants to be mayor of Albuquerque in order to initiate a major urban development project, nothing less than building a Venice in the city, with canals full of Rio Grande water and casinos and gambling spots all along the canals. To create this fantasy world, Dominic will need to control the water rights of the Pueblo Indians and the Hispanic villages of the north. His project requires privatizing water, and he is already in negotiations with Indigenous communities. Here Anaya, through his character Dominic, is at the same time echoing and critiquing the words of the chairman of transnational behemoth Nestlé, Peter Brabeck-Letmathe, who in 2005 said that all water ought to be privatized.[266]

Alburquerque—a spelling that harkens back to the original Spanish colonial figure (El Duque de Alburquerque) for whom the city is named—sets the stage for a confrontation between a corporation, Río Grande Entertainment, which promises Pueblos a percentage of casino profits if they sign a contract relinquishing their water rights, and the local Hispanos/as who refuse to consider it: "To give up the water rights of the Hispanic land grants was unthinkable, the Indians selling their water was just as preposterous. Yet Dominic was convinced they all would sell."[267] And in spite of resistance from some quarters, already the Indian Council of Santo Domingo is voting to sell their water rights. In this way, in *Alburquerque* Anaya presents a New Mexico that is again undergoing transformation, facing new enclosures imposed not by cattlemen, farmers, or railroads but by housing and entertainment enterprises in the shape of casinos and elite housing. The novel's driving plot centers on a young boxer who has just discovered he is adopted and wishes to discover who his father is. Identity through paternity thus figures, too, as a central issue in *Alburquerque*, while at the same time providing the background for a critique of a New Mexico undergoing a new round of enclosures and new forms of dispossession in the twenty-first century.

Water is taken up again in another Anaya novel, *Jemez Spring*, where the detective Sonny Baca finds the evil villain, Raven, allying with Dominic. In the middle of the assassination of the state's governor and a bomb threat on Jemez Mountain, supposedly planted by Al Qaeda but actually a plot worked out by Raven, Sonny hears that several Indigenous groups—allied as Green Indians—are meeting in Algodones to try to find a way to protect their water rights. The authorities, including lawmen in collusion with businessmen like Dominic and Raven, are seeking to stop the meeting: "Now [Sonny] knew a wider conspiracy was taking place, and it revolved around the most precious element in the drought-stricken region: water."[268] Dominic continues to plot to gain control of the Río Grande water rights, promising, as he puts it, "to work closely with all the Indian and Hispanic farmers in the valley."[269] He proposes to build underground aquifers to store water, which his corporation will manage. But as environmentalists caution: "Placing water rights in a private corporation run by [Dominic] was like giving up the baby with the tub."[270] Vandana Shiva in her work *Water Wars*, speaks to this new site of enclosure when she quotes the vice president of the World Bank as saying in 1995, "If the wars of this century were fought over oil, the wars of the next century will be fought over water."[271] In this regard, the novelist Anaya is drawing an important connection in his works by representing the linkage between different forms or modalities of enclosure and their impact on the inhabitants (past and present) of New Mexico; land and water go hand in hand, then and now.

These water issues, part of the arc of what could also be considered Anaya's eco-poetics in several of his novels, are among the ecological issues presently affecting New Mexico and other parts of the United States, like the Dakotas. Fracking in Chaco Canyon, the pollution of 88 percent of New Mexico rivers from the dumping of toxic chemicals, and the mining and drilling in Otero Mesa that threaten the drinking water and critical habitat of a thousand native species are but a few of the ecological threats currently facing Nuevomexicanos/as. In all cases, their water sources are vulnerable and at risk.[272] This major case of enclosure of vital resources and the ensuing dispossession will affect Pueblo Indians, Hispano/a farmers, and all residents alike. Anaya's signaling of the dangers and potentially catastrophic effects of the loss of water rights on the horizon can be read as drawing on a historical awareness and shared memory of the consequences of depriving people access to the means and resources for survival, whether by dispossession of land or, in this case, water.[273] The novel is discursively bearing witness and connecting to what is already happening in the United States, Africa, India, and in the Middle East and, as such, offers a clear warning of what is to come.

Enclosures serve to dispossess inhabitants of land, water, salt, wood, grassland, wild animals, and other resources necessary for subsistence. Like land, water has also been an especially contentious issue and the site of struggle and spatial violence in the form of enclosure, especially given its scarcity in South Texas, as we shall see in chapter 4.

4

Texas Narratives of Dispossession

WHEN THE LAND BECAME REAL ESTATE

We have argued that it is through narrative that we can grasp the multiplicity of temporalities in history and the emplotment of the history of class struggle.[1] Literary texts offer an interpretation of history and, in the case of Tejano/a writers, a positioning with respect to enclosure. Narratives not only bear witness to the multiple forms of discursive violence attendant to processes of dispossession but at the same time construct Tejanos/as as historical subjects.

Writers considered in this chapter demonstrate the constitutive relationship between land and identity in what we might term regionalist family narratives that configure characters' lived experience of a traumatic historical moment that changes the geography as well as the mode of production. In many texts there is a perception of entropy at all social levels as the characters recall the demise of an idealized colonial society and witness the decline and end of the semifeudal Mexican ranchero system in Texas after 1848. In its place emerges an agro-industrial capitalist system, already consolidated back east but developing in late nineteenth-century Texas with Mexican and Black wage labor working the cotton fields.

The land narrative in much of twentieth-century Chicana/o writing reconstructs the Spanish/Mexican past in relation to the spatial violence brought on by the US-Mexican War, which came to dominate the region and separated the Spanish/Mexican landowners from their means of production. Dispossession by US invaders and settlers meant not only land loss but also loss of political and economic power. With subordination came both state and mob violence against ethnic Mexicans. Loss of access to the land in the midst of changes in relations of production brought, in time, proletarianization of the former landowners. This powerlessness within a new political and economic system is the result that characters in these narratives both resent and come to accept. Generally speaking, Tejano/a novelists set out to construct a Tejano/a historical subject with a supposedly heroic colonial Spanish past (often ignored in dominant Anglo accounts of Texas history that stress the superiority of whites) that brought "civilization" to the hinterlands. These colonists would be figured as criollos, as white, despite being historically mostly mestizos. These accounts by and large ignore pre-eighteenth-century Texas, when the land was Indigenous territory marked by different commons that would be expropriated by Spanish explorers, conquerors, and landowners.

In the Tejano/a land dispossession narrative, locality and region are always central, especially the notion of land not only as private property but as territory, as region, as cultural geographic space. The story of how the Spanish- and Mexican-origin population was dispossessed through invasion and violence, through financial and state policies, and through a shift in the mode of production is told through an often nostalgic reconstruction of the particular mores of the upper classes of the past. Peons, vaqueros, and servants enter the accounts occasionally, primarily to supply the folklore or local color of the period. What is most important in these narratives is that, in the process of figuring a past, a variety of identities or elite subjectivities are constructed to counter disparaging notions of inferiority expressed by the hegemonic power: the Anglo. These land narratives are novels of domesticity of a sort that figure not feminine but patriarchal domains centered on the hacienda or rancho that face loss and family fragmentation after the major 1836 and 1846 events. Importantly the family narrative here is not, as often elsewhere, an allegory for the nation but rather an allegory of the fractured Rio Grande Mexican region. Reconstituting family is consequently crucial, and for that reason the marriage trope is often central to these works as new constructs of the home space replace former ones. Key in these narratives is the Tejano/a family's adaptation or refusal to acquiesce to the new social relations that ensue. Economic transformations bring changes in everyday life and shifts in the systems of consensus and coercion as well and in the relations between invaders and the conquered. As many of the affected note, the conquered, who consider themselves natives of the region, become the foreigners. Conversely, the foreigners, the incoming Anglo settlers, envision themselves as the real Americans, the real Texans. Left out of this clash-of-cultures narrative is that this land was Native American land.

Discussions of the nineteenth-century US Southwest sometimes assume that the situations in Texas, New Mexico, and California were homogeneous and that the dispossession that occurred affected residents of Spanish and Mexican origin in similar ways. But these different regions varied greatly in terms of the presence of Indigenous communities, the status of the original colonial settlers, and internal class divisions involving indebted peons, servants, and vaqueros. It bears remembering that the first to be despoiled were the Indians, who were dispossessed in East and Central Texas (north of the Nueces River) by Spanish and later Mexican soldiers, their settler families, and a few missionaries; in the 1820s and thereafter, Indigenous people would be dispossessed by Anglo settlers and after 1836 removed to Indian territory. In South Texas, it would be mestizo and criollo landowners from Nuevo Santander in northern Mexico who were involved in the displacement and dispossession of Indians and their reduction to servitude through the establishment of large landed haciendas or ranchos. Most of the texts discussed in this chapter deal with South Texas, which was not considered part of Texas by Mexicans at least until 1848.

In these literary renderings of history, there are omissions and absences, but novels provide us an account (however partial, in both senses) of dispossession, displacement, discrimination, and abuse at the hands of Texas Rangers and speculators, practices that provoked resentment, rebellion, accommodation, and assimilation. Central, too, in three of the novels we examine is the perspective of female characters, generally absent in historical accounts or fiction.

This history of enclosures requires periodization. Geography, too, has been key. Whether in the form of travelogues, court records, or literary narratives and corridos, movement through space in the form of migration and immigration, or in the forced relocation by dispossession, colonization, or war, geography has been recorded and serves to situate the population of Spanish, Indigenous, mulatto, and mestizo origin socially and politically within the lands of the Southwest. In broad strokes, four main periods in Texas can be identified: a Native communal system of production, a semifeudal mode of production under Spain and Mexico, a capitalist system after the US invasion, and a transnational capitalist and agribusiness system in the twentieth century. As noted by Enrique Semo, these various periods were heterogeneous, with more than one mode operating at any given time.[2]

Sociogeographic relations are important factors in that they mark key differences across regions. First, Texas was not colonized primarily by Spanish missionaries, as was the case in Alta California, as that attempt failed. Second, Texas could be said to have involved four different colonization efforts in four different regions: the Nuevo Santander settlement in northern Mexico, which extended from Tampico to the Nueces River in what is now Texas; the area north of the Nueces River, called Texas, which initially included failed missions and forts in East Texas and that later saw settlement primarily by Anglos and their slaves; the area of San Antonio in Central Texas; and West Texas, including the area of El Paso, Presidio, and El Llano Estacado, more closely related to patterns of New Mexican colonization. Texas is a big state, and people of Mexican origin in Texas call themselves Tejanos/as, but those residing south of the Nueces River have not always been Tejanos/as, since Texas proper began north of that river. This historical division contributed to a fluid identity.[3] People residing in what came to be the Republic of Texas in 1836 were technically Mexicans only for a relatively short period of time: from 1821 until 1836. Fifteen years is not long enough to create a national identity, a sense of belonging to an imagined community. The disconnection from Mexico is easier to understand in Central and East Texas. In what came to be South Texas, the Rio Grande region, geography was key in establishing a closer identity with Mexico after 1836 and especially after 1848.

In his cultural geographic work *Tejano South Texas*, Daniel D. Arreola argues that South Texas is "a unique subregion of the Mexican American borderland."[4] Historians recognize that the space of South Texas needs to be constructed separately given its history and people's lived experience of this space.[5] Arreola further claims that South Texas was "not seen as a differentiated region until quite recently," but this is really not the case, since, as previously noted, the land south of the Nueces was historically separate from Texas, as it was part of Nuevo Santander and later Tamaulipas.[6] It was not conceived as part of Texas until 1848, for its inclusion was contested by Mexico when it was claimed in 1836 by Texans and later in 1845 by the United States, when it became part of the Union.[7] We use "South Texas" to refer to the lower Rio Grande valley or El Valle, an area that has always had a distinct cultural significance. In the fiction of Chicano/a writers, focusing on South Texas has meant a focus on the lower Rio Grande valley and not on San Antonio or Laredo. It is the lower Rio Grande valley that has been richly configured in the work of Jovita González, Américo Paredes, and Rolando Hinojosa. It is perceived, conceptualized, and lived as a unique region, and those born there have a particular identity marked by language, culture, and residence in a chromosomatically ethnic Mexican majoritarian space.

What Is Left Out: The Dispossession of Indigenous Populations

The Indian side of the story of Spanish/Mexican violence and dispossession of Indigenous populations is generally sidestepped in Chicano/a historiography and literature, although in more recent historiographic accounts by Omar S. Valerio-Jiménez, Raúl Ramos, and Andrés Reséndez, thicker, more nuanced readings are emerging.[8] Others, such as Armando C. Alonzo, deal less with Spanish dispossession of the Indigenous populations, if at all.[9] Dispossession entailed separating Indigenous populations from their means of survival, the land. In Texas, Indians would resist colonization, especially in East Texas where Indigenous social relations depended on the commons, used for farming and hunting; separating them from the land and from hunting grounds would prove disastrous. Spanish colonizers also attempted to separate Indigenous populations from their culture and religious practices, but this type of enclosure through missionization would largely fail in East Texas. As Indians learned to ride horses and acquired guns and gunpowder, primarily from the French, they defended themselves and in some cases gained some leverage, as it proved less costly to trade and appease them with gifts, as the French did, than to adopt the violence of extermination that the Spanish soldiers had sought to impose.

The history of the land to be called Texas began more than twenty thousand years ago for Indigenous peoples who resided and continue to reside in the Southwest. As one of Hinojosa's characters tellingly notes, it's important to go to the cemetery on the Texas side of the river "para ver quién llegó aquí antes que nadie" (to see who arrived here first, before anyone else).[10] Clearly there are no marked cemetery plots for Indigenous populations massacred in Texas. In fact, Indigenous burial grounds were not individualized and often were subsequently desecrated by soldiers, ranchers, and corporations interested in mining—and today fracking. If who got here first is the question, then of course it was not the population of European origin.

In his work *Tejano Legacy*, Alonzo finds that Tejano/a history begins in the 1730s or 1750s, a period when large numbers of Spanish settlers received land grants, at least south of the Rio Grande. We argue that Texas history proper goes farther back, to pre-Spanish and pre-French days when the Coahuilteca Indians were spread across South Texas, from Galveston Bay west to San Antonio, south to the Rio Grande and beyond, and then west to the Pecos.[11] North of this area were numerous other Indian nations, some nomadic, some sedentary, some semisedentary, encountered by Spanish missionaries, explorers, and settlers who first began colonizing Texas in the late seventeenth century.[12] Anthropologist W. W. Newcomb's work *The Indians of Texas* offers a detailed cultural history of Indigenous groups in Texas from the sixteenth to nineteenth centuries. South and Central Texas were home to Coahuiltecan tribes and Jumanos and the Karankawa tribes in the south coastal area. Pueblo Indians resided close to what is now New Mexico and in the Llano Estacado in the Texas Panhandle; farther south were the Comanches and the Apaches: the Kiowa Apaches, the Mescaleros, and the Lipan Apaches. North of the Karankawa were the Atakapans, the Kadohadacho, and the Caddos, among them the Hasinai. The Caddos descended from mound-building Indians and shared cultural traditions with the Creeks, Chickasaws, Choctaws, Cherokees, and Natchez.[13] How many thousands there were is not certain, but what is clear is that their contact with colonizers was deadly: "The facts of history are plain: Most Texas Indians were exterminated or brought to the brink of oblivion by Spaniards, Mexicans, Texans, and Americans who often had no more regard for the life of an Indian than they had for that of a dog, sometimes less."[14] Their vast area caught the interest of Europeans early on; Álvar Núñez Cabeza de Vaca would be the first explorer of Texas territory (1528–36), although already in 1519 Alonso Álvarez de Pineda's voyage through the Gulf of Mexico had led to Spanish claims to the area.[15]

Ironically, when Chicanos/as stress that they are a mestizo population, the association with Indian ancestors is generally with Aztecs or Mayas. Rarely do they write of Coahuilteca, Karankawa, or Jumano ancestors. The tale of bloodshed and Indian genocide is not one that appears much in the fiction of Chicano/a writers, with one notable exception.[16] When Indigenous peoples are mentioned in works dealing with the nineteenth century, it is usually to describe savage Indian raids on Spanish or Mexican settlements. The fact that this was Indian land is set aside or conveniently occluded. These writers prefer to see the Southwest as Spanish/Mexican land before it was invaded by the Americanos. And yet the "kingdom of Tejas" was one of three confederations of the Caddos, the Hasinai from which the state gets its name.[17]

Historian Valerio-Jiménez stands out for recording Spanish colonists' spatial violence in the form of encroachment onto Indian land, the enslavement of the Indians, their use as forced labor, and the creation of an indebted servant class of Indian peons.[18] Spanish colonists were largely criollo and mestizo, but their laborers were Indians, mulattoes, and members of other *castas*. As he explains, the colonization of northern Mexico "created a population catastrophe among Nuevo Santander Indigenous nations."[19] When the Spanish colonists arrived in 1749, some fifteen thousand Indigenous people lived in the area; by 1798 there were some 650 survivors, the dead succumbing to warfare, disease, and hunger. And he adds, "New Spain's state formation in the northern villas ultimately fostered genocide and cultural eradication among the region's Indians."[20] By 1821, Indians in Texas had been decimated, killed by soldiers or settlers or wiped out by smallpox and other epidemics. The first Spanish/Mexican settlers in the Southwest were thus slayers, oppressors, and exploiters of Indigenous peoples as well as their dispossessors.

Colonization and Dispossession

The Spanish presence in Texas needs to be seen in relation to other Spanish explorations in Florida, the Carolinas, Georgia, the Mississippi River, Louisiana, and East Texas and especially in relation to French exploration of the Gulf of Mexico area.[21] The French presence was seen as a threat and led to failed Spanish colonial attempts to occupy the Gulf region through missions and presidios. In 1716, the new viceroy in New Spain ordered the establishment of a way station between the Rio Grande and the struggling East Texas missions, and two years later the governor of Texas established the presidio San Antonio de Béjar and a mission named after the viceroy: San Antonio de Valero (later, the Alamo). He also established the municipality or villa of San Antonio, called Béjar.

Seeking to claim the area west of Louisiana by increasing the number of settlers in the northern province, Spain recruited people from the Spanish-held Canary Islands off Africa to come to Texas. In 1731, fifty-six islanders (fifteen families) arrived to establish the first formal municipality in San Antonio. There were by then a few other settlers tied to the missions. As enticement, the new colonists from the Canary Islands would be designated hidalgos, the lowest rank of nobility, in perpetuity, in turn creating tension between them and earlier settlers.[22] These are the only official hidalgos named by the Spanish Crown in Texas, although fiction writers, like Jovita González, used the term quite broadly.[23]

In what became South Texas and San Antonio, the Spanish/Mexican colonists established a semifeudal rancho system based on the exploitation of Indian labor, peons who were subordinated and indebted to the colonial settler landowners, the patrones. This was a continuation of the ranchero system in place already in northern Mexico, which Semo has described fully, based on the dispossession of the Indians and on the maintenance of a landed oligarchy allied to the Church, the Spanish viceroy, and later the Mexican state.[24] Spanish/Mexican colonizers from New Spain, later Mexico, were at first unwilling to move north to what was considered wild territory, a no-man's-land distant from any colonial centers; in East Texas, Spanish presidios and missions were closer to French forts and trading posts than they were to New Spain. Maintaining far-flung empires proved costly for European colonial powers: in 1762, with the Treaty of Fontainebleau, France ceded Louisiana to Spain as it had become a financial liability. By 1800, however, Spain would trade Louisiana back to France, and Napoleon would turn around and sell the area to the United States in 1803.

Settlement in Nuevo Santander

By far the most important settlement in South Texas would be the one established by José de Escandón in the mid-eighteenth century (1747–67), primarily south of the Rio Grande.[25] Since the Gulf of Mexico region in the northern part of what today are the states of Tamaulipas and Coahuila was not settled, the Bourbon monarchy determined to try a new method for colonizing this area from Tampico to the Nueces River. The plan called for a new colony to be settled by colonists rather than by missionaries and soldiers.[26] In 1746, the viceroy of New Spain and his council selected a plan for settler colonization submitted by Escandón, a wealthy officer and Indian fighter, to head this private-public enterprise. He would establish villages comprising residents from neighboring provinces, induced by land grants and funds for relocation.[27] In a shift in tactics, in Escandón's colony, called Nuevo Santander, Indians were to be hired as workers and paid wages. Those not willing to submit would be killed. Many fled. Although estimates by historians vary, David

Weber indicates that by 1821 only around two thousand Indians remained.[28] Genocide and forced labor were both effective strategies to vacate lands.

All of the villas that Escandón established were south of the Rio Grande, but in 1750 José Vásquez Borrego established a ranch settlement, the Hacienda de Dolores, on the north bank, near what is now Laredo, and in 1754 the town of Laredo was founded.[29] Settlers in these various villages were mestizos, criollos, or *peninsulares*.[30] Some thirty years later, criollos and peninsulares were outnumbered by the Indians, mestizos, mulattoes, Blacks, and other castes.[31] In 1755, Escandón could report that there were twenty-three settlements in Nuevo Santander, with over six thousand settlers and close to three thousand Indians living in missions administered by Franciscan missionaries.[32] At this point lands were held in common, but settlers began requesting the partition of lands into individual allotments. In 1771, commissioners awarded private land grants to more than one thousand *pobladores* of New Santander.[33]

Valerio-Jiménez notes that these settler colonists were landless families seeking land grants and that land distribution was based on military rank and class.[34] While the first grants were royal grants to settlers for the purpose of ensuring the occupation of the land, by the 1770s new settlers were arranging to buy *sitios* from the owners of large grants south of the Rio Grande.[35] Petitions for land grants continued, but once granted, lands were often sold. At what point grantees began paying for the land south of the Río Grande is not clear, but by the late eighteenth century those requesting land grants were paying for the sitios. Land as real estate was thus already a practice in Nuevo Santander.

The proximity of settlements south of the Rio Grande to each other created a sense of community among ranchero families in the Rio Grande valley. Most of the allotments were for ranchos, with few large haciendas.[36] Although Alonzo reports that there were no indebted peons, David Montejano and Omar S. Valerio-Jiménez disagree, noting the existence of indebted peons on these haciendas and ranchos, as does—importantly—novelist Jovita González in *Caballero* and *Dew on the Thorn*.[37] These early Spanish settlements were undoubtedly patriarchal and semifeudal, with both indebted peons and servants.[38] Indian laborers earning wages under Escandón became indebted peons in short order. Valerio-Jiménez is more explicit and less willing to idealize the past. He notes that local Indigenous people were transformed into subordinate workers; children worked for the Santander families as *criados*, a euphemism for slaves, he notes.[39] Indian children were either kidnapped, war captives, or traded by their parents for goods. Indian slavery of that type, as we have seen, was also common in New Mexico.

Mexico's Ill-Fated Open-Door Policy in Texas

Colonists soon requested land north of the Rio Grande and south of the Nueces River for cattle grazing.[40] By 1800, some of these haciendas encompassed thousands of acres. When in 1821 Mexico gained its independence from Spain, Nuevo Santander became the state of Tamaulipas, and Texas (the land north of the Nueces River) became part of the state of Coahuila. Coahuila was now in charge of the disposition of public lands in Texas, and it turned over a good part of the land to foreigners. In fact, as Weber notes, "the alienation of public lands in Texas by Coahuila became such a scandal that, as one contemporary noted, the term *empresario* is justly considered equivalent to that of a swindler."[41]

By 1821, there were some four thousand Mexican settlers north of the Rio Grande.[42] That year, Moses Austin renewed his application (made previously under Spain) to introduce a colony of families into the Texas province, marking the beginning of a new settler colonist endeavor, but still under Mexican authority. Austin was offered a 200,000-acre tract, on which he was to settle three hundred families; each colonist was to build a house and cultivate the land, receiving 640 acres, 320 acres for his wife, 160 acres for each child, and, notably, 80 for each slave. The newly minted independent Mexican state of Coahuila allowed additional empresarios to bring colonists from the United States to the province of Texas.[43] While settlers were streaming in, Mexico passed two colonization laws in 1823 and 1825, "which provided for a general policy of colony promotion."[44]

By 1830, more than seventeen Anglo empresarios had signed contracts with Mexico to bring colonists, but only two (Austin and Green de Wit) would meet the conditions of the colonizing contract.[45] Land received was to be purchased. The Mexican government permitted immigrants to purchase up to eleven leagues, at $100 per league for pastureland, $150 for nonirrigable farmland, and $250 for irrigable farmland. This translated to a rate of 2.5–5.6 cents an acre.[46] This was a good deal in comparison with what was offered in the US territory, where the price for its land was $1.25 an acre, to be paid in cash on the day of sale—a price considered too high. In Texas, Anglo settlers had to become Mexican citizens, and even early on, concern over the growing Anglo presence led to the creation of a commission headed by General Manuel de Mier y Terán to investigate land holdings, immigration, and the flora and fauna of Texas.[47]

Of course, given this influx of settlers, setting boundaries became an important task for both Mexico and the United States. The Adams-Onís Treaty of 1819 had previously set the border between Spain and the United States, but after Mexico's independence actual boundary lines needed to be defined. The boundary commission headed by Mier y Terán traveled across Texas, from Laredo to San Antonio to Austin toward Nacogdoches, surveying the area and noting the geography, Indigenous populations, natural resources, and the large number of immigrants in the territory, with reports on the three towns of Béjar, La Bahía, and Nacogdoches, his headquarters, as well. From there he explored East Texas, visited Indian communities, noted the growing Anglo population, and found conditions worrisome. By 1828, Anglo settlers as well as Mexicans in Texas were asking that Texas be separated from Coahuila as a separate territory.[48]

Surveying the Terrain: Too Little, Too Late

Mier y Terán was especially concerned with the fact that the population in East Texas was increasingly from the United States, and he argued for greater Mexican occupation of Texas (north of the Nueces River) lest Mexico lose it forever. He was instrumental in preparing the Mexican Congress Law of April 6, 1830, which prohibited further immigration from the United States, rescinded empresario contracts not yet fulfilled, and prohibited the introduction of slaves into the territory.[49] Some, like Minister of State Lucas Alamán, saw through the settlement scheme: "Where others send invading armies, [the Americans] send their colonists."[50] The 1830 law meant to end the flood of immigration to Texas from the United States, but, without the necessary military backing, enforcement was lax.[51] Armed adventurers also began arriving through New Orleans. Settler colonialism and filibustering thus would prove quite effective as weapons of expansionist policy, even if not official US government policy, as Alamán and Mier y Terán feared.

When the Mexican government tried to stop immigration and outlawed slavery in its territories, colonists in Texas were alarmed and began protesting.[52] In the meantime, rumors spread about an imminent US invasion; US ambassador Joel Poinsett tried to buy Texas from Mexico, but the offer was rejected three times. In 1832, a frustrated Mier y Terán, faced with conflicts in the Mexican capital, an approaching insurrection in Texas, and his failure to attract Mexican settlers to Texas, committed suicide.

The decade of the 1830s brought the serially vacationing Mexican president Santa Anna back to power, declaring his plans to establish a centralist government in Mexico and a new constitution. The federalist versus centralist conflict in Mexico became a fraught issue in several states, including Texas.[53] Opposition to the new constitution led Texas to declare that it would remain with Mexico if the 1824 constitution was retained, but, if not, it would declare independence. In 1836, after Texans declared their independence, Santa Anna set out with his army to ensure that the Texan rebels were defeated. Many men arrived from the United States to join the fight against Mexico, especially after the battle at the Alamo. As it warrants special attention, the varying and conflicted interpretations and representations of events at the Alamo are addressed in subsequent sections.

The success of Texan filibuster maneuvers led to the defeat of the Mexican army and US recognition of Texas's independence.[54] The demographic shift was dramatic: a ten-to-one ratio, similar to what would take place some ten years later in California. By 1836 there were in the territory some 30,000 Anglo-Americans, 3,470 Mexicans, and 2,000 Blacks, almost all slaves.[55] Estimates differ, but it is estimated that by 1844 there were 51,000 Anglo-Americans, 4,000 Mexicans, and 10,000 slaves, as immigration from the US South increased markedly after 1836. In the case of Texas, that is, in the territory north of the Nueces River, the settler colonists were thus both Anglos and Mexicans, although by 1836 the vast majority were Anglos.

Texas independence did not bring immediate admission into the Union because of debates in Congress over slavery; the antislavery North did not want to admit another slave state.[56] During the ten years of Texas independence, it is estimated that thirty million acres that once were Indigenous, Spanish, and then Mexican lands were granted to US settlers. Texas used land to pay off its debts but was unable to pay them all off. Five years after US annexation in 1845, the state of Texas sold 78,842,880 acres of its western lands to the US government for $10 million and thereby retired its outstanding debt.[57]

Mexico did not recognize Texas independence in 1836 nor its claims that Texas reached to the Rio Grande. In 1846, a year after US annexation of Texas, when Mexican troops crossed the Rio Grande into what was for them Mexican territory and fired on what were seen as invading US troops, President James K. Polk immediately declared war, invaded Mexico, and took over half of the northern Mexican territory. At war's end, Mexico was forced to transfer its lands in the Southwest for $15 million and accept the Treaty of Guadalupe Hidalgo. This ostensible purchase was nothing more than blood money, paid by the United States for the war, invasion, and occupation of Mexican lands that it then kept. A few years later, the United States paid Mexico $10 million for the comparatively minuscule Gadsden Purchase in Arizona and southern New Mexico. Although not the first empire-building war the United States embarked on, in view of its filibustering in Texas in 1836 and its many wars against the Indians to displace them and enclose their territory, the war of 1846–48 was a benchmark: the United States' first major imperialist war. Juan Gómez-Quiñones notes: "today, nearly all historians agree that the United States was clearly the aggressor."[58] Even H. H. Bancroft called the war "a premeditated and pre-determined affair . . . the result of a deliberately calculated scheme of robbery on the part of the superior power."[59] US interest in the acquisition of Texas was clear long before 1836, after it acquired the Louisiana Purchase in 1803, but it was in fact the Mexican state that willingly opened the door to the flood of Anglo settlers. The United States did not force settler colonies on Texas as England and the Zionists forced Israeli settlements on Palestine, with warfare, but the United States would, later in 1846, use military force to retain the Texas territory, when Mexico continued to claim South Texas.

There are different estimates of the Mexican population in Texas in 1836, and clearly Anglos were the absolute majority in the area north of the Nueces River but not south of the river. By 1847, some thirty years after Anglo colonization started in earnest, the white population in Texas north of the Nueces River was over 100,000, with over 35,000 slaves.[60] Three years later, the numbers had grown to 120,000 Anglos, with 2,500 Anglos south and west of the Nueces River.[61] After 1848, the few thousand Mexicans in what was now Texas, going all the way to the Rio Grande, found themselves not only outnumbered but disempowered as well, and subject to racism, abuse, segregation, and violence, including lynchings. This would only escalate during the second half of the nineteenth century, especially harassment by the Texas Rangers, the shock troops of Anglo ascendancy. As noted by Weber, "Hispanophobia lasted longer in Texas than in any of Spain's former North American provinces," noting further, "After their victory in 1836, Anglo-American rebels controlled not only Texas, but the writing of its history."[62] It is this racist history of white supremacy that Chicano/a historians and fiction writers have sought to document, challenge, and counter.

Post-1848: Under New Management

The US invasion would affect subject formation and identity in the case of Mexicans residing north of the Rio Grande. They would now be seen as Tejanos/as and as US citizens, despite not having considered themselves part of Texas before; the class status of landowners would be dramatically affected as they underwent—either rapidly or gradually—wholesale dispossession after 1848, as Indigenous peoples had at the hands of Spanish, Mexican, and US invaders, but not necessarily in the same way. Vastly outnumbered in the state, the Tejano/a population in the Texas Valley north of the Rio Grande nevertheless grew during the second half of the nineteenth century, from 15,210 in 1860 to 79,925 by 1900, despite xenophobia; in some five counties in South Texas the population was over 90 percent Mexican.[63] Land loss would come through legal and extralegal means.[64] Spatial violence in the form of land dispossession was widespread, especially in the coastal counties of Cameron and Nueces, but in counties where Mexican Texans were the majority, ranchers retained landownership for longer periods, says Valerio-Jiménez, agreeing in this case with Alonzo.[65] It is also the case that with the military occupation of 1846 and subsequent annexation, many Mexicans fled south of the Rio Grande and settled in towns across the river; new refugee towns were also established, says Montejano: "Despite these refugee movements, Texas south and west of the Nueces River remained predominantly Mexican in population."[66] How this spatial dispossession took place is variously described in the work of Jovita González and Rolando Hinojosa.

Tejanos/as in South Texas have been acutely conscious and resentful of their dispossession since 1848, as noted by Graham, even today.[67] Fort Brownsville was established by Zachary Taylor's army on Mexican land for which no payment was ever made. Visitors to Brownsville, like Abbé Emmanuel H. D. Domenech, recall seeing Mexicans "flogged to the point of death." Mexicans were lynched without trial, and Comanche raids continued.[68] According to Frederick Law Olmsted, "Mexicans were regarded in a somewhat unchristian tone, not as heretics or heathens to be converted with flannel and tracts, but rather as vermin, to be exterminated."[69] Ironically, like the Indians, previously denigrated by Spanish and Mexican settlers, Tejano/a communities would now also be described in derogatory terms.[70]

These demeaning descriptions are later opposed by romanticized portrayals of the Spanish period of occupation by Tejano/a writers, descendants of the early settlers. As in the case of Nuevomexicanos/as, what is emphasized in these literary representations of colonial times is Spanish cultural heritage. Here it perhaps needs restating that these early colonizing settlers should not necessarily be seen as "our ancestors," since most people of Mexican origin in the United States today are descendants of immigrants who came north after 1900. In South Texas, on the other hand, some Tejanos/as do in fact trace their descent to eighteenth- and nineteenth-century settlers.

The economic and political situation of this Rio Grande Tejano/a post-1848 community can be examined best through the prism of the dominant economic force in South Texas, the King Ranch. Histories of the King Ranch and of Mexican dispossession are intertwined, as are the racism and lynching of Mexicans that, in turn, led to turmoil.

"My Land": New Landowners

Don Graham's *Kings of Texas: The 150-Year Saga of an American Ranching Empire* provides an account of the King Ranch, an 825,000-acre family-owned ranch established in 1854 that became a transnational corporation by the mid-twentieth century.[71] The founder, Richard King, was a former boat pilot who came to Texas in 1847, freighted passengers and goods from Brazos Santiago to Matamoros and along the Rio Grande, and bought the Santa Gertrudis de la Garza land grant.[72] Like King, other US settlers, businessmen, soldiers, and speculators began buying Mexican ranches at a low cost after 1848. Some landowners had fled during the US-Mexican War or had been forced out of their lands, but others had long been absentee landlords who had a few cowboys and servants living on their land.

Purchase of abandoned land grants was one way that incoming Anglo settlers acquired land, but it was not the only way. In some cases, Tejano/a lands were simply occupied by squatters, and in others Rangers killed or ran off the landowners. Shrewd lawyers who transferred Tejano/a land titles to land-hungry Anglo-Texans facilitated Tejano/a dispossession.[73] Graham also notes that those Tejanos/as unable to pay their debts or taxes had their lands auctioned off and purchased by Anglos.[74] In fact, Texans used every means from lynching to scare tactics to drive the Tejanos/as away from their land: "Once the Mexicans fled, as many of them did, their lands could be transferred to Anglo ownership."[75] The Mexican response to the violence and dispossession would take a variety of forms: "legal, extra-legal, violent, non-violent, and individual as well as collective, cultural, economic, juridical and civic."[76] An example of these responses concerns a landowner named Juan Cortina.[77]

Juan Nepomuceno Cortina, who owned property on both the southern and northern sides of the border, lived on Rancho El Carmen, a few miles from Brownsville, and had difficulties with Anglos over land grants. In 1859 he shot a Brownsville marshal who was pistol-whipping a Mexican who had worked on Rancho El Carmen.[78] After fleeing across the border, he organized a group of men who were fed up with the mistreatment of Mexicans and wanted the US government to settle the issue of land claims, which is evident in Cortina's appeal to Sam Houston. Feeling powerless, Cortina saw the situation as hopeless unless they formed a new republic. He had seen both his mother and aunt lose thousands of acres of the Espíritu Santo grant to Anglo lawyers.[79] In 1859, Cortina's small guerrilla army rode into Brownsville with about a hundred men, shooting five men, among them four Anglos who had killed Mexicans. Cortina then came out with a proclamation pledging to defend Tejanos/as against those seeking to spread terror among them to compel them to abandon their lands.[80] The Cortinistas voiced grievances against US judges and law enforcement officers.[81] Asserting their US citizenship, they also denounced the use of Mexican troops from Matamoros to put down their protest.[82] Anglo citizens of the border area began preparing for a second attack. In late December 1859, US troops and Texas Rangers were able to defeat Cortina, who supposedly left the area but remained connected to Mexican liberals on the border and US Union forces.[83] Although often seen as a bandit and a rabble-rouser, Cortina in fact was a hero to many Tejanos/as, as his actions called attention to their dispossession and abuse. As Gómez-Quiñones indicates, Cortina "had the most explicit consciousness of fighting foreign domination. He put forth a call to arms in a manifesto that contained ideas on political and economic organization."[84] Armed resistance in South Texas would again resurface during the US Civil War.[85]

The dispossession of Tejano/a landowners through vigilante and Texas Ranger violence proved profitable to ranching operations like those of Mifflin Kenedy and Richard King, who took over sacked and burned properties. Cattle rustling was the perfect excuse for killing and dispossessing Tejanos/as, whether they were accused of the act or of harboring the raiders. Enter Leander H. McNelly as head of the Rangers, who was willing to use whatever method it took to suppress "cattle-rustlers."[86] McNelly is the basis for the portrayal of MacDougal in Paredes's *George Washington Gómez*.[87] The King family is the not-so-veiled correlate for Hinojosa's Klail-Blanchard-Cooke Ranch family and for the Benedict family in the Edna Ferber novel *Giant*.[88]

Further Displacement and Disempowerment with the Coming of Commercial Farming

The end of the nineteenth century brought commercial farming to Texas on a scale hitherto unknown. The discovery of underground water led to the digging of wells, a practice that furthered exploration for oil as well.[89] Local ranchers, seeing the disinterest of the Southern Pacific in building a rail extension into South Texas, opted to build the railroad themselves.[90] Overproduction of cattle and the difficulty of getting it to market led ranch owners to shift to commercial agriculture. Ranch lands were then divided into farm tracts, and with the railroad came farmers, land developers, irrigation engineers, and produce brokers. Access to outside markets stimulated settlement in South Texas, and new towns sprang up. Migration from the Midwest brought thousands to South Texas, more than tripling the population from 79,934 in 1900 to 322,845 in 1930. Thousands of farms were created in what was called the Winter Garden area.[91] Yet despite this growth in the number of Anglo newcomers, Tejanos/as continued to be the majority population in South Texas, as Mexican nationals now migrated north of the Rio Grande to work on Texas farms.[92]

This twentieth-century economic transformation in Texas, which saw the collapse of the cattle ranch and the emergence of the farm economy, led to conflict between ranchers and farmers, or more specifically between transplanted Midwesterners and Tejanos/as. Historian David Montejano quotes writer Jovita González in noting that it was "a struggle between the New World and the Old," later putting a finer point on it by signaling that it was "at the same time a race struggle."[93] The conflict was most acute in the "densely settled Lower Rio Grande."[94] It was especially painful for the old Tejano/a "landed aristocracy" as well as for the merchants, artisans, vaqueros, and peons who found themselves rapidly displaced.

The cotton industry, first introduced by Austin in Texas in 1821 with settlers from the South who brought their Black slaves with them, required workers to pick the cotton. In a time before the mechanization of cotton farming, growers were especially interested in Mexican farm laborers and Tejanos/as who had lost their land. In an early example of a pull factor drawing Mexican migration, growers requested that literacy and head tax payment be waived for Mexican immigrant workers in view of the shortage of agricultural workers in the cotton fields of East, Central, and West Texas.[95] Mexican workers were seen as cheap labor, inferior creatures "somewhere in between a burro and a human being," according to an agent for the Farm Bureau in Ysleta, Texas.[96]

The early twentieth-century new commercial farming economy saw proletarianized Tejanos/as and Mexican immigrants working as sharecroppers and migrant field-workers, especially as cotton pickers. Neil Foley notes that the cotton world was divided into landowners, tenant farmers, sharecroppers, and Black and Mexican field-workers. The Mexican elite, on the other hand, "who wished to be recognized as American and white," found themselves increasingly in conflict with Mexican working-class progressive movements that they felt "reinforced stereotypes that Mexicans in general were poor, dirty and politically radical."[97] This class division is clear in the fiction that we examine in what follows. By 1900 Tejanos/as had generally been reduced, except in a few border counties, to the status of landless wage laborers; the landowners were now Anglos and the workers were Mexican.[98] Montejano further notes, "Mexicans now found themselves treated as an inferior race, segregated into their own town quarters and refused admittance at restaurants, picture shows, bathing beaches and so on."[99] Former landowners and peons were all treated alike, painted with the same brush, as "Mess'cans" by Anglo Texans.[100] According to Montejano, while Mexicans continued to be harassed and lynched by the Rangers, Tejano/a leaders began to denounce lynchings, calling for an end to educational discrimination and urging Tejanos/as not to sell their land.[101] It is in this context that border troubles increased and the Plan de San Diego was developed.

In the midst of the Mexican Revolution, in 1915, several Tejanos/as came up with the Plan de San Diego, a radical manifesto calling for the secession of South Texas from the United States and the formation of an army made up of Mexicans, Blacks, Japanese, and Indians to create an independent republic that would include Texas, New Mexico, Arizona, Colorado, and California.[102] These *sediciosos* are believed to have been influenced by the Mexican Revolution and the anarchist Flores Magón brothers, their newspaper *Regeneración*, and the worldwide anarchist movement. The Plan de San Diego can be seen only as a reaction to the rampant anti-Mexican violence, dispossession, and persecution in its call for an uprising of the Mexican people to redress these wrongs and to return to territory lost in 1836 and 1848. Tejanos/as who had finally had their fill of murderous tactics burned down the main house at King Ranch. The seditionists engaged in various encounters with the Rangers. Photos of Rangers who tied up the corpses of Mexicans with rope, as if they were cattle, served to infuriate the Tejano/a community further. Texas Rangers were seen as "a major cause of the border trouble."[103] Bodies of dead Mexicans were found everywhere, and Tejanos/as began to flee across the border.[104] The violence would subside around 1917 with the intervention of both the US and Mexican governments, but the racial mistrust and hatred would live on for years. The origins of the Plan de San Diego are in doubt, with some attributing the manifesto to the Carrancista Revolutionaries across the border during the Mexican Revolution, but Gómez-Quiñones rightfully points out that the plan was more likely than not "a militant response and reaction within a particular set of historical circumstances."[105] This topic is taken up later as it is a key part of Paredes's novel *George Washington Gómez*.[106]

Transfiguration of the Social Structure: A Rude Awakening

With the incorporation of the Tejano/a communities into the state of Texas, much would change, not only in terms of violence and racism but also in terms of the social and economic structure of the state. The new farm order and the cotton boom would lead Tejanos/as to become field-workers, cotton pickers, and in some cases tenant farmers, like Feliciano in Paredes's *George Washington Gómez*. Montejano cites Jovita González, describing the "rude awakening" of the once-landed aristocracy: "It was a blow to see these new arrivals ruthlessly appropriate all that had been theirs, even the desert plains."[107]

Few continued to be landowners. Differences aside, what historians do agree on is that "land loss among the mexicanos in the Southwest after 1848 resulted in their reduction to second-class citizens."[108] The disagreement among historians concerns the speed with which dispossession took place. While some historians argue that Tejano/a rancheros were quickly dispossessed after 1848, Alonzo sets out to demonstrate that not all the Tejanos/as lost their land in South Texas. Tejanos/as in the lower Texas Valley persisted and prevailed until the 1880s, he notes.[109] Despite tensions, violence, and hostility, Alonzo considers the years after 1848 as a period of accommodation that brought cooperation between Anglos and Tejanos/as in trade, commerce, and the livestock industry.[110] He tries to put a positive spin on this period of modernization in South Texas, highlighting cooperation between the well-to-do and skirting the blatant racism operating against Mexicanos. Gómez-Quiñones explains that during this period and up until 1941, "when overt anti-Mexican chauvinism was most intense, members of the middle class [ranchers, professionals, merchants, and teachers] struggled to both maintain themselves as members of a modestly advantaged economic sector" and to assimilate to the now-dominant Anglo society.[111] While it is clear that the population of Tejanos/Mexicanos in the lower Texas Valley region continued to grow, becoming 85 percent of the total population of about 90,000 by 1900,[112] for the increasing number of landless workers, the situation was challenging at best and dire at worst.

More changes were in store for Tejanos/as. In South Texas, dispossession and both spatial and discursive violence would in time lead Tejanos/as to various forms of resistance: social banditry, armed uprisings, and clandestine organizations. Some took up legal battles against fraud and land seizures. Industrialization and the military mobilization produced by World War II and the Korean War, along with the aftereffects of the Mexican Revolution of 1910, led to massive immigration from Mexico, migration to cities, new labor markets, and the "politicization of Mexican American veterans."[113] With growing urbanization, some displaced people of Mexican origin would become unskilled laborers; some became service workers or semiskilled urban workers ready to fill the needs of the ebbs and flows of the twentieth-century US economy.[114]

What especially concerns historians such as Alonzo, however, is the lack of recognition of the many contributions of Tejanos/as in South Texas and the Anglo failure to acknowledge that before their arrival, lower South Texas was not a vacant frontier but an area populated by Mexicanos.[115] It is precisely this concern for the recognition of a Tejano/a historical subject engaged in the development of South Texas that is central to much of the literature as well. For many Chicano/a writers, whether historians or fiction writers, recognition of contributions and inclusion as "Mericans" is an overriding concern.[116] Being seen as part of the US nation-building narrative all too often colors writers' readings of the harsh reality that was and is Texas.[117] On the other hand, countering the representation of Tejanos/as as inferior beings leads at times to an idealization of the landed elite. How fiction writers respond to the Hispanophobic history noted by Weber, and to a history of colonization, independence, racism, and acculturation is the focus in what follows.

Literary Representations of Spatial and Discursive Violence

In literary assessments of the past, what needs close accounting is the standpoint or positionality from which one addresses and represents the past—and the type of historical subject that is constructed in relation to the land. All of the works examined here were written by twentieth-century writers, some looking at the mid- or late nineteenth century from the perspective of what was already clearly lost by the early twentieth. Others begin in the early twentieth century and examine what occurred in the first half century, with a few referencing what came before. Still others begin their time frame in the 1930s, looking particularly at how South Texas changed up to the 1960s. Historical standpoint is crucial in setting up the historical horizon within which the narrative plots are developed. Ideologically, the novels represent not only the resentment of the dispossessed but at the same time underscore the distinct regional identity of the residents of South Texas. Chicano/a historians and novelists, in representing the dispossession of ethnic Mexican landowners, face both ethnic and class issues. More often than not, ethnicity and class in tandem win out, with a defense of the Tejano/a landowner suffering Anglo Ranger attacks, rather than a defense of the peons on the ranchos subject to that same violence.

To be sure, land in these novels is equated with capital and power. But it also represents the homeland, more regional than national since Texas was part of Mexico briefly, for only fifteen years. And yet, given the US invasion and the subordination of the Tejanos/as as well as the subsequent immigration flows from Mexico, a well-defined Mexican ethnic identity developed quickly in Texas, along with a fluid sense of citizenship. Tejanos/as became US citizens after 1845 but were not treated as such.[118] Conflict and racism make ethnic identity vis-à-vis the Other a form of disidentification with the dominant national and racial identity of Americanos. But with the Mexican Revolution of 1910 and the large and recurring immigration waves from Mexico after 1900, matters changed, and Mexican ethnic identity became the dominant form of identification, at least in Texas. A Mexicano in Texas is not necessarily an immigrant from Mexico. Native-born Tejanos/as also consider themselves Mexicanos, and both are often "jus Mess'cans" to most Anglos, without distinction.

Although the Texas novels discussed here were written in the twentieth and twenty-first centuries, they are all distinctively different. Not only is the range of projects disparate, but the techniques, the coding of history and social realities, and the cultural logic vary widely. Some novels are in part realist with residual romance elements and emergent modernist elements. Twentieth- and twenty-first-century ethnic or regional realism is what some critics term "peripheral realism," with a focus on groups defined by race, ethnicity, gender, and sexuality.[119] In Chicano/a realist fiction, class is always a factor as well, and the narrative perspective is critical. What these texts provide is a depiction of historical forces in motion, in other words, of the social contradictions in society, even while focusing not only on the impact of invasion and dispossession but also on the willingness (or not) to capitulate before the cultural and economic avalanche brought on by invasion. The land narrative in twentieth-century Chicana/o narratives is thus told in relation to dispossession, not only of land but of power and cultural practices, including language. Ties to Mexico are especially important in novels of the lower Rio Grande valley. An example: Américo Paredes's notion of a "Greater Mexico" makes sense in South Texas where, since the eighteenth century, families lived in villas on the south side of the Rio Grande while grazing cattle on the north side.[120] Although 1848 would split the region politically and economically, culturally, linguistically, and kinship-wise the two sides of the Rio Grande would continue to see themselves as one area, as Nuevo Santander and later as Mexican, *de éste y del otro lado*, for at least half a century.

In their introduction to *Recovering the Hispanic History of Texas*, Mónica Perales and Raúl A. Ramos suggest that fiction can be seen as offering "an oppositional narrative," as in novels by Américo Paredes and Jovita González.[121] That these novels provide oppositional narratives is perhaps an overreach. What they do show is how the dispossessed and subordinated came to accept their defeat and accommodated, in part through marriage, to the dominant economic and political perspective; residence in a majority Mexican South Texas region would, however, allow them to retain a distinct ethnic and cultural identity even while being assimilated into Anglo Texan hegemony. In the two González works we examine, land in South Texas is viewed in a complex and often contradictory matrix, economic, political, and cultural in nature. For González, land is the ranchero's patrimony, wealth, kingdom, where he reigns supreme over peons, vaqueros, servants, and family. When his ranch is threatened by invasion, *rinches* (Texas Rangers), violence, and gringos, so is his livelihood, his culture, his identity, his power, his manhood—everything he stands for. Land here is the place of a residual but disappearing feudal system. Precapitalist accumulation, along with social location, is lost when he loses the land.

Jovita González: Lamenting the End of an Era

Born in Roma, Texas, into a family of educators and artisans, Jovita González (1904–83) descended from early Escandón Nuevo Santander colonists.[122] She produced two historical regionalist novels about nineteenth- and early twentieth-century South Texas, that is, about the lower Rio Grande valley, the land, its people, and its culture. Cultural critics from György Lukács to Fredric Jameson speak of the historical novel as a narrative form generated by the transition from an older order to a bourgeois society as well as the representation of that historical passage.[123] In González's novels it is the war of 1848 between Mexico and the United States that brings about political change and the passage from a semifeudal to a capitalist order, from a ranching to a farm order, and from a dominant Spanish/Mexican political structure to a dominant Anglo structure. The historical novel also demands a multiplicity of voices or standpoints; here, although a range of class positions is suggested, it is the landowner's perspective that is dominant. Her two longer works, *Caballero* and *Dew on the Thorn*, written between 1926 and the late 1940s, are not about workers, peasants, or peons (tangentially presented) but about the wealthy landed rancheros and hacendados, with vast holdings.[124] It is worth remarking, however, that the standpoint of women is prominent in her fiction.

In these narratives, the female narrator offers a view of an irretrievable past with a political and ideological reflection on what happened and what came later; this is the perspective of the narrator who looks back, points to the wrongs and abuses of the old system, sympathizes with the dispossessed rancheros despite their faults, and decries the end of an era but is willing to accept that survival meant accommodating to the new regime. González's novels are critical of the insurrectionists (described as thieves), of the rancheros (criticized as dictators), of the feudal culture (abusive of peons and women), and of the feudal mode of production (the peons were like chattel and always indebted). The new order brings change, violence, and discrimination as well as commercial farming, a new language, a new political system, and new laws, but culturally, where the Tejanos/as are the majority population, they are able to maintain their language and their ways. While politically and economically displaced, most of the Tejanos/as are not geographically displaced. They continue to reside in the Rio Grande valley, now, for the most part, as laborers. The displaced are the Mexican immigrants who come north.

The post-1846 invasion period and its long aftermath are the focus of González's works. The first novel, *Dew on the Thorn*, and the second, *Caballero*, written with Eve Raleigh in the 1930s, present contradictory visions of the post-1846 period. González's historical romance, *Caballero*, is a costumbrista novel, with sketches of manners, like many nineteenth-century Latin American romances, that provides a view of the changes faced by South Texas landowners like Don Santiago de Mendoza after the outbreak of the US-Mexican

War. The social fragmentation of the Mendoza clan serves as an allegory for Mexican South Texas. Like the territory, the rancheros face a losing battle in the economic contest with the invaders and find themselves unable to withstand dispossession and the onslaught of US capital, laws, and military might. Some landowners accommodate to the new system, however, in hope of retaining their lands. In *Dew on the Thorn*, by contrast, also written in the costumbrista mode with vignettes and sketches of manners, the perspective is less optimistic since, by the early twentieth century, the setting of the novel, Tejanos/as now face almost total dispossession with the massive arrival of Anglo migrants and a new commercial agricultural-industrial order.

Through narratives of two families, the Mendozas in *Caballero*—initially titled *All This Is Mine*—and Olivares family in *Dew on the Thorn*, González provides an accounting of Tejano/a land loss and cultural and political changes in South Texas. These historical novels project a new sense of history. With the decline of the ranchero system comes the decline of other social practices. A new class perspective emerges, although this change is gradual. In *Caballero*, the *rancho patronal* system, with the workers indebted to and controlled by the patrón, remains after 1836. But as South Texas falls under the control of the United States, workers on Don Santiago's ranch begin to seek better working conditions (with Anglo ranchers). The end of the century brings an emerging farming capitalist order, producing new social relations, as is evident in *Dew on the Thorn*, though by 1904 things have not changed radically. The ranchero system is still somewhat in place, but politically things are changing at the local level. Rancheros who feared total dispossession in *Caballero*, that is, in the mid-nineteenth century, have not been altogether dispossessed, although widespread dispossession is well on its way, gradually reducing landowners to field-workers, and ranches to farms.

Workers now earn wages and are free to live wherever they like—or rather, can afford. Thousands of Mexicans immigrate north to escape the violence of the 1910 Mexican Revolution. At a cultural and social level, fathers continue to think that they can marry off their daughters regardless of the women's wishes, but now the daughters have the option to refuse. Sexual abuse, however, continues, as is evident in *Dew on the Thorn*, since the patrón and his sons continue to expect sexual access to the women on the ranch. Some things change more slowly than others. Unlike other collectivities that undergo a diaspora, Rio Grande Tejanos/as by and large remain in place; a shared language and customs and a majority population status in El Valle favor survival of the culture.

González's *Caballero: A Historical Novel*

Caballero looks at the period between 1846 and 1849 and attempts to provide, as the novel states outright, "the Mexican side of the war of 1848 [that] has never been given"[125] As González indicates, "We picture the Mexican hidalgos with their faults as well as their virtues, with their racial and religious pride, their love of tradition and of the land which they inherited from their ancestors."[126] Calling these landowners "Mexican hidalgos" would assume that they were Spanish nobles. And though titles of nobility could, by the eighteenth century, be bought, the settlers on the frontier rarely were considered to be part of the nobility, although the terms "Don" and "Doña" meant a higher status. In time, those titles would be used in Texas as a form of address to show respect for an elder, irrespective of their social status.

Gesturing toward objectivity, González also notes that the novel presents "the American officers, their kindness to the conquered race" as well as the racist pillagers who hate everything Mexican.[127] Clearly, González seeks to present an evenhanded story of conquest and dispossession without overly antagonizing the Anglo community, although she admits that there were anti-Mexican racists among the invaders. At the same time that she presents the Mexican landowner as proud and genteel, she also recognizes that the peons were not happy with their semifeudal work arrangements and were ready to leave the paternalistic arrangement in favor of wage labor. This romantic-realist novel acknowledges a distant past and a lost economic, social, and cultural structure. While seeing advantages in the change, the narrator also mourns the loss of Spanish/Mexican land and power. Missing here and in other works dealing with the nineteenth century is a recognition of Spanish settler colonialism that dispossessed Indigenous populations. Redressing this lack has fallen to more recent historians, fiction writers, and cultural critics, as previously noted.

Caballero's plot itself, in dealing with family fragmentation, provides a series of short subplots in which marriage especially plays a major role: the dilemma of young lovers separated by ethnicity and war (Susanita and Warrener), the plight of Inez, who falls for a gringo Ranger; the case of the younger son Luis Gonzaga, who dreams of becoming an artist but is ridiculed for seeking what his father considers an effeminate career and who will follow Captain Devlin to Baltimore to study painting; the case of the daughter Angela, who will choose to marry the wealthy Red McLane for the opportunities he offers her to do charity work; the willingness of Don Santiago's best friend,

Don Gabriel, to negotiate with the invaders and file his title to the land; the case of the widowed aunt Dolores, who late in life discovers her love for Don Gabriel; the libertine life of Álvaro, who as the eldest male son can do as he pleases, joins the guerrillas, and is finally shot by a Texas Ranger; and, finally, the loveless marriage of María Petronila and Don Santiago.

Love, Don Santiago tell us, is not important for marriage. He himself did not marry María Petronila for love. Their daughter, Susanita, however, wishes to marry for love.[128] The thought of her marrying Warrener, an invader, and her visit to the military camp to plead for her brother's life lead Don Santiago to accuse her of going against the stern codes of honor that Mexican caballeros expect their women to follow. To this the narrator reacts: "Honor! It was a fetishism. It was a weapon in the hand of the master, to keep his woman enslaved, and his fingers had twisted upon it so tightly he could not let go."[129] Women, like land, are viewed as chattel, and marrying a foreigner is a type of dispossession as well. Wanting to be strict, Don Santiago disowns his daughter and sentences her to live apart from the family or else leave the hacienda. Insulted and wronged, she keeps her head high and, that night, leaves the hacienda with an old servant, traveling incognito to Matamoros, where she marries Warrener. Like other romances, the novel uses marriage as a means to bridge the Mexican-US divide and to move from conservative traditionalism to modernity. In this fashion, the narrative of domesticity in *Caballero*, with its focus on the patriarchal hacienda, allows for the story of enclosures via family fragmentation and the dethroning of the patriarch, Don Santiago Mendoza y Soría, a sexist, machista, dictatorial father; it is an allegory of the end of the semifeudal system in South Texas and the loss of land and power of the rancheros in the lower Rio Grande valley.

Different Forms of Resistance

Importantly, the trope of family fragmentation within the domestic sphere coupled with successful female rebellion against patriarchal norms is represented against the backdrop of an unsuccessful Tejano/a insurrection against the US invaders. The novel, through a priest character, makes a case for accommodation to the new capitalist order and assimilation to the Americano economic and political system while safeguarding Tejano/a culture. Cultural resistance along these lines seems to be the dominant motif in Southwest literature dealing with the nineteenth century, although it did not impede dispossession. Faced with a losing battle, rancheros like Gabriel del Lago begin seeking legal alternatives to armed resistance. Misconceptions and biases about the Tejano/a Other are counterproductive, the novel argues in the end, preferring to stress commonalities among the well-to-do on both sides, but noting, too, the coarseness and violence shared by the "lower orders" in both groups. In these representations, the novel is clearly cut across by class bias.

González's narratives were written when farms had replaced ranching and outsiders from other states had come to increase the overall population in South Texas. Thus by the time González wrote, few of the original Tejanos/as had been able to hold on to their lands, and some had become tenant farmers. Land loss went with lost status and political power in society. Gone, too, was a way of life that could not be recovered. Interestingly, if not ironically, in the early twentieth century, with increasing immigration from Mexico, especially during the Revolution of 1910, incoming wealthy Mexicans also began buying Texas land, with the end result that Mexican culture would be reinforced, but not the elite Tejano/a ranchero way of life and culture that González describes.[130]

Narrative Perspective: Gendering Transitions and Positionality

In *Caballero*, character portrayals are by and large one dimensional, provided by an omniscient narrator who does, however, recognize that changes in social standing affect the character's agency. In the case of Don Santiago, for example, he is not presented as a villain; he is presented as a man of the past, out of time and place. Women's attitudes, on the other hand, shift with change; it is striking that the novel's female characters are more amenable to the dominant Anglo perspective and are willing to counter retrograde misogynist Tejano male mindsets. Changes brought on by invasion open the door for women now able to counter their fathers' wishes and accept Anglo men as spouses. Both daughters in *Caballero* see Americanos as the best choices for husbands, despite their father's refusal to concede their hand in marriage (forbidding it, in fact). The women are like the land. They can be productive under one regime or another, as long as they are well cared for, and clearly, the novel suggests, they will be better off with Anglo men.

There are thus two crucial standpoints in the novel: that of those who resist and that of those who accommodate. Among the first are those who wish to resist through insurrection, and among the second, those of higher class who accommodate to survive. Class status, the novel suggests, is the overriding force that can unite the cultured well-to-do Tejanos/as and the cultured well-to-do Anglos, for the upper classes of both groups are seen to have much in common. *Caballero* is a narrative, then, about the disintegration of a traditional community and the imminent loss of land. The collectivity will survive, yes, despite enclosure, but its place and status will be definitively altered. Under Anglo domination, Tejanos/as will be decentered in South Texas and more precariously situated.

A World Irretrievably Gone: *Dew on the Thorn*

Some twenty years before *Caballero*, González's first novel, *Dew on the Thorn*, is written in an ethnographic vein about the customs and traditions of Tejano-Mexicano rancheros toward the end of the nineteenth century and the early twentieth century and includes numerous intercalated folktales. It is in keeping with an early twentieth-century literature, with a modernist longing to recapture or re-create the past, but written like a nineteenth-century costumbrista narrative.[131] There is then in González's *Dew on the Thorn* a definite attempt to record the historical roots of what is represented as a disappearing class, one facing extinction in Texas. In a way there is less idealization of the ranchero period in *Dew on the Thorn* than in *Caballero* as it critiques several aspects of a disappearing Tejano/a lifestyle while simultaneously recovering and safeguarding others.

Dew on the Thorn cannot be taken as a full-fledged novel as it is a compilation of several folkloric sketches; like *Caballero* it is a story of patriarchal domesticity in large part and of folk culture, but it does not focus solely on the rancho, as the narrative moves away from the ranch to a town in South Texas. The town, no longer south of the border as in *Caballero*, includes commercial, religious, and political spaces. Most of the action, however, takes place in the countryside; this rural space allows for the inclusion of all kinds of folktales, melodramatic elements, and costumbrista sketches, some of which have been collected and published separately in the collection *The Woman Who Lost Her Soul*.[132] The tales included in the novel are quite varied. The central opposition in this work, as in *Caballero*, is that between the remaining Tejano/a landowners and the new invaders (the Anglo farming settlers), that is, between residual and emergent cultures and socioeconomic systems. The novel traces the spatial violence of land loss along with the discursive violence of the loss of cultural primacy.

The narrative looks back on the history of the Olivares family, who came to

South Texas in 1764 to live on the family grant. The narrator underscores that the founders of these border towns and ranches were in the majority criollos or Spaniards, *gente de razón*—literally, reasoning people—unlike the ignorant and uncultured peons. This historical subject is racially marked as white and of Spanish heritage, as in *Caballero*. Again, there is no mention of Indigenous people residing in the territory before the Spanish soldiers and settlers arrived, nor that these Indians would be dispossessed by the incoming cattle ranchers who kept their families in Mexican towns south of the Rio Grande, except to signal the continuing danger of Indian assaults. The pioneer's son, Don José Alejandro, would inherit the ranches north of the river and move his family there, establishing what became El Olivareño.

It is Don José Alejandro's son, Cesáreo, already the third generation on these Rio Grande valley lands, who hears in the 1820s that Americanos have been granted permission by Mexico to settle in Texas. In 1836, he hears of what occurred at the Alamo, and though sorry about the deaths, voices the opinion that the Americanos should not usurp Mexican land. Besides, Cesáreo argues, these new colonists were heretics, enemies of Spain and, ergo, enemies of the Olivares. When an Americano threatens to take possession of his land and Don Cesáreo protests, the Americano shoots and kills Cesáreo's foreman. There begins what the novel terms outright "the struggle for possession of the land the Mexicans owned and the Americans coveted."[133] The conquered, the Tejanos/as of El Valle, would be on the losing end of that struggle. The novel makes the tension and friction between the two groups abundantly clear, much more intensely than in *Caballero*.

Additional murders by Americanos force Don Cesáreo and his wife, Doña Ramona, to abandon "the land won by the sweat and blood of his ancestors," crossing the Rio Grande to live on the Mexican side.[134] The narrator remarks that the thought of losing the heritage of his ancestors crushed his proud spirit, and he dies a brokenhearted man. Doña Ramona looks after his land in Mexico and teaches their three children to hate Americanos, their enemies who had despoiled them and others of their land and killed members of their family. If they were to meet these enemies later in life, she says, their job would be to kill them without mercy, just as the killers had shown no mercy to their uncle and father.

Dew on the Thorn begins with a brief account of the atrocities committed against Tejanos/as, recounting the rise of some, like Cortina, who dared to respond in kind. According to the novel's editor, José E. Limón, González edited out several passages, likely deemed too critical of Americanos.[135] One such omitted passage refers to Juan Nepomuceno Cortina, whose rebellion against Texas's invaders, especially Rangers and sheriffs, is also mentioned, albeit negatively, in *Caballero*, with one Cheno Cortina joining up with the rebels, who are described as thieves. In *Dew on the Thorn*, on the other hand, it is noted that Cortina became a Robin Hood of the border who fought to right the wrongs committed against Tejano-Mexicanos. The fact that this information has been circumscribed or "bracketed" is most revealing, as if the mention of armed resistance and "the hated Americans" were taboo in Anglo-dominated Texas.[136]

While there is no Red McLane, the good gringo of *Caballero*, in *Dew on the Thorn*, there is an ex-Confederate soldier who, after his side loses the war, shares the Tejanos/as' sense of injustice. John Warren Preston will marry a cousin of Doña Ramona and show that not all Americanos are "cruel, heartless, avaricious men"; he will help the Olivares family and other Tejanos/as reclaim some of their Texas lands.[137] Again, the US legal system is presented as able and willing to aid the dispossessed although historically that was not the case. The return of wealthy Texas-Mexican families to the US side ensures, the novel argues, that their culture will again dominate South Texas. The loss for the older Olivares generation is absolute, as the widowed Doña Ramona never returns to Texas, but her children prosper there. Demographics and lineage are underscored; class and culture are upheld as defining.

The narrative goes on to note, "Interracial peace returned. In towns, Americans, Germans, and French migrants intermarried with the descendants of the old Mexican families, and Spanish became again the language of society."[138] Despite the novel's asseverations, interracial peace did not return toward the end of the nineteenth century. Paredes's *George Washington Gómez*, for example, provides ample evidence that widespread racial violence and discrimination continued. González, writing at approximately the same time as Paredes, knows well how things turned out, but she prefers to make it seem as if harmony reigned in South Texas, that is, until the last few pages of her novel. In 1904, the time of *Dew on the Thorn*, descendants of the Olivares family are still in South Texas and have retained their lands. The Olivares family is much like the Mendozas, but with fewer high aristocratic airs and less wealth than mark the family in *Caballero*. In the first decade of the twentieth century, South Texas is still very Mexican. Don Francisco Olivares's ranch was "one of the richest estates on the lower Rio Grande," and he, a man of wealth, of Spanish descent, and a cultured gentleman, was fit to interact with well-to-do Americanos. Upper-class standing is again seen to bond individuals.[139]

It is interesting to note that more explicit and concrete historical information is presented in the shorter *Dew on the Thorn* than in *Caballero*. For example, not only is the Escandón expedition described in the earlier work, but so is the semifeudal ranchero system. Don Francisco, a criollo, is described as "a feudal lord," "accustomed to command," "master of everything, not only of the land he possessed but of the *peones* who worked the soil."[140] The life of his indentured servants and peons was one of submission and generational bondage. In this way the novel acknowledges historical debt peonage when it explains that because the remuneration was small, "they were always in debt to Don Francisco and this formed a debt which the *peones* could never hope to pay."[141]

While pointing out the abusive treatment of the peons, the novel's narrator nonetheless goes to great pains to be both critical and understanding, trying to explain away what is obviously condemnable. The narrator is thus quick to point out that Don Francisco was not "cruel or unjust."[142] As in *Caballero*, the ranchero in *Dew on the Thorn* merely followed the customs of an inherited system, as if the custom of abuse justified it, suggesting that neither the master nor the peon knew better—a rather naive or disingenuous notion that clearly sets out to justify the exploitation and subjugation of the peons, many of them Indigenous and mestizos. Telling, too, is the fact that González's novel engages in an act of discursive violence when it marshals the trope of "foreign" against the peons and further others them by identifying them as "immigrants" from Mexico, although they had been with the Olivares family for generations, since well before 1848.[143] The positioning and contradiction are even clearer with the landed Tejanos/as claiming autochthonous, Indigenous, native status in the region when in fact their ancestors had migrated from south of the Rio Grande as well.

There are, however, brief nods to characters who offer a more progressive perspective in *Dew on the Thorn*, like the teacher, Don Alberto, educated in Mexico, who runs a school for boys and is willing to educate not only the sons of the rancheros but those of the peons. The novel in this way points to the coexistence of multiple temporalities: semifeudal and capitalist, conservative and modernizing. The narrative is critical of the class structure in South Texas, although stratification is seen as inherited and therefore natural and normal. It will be Don Alberto who teaches the boys about "the robbery of Texas by the insidious cupidity and avarice of the Colossus of the North."[144] Here Martí's notion of the imperialist "Coloso del Norte" is evident, as is Mexico's resentment over the loss of half its northern territory.

Dew on the Thorn likewise addresses economic changes taking place with the introduction of commercial farming in the early twentieth century. In the process, it distinguishes between two types of Anglos: those earlier arrivals like Preston, who came to the valley and assimilated into Tejano/a culture, and the newcomers who are bent on taking over the lands of the remaining Tejano/a landowners, dispossessing them anew. Whatever happens, this time the Olivares family will not leave, as Don Francisco's wife, Doña Margarita, notes: "This land is ours. It was blessed by the blood of the fathers who made it a Christian land. . . . The Americanos may come. They may take the land, but our spirit, the spirit of the conquerors, will live forever. Texas is ours. We stay."[145] What is enshrined by saying, "Texas is ours," is the memory of having conquered a land occupied by Indigenous peoples who were decimated and subjugated to work their lands; it is this that makes them proud. There is no critique of this foundational dispossession in either novel, but instead a culturalist, almost nationalist, identification with the land not as real estate, not as an alienable, saleable commodity, but as spirit, as immaterial *geist*.

Both of González's novels on dispossession are told from the perspective of the constructed historical subject, the landed, the elite. Later narratives, like those of Tomás Rivera, provide different approaches to land loss and migration in mid-twentieth-century texts that construct the perspective of other subjects and historical actors: the producers, the farm laborers, workers for whom the land is a place or site constructed through their labor, not an idealized harkening back to a world and time past.[146]

Writing Wrongs:
Emma Peréz's *Forgetting the Alamo, or, Blood Memory: A Novel*

While the dispossession of Tejano/a land in Texas has been the subject of a number of histories and the backdrop of several novels, Tejano/a and Chicano/a literature is also characterized by a glaring absence of any mention of dispossessed Indigenous peoples. In effect, these works buy into and share in the hegemonic—both Spanish and Anglo—revisionist historical erasure of the Native American presence and history on the land where colonists serially and unrelentingly arrived. When mentioned in Chicano/a literature, Indians are generally the Aztec population and its culture, but the northern tribes of what became southwestern Texas are seldom recalled, other than being portrayed as threats for their attacks on settlements. Even in Chicano/a fiction dealing with nineteenth-century Texas, Indigenous peoples are seldom mentioned.

Emma Pérez's 2009 *Forgetting the Alamo, or, Blood Memory: A Novel* is, however, the notable exception to the norm. The novel is narrated by the main character, Micaela Campos, who in 1836 travels across South and southeastern Texas dressed as a man. Pérez's novel provides a geographical adventure that unites episodic and linear historical events. Cross-dressing is a strategy that allows an eighteen-year-old woman to move around Texas, visiting saloons, stables and blacksmiths, farm labor sites, gambling halls, brothels, and Indian encampments, while riding her horse in open country seeking the marauders who raped and beat her mother, raped and killed her young sister, and murdered her young brother. Her disguise does not deceive those who are observant—especially women—but others seem to be easily fooled. Along the way, Micaela takes note of the dead bodies in the San Antonio streets after the siege of the Alamo, and later more bodies, including that of her father, after the battle of San Jacinto; she meets slaves, sees the brutal massacre and scalping of Apaches and Comanches, and the raping of Indian women, and describes the racism and lynching of Mexicans, all against the backdrop of the ongoing major land grab that dispossesses Tejanos/as. In the late 1830s, "Texas is a hellhole," as succinctly noted by the Black slave Lucius.[147]

Unlike González's main characters, who all stand out for being criollos, white, blue-eyed, and wealthy, the characters in Pérez's novel are mestizos, of Spanish or French or Anglo and local Indian blood. Micaela's mother's ancestry was Tonkawa and her father's was Comanche, and Micaela falls in love with a woman whose mother was Karankawa, a coastal tribe. At one point she rides into the encampment of Comanches called the Honey Eaters, where she meets Eagle Mother, who seems to have been expecting her and who tells her that "blood preserves memory," hence the novel's title.[148] In the narrative, history is in the blood; it is ingrained ethnic history, but it can be erased and replaced by hegemonic histories, reminding us that Texas continued to be Indian country into the mid-nineteenth century. Pérez's novel is a rejoinder, a corrective to dominant history on Texas; it is primarily a history of settlement and displacement, but it is also a history of massacres, butchery, and genocide, a history of wholesale dispossession along with and tied to a history of sexism and male dominance. Importantly in Pérez's work, Indigenous peoples are not evacuated from Texas history.

In 1836, Micaela's family is land rich, holding 49,000 acres, but financially strapped. Once the father is killed at the site of the San Jacinto battle, the land is worked by a supposed friend of his, who in fact murdered him and who is the father of Micaela's cousin Jedidiah, killed by the same men that raped

Micaela's mother and sister. Later she is accused of murdering Jedidiah by the evil colonel, who massacred Indians and who as judge controls the legal system in San Antonio. He tries Micaela in a kangaroo court and condemns her to be hanged, after which he takes over Micaela's property, saying it's the court that seizes the land. Says the colonel: "I got all the rights from here on out, missy. I am the law. Get used to it or get yourself on back to Mexico. If you don't like it."[149] Micaela's lover and her mother work out a jailbreak prior to execution so that she can escape to Mexico, where she hides out in a convent.

While the novel stresses the sensationalist aspects of the story of a lesbian dressed as a man riding through Texas avenging wrongs, at the same time it provides snapshots of the area's tensions and conflicts in the face of conquest and dispossession, first of Indigenous peoples and later of Tejano/a landowners, as spatial violence played out sequentially in the US Southwest. Spanish/Mexican settlers would be displaced by Anglo settlers in a new form of settler colonialism. Unlike González's novels, Pérez's does not construct the law as favorable to the rancheros' cause. Here the judge's abuse of the law to his personal advantage and the foreignizing of Tejanos/as by threatening to repatriate them back to Mexico constructs both the dispossession and oppression faced by Tejanos/as in post-1836 Texas but is eerily contemporary to the twenty-first-century reader.

Reimagining the Alamo: Rebuttals

The Alamo is iconic in Texas culture, with much written and filmed about the 1836 event, commercializing the myth in most cases with little faithfulness to fact or analysis of what actually took place. What is incontrovertible is that the rallying cry "Remember the Alamo!" was deployed (and continues to signal) Anglo privilege and righteousness against Mexican aggression, with an eye to validating Anglo dispossession of Tejanos/as. In the work of Pérez, González, Taibo, and Flores, we find a variety of counterreadings of the Alamo myth.

Given the title of the novel *Forgetting the Alamo*, one would expect events at the Alamo perhaps to figure more centrally, but the battle at the Alamo and the mythification of what occurred there are not taken up in detail, except to mention the cadavers that remained on the street, among them that of Micaela's uncle, Tío Lorenzo, found dead outside the walls. One of the characters, Miss Elsie, demythifies the so-called heroes, calling Bowie a drunk, and others abusers of women: "Them boys ain't heroes. They ain't no better than a buncha drunks who come here whoring, expecting me to open my doors when they want."[150] It is the novel's point to stress that the Alamo is not the iconic site of loss of life of Anglo Texan pioneers that ought not to be forgotten, a foundational moment of the Texas Republic, but rather the locus of what took place in all of Texas, where the victims are Tejanos/as, not Texans.

The debunking of the Alamo myth is taken up, ironically, not as much in Chicano/a literature (with the exception of the Pérez novel) as in Paco Ignacio Taibo II's work on the Alamo. In *El Álamo: Una historia no apta para Hollywood*, the Mexican writer sets out to explore facts of this event that are rarely discussed and to debunk, like Miss Elsie, many of the myths about the supposed Anglo heroes of the Alamo.[151] He notes in the first place that the defenders of the Alamo were for the most part not Texans or Tejanos/as.[152] They were newly arrived *filibusteros*, immigrants from the United States. The few survivors included slaves, children, and a few women, all of whom gave various versions of what they had seen or failed to see.[153]

Taibo sets out to de-romanticize the protagonists of the Alamo and lay out events that have been distorted as well. In his brief discussion of the aftermath of the battles for Texas independence, Taibo writes that the Mexicanos, both those who supported the uprising and those who opposed it, would ultimately largely lose their lands through fraud, false transfers of land titles, and litigation that went on for years. Taibo notes the contradictory attitude taken by Chicanos/as today regarding the Alamo; some want to identify with the defenders of the Alamo and to make clear that Tejanos/as, too, fought for and liberated Texas; others reject the heroic-racist imperialist version of what occurred at the Alamo.[154] Taibo is on target that some Chicanos/as identify with the defenders of the Alamo, as is evident, for example, in the movie *Seguín*, where the Chicano filmmaker tries to pass the Tejanos/as off as "red-blooded Americans," as if to say, "See how patriotic we are."[155]

Aside from those historians already mentioned, the range of current scholarship on the Alamo speaks to the continuing—and contentious—discursive power of the site. The titles are telling: *Remembering the Alamo . . . Forgetting the Alamo . . . Beyond the Alamo*. One such recent work from a Chicano perspective is *Beyond the Alamo*, by Raúl Ramos, who notes that a number of Tejanos/as left Béjar before Santa Anna's arrival for reasons of family survival and not because they were against the Texan rebellion.[156] Another work is *Remembering the Alamo: Memory, Modernity, and the Master Symbol*, by Richard R. Flores. His analysis is grounded on the notion of the Alamo as a "master symbol of modernity" that has affected identity formation.[157] For Flores, the Alamo "serves as a critical map for the exploitation and displacement of Mexicans, legitimized by the Texas Modern."[158] In any case, Tejano/a actions defy clear categorization as sympathizers of Anglo-Texans or Mexican troops. In San Antonio where the Alamo is hallowed ground for tourists, a shrine to the heroes of Texas independence, the Alamo story has been foundational for one Tejana who worked to enshrine the site: Adina de Zavala, whose efforts are documented in *History and Legends of the Alamo and Other Missions in and around San Antonio*.[159] In the early twentieth century, the granddaughter of Lorenzo de Zavala, the previously discussed Mexican political turncoat who favored the independence of Texas from Mexico, dedicated herself to preserving the Alamo as a historical museum, despite a number of obstacles detailed by the editor of her history, Flores. Montejano, too, notes that in Texas history, the Alamo in particular was a prevalent rationale for anti-Mexican discrimination and racist practices; as late as the 1940s, Anglo Texans described Mexicans as murderous individuals who had killed their kin at the Alamo and still threatened to cross the border at any time and invade Texas.[160] Racist notions of Mexicanos as bloodthirsty, ostensibly given their Indigenous ancestry, are not peculiar to Texas, as the same words were used to justify violence against Chicano zoot-suiters in the 1940s in Los Angeles; threats of invasion from the south still hold currency today as well, as President Trump also proclaims.

Attempts on the part of some Chicanos/as or Tejanos/as to connect with the mythic, hegemonic, heroic events of the Alamo to validate their claims and even presence in the United States speaks volumes to the effects of ideology, discrimination, and exclusion of many years; this "we too" emphasis is understandable, if lamentable. What is, however, clear is that the racism and dispossession of the Tejanos/as in Texas did not require the memory of the Alamo to promote or justify it. The accumulation of land capital was the overriding impetus for dispossession; racial animus was its handmaiden; discourses emerged to justify both; one type of violence relies and feeds on the other.

The US Civil War and Its Aftermath

During the US Civil War, Tejanos/as' internal class divisions came to the forefront as the landed elite, not surprisingly perhaps, identified politically with the Confederacy. As noted by Gómez-Quiñones, some of the Tejano/a landlords had become slaveholders, like the Benavides family before the war, and some even supported the Ku Klux Klan during the war, another aspect of Texas history that is not generally recalled in Chicano/a literature.[161] Other Tejanos/

as, like Cortina, would support the Union. In his memoir *A Life Crossing Borders*, Santiago Tafolla, a New Mexican man who lived in Texas during the Civil War, recalls that he joined the Confederacy after serving in the US Army.[162] In California too, Californios like Antonio Coronel in Los Angeles would support the Confederacy, although in the north, Californios like the Vallejo family supported the Union. Valerio-Jiménez notes that some 2,550 Tejanos/as were conscripted into the Confederate army and fewer, only 960, joined Union troops; the fact that the former was involuntary no doubt goes far in explaining the differential in numbers, making the 960 Tejanos/as who—despite Texas belonging to the Confederacy—joined Union forces all the more striking.[163] In this context it bears remembering that Mexico had outlawed slavery long before the United States did.

The period after 1865 would bring both more economic integration and "increasing social and political discrimination" to Texas.[164] As previously noted, by the end of the nineteenth century and the early twentieth century, the commercialization of agriculture, especially the booming cotton industry, would drive more and more Mexicans to migrate to different parts of Texas where previously the Mexican population had been small or nonexistent. While in East Texas, Blacks worked the cotton fields, in South and West Texas the *piscadores*, the field hands, would be Tejano/Mexicano, following the crop circuit north to Kansas, Missouri, Iowa, and other states. Thousands of Mexicans from south of the border came to work in the cotton fields, especially during the 1910–20 Mexican Revolution, as described in *Under the Texas Sun* by Conrado Espinoza, a 1926 novel about Mexican immigrants who pick cotton in Texas under harsh conditions. Espinoza focuses on the sense of helplessness that overtakes the family. Nor is the much heralded American Dream attained by the three other immigrants who ride in the same truck with them, a father and his two sons; they, too, struggle to make enough to return to their family in Michoacán as they work on the railroad, where one of the sons will be killed by a train. Undeniably didactic in intent, a tale to warn would-be immigrants about coming to Texas, *Under the Texas Sun*, like Daniel Venegas's 1928 *Las aventuras de Don Chipote*, situates these immigrants as an important part of the labor force in Texas in the period of early twentieth-century commercialization of agriculture and the emerging oil industry. It is a caveat registering their exploitation and dehumanization.

In addition to this increasing working-class population, especially of fieldworkers, and especially in the lower Rio Grande valley area, there was however a growing Tejano/a middle class made up of small-scale retail merchants, agriculturalists, ranchers, professionals, and semiprofessionals, including journalists and intellectuals, especially among more recent émigrés from Mexico, who sought to assimilate into the dominant Anglo population.[165] Then, as now, the Tejano/a population has never been monolithic or of one mind, as their allegiances then and now bear out.

Brito's *El Diablo en Texas*: Multiple Temporalities in South Texas

This story of Anglo encroachment on Tejano/a land continues beyond South Texas in the early twentieth century, as recalled in *El Diablo en Texas*, by Aristeo Brito. Brito's novel is unique in that it deals not with the lower Rio Grande valley but with the Southwest story of Presidio, Texas, around three distinct dates: 1883, 1942, and 1970. The innovative fragmented structure includes a variety of dialogues, including those of ghosts that still roam the area, the monologue of the devil, identified with the oppressive and exploitative land baron Ben Lynch, and the dialogues of living Tejanos/as who continue to work the land they no longer own. The novel lays out the landownership system between 1846 and 1904. There are the rancheros who own the land, the vaqueros and peons who work the land, and the Anglo invaders who appropriate the land, dispossessing the Tejanos/as.

Presidio is a border town on the upper Rio Grande in southwest Texas, across from Ojinaga, Chihuahua, mentioned already by Cabeza de Vaca in 1535 as the place where three rivers meet. Indian and mestizo towns had long been established on both sides of the river, and after 1848 the area attracted Anglo ranchers and scalp hunters, among them Ben Leaton, who appears in the novel as Ben Lynch. In Brito's novel, the former Ranger Lynch dispossesses the Tejanos/as of Presidio through fraud, bribes, and force and reduces them to wage laborers, some of whom, instead of being paid by Lynch, are killed in a massacre of protesting workers. Aptly named, Lynch controls the town and gets away with murders—plural. Theft and murder are shown to be foundational in Presidio. The fictional killings in the novel occur a few years before the historical 1918 massacre in the village of Porvenir in Presidio County by Texas Rangers, army cavalry, and local vigilantes, but register in fiction the ongoing violence against ethnic Mexicans in Texas throughout the nineteenth and twentieth centuries.

In the subsequent two temporalities of Brito's novel, things do not improve in Presidio. By 1942 former Tejano/a landowners are now tenant farmers growing cotton, like José, and the workers are undocumented migrants from

Ojinaga, always hiding from the Migra, which comes around and kills those it can find. In the last section of *El Diablo en Texas*, set in 1970, José's child has grown up and left Presidio, unable to stand seeing his father José consumed by resentment, forever hating those who deprived him and his family of their land and livelihood. The three periods of Presidio history are superimposed, as it were, and shown to coexist in the palimpsest of the narratives; the temporalities of dispossession and exploitation intersect with more recent temporalities within the modern capitalist order. Whether in 1843, 1943, or 1970, Presidio suffers similar land dispossession issues and spatial violence that mark Tejano/a inhabitants of South Texas.

The painful passage from an older semifeudal rural order to modern and increasingly urban capitalism—with remnants of previous temporalities still present—is taken up by these various writers: while González looks back and focuses on the end of an era, Paredes's novel centers its lens on the end of one and the beginning of another. In Hinojosa's works, the *Klail City Death Trip Series*, on the other hand, we move from social and economic relations in earlier phases of emergent capitalism to those of late capitalism in all their hybridity and contradiction, as we shall see.

Different Takes on Dispossession:
Paredes, Hinojosa, Cisneros, and the Long Twentieth Century

The importance of space and place and spatial violence continues in the literature dealing with twentieth-century Texas. While literature set in nineteenth-century Texas deals pointedly and poignantly with the violent dispossession of the Tejanos/as' lands, assisted by force and threats that led many to sell and others to flee and abandon their lands, literature focusing on twentieth-century South Texas presents this dispossession as a fait accompli. It deals with the aftermath of this dispossession in a new moment characterized by a new farm order, increased migration of Anglos and immigration of Mexicanos to Texas, a new division of classes, and the creation of new power structures.

Discrimination and unfair treatment before and under (and outside) the law would continue during the twentieth century. With the increased number of Mexican immigrants coming to the Southwest during the period of the Mexican Revolution of 1910–20 also came the dehumanizing and humiliating abuses at the border for those wanting to cross, as recounted, for example, in *Las aventuras de Don Chipote*. In Texas, as elsewhere in the United States, the Depression would bring repatriation of Mexicans in the 1930s. Lynchings,

Ranger aggression, police brutality, deportations, segregation, violence, and racism, and "No Mexicans or Dogs Allowed" signs (still in evidence in Texas in the late 1950s and 1960s) led some early twentieth-century authors to write to reconstruct a past that spoke of the Spanish/Mexican's population's right to Texas by reason of first occupation. As noted earlier, the fact that they had taken the land from Indians by force seldom came into play in these writings bent on affirming place and belonging. The works of Paredes and Hinojosa are interventions of a different sort. They foreground matters not previously expressed in narratives and present a view of life in South Texas from the inside even while still pointing to a process of increased integration of the Tejano/a community into larger national US society. While this integration is nowhere near harmonious and in some cases never occurs, there is a certain resentful resignation to Anglo hegemony on the part of the Tejanos/as, particularly after losing the Plan de San Diego sedicioso struggle.

Paredes's Conflicted George Guálinto Gómez

The narratives' standpoints vary widely, however. In González, as we have seen, it is not the laboring working-class experience that is central but rather the elite ranchero experience. In Paredes, on the other hand, the land has been lost, and now the dispossessed seek work in a variety of low-wage occupations; their condition, especially during the Depression, will be one of near destitution. But while Paredes's García-Gómez family suffers racism and segregation, as do other Tejano/a families in Jonesville, there is limited social mobility. The conflicted identity formation of the son, Guálinto, is key. Hinojosa's narrative perspective is different. There is pride in family history among some characters, for whom identity is not in question; knowing full well who they are, they see their land, their valley, under transformation.

Paredes's novel *George Washington Gómez* begins with the early twentieth century. Like González's novels, this realist novel begins with an acknowledgment of land dispossession but quickly shifts to focus on the situation of a now landless, poor Mexican family; through its trials and tribulations, we gain insight not into how Anglo invasion affected the elite class but rather into what it meant for the dispossessed and proletarianized, that is, for those who became laborers, especially farm laborers. The dispossessed family—consisting of Feliciano García, his elderly mother, his younger sister Maria, her husband Gumersindo Gómez, and their three children—lives in a one-room shack, with no doors or windows, in San Benito, Texas, near the Rio Grande.

Land in this Paredes novel, written in the 1940s but published much later in 1990, represents the lower Rio Grande territory and a Tejano/a community now cash and land poor. The land issue becomes not only economic and political but cultural as well. Mexican immigration to the United States during the Mexican Revolution would increase the population of Mexican origin and strengthened the sense of being part of "Greater Mexico."[166] Mexican immigrants per se, however, do not figure much in this novel. The characters are native Tejanos/as, some fourth-generation Tejanos/as, like Feliciano, who can trace his family roots to a great-grandfather: "I was born here and so was my grandfather and his father before him."[167] Feliciano's landowning ancestors were dispossessed of their land by the King Ranch. As he puts it, the Anglos came and took it, stole it and called it theirs. For the novel's characters, the land's rightful people are the Tejanos/as, with or without the papers to back their claims. Here, too, the revisionist historical blind spots regarding Native Americans as the original occupants of American lands are in evidence.

Still, it is because of the sense of connection and entitlement regarding the land that the characters involved with the sediciosos and the Plan de San Diego are ready to fight to reclaim the land for the Tejano/a collectivity, their homeland in South Texas. As Feliciano says, "They tell you, these Gringos. 'If you don't like it here, don't want to be American, get out. Go back to your own country.' Get out? Why? Let *them* get out, they came here last. And go where? *This* is our country. *This* is our home. They made it Gringo land by force, we cannot change that. But no force of theirs can make us, the land's rightful people, Gringo people."[168] Unfortunately, the novel shows that the forces at work prove otherwise; they are in fact capable not only of dispossessing Tejanos/as of their land but of making a Tejano become *agringado* and a betrayer of his own.

Paredes's novel *George Washington Gómez* is a bildungsroman that uses a young boy, Guálinto, as a vehicle for exploring relations between races and classes in the lower Rio Grande valley in the early twentieth century. In a bildungsroman, a young man is "an instrument for exploring new possibilities of bourgeois society."[169] And while Guálinto, the "Washington" of the novel's title, does not initially deal with a bourgeois social order, he is faced with the onslaught of modernization, the new capitalist farm order, and Anglo dominant culture. In this type of novel, the young man, following Jameson, is a kind of gauge or registering device, and Paredes offers us a laboratory situation in which numerous possibilities and avatars are acted out before our eyes. The laboratory here is Jonesville (Brownsville), a border town across from Morelos (Matamoros); Guálinto, notably, is never shown to cross the border, but his uncle Feliciano does, often. The border Guálinto does traverse is the one that takes him from his barrio to school, from a Mexican culture to what the novel calls "Americanization." The early twentieth century is narrated in terms of the relationships, the solidarities within the community, the discrimination faced by Tejanos/as, and especially the education of Guálinto, his childhood fantasies, and the emergence, especially during his adolescent years, of ethnic and class shame and resentment.

Understandably, since the novel is narrated from a standpoint that looks back on the past, it posits no possible different outcome. The Tejano/a territory had been irretrievably lost to the United States in the war, even though for a while some of the landowners survived and retained their lands, but now they, too, have lost the land. This new order is resisted by a group of *secesionistas*, but this struggle, too, will fail, while the larger Tejano-Mexicano collectivity continues as an oppressed population that experiences discrimination. Paredes begins the novel with the atrocities committed by the rinches against the Tejano-Mexicanos, but the violent tactics of the seditionists are also critiqued. A few pages later, with the failure of the secesionistas' Plan de San Diego and the leaders' flight to Mexico to join the Mexican Revolution there, the novel moves to focus on the everyday life of Guálinto and the Gómez-García family.

The 1915 Plan de San Diego in *George Washington Gómez*

The early twentieth century is a period of "pervasive and brutal segregation," with the Tejanos/as marked by both race and class. Montejano writes that while "a segment of the Mexican elite still held on to the land," there was a certain "accommodative 'peace structure' with the Anglo political and commercial elite," that is, "until the ranch order was confronted with a 'newcomer' farm society at the turn of the century."[170] This conflict and the resultant uprising took place in 1915 and would be in part configured in Paredes's novel.

In Texas, armed responses to injustice were not uncommon in the late nineteenth century and in a way, as previously noted, served as precedents for what came to be known as the Plan de San Diego.[171] Paredes's novel offers historical documentation that the community of Mexican descent in the United States was not all marked by conservatism or complacency, as portrayed by some.[172] This secessionist uprising would turn "the Valley into a virtual war zone during 1915–1917."[173] Of course some Tejanos/as fought against the sediciosos, like attorneys and political bosses and, as expected, *kineños* (as workers on the King Ranch were known) stayed loyal to the ranch.[174] In Paredes's novel, the well-to-do, like Osuna, join the white capitalists and distinguish themselves by identifying as "Spanish" as they join in the repression of the sediciosos. The uprising of the seditionists was brutally suppressed by the Texas Rangers, and in the process hundreds were killed, thousands dislocated, and property "worth millions of dollars was destroyed."[175] The sediciosos' armed struggle was eventually put down, but, as Graham states, it left in its wake "a legacy of racial mistrust and hatred that would be slow to die along the border."[176]

Anglo ranchers and farmers divided the Texas Mexicans into good and bad Mexicans, submissive and uppity. In Paredes's novel, the character Gumersindo is described by the Anglo doctor as a "good" Mexican, but despite being fair skinned and red haired, he will nevertheless be shot dead by the Rangers for being related to the sedicioso leader, Lupe García. The murder of Gumersindo by rinches seeking to discover his brother-in-law's whereabouts will leave the family with no means of support. The uncle, Feliciano, is forced to set aside his political leanings in favor of the sediciosos to ensure the family's survival; he will move his widowed sister and children to Jonesville to get them away from Ranger danger. Faced with Ranger threats on the road, he is saved by another Anglo, Judge Norris, who happens by at that moment; Feliciano is offered a job by Norris in a saloon as well as a part-time political job as a ward worker, hired to get out "the Mexican vote" on election day. This shift from rural to urban work will allow Feliciano to buy a two-room house, a former saloon, from Judge Norris. As the narrative progresses, Feliciano is first a worker at the saloon, then a storekeeper; later he becomes a tenant farmer and finally a small landowner again, farming his own land.

Guálinto's Education

Feliciano García represents the first postinvasion generation of Tejanos/as dispossessed of the land, but his nephew, George Washington Gómez, called Guálinto, represents an assimilated generation dispossessed not of land but increasingly of its culture and identity. The loss of this identity is shown to be a product of his education and his buying into the individualist mindset over the collective. The outlook for Guálinto, born in 1914, is not good if he stays a Mexican: "Born a foreigner in his native land, he [Guálinto] was fated to a life controlled by others."[177] His father and mother, however, have great expectations for Guálinto: he is to "grow up to be a great man who will help his people."[178]

These expectations and Feliciano's promise to fulfill his dead brother-in-law's dream become an onerous weight as he gives up his own life to meet the needs of his sister María's family. Ultimately his nephew Guálinto will reject this calling to come to the aid of his family and be a "leader of his people."

Dispossession does not necessarily imply displacement or relocation from the region; the characters continue to reside in South Texas, now in an urban setting, Jonesville (Brownsville), a small town on the border. Here education is difficult for Tejano/a children who enter a racist school system that divides students by ethnicity into high and low tracks. The novel posits that education interpellates students to assimilate while the family influences them to remain Tejano/a. Feliciano brings Guálinto up to be conscious of his Tejano past, even though he is unaware of the full extent of the Ranger violence or how exactly his father died until his senior year in high school. In the end, the revelation that his father died at the Rangers' hands will prove meaningless to Guálinto, who in fact marries the daughter of a Ranger.

Conscious as a child of being Tejano, as he grows up, education begins to fracture that consciousness. His assimilation is slow because, as the novel notes, he was not an immigrant "come to a foreign land. Like other Mexico-Texans he considered himself part of the land on which his ancestors had lived before the Anglotexans had come."[179] Assigned to an Anglo teacher's classroom, "he began to acquire an Angloamerican self and as the years passed, under Miss Huff and other teachers like her, he developed simultaneously in two widely divergent paths."[180] The idea of a developed double consciousness in the lower Rio Grande valley (where more than 90 percent of the population is of Mexican origin) is perhaps unlikely but, in any event, quite Du Boisian. Later, Guálinto becomes aware not only of the two antagonistic selves within him but of multiple identities. This notion of a split, conflicted subject and multiple subjectivities is quite modern and even postmodernist, and it is possible that Paredes revised his novel before its 1990 publication: "It would be several years before he fully realized that there was not one single Guálinto Gómez. That in fact there were many Guálinto Gómezes, each of them double, like the images reflected on two glass surfaces of a show window. The eternal conflict between two clashing forces within him produced a divided personality, made up of tight little cells independent and almost entirely ignorant of each other, spread out all over his consciousness, mixed with one another like squares on a checkerboard."[181]

Enclosure of Tejano/a land thus leads not only to dispossession but to fragmentation of subjectivity. In this novel of social mobility and assimilation, the

"Anglo American self" will win out, in part, perhaps, because Guálinto is fair skinned, with light brown hair, and finds it easy to blend in. The novel presents Guálinto's assimilation and accommodation to the system, not in positive terms, but as a failure of sorts. Already in school Guálinto "secretly desired to be a full-fledged, complete American without the shameful encumberment of his Mexican race."[182] He is conflicted in many ways: ashamed to be a Mexican and yet, at the same time, ashamed to think that his uncle Feliciano was a coward and hadn't been a seditionist; ashamed that his class status works against him when he falls for the pretty María Elena, daughter of the well-to-do Tejano Osuna; and disgusted when his sister runs after an Anglo boy, Bobby Goodman.

The US Depression in the 1930s causes Judge Norris's bank to go bankrupt. The bankruptcy will lead in turn to Feliciano's loss of money in the bank, the store he rents, equipment, and unsold goods. Fortunately for Feliciano, he had not put all his money in the gringo bank, and he is able to use his cash to buy the eighty acres he has been leasing because the owner is now pressed for cash. He then buys eighty acres more. In what is an ironic turn, the Depression allows Feliciano to restore to himself part of the land his ancestors had lost to the gringos.

That, within this majority-Tejano/a Rio Grande valley, space is divided along racial and class lines is never clearer than during the US Depression. A new type of enclosure becomes evident as Tejanos/as realize they are dispossessed of all sorts of social entitlements available to Anglo citizens. The novel's description of life in South Texas during the Depression focuses on the breadlines, unemployment, and the government's racialized practices, and here the novel is explicit in its critique. When emergency relief agencies are set up, like the Reconstruction Finance Corporation, Tejanos/as find themselves cut out: "The Mexicotexan has a conveniently dual personality. When he is called upon to do his duty for his country he is an American. When benefits are passed around he is a Mexican and always last in line."[183] When it comes to employment, Mexicans are considered only for manual labor. Those with schooling are seen by employment agencies as presumptuous: "Then they start thinking they're as good as white people."[184] Ethnicity and class come together, and Paredes lays bare the ongoing discursive violence—what whites think of "Mess'cans"—years after the Rangers are no longer meting out physical violence. Interesting, too, is that Paredes does not mention continued Mexican immigration or government repatriation, even of US citizens. The main characters are Tejano/a natives of South Texas.

Years later, Guálinto, now George G. Gómez, an intelligence officer in the army with a law degree and totally alienated from "his people," will be more than willing to spy on Tejano-Mexicanos on the border and on his former childhood friends who are trying to organize politically to elect a Tejano/a to public office. George also has no problem with the creation of jobs in Jonesville only for whites. If digging ditches is all Mexicans can do, then so be it, he says. He thinks his politicized friends are fools, but Elodia, a former classmate, sees him for what he is: possibly an FBI spy, a sellout. Totally disillusioned, Elodia screams at him: "Cabrón. Vendido sanavabiche!"[185]

Guálinto, who was supposed to be the leader of his people—had he not been named George Washington Gómez in anticipation of all he would do for Mexicans in South Texas—sees his people as backward, decadent, and incapable of organizing, but capable of betraying the US government by being spies for Germany. In fact, Guálinto is disgusted with "his people" and sees no future for them. His uncle Feliciano, who had given up a chance for a life of his own to look after his sister's family and especially for Guálinto, is the one who is shortchanged. This bildungsroman examines how Guálinto becomes increasingly estranged from his community. To his mind, anyone who speaks out, like Elodia, could be dangerous. He no longer identifies as a Tejano. Jonesville is now "this filthy Delta," a place to get away from, as far away as one can get. In his mind, leaving the delta will enable his classmates to "get rid of their Mexican Greaser attitudes."[186] Guálinto has taken on the gringo way of thinking: "Mexicans will always be Mexicans."[187] Education is thus presented as a means of brainwashing Tejanos/as. Feliciano harbors little hope for Guálinto, and he finds it pathetic that he ever could have thought that Guálinto could be "the leader of his people."[188] For Feliciano, dispossession had entailed the loss of property but not of identity. For Guálinto, education would achieve that alienation, not of property but of identity, as he no longer identifies with the collectivity of Tejanos/as.

The novel is thus an allegory of the fragmentation of the Tejano-Mexicano collectivity, alienated from itself and willing to serve hegemonic interests. In contrast to the sellout—Guálinto—stands Feliciano, in fact the novel's central character. He has sacrificed much and has at least marginally integrated into the emerging farm order by acquiring his own land. He, too, is part of the system now but with a consciousness of his history and his identity as a Tejano-Mexicano. In *George Washington Gómez*, Paredes thus provides us with a regional narrative that traces dispossession, racism, and subordination in the lower Rio Grande valley. The political climate leads variously either to insurrection and political organizing or to assimilation and alienation from everything Mexican. In the novel through the bildungsroman narrative of Guálinto, assimilation begets accommodation and a rejection of the Tejanos/as who still see the valley as home despite no longer owning the land. This moment of transition in the Rio Grande valley is also the subject of Rolando Hinojosa's novels.

Time and Place: Hinojosa's *Klail City Death Trip Series*

Like some New Mexican Hispanos/as, as Montejano indicates, a limited number of Tejanos/as did manage to maintain their landholdings post-1848.[189] The story of those who were able to do so, at least in part, is told in Hinojosa's *Klail City Death Trip Series*.[190] In these novels, we find that four of the valley landowners, the Vilches, Campoy, Buenrostro, and Villalón families, are among those who were able to hold on to some of the lands granted to them in the eighteenth century.[191] The Klail City series also narrates the enmity among these Tejano/a families, divisions that contribute to their political weakness and aid in their dispossession. Valley residents, like Echevarría in his old age, despair over what they see: "The Valley is disappearing."[192] The valley is not the land but the consciousness of the land as culturally, linguistically, and demographically Tejano-Mexicano.

Land loss leads concomitantly to dissolution of home and community and the loss of cultural traditions, producing in its wake a sense of displacement, as old Echevarría notes, when by the 1960s he is one of the few remaining men of his generation to remember what happened in the valley in the past century. The loss is great; many have left and gone north, says Echevarría; his "sense of place" is gone, but those who stay on, like the young Jehú Malacara and Rafa Buenrostro, are busy constructing a new sense of place. What is however true is that if many left, hundreds of thousands more arrived, not only from the Midwest but especially from Mexico. Importantly, the main characters do not fully relate to them. Thus the land, whether alienated or not, continues to give rise to an imagined community and a distinct sense of place or regional identity. In Hinojosa's late twentieth-century narratives, there are no long descriptions of landscapes; the land is increasingly the socially constructed place wherein the people live. By contrast, Cabeza de Baca includes detailed descriptions of geographical features of the Staked Plains and mountains of New Mexico, physical markers that serve to construct the particular sense of place that she recalls. In all of these works, however, the perspective is that of natives of Texas, New Mexico, and California, whose ancestors inhabited the Southwest since the eighteenth century or before, not that of the newcomers (whether Anglos or Mexicans that came to the region at a later date).[193] In any event, land is central to Hinojosa's construction of a cultural regionalism in South Texas. El Valle, or the Valley, as the lower Rio Grande area in South Texas is known, was no lush valley; these are semiarid, desert-like plains. A magical transformation through irrigation and wells allowed this land to produce not only cotton but a range of fruits and vegetables on a commercial scale, repurposing it away from the grazing/cattle economy that had defined it previously. Still, it bears noting that wells and irrigation were already part of the Spanish/Mexican settlements and not first introduced by the Anglo immigrants, as is often suggested.

The erosion of Tejano/a landholding in South Texas after 1848 would be gradual, although a few, like the Buenrostro family in Hinojosa's *cronicón*, still own a good portion of the El Carmen Ranch in 1970. With its mid-twentieth-century setting, Hinojosa's fiction looks back to the Escandón settlers who first came to the Valley in the eighteenth century and of whom several of his characters are descendants. None of the Indians whose lands were taken appear in Hinojosa's chronicle of Belken County, although Echevarría mentions Indian raids (in *Claros varones* and in *The Valley*). Hinojosa does not specifically distinguish between different Tejano/a classes, but the social hierarchy is clear when the Buenrostros distribute some of the land to their workers. The focus falls on different generations of Tejano/a residents of Belken County; the central characters are the descendants of the pioneers: the Buenrostro, Villalón, Campoy, Garrido, Vilches, and Malacara families. Belken County is the fictitious name for the lower Rio Grande valley area that historically includes towns and cities like Brownsville, San Benito, Harlingen, McAllen, and others. Although there is no single county that includes all the towns pictured in the map included in *The Valley* novel, Belken could be said to include parts of four Texas counties: Cameron, Hidalgo, Willacy, and Starr, all near the Rio Grande. The central site is Klail City, modeled perhaps after Kingsville, but in the novel it is much closer to the border than Kingsville. All the Belken County towns are south of the Nueces River and thus part of the Nuevo Santander territory that later was part of the state of Tamaulipas. Texas proper, we need to recall, began north of the Nueces River. The Klail City series serves as an allegory of twentieth-century South Texas history.

Although early incoming Anglos initially settled north of the Nueces River, toward the end of the nineteenth century and the early twentieth century many began migrating south to the lower Rio Grande valley in search of farmland. Also arriving in the late nineteenth century were Mexicanos, like the Leguizamón family, which arrived around 1867 after residing south of the border since 1858; once in Texas they allied themselves with the Anglos and Rangers and "grabbed land," that is, they participated in dispossessing fellow Tejano-Mexicanos, making crooked deals and exploiting other Tejanos/as. Hinojosa presents them as claiming to be old pioneering Mexicans, later whitening themselves up and claiming to be Spanish, and afterward claiming to be good US patriots, not by joining the army but by making money and "shafting one's neighbor."[194] Hinojosa goes on to state that they accommodated to the prevailing winds and thrived.

Pinches Rinches and Other Affronts, or
"No tener dónde caerse muerto"

Like other Tejanos/as, the descendants of early settlers would also be subject to Ranger raids. They first attacked the Vilches family and later the Buenrostros at their Carmen Ranch, but the two families defended their lands: "Los rinches stopped their harassment at the end of the Valley when the mexicano ranch hands started firing back at them."[195] Hinojosa shows Tejano/a families to be willing to die for their land: "Those who died in these affrays died facing North and with their backs to the Rio Grande; as they said, 'We were born here, we may as well die and be buried here, too. Come on, you rinche bastards.'"[196] *Claros varones* is clear on the issue of land, as it recalls the words of Jesús Buenrostro, Rafa's father: "The land, in part, was taken away from the old people; in part, we ourselves also lost it and others sold it. That's all in the past . . . and, anyway, the land neither dies nor goes off anywhere. Let's see if my children or theirs, when they have them . . . let's see if they keep it or recover some of it. If they also take away or if we lose or sell our language, then there will be no remission. The day Spanish dies, this will no longer be the Valley."[197] Land and culture go together in Hinojosa's re-creation of the Tejano Valley world, and the Spanish language in particular is central to maintaining the culture.

More so than for later generations, for the earlier generation of Tejanos/as, Mexico played an important role in their lives. Some of the older Texas-born residents, like Don Manuel Guzmán, felt called upon and fought in the Mexican Revolution of 1910, and it is while fighting in Mexico that Don Manuel's wife, Doña Josefa, lost control of their Texas lands. Having family on both sides of the Rio Grande and crossing the border to go eat, visit family, go shopping, and so on, is and has been a daily occurrence for residents of these South Texas border towns. Consequently, as Valerio-Jiménez points out, identity and allegiances are not binary but fluid. Again, in Hinojosa's texts different modalities of the lived experience of border areas do not allow for wholesale generalizations regarding identity formation, a danger evident in some critical approaches and formulations regarding border identity.

Hinojosa is especially keen to trace how with dispossession and Anglo migration into Belken County also comes the loss of Tejano/a political and economic power. We learn that the Klail-Blanchard-Cooke (KBC) Ranch controls the economy and the land, not only in Klail City but throughout Belken County. Politically they determine who is elected to local, county, and congressional offices. They also own the bank and the savings and loan and control all financial matters. They control the police and have their own man as sheriff. They determine elections and run candidates who support their interests. They control all the social clubs, but if they want something, like setting up a Mexican to run as a candidate, they can have his Mexican/Chicana wife admitted to the Women's Club, where Mexicans are as a rule not admitted. Nothing happens without KBC pulling the strings. Unlike the real King Ranch, however, Hinojosa's KBC Ranch, owned by the Klail, Blanchard, and Cooke families, is a local enterprise. Klail City is named after the founder of the ranch, much as Kingsville is named after the founder of King Ranch. Junior Klail is the official head of KBC interests and worth some $37 million, but the bank and other financial interests are managed by Noddy Perkins, husband of Blanche Cooke. Marriage is again shown to allow for a merger of white interests.[198] Perkins, like other Valley Anglos, speaks Spanish. His daughter, Sammie Jo, marries twice, but these are business mergers rather than love affairs. Her father opposes her teenage interest in a Tejano like Rafa Buenrostro. Many years later, however, when Rafa returns from Korea and later from the university with his law degree, he becomes a policeman and then a detective and marries Sammie Jo. Here, as in a number of Tejano/a novels, marriage is posited as a resolution or reconciliation of the underlying Anglo-Tejano/a conflict.

Hinojosa's novel makes clear that some Tejanos/as have retained possession of their land or have purchased land post-1848. The three Buenrostro brothers own the Tierras del Carmen, and Jehú checks to see that land titles are in order at the county courthouse. Buenrostro lands are to be divided equally between the three brothers, and Rafa decides to give some of his land to those who worked his father's land but did not own it: "repartí más tierras entre cierta gente o sus descendientes que trabajaron las tierras del Carmen."[199] In transferring this land to individuals connected to their ranch, seen as a positive economic and cultural measure, he follows the practices of his father, who had also distributed land near the town of Bascom. Later when old man Echevarría is about to die, Rafa decides to give the rest of his land to his own brothers, Aaron and Israel. And as Jehú notes in a letter to Rafa, "parte de la raza va recobrando terrenos y parcelas que se habían perdido años y años atrás," even though "la bolillada todavía is sitting on top of the pile of money, pero el tiempo dirá" (Some of the race is recovering lands lost years before, even though the Anglos are still sitting on top of the pile of money, but time will tell).[200]

Land thus figures in Hinojosa's Tejano/a lower Rio Grande valley in various ways, as capital, as heritage, as roots, as culture, but economic clout, centered at the KBC bank, is increasingly the site for retaining and acquiring it. By the 1960s and 1970s, Klail City Bank is involved in all manner of financial deals, selling insurance through KBC underwriters to buyers of KBC businesses, like a car dealership, through KBC loans. Under this new order, land has become a commodity—as real estate—and, as such, a means for KBC financial speculation. The biggest KBC deal will be setting up an academic institute—a nonprofit enterprise—a shell company that then buys businesses that are run by the KBC to avoid taxes. Extralegal and illegal means, otherwise known as standard business practices, are used for continued dispossession, even if that no longer requires the services of the rinches, but rather of attorneys, CPAs, and lobbyists.

In his tracing of the power structures at work in Belken County, Hinojosa notes that in the decade of the 1970s, for example, capitalist interests operated on both sides of the border, unconcerned about how—or where—money was made; what mattered was their profit margin, their return on investment. For example, wealthy Mexicans from the other side involved in drug trafficking are able to buy land in Texas. The Gómez brothers, for example, in *Ask a Policeman*, are worth millions and have condos at Padre Island, farmland in Belken County, extensive landholdings in Dellis County, Arabian horses, and fighting roosters.[201] Their ties to land are not ancestral (as in the case of Tejanos/as), but rather rooted in diversifying their investment portfolio with real estate in Texas.

Dispossession in Hinojosa's work continues under twentieth- and twenty-first-century capitalism and always implies lack of political power. Politically, as previously noted, KBC exerts its power from the boardroom to the bedroom; it controls elections, from the local to the regional. In this new Rio Grande valley, the main characters—Rafa Buenrostro and Jehú Malacara—are conscious of their Tejano/a past and are supportive of other Tejanos/as who want to keep their lands, but they, too, end up becoming part of the dominant economic machine and therefore the status quo. Jehú is rehired by the KBC bank and assists Perkins in his capital accumulation deals. Rafa not only marries the daughter of Noddy Perkins but joins the police force and becomes a detective. The idea in Hinojosa's narratives seems to be that rising up is no longer an option; if you can't beat them, join them. Infiltrate; at least that way you'll know what they're doing. Accommodation here is not linked to a loss of identity, as in the case of Paredes's Guálinto, but it does point to the end of resistance.

Litigating Land Grants in the Twenty-First Century:
Looking at Cisneros's *The Land Grant*

As the previous discussion of mid- and late twentieth-century writers shows, the sense of land dispossession in its various manifestations continues as a defining issue for contemporary Tejano/a and Chicano/a writers, but with important differences. It should be more than clear that in Texas, as elsewhere, physical violence was never the only way to dispossess Tejanos/as. The legal system served the invaders well, but from the nineteenth century to the present also led to Tejano/a legal struggles over lost land grants. Unlike New Mexican land claims taken to court, not many Texas claims have been in court news, perhaps with the exception of the Ballí case on the Texas coast.[202] In his 2012 novel *The Land Grant*, Carlos Cisneros uses the premise of a fictitious court battle for lands fraudulently taken from the heirs of Arturo Monterreal to expose a corrupt legal system in Texas.[203] A Brownsville, Texas, lawyer himself, Cisneros knows the ins and outs of the system, the legal jargon, the legal strategies used to delay hearings or speed up decisions, and the sometimes suspect and subjective nature of judges' decisions, especially of those who collude for personal or political gain. In the novel, the party being sued for fraudulent dispossession of the La Minita land grant is none other than the Catholic diocese. Its powerful bishop, Salamanca, and its Agnus Dei Foundation make billions through the foundation's leasing of the La Minita grant lands to major oil and gas producers and from their interests in telecommunication companies, railroads, wind farms, and shrimp farms, as well as from drug and human traffickers connected to the drug cartel in Matamoros. Any lawyer taking on the case on behalf of the now landless Tejano/a heirs to the La Minita land grant is at best naive and at worst dead, as are the two previous lawyers that took on the case. As the novel begins, the La Minita case, lacking lawyers for the plaintiffs, is about to be thrown out. Even if there were a lawyer willing to pursue the case, the case can be dismissed with a summary judgment, if the defense, that is, the diocese, has the right judge. And the powerful diocese, of course, can always get the best judge money can buy.

Enter Alejandro del Fuerte, partner in the law firm of del Fuerte, Fetzer and Montemayor, who is asked by the lieutenant governor of the state, Rene Yarrington, to look into and possibly take the case, as a favor to his Tejano/a constituents. The novel provides details on the land grant case, but deals especially with the personal problems that del Fuerte will encounter, the threats and danger that he and his fiancée, Gigi Montemayor, a partner in his practice, will face; matters do not go well for Alejandro del Fuerte. Tejanos/as are now lawyers, judges, and politicians, holding middle-class positions but not necessarily wielding much power. The preliminary judge, who is indebted to Bishop Salamanca, will be dismissed upon the plaintiffs' request and a new judge, Cienfuegos, appointed. The case involves the La Minita land grant, covering half a million acres (690,000 acres, to be exact), awarded to the Spanish settler Arturo Monterreal. His heirs, descendants of Candelario Santibáñez, a seven-times-great-grandson of Monterreal, had spent the last twenty years suing the Agnus Dei Foundation to get their land back. The diocese argues that it inherited the land from Austin McKnight, the last heir to the land, who married two of Santibáñez's great-great-granddaughters, who upon dying had left the estate to the diocese. Questioning the legitimacy of that land transfer, del Fuerte and his legal team find that Candelario Santibáñez in fact willed the land to an illegitimate son, Arturo Santibáñez, and that this will was duly filed in the Cameron County property records in Spanish.

The powerful Bishop Salamanca, who lives a life of luxury and sends millions to the Vatican with the expectation of being named cardinal, and his many lawyers, representing all the commercial interests on his property, are not about to lose the case. A video of del Fuerte in bed with a porn star a few days before his marriage to Montemayor surfaces, and he is threatened with blackmail: either he loses the case or the video will be posted on YouTube. His life, personal and professional, is in jeopardy—notwithstanding that he was drugged while having a drink in a bar. Del Fuerte will also be tracked and stopped by one of Salamanca's dirty cops and given a speeding ticket, allowing the cop to plant drugs in del Fuerte's vehicle. These drummed-up charges can cause him to lose his license to practice law, but he is told the charges can disappear—if he cooperates. Shortly thereafter, on his way back from Matamoros, del Fuerte is kidnapped by drug traffickers, beaten, and again forewarned about what can happen to him if he does not "cooperate"; it seems the La Minita land is also now used to smuggle drugs and undocumented workers. The Mexican traffickers kill a boy, drowning him in a brown liquid before del Fuerte's eyes. Afraid and horrified, he is ready to do anything to save his career, his relationship to Gigi, and his life. In his face-to-face talk with Bishop Salamanca, he capitulates; he agrees to lose the case for the return of Santibañez's lands, but when he puts Salamanca on the stand and asks—hypothetically—about drug trafficking on the land, he has crossed the line, and the evil bishop is set on revenge against him. It is then that Salamanca takes the sex video public, and—of course—Gigi breaks off their engagement; she is subsequently kidnapped to put further pressure on del Fuerte. In court, the judge makes it appear as if the jury is set to rule against Salamanca, leading the bishop and his allies to negotiate a settlement. The win proves quite profitable for del Fuerte and his firm, but the kidnappers in the meantime take del Fuerte for all he's worth to release the kidnapped Gigi and his newborn baby. At novel's end, the corruption of the powerful includes not only the bishop, *narcotraficantes* in Mexico, and the Drug Enforcement Agency but even the Texas governor's office.

Cisneros's novel is a legal thriller with all the constraints of that genre. Nonetheless, the narrative makes clear that the processes of enclosure and dispossession continue today—in different ways—and are increasingly complicated and corrupt legal affairs that involve officers of the state, the Church, narcotraficantes, mass media, and the judicial system. It is now not about fencing a tract of land or bringing in the Rangers as muscle to enforce dispossession, nor is it limited to legislative or congressional acts that dispossess and remove people from their lands; it is now—as in the past—accomplished through a range of tactics and strategies, through criminal acts and the collusion of the legal system; fighting them in the present—as in the past—is shown to be next to impossible.

Land as private property, as homeland, as place of identity, as region, as the space of culture, as the space of the collectivity, all these constructs appear in Tejano/a literature focusing on the nineteenth and twentieth centuries. The dispossession of this land—and all that goes with that—by those in power, making use of all sorts of means, is foundational in these works, leading to a strong regional consciousness grounded in the fact that this land was once Tejano/Mexicano land.

Conclusion

SPATIAL MOORINGS AND DISLOCATION

In the preceding chapters, we have been concerned with examining the process of enclosure, by reviewing first the history of Indigenous dispossession by Spanish, Mexican, and US troops and settlers, and then the dispossession of Mexicans in the Southwest by US troops, land speculators, and settlers. This historical background of multiple instances of spatial violence has been brought to bear in looking at narratives of land dispossession produced by those who have inhabited and continue to inhabit these lands, that is, primarily but not exclusively, by Chicanos/as and Native American writers. Historians of the Southwest have addressed and continue to address and offer readings of the area's complex history; that has not been the intent here. We have sought to consider how these processes of enclosure regarding land, with its quite different modalities, get configured, both in history and especially in literature. Some historians voice concerns that what is often not considered in historical accounts is the socioeconomic and cultural impact of dispossession on the land's residents and the perspective of the dispossessed; we argue that literature is able to provide insights into this community perspective and that Chicano/a land narratives in differing ways respond to, reject, or acquiesce to hegemonic narratives of US settlement of the Southwest. In some Nuevomexicano/a, Tejano/a, and Native American cases these narratives omit or distort important social relations, but in other cases they transmit a historical or cultural memory often ignored or disavowed in mainstream accounts, thereby providing instances of critical memory, a peripheral (complementary if not complimentary) perspective not offered by other narratives.

As the Latino/a population of the United States increases, especially the Mexican-origin population, it becomes ever more important to look back to register not only the anti-Mexican spatial and discursive violence in this country, but also the anti-Indigenous violence in which all have participated, including Mexicans. This violence has been in large measure spatial because of the centrality of land, which can be mapped in literature as a sociospatial construct in a variety of ways. It can be figured as a physical location, a property, a space of production and subsistence, a landscape, a nation or homeland, a place. It is also a malleable construct that can be manipulated and redefined. Take for example the place name of Aztlán. According to León Portilla, in his essay "Los aztecas: Disquisiciones sobre un gentilicio," the Indigenous group called Mexicas left the land of Aztlán to escape the tyranny of the Aztecas; the Mexicas were the *macehuales*, the subordinate group and workers of the Aztecas; henceforth they called themselves Mexicas, rather than Aztecas, following the words of their high priest Huítzitl. Many years later, Aztlán, the place of tyranny, was given a positive spin as an ur-narrative of place of origin, first by Tlacaélel, the adviser to the Mexica rulers Itzcóatl and Motecuhzoma Ilhuicamina in the late fifteenth and early sixteenth centuries.[1] Later, it would be picked up in the 1960s by cultural nationalist Chicanos/as, who considered the US Southwest the mythical fatherland of Aztlán.

Land, then, can be not only symbolically constructed as a homeland and as a mythic space, but also, and more importantly, valued as a habitable space that can sustain life, as a space of production, reproduction, and subsistence. When this physical space is closed off or taken away by outsiders, whether invaders, settlers, or missionaries—or, usually, a combination of these—the resulting displacement can be devastating. Under the capitalist order, land becomes a symbol of loss and dispossession, of displacement, of injustice, and of de facto and de jure violence against, in the particular case of the US Southwest, Indigenous and Latino/a populations. Land then becomes commodified, real estate, so to speak. Understandably then, notions of land loss and betrayal have figured prominently in historical fictions about Indigenous, Hispano/a, Tejano/a, and Californio/a lands. Whether the dispossession came suddenly by force or gradually, the motif of loss and disenfranchisement has been central and a constant. While this configuration of land dispossession has been a response to very real and material enclosures, the displacement or loss itself has also been figured as a traumatic experience of the violence that continues to be relived throughout history as if imprinted on the collectivity's DNA, as expressed figuratively in Pérez's notion of blood memory, or as the "lived experience," for example, of characters in narratives dealing with migrations, displacement, and dispossession.

For Tejanos/as, loss of land and shifts in the mode of production post-1836 gave rise to displacement and migration to seek work elsewhere, either with other Texas landowners, or by going north. Migration—writ large—is the subject of a multitude of corridos, short stories, films, and novels. In 1900, some dispossessed Tejano-Mexicanos did not actually move far from their home ground but, like Gregorio Cortez, ended up as sharecroppers on Anglo-owned land, as noted in the corridos.[2] By the middle of the twentieth century many families in Texas boarded up their homes and spent part of the year on itinerant farm labor circuits that took them as far north as Iowa and Minnesota, and as far west as the states of Washington and California. Former landowners and peons became farmworkers and migrant workers, as in Hinojosa's already discussed *Klail City Death Trip Series* and Tomás Rivera's *Y no se lo tragó la tierra*. Rivera's work stands out as possibly the best-known Chicano/a narrative of native migrant workers from Texas. Land here is reconfigured principally as a place of production, with shelter becoming an urgent spatial issue; but the sense of place is also linked to a sense of identification, as we find acutely narrated especially in some of Rivera's short stories.

Narrative can become a way of figuring a critical memory of the past, a way of reading the collective scars left by history and, more concretely, the psychosocial marks left by the spatial and discursive violence of dispossession. Our work here has been concerned with examining how literary texts configure enclosures and deal with the political-economic events that gave rise to the dispossession of Indians and Latinos/as, bearing in mind that these events can be dehistoricized, naturalized, mystified, and distorted in literature as well. Enclosures are serially established and ongoing; they are not merely a phenomenon in the early modern period or limited to a specific location; they mutate, as it were, taking different forms, and are continually generated within a variety of spaces. Our particular interest in the phenomena of enclosures, both old and new, requires that we be aware that since in distinct periods they have been actualized in different ways, we need to look at the various historical periods and different regions in the US Southwest. Periodization has been important for our project of distinguishing different phases of economic production during which the population of Spanish-Mexican origin in what is now the US Southwest has undergone substantive changes, both quantitative and qualitative.

As they evolve across time, the processes of enclosure generate new subjects, including waged workers, migrants, and displaced people, subjects who become to greater or lesser degrees integrated into the developing capitalist order, generating identities or subject positions that correlate with the space and place occupied in the social order. The US invasion of the Southwest would bring enclosures that defined, regulated, and shaped subjects within complex and often contradictory capitalist social relations that in many instances revealed residual social relations coexisting with newer ones. As we saw, the loss of Tejano/a lands led to new subjects: field workers, ranch workers, sharecroppers, and tenant farmers, but also conservative Tejano/a ranchers who would keep their lands, support the Confederacy during the Civil War, have slaves, and accommodate to the new dominant paradigm. Works of fiction register the nuances of new subjectivities, emphasizing the notion of a citizen-subject presumed to have a voice and access to self-representation and aligned for the most part and in varying degrees with the new dominant economic and political order. Many of the texts discussed here speak to these shifts.

As we have seen as well, and as pointed to by De Angelis and others, enclosures take different forms, but in all cases they have the effect of separating the producers from access to their means of production.[3] And as enclosures—more broadly conceived—are projected into our present moment, we can see that they can emerge from direct or indirect expropriation of land, land pollution, water privatization, urban planning, eminent domain for road building, cuts in social spending, cuts in entitlements, and control of intellectual property rights. These mechanisms of enclosure involve privatization and the elimination of communal property and produce deprivation, uprootedness, migration, and homelessness. Debt itself, whether to the company store or to the bank, is yet another form of enclosure, as Silvia Federici reminds us.[4] Whatever drives one from or deprives one of the means of subsistence, whether it is violence, barbed wire, famine, plague, debt, or the courts, and leads to migration or to work in factories, office cubicles, plantations, and reservations, or as cargo on slave ships or eighteen-wheelers, is a form of enclosure.[5] State debt itself can drive a nation to enclose land, as occurred in Mexico when the Salinas government complied with World Bank and International Monetary Fund dictates, repealed article 27 of the Mexican Constitution, and sold off peasant lands.[6] At present, neoliberalism, including debt restructuring, the establishment of free enterprise zones, and gentrification as well as the imposition of trade agreements, as in the case of NAFTA—all new forms of enclosure—have also displaced workers who have subsequently had to migrate. Of course, displacement can also be the product of what De Angelis calls "negative externalities," like the destruction of forests, rivers, and the environment in a variety of forms that are often the product of capitalist investments, as in the case of the Dakota Access pipeline or the Canada-to-Nebraska segment of the Keystone XL pipeline, or fracking or mining that destroys water reservoirs. Indigenous populations in the Andes region as well as in the United States are protesting not only the privatization of nature and its resources, like water, but the creation of ecological disasters, even as experts see the striking acceleration of pollution, with increasing levels of fossil fuel burning and climate-warming carbon emissions on Planet Earth. Scientists today speak of a new geological epoch, the Anthropocene, since human beings and their actions are having catastrophic impact on the planet. Others rebut that it could more aptly be called the Capitalocene epoch in view of the fact that the nature of capitalist production with its attendant commodification of resources plays a central role in this contamination, the extinction of species, and the transformation of land by erosion and deforestation.[7]

Whether enclosures are imposed by the state or by capital (or in conjunction, as is more usually the case), they are meant to allow land to be taken and redirected for capitalist production, whether for agribusiness, energy production, water reservoirs, lithium mining, and oil production today, or for gold, timber, or cattle as in the past, in the process generating discourses legitimating the enclosures and ensuring dispossession. These enclosures inevitably also generate struggles to resist the particular type of enclosure, whether as a movement of those without land, as in Brazil, or the Zapatista resistance in Mexico against attempts to sell off Indigenous common lands, or the uprisings in Zambia in 1986 against International Monetary Fund austerity measures, and, as Federici and others note, any number of other examples of enclosures that separate producers from their means of production.[8] Today workers live ever more precarious lives; they are uprooted, deprived of their right to make a living, and forced to migrate or emigrate to seek a livelihood for themselves and their families in Europe, Africa, or the United States. Enclosures and their contemporary incarnations are represented, especially today, in works on immigration, like Graciela Limón's *The River Flows North*, in which we see the impact of NAFTA, agribusiness, and the dispossession of Indigenous people in the Américas leading people to cross the deadly Sonoran Desert to get to the United States.[9] Enclosures also impact all types of communal control, including what De Angelis calls the "knowledge-commons," as in the case of schools, universities, and the internet, which are being privatized, making knowledge accessible to some and not to others.[10] Tragically, one area in which this can be seen is in the catastrophic loss of Indigenous languages.

New enclosures of the twentieth and twenty-first centuries have led to the displacement of US Latino/a populations within urban spaces through gentrification, privatization, restructuring, and eminent domain. We can find textualizations of these more recent types of enclosure in urban Latino/a contexts—and the resulting sense of dispossession—represented, as noted in chapter 1, as translocal spaces, in the work of Ernesto Quiñónez, Helena María Viramontes, and Culture Clash. These are, however, but samples of the whole range of enclosures taking place throughout the world, cases of dispossession and social and economic precarity that in turn produce shared sites of commonality and create translocal communities. Today, enclosures in urban sites are more often the product of foreclosures as well as gentrification, as is now evident not only in Los Angeles and Harlem in New York, but also in East Austin, where Blacks and Latinos are being pushed out, or in Houston, Dallas, San Antonio, Fort Worth, Albuquerque, and even Oklahoma City. But this, too, is part of a global practice of growing urban enclosures, as much the case in Los Angeles as in Rio, as in Detroit, as in Mexico City. We argue that we need to look at these sites with new eyes to find in the process of contemporary enclosure the potential for new agencies, new strategies and tactics of active resistance, and new alliances.

In our work, we have examined a variety of narratives that provide what is an always partial and necessarily incomplete rendering of the historical contradictions that drive enclosures. Fiction that does not address these historical contradictions and what drives them ends up offering only a pastiche of a particular period if it ignores the complexity and layering of mechanisms and discourses, including those of race, ethnicity, sexuality, gender, and especially class. When history is mere backdrop, without depth, all we have are simulacra. Cultural representation serves as constructed memory. It can be a catalyst for resistance, for change, for raising consciousness of dispossession and enabling awareness of and connection with other groups and nations undergoing dispossession throughout the world, as in the case of the Palestinians and the many Indigenous populations in the Américas. In and of itself, cultural production does not produce change or decolonization or liberation. Culture cannot be privileged and should not displace our awareness and connection to the historical and material. Real transformation only comes about through political and social action. But in order to catalyze activism, there needs to be awareness, knowledge, and analysis, and cultural production can be generative of this *concientización*. Knowing one's history and what others have said about it is fundamental. Critical memory, a critical assessment of enclosures, both historical and present, can be part of that process.

What is crucial, then, is the standpoint from which one addresses the past. We have argued that historical standpoint is important in setting up the horizon within which the narratives configure enclosures. Ideologically, the texts we have considered render not only the resentment of the dispossessed but also the regionalism of the residents, a regional identification that is today receding for a number of reasons, including class status, generation, assimilation, migration, language, and education. Ethnicity, in fact, comes to replace regional identity in many cases. All of these works, however, offer insights into the complex social systems of the past and the present, insights that other representations of historical moments or collectivities often fail to fully provide. The texts, moreover, make clear that land is always both a material and a cultural space that constitutes place-bound identities. It remains a powerful construct. Even under enclosures, even when land becomes real estate, even when home is a homeless person's tent, it is the basis for a powerful sense of place, a sense of sociospatial location linked to specific if highly variable social relations.

As spatial mobility increases, regional identification recedes. Sometimes place identity is no longer with a region, nation, state, or city, but with a barrio, a street, or even a building. There is a new reality today among working-class people especially when precarity forces one to move often as rents rise, or when gentrification leads to eviction and relocation, or when loss of a job leaves one disconnected. With economic insecurity, nothing is seen as stable. Notions of family and home are no longer necessarily linked to specific places; it's as if family as a site of foundational identity has run its course. Migration also uproots populations and, with the passing of time, the sense of belonging somewhere is diminished. Homelessness, too, leads to a sense of disorientation, and perhaps all one can count on is identification with a particular street corner, parking space, park, or bridge.

Place, then, is variable; in a way it can be a free-floating construct. In this current climate of alienation, with its sense of social dysfunction and displacement, other sites come to assume prominence. New coordinates, not necessarily place based, come into play; land—much less landownership—is no longer the cornerstone of identity (as it still is in the great majority of texts discussed here). Social location or positioning replaces those geographical mappings, and people come to identify in terms of gender, race, ethnicity, sexual orientation, education, profession/occupation, or class. While this may be the case, these new identities must perforce be grounded. One does not exist in a vacuum, in the abstract; one is always positioned geographically. These social locations inevitably assume a place, a physical space where they can be experienced or carried out.

In this regard, we want to end by turning to two of Tomás Rivera's narratives to suggest that they can be viewed as anticipating new relations to place, perhaps foreshadowing what is to come in terms of the short- and long-term effects of dislocation.[11] Rivera's stories on migratory Texas farmworkers present a social reality where the variables of displacement predominate rather than a specific grounding in a particular place/region or land; property and ownership of the land cease to be the determining factors. Rivera's "Zoo Island" is especially noteworthy as a register, not of land loss per se, but of the symptomatology, as it were, of the sense of uprootedness that is the product of social dislocation and subordination. Here the young characters have a need to establish and mark their space, no longer through land ownership and tenancy but through constructing identities of their own—a type of branding, one might say—and representation. Farm land is alienated, that is, the property of a white man, but the chicken coops where the workers live during the seasonal harvest constitute their place, and migrants claim this space—own it, in current parlance, figuratively—making it their own when they name it Zoo Island and put up a sign with the name and population. They respond to objectification by Anglos who drive by to make fun of their living conditions with affirmation, textualizing or inscribing their presence in a given space by naming it. Importantly, it is a collective act. Here, too, land and place of identity are closely related, as in much of Chicano/a literature, but in a noticeably different way as the characters are not "from there" but "are there" for now; they are in transit but exert what agency is available to them (in representation) to make that place theirs, to "belong" to the space they name and occupy.

In another Rivera story, "The Salamanders," the adolescent character, aware of the extreme poverty and precarity of his migrant family, with no place to stop to look for work while it rains or even to set up a tent to sleep, becomes increasingly alienated from his family and begins to detach from and disidentify with his parents. Searching both for work and for shelter, the family finally finds a farmer willing to let them set up their tent at the foot of a flooded beet field. Glad to have the space to at least stretch out rather than sleeping in their car, the displaced family will feel further displaced when it is rudely awakened in the middle of the night by an invasion of salamanders, bent on repossessing or reclaiming their space. The family's violent response to the salamander incursion or "attack" will in the end bond and bind the boy again to his family: "I don't know why we killed so many salamanders that night . . . Now that I remember, I think that we also felt the desire to recover and reclaim the foot of the field."[12] The boy finds in this collective (and violent) resistance against the salamanders renewed solidarity and identification with his own family. This interspecies conflict and spatial violence, pitting humans against salamanders, points to displacement as not only a physical but also a psychological trauma of "unrootedness," of feeling unmoored or untethered. Rivera's narrative allegorizes dispossession and the importance of space, solidarity, and communal resistance. Written from the standpoint of an impressionable young boy who intuitively senses the symptoms if not the cause, the story registers the lived experience and consequences of dispossession and loss of different orders. That physical, deadly but justified, violence against another, in this case another species, is called on and ends up being therapeutic for the family suggests the need for collective action. Obliquely perhaps, in these intriguing stories Rivera insightfully taps into and represents the transformative changes that ensue when traditional identifications, conventional moorings, as with a land or a home place, no longer exist or are inoperative, when people have been deprived and displaced from their home turf by multiple processes of enclosure and multiple violences—past and present.

The space then that gives rise to a sense of belonging and identity need not be one's own land; any type of displacement or dislocation elicits a need for relocation, some act of affirmation and regrounding. In the past, land was the material and cultural space that on the one hand constituted place-bound identities and, on the other, was coveted by invaders, speculators, and settlers. Today the space coveted and subject to enclosure is not necessarily land, but rather any productive space from which gain or profit can be extracted, whatever that may look like and wherever that space may exist. In discussing the historical spatial violence in the US Southwest, we hope to have shown that literature offers a symbolic representation of land and land loss, with the potential for constructing in the process a critical memory of the past. We argue, too, that literature has served—and continues to function—as a sensitive register to gauge changes that are taking place today, as new enclosures (some of very different orders) are being put in place in our neoliberal moment. In the process of rendering the effects of enclosure, new and old, fiction not only constructs narrative spaces that can transcend the local but at the same time, in catalyzing critical memory formation, enables new imaginaries. Seen in this way, as a space or site from which to resist new enclosures, we need to continue to look to cultural production, and to literature more specifically, to see how it is attesting to the latest instantiations of enclosure, registering how the new forms of spatial and discursive violence are being experienced.

Notes

Introduction

1. Caffentzis, "Tale of Two Conferences," 6.
2. See Harvey, *New Imperialism*, 137.
3. De Angelis, "Separating the Doing and the Deed."
4. See also Perelman, *Invention of Capitalism;* and Caffentzis, "Power of Money."
5. De Angelis, "Separating the Doing and the Deed," 75. De Angelis uses "primitive accumulation" and "enclosures" as interchangeable terms. Marx himself noted that the difference between accumulation and primitive accumulation is not a substantive one and that it continues. In the *Grundrisse* Marx notes, "Once this separation is given, the production process can only produce it anew, reproduce it, and reproduce it on an expanded scale" (461). Consult, too, Midnight Notes Collective, *Midnight Oil*.
6. See Marx, *Capital*, 724.
7. Viñas, *Indios, ejército y frontera*. His work is unfortunately little referenced by US historians but has much to add to a deeper and layered understanding of enclosures and dispossession in the Américas, North and South.
8. For an analysis of Foucault's notion of governmentality, see Dean, *Governmentality*.
9. Wallace, *Long Bitter Trail*, 4.
10. Wallace, *Long Bitter Trail*, 73.
11. Wallace, *Long Bitter Trail*, 74.
12. Foucault, "Governmentality."
13. Amin, *Accumulation on a World Scale*, 3.
14. De Angelis, "Separating the Doing and the Deed," 57.

15 De Angelis, "Separating the Doing and the Deed," 60.
16 Harvey, *New Imperialism*, 232.
17 Wood, "Logics of Power."
18 Caffentzis, "On the Notion of a Crisis," 2.
19 Olivera and Lewis, *Cochabamba!*
20 De Angelis, "Separating the Doing and the Deed," 71.
21 See De Angelis, "Separating the Doing and the Deed," 77, for a typology of new enclosures.
22 De Angelis, "Separating the Doing and the Deed," 82.
23 Newkirk, "Great Land Robbery."
24 De Angelis, "Separating the Doing and the Deed," 58.
25 De Angelis, "Separating the Doing and the Deed," 59.
26 Another instance of a concept having a determining if not explicitly enunciated role can be found, for example, in Rene Girard's work on scapegoats. Girard finds that in narratives where there is no direct mention of scapegoats, scapegoating is often the controlling principle. See Girard, *Scapegoat*, 119–20.
27 Gates, *History of Public Land Law Development*.
28 On Lefebvre, see Harvey, *Cosmopolitanism*, 134.
29 Turner, "Significance of the Frontier," 2.
30 Stedman Jones, "History of U.S. Imperialism," 217.
31 Rana, *Two Faces of American Freedom*, 8–19.
32 Rana, *Two Faces of American Freedom*, 7.
33 Benson, "Historian as Myth Maker," 3. See also Decker, "Great Speculation," 358.
34 Dunbar-Ortiz, *Indigenous Peoples' History*; Goeman, *Mark My Words*.
35 See Smith, *Uneven Development*.
36 For a discussion of the California process of spatial and discursive violence and the place of the *Californio testimonios* in these, see Sánchez, *Telling Identities*.
37 Harootunian, *Marx after Marx*, 5.
38 Harootunian, *Marx after Marx*, 201.
39 Harootunian, *Marx after Marx*, 211, 216.
40 Quijano, "Coloniality of Power, Eurocentrism, and Social Classification," 181–82.
41 Quijano, "Coloniality of Power, Eurocentrism, and Social Classification," 194–95. Transmodernity is discussed by Quijano. See also Dussel, "Philosophy of Liberation," 345.
42 Mignolo, "Geopolitics of Knowledge," 234.
43 Mignolo, "Geopolitics of Knowledge," 238.
44 Harootunian, *Marx after Marx*, 64.
45 Tomba, "Marx's Temporal Bridges," 90.

46 Harootunian, "Piercing the Present with the Past," 64.
47 Harvey, *New Imperialism*, 137.
48 Jameson, *Valences of the Dialectic*, 531.
49 Culture Clash, *Oh, Wild West!*
50 Viramontes, *Their Dogs Came with Them*.
51 Smith, *Uneven Development*, 200; Quiñonez, *Chango's Fire*.
52 Briggs and Van Ness, introduction to *Land, Water, and Culture*, 6.
53 Briggs and Van Ness, introduction, 6.
54 Briggs and Van Ness, introduction, 8.
55 Poyo and Hinojosa, "Spanish Texas and Borderlands Historiography in Transition," 411.
56 Truett and Young, "Borderlands Unbound," 326; Mikesell and Murphy, "Framework for a Comparative Study."
57 Hämäläinen and Johnson, *Major Problems in the History of North American Borderlands*.
58 Poyo and Hinojosa, "Spanish Texas and Borderlands Historiography in Transition," 413.
59 Weber, "John Francis Bannon and the Historiography of the Spanish Borderlands."
60 Cuello, "Beyond the 'Borderlands,'" 292.
61 Ramos, *Beyond the Alamo*. See also Valerio-Jiménez, *River of Hope*.
62 Poyo and Hinojosa, "Spanish Texas and Borderlands Historiography in Transition," 415–16.
63 Harvey, *Cosmopolitanism*, 135.
64 Ricoeur, *Memory, History, Forgetting*; Baker, "Critical Memory and the Black Public Sphere."
65 Jameson, *Postmodernism*, 19, 21.
66 Jameson, *Postmodernism*; Baker, "Critical Memory and the Black Public Sphere," 7.
67 Baker, "Critical Memory and the Black Public Sphere," 7.
68 Sturken, *Tangled Memories*, 3; Pierre Nora's work on memory is reviewed in Ricoeur, *Memory, History, Forgetting*, 406; Maurice Halbwachs's notion of collective memory is also taken up in Ricoeur, *Memory, History, Forgetting*, 408.
69 Ricoeur, *Memory, History, Forgetting*, 444.
70 Jameson, *Political Unconscious*, 266.
71 The connections between place and memory are nicely drawn out in David Harvey, "Place as the Locus of Collective Memory," in *Justice, Nature, and the Geography of Difference*, 304.
72 Harvey, *Cosmopolitanism*, 137.
73 Weber, *What Caused the Pueblo Revolt of 1680?*, 3–18.
74 *Shaman Winter* is part of Anaya's detective tetralogy that includes *Zia Summer*, *Río Grande Fall*, and *Jemez Spring*.

75 Pérez, *Forgetting the Alamo*.
76 Esty and Lye, "Peripheral Realism Now."
77 Esty and Lye, "Peripheral Realism Now," 278.
78 Morales, *Reto en el Paraíso*.

Chapter One. Spatial Violence and Modalities of Colonialism

1 In the case of Australia, the elimination of Aboriginal peoples, that is, the native population, took a similar form, according to Patrick Wolfe, who in his work on settler colonialism in Australia explains what happened there by distinguishing between colonialism and settler colonialism. See Wolfe, *Settler Colonialism and the Transformation of Anthropology*.
2 Marx, *Capital*, 723. In Australia the strategies were also cultural and legal. The European settlers manufactured their justification with a gendered bent through what Wolfe calls "nescience," false rumors about female promiscuity and uncertain paternity that led to official rejection of the rights of Aboriginal children to inherit their father's land once the father's paternity was placed in doubt (Wolfe, *Settler Colonialism and the Transformation of Anthropology*, 26–27).
3 Roxanne Dunbar-Ortiz cites Cree scholar Lorraine Le Camp, who calls this kind of erasure "terranullism." See Dunbar-Ortiz, *Indigenous Peoples' History*, 230–31.
4 Gates, *History of Public Land Law Development*, 33.
5 Berle, "A Few Questions for the Diplomatic Pouch," 3, 32.
6 Veracini, *Settler Colonialism*, 21.
7 Veracini, *Settler Colonialism*, 25.
8 Veracini, *Settler Colonialism*, 26, 27, 33, 29. "Improvement" may come, on the other hand, through mestizaje. Children of mixed parentage in Australia, for example, were deemed non-Indigenous and thus belonged to the white population; in this way the Aboriginal race was reduced, as no half-caste children were allowed to remain in native camps, nor were they able to inherit, in effect separating children from their mothers and "breeding them white" (Wolfe, *Settler Colonialism and the Transformation of Anthropology*, 11).
9 Marx and Engels, *Ireland and the Irish Question*.
10 Marx and Engels, *Ireland and the Irish Question*, 29.
11 This midcentury catastrophe occurred at the same time as another agricultural revolution that enabled landlords to produce through the use of machinery and modern systems of agriculture, leaving farmworkers without work and land. The Irish were not only dispossessed but pauperized and forced "to cross the sea in search of a new country and of new lands" (Marx and Engels, *Ireland and the Irish Question*, 66). Enclosures and the forcible eviction of Irish peasants led to the emigration of 1,200,436 Irish agricultural workers to the United States between 1847 and 1852.

12 Brenner, "Agrarian Class Structure and Economic Development," 12.
13 Brenner, "Agrarian Class Structure and Economic Development," 23.
14 Vicens Vives, *Economic History of Spain*, 184, 186.
15 Vicens Vives, *Economic History of Spain*, 316.
16 Vicens Vives, *Economic History of Spain*, 317.
17 Vicens Vives, *Economic History of Spain*, 386.
18 The story of colonists in Virginia and more specifically of one convict/colonizer is told in Daniel Defoe's *Moll Flanders* (1722). While the novel traces the plight of an indentured servant/convict in the early Virginia colony and provides a good view of English class structure, it does not focus at all on the foundational dispossession of the Indians in the colonies, who are largely absent from the work.
19 Weber, *Bárbaros*, 10.
20 Semo, *Historia mexicana*, 11.
21 Some communal lands, however, survived after independence, despite efforts in some cases, as in Mexico, where the liberal Benito Juárez set out to eliminate all corporate holdings, including both Church holdings and Indigenous communal holdings.
22 Weber, *Spanish Frontier in North America*, 78, 84.
23 See Barr, *Peace Came in the Form of a Woman*, 67.
24 Barr, *Peace Came in the Form of a Woman*, 120.
25 Weber, *Bárbaros*, 102.
26 Weber, *Bárbaros*, 103.
27 As Weber notes, "Secularization also implied that Indian communal property, held in trust by missionaries, would be returned to the Indians and the surplus would enter the public domain." See Weber, *Mexican Frontier*, 46.
28 Park, "Spanish Indian Policy in Northern Mexico," 222–23.
29 Weber, *Bárbaros*, 105.
30 Valerio-Jiménez, *River of Hope*, 35.
31 Vicens Vives, *Economic History of Spain*, 636, 638–39.
32 Semo, *Historia mexicana*, 84.
33 See Viñas, *Indios, ejército y frontera*, 11–13.
34 The emergence of twentieth-century Indigenous movements in Bolivia, Ecuador, Peru, Guatemala, and Mexico and the recognition of Indigenous rights by the United Nations (Declaración de Naciones Unidas sobre Pueblos Indígenas, 2007) point to renewed efforts at recovery of land rights. Albó, "Del indio negado al permitido y al protagónico," 1.
35 Viñas, *Indios, ejército y frontera*, 27, 31, 33.
36 Viñas, *Indios, ejército y frontera*, 40–44.
37 Albó, "Del indio negado al permitido y al protagónico," 10–11.
38 Stedman Jones, "History of U.S. Imperialism," 213.
39 Harvey, *New Imperialism*, 43.

40 Byrd, *Transit of Empire*.
41 Stedman Jones, "History of U.S. Imperialism," 217.
42 Gates, *History of Public Land Law Development*, 51.
43 Gates, *History of Public Land Law Development*, 56.
44 Lee, introduction, xv. Gates's essay on California was first published in 1958.
45 Gates, *Land and Law in California*, 5.
46 Gates, *History of Public Land Law Development*, 35–36.
47 Gates, *History of Public Land Law Development*, 35–36.
48 Gates, *History of Public Land Law Development*, 38. While men like Jefferson advocated for granting small allotments of land to settlers and the right of squatters to occupy vacant lands, his work in the Virginia legislature and later as president did not block speculation on public lands, and he ordered that troops remove those illegally settling on public lands (Gates, *History of Public Land Law Development*, 3, 63).
49 Cited in Gates, *History of Public Land Law Development*, 303. See also George, *The Land Question*.
50 Gates, *History of Public Land Law Development*, 147.
51 Interesting in the approval of these acts is the policy on immigrant rights if the immigrant intended to become a citizen. The Preemption Act of 1841, considered a "frontier triumph" (Gates, *History of Public Land Law Development*, 236), finally authorized squatting on both surveyed and unsurveyed land and stipulated that "persons eligible for preemption were heads of families, widows or single men over 21, who either were citizens or had filed a declaration of intention to take out citizenship" (238). The mere intention of white settlers to become citizens was enough to justify treating them like citizens, unlike today.
52 Gates, *History of Public Land Law Development*, 440.
53 Gates, *History of Public Land Law Development*, 77.
54 Gates, *History of Public Land Law Development*, 79.
55 Gates, *History of Public Land Law Development*, 80.
56 Gates, *History of Public Land Law Development*, 452.
57 Gates defends the government throughout: "Undoubtedly some hardships did result but they were caused by the fact that confused, ill-defined, overlapping, and inadequately documented but valid claims or rights were intermixed with fraudulent claims (Gates, *History of Public Land Law Development*, 96).
58 Gates, *History of Public Land Law Development*, 96.
59 Gates, *History of Public Land Law Development*, 99, 101.
60 Gates, *History of Public Land Law Development*, 190.
61 Gates, *History of Public Land Law Development*, 187.
62 Dunbar-Ortiz, *Indigenous Peoples' History*, 187.
63 Dunbar-Ortiz, *Indigenous Peoples' History*, 155.

Chapter Two. Indigenous Spatial Sovereignty and Governmentality

1. Goeman, *Mark My Words*, 4.
2. These three forms of control are analyzed by Michel Foucault in his seminal essay "Governmentality," 87–104.
3. Wallace, *Long, Bitter Trail*, 24–26.
4. Wallace, *Long, Bitter Trail*, 26.
5. See Dunbar-Ortiz, *Indigenous Peoples' History*, 80.
6. Wallace, *Long, Bitter Trail*, 27.
7. In 1814 General Andrew Jackson went south, entered Creek country, defeated them, and forced them to sign the Treaty of Fort Jackson, ceding most of their lands in Georgia and Alabama, some 23 million acres (Wallace, *Long, Bitter Trail*, 50). Some Creeks escaped into Florida, where they became known as Seminoles and were joined by runaway Black slaves; together they held out for many more years (from 1817 to 1842), although hundreds were slaughtered by Jackson's armies. See Dunbar-Ortiz, *Indigenous Peoples' History*, 99.
8. Wallace, *Long, Bitter Trail*, 43.
9. Wallace, *Long, Bitter Trail*, 44.
10. Wallace, *Long, Bitter Trail*, 55.
11. Wallace, *Long, Bitter Trail*, 68.
12. Quoted in Wallace, *Long, Bitter Trail*, 74.
13. Wallace, *Long, Bitter Trail*, 71.
14. Wallace, *Long, Bitter Trail*, 85.
15. Dunbar-Ortiz, *Indigenous Peoples' History*, 110.
16. Wallace, *Long, Bitter Trail*, 7.
17. Wallace, *Long, Bitter Trail*, 8.
18. Cited in Magdoff, "Twenty-First-Century Land Grabs," 4.
19. See, for example, Estes, *Our History Is the Future*.
20. Wallace, *Long, Bitter Trail*, 105.
21. Prucha, *American Indian Treaties*, 184.
22. Wallace, *Long, Bitter Trail*, 106–7.
23. Dunbar-Ortiz, *Indigenous Peoples' History*, 142.
24. Dunbar-Ortiz, *Indigenous Peoples' History*, 77.
25. Wallace, *Long, Bitter Trail*, 109.
26. The "shock of the near disaster," as Wallace (*Long, Bitter Trail*, 111) calls it, led to changes within Seneca society, but among the Tonawanda, who refused to move, the entire episode left them with a sense of disgust for white man's Christianity and Christians like the Reverend John Schermerhorn, who had actively sought their removal and forced the treaty on them. The Tonawanda thereafter worked to revive their old-time religion and prophecies. Cultural resistance was one of their last strategies of resistance in the face of destitution and displacement.

27 Wallace, *Long, Bitter Trail*, 117.
28 Previously, as noted by Gates, the government had used Indian treaties as a modality, a way to create a facade of legality, when in reality it took Indigenous lands through force and means of deception. Another important factor, supported by speculators, was that Indian lands were not to become public lands; this way they could be sold at public auctions without being open to preemption. Those managing Indian lands profited from these sales. See Gates, *History of Public Land Law Development*, 452–53.
29 See Gates, *History of Public Land Law Development*, 464.
30 See Lefebvre, *Production of Space*, 27.
31 For further discussion, see Kamins, "Ethnic Cleansing: We Have It Here Too!"
32 Goeman, *Mark My Words*, 91. Distribution of individual allotments did not lead, however, to assimilation and self-reliance among Indians. Gates's quasi-apologetic explanation of the failure of this government action seeks to justify the dispossession imposed on Indians as a simple miscalculation or mistake (*History of Public Land Law Development*, 465–66). It clearly was not a mistake but the plan all along; there was, literally, no place for Native Americans in a white man's world.
33 Debo, *And Still the Waters Run*, 22; Prucha, *American Indian Treaties*, 319.
34 See Debo, *And Still the Waters Run*, 33.
35 Debo, *And Still the Waters Run*, 35.
36 For discussion of the Indian Reorganization Act of 1934, see Dunbar-Ortiz, *Indigenous Peoples' History*, 171; and Goeman, *Mark My Words*, 91–92.
37 Angie Debo indicates that the original form of the bill was modified before it passed, but that it did stop further allotment; it authorized $2 million for the acquisition of land for now landless Indians and permitted the organization of tribal governments. For further discussion, see Debo, *And Still the Waters Run*, 368.
38 Debo, *And Still the Waters Run*, 368–69.
39 Debo, *And Still the Waters Run*, 371.
40 Debo, *And Still the Waters Run*, 372–74.
41 Debo, *And Still the Waters Run*, 323.
42 The dispossession of Indigenous peoples continues today in Jamaica, Mexico, Haiti, and other parts of Latin America as well as in Africa, "the target of much of the land grabbing," and in Indonesia and China (Magdoff, "Twenty-First-Century Land Grabs," 9–11). China's current privatization of land formerly worked by communes is leading to the displacement of millions and is arguably akin to what happened with the privatization of Indian reservation lands (12).
43 Hogan, *Woman Who Watches Over the World*.
44 De Angelis, "Separating the Doing and the Deed."
45 Rosemont notes that in the last couple years of Marx's life, "to a far greater

degree than ever before, he focused his attention on people of color, the colonized, peasants, and 'primitives.'" See Rosemont, "Karl Marx and the Iroquois."
46 The power of Seneca women in Iroquois society would also impress Marx, even though it was the male council of chiefs that allowed women the right to speak. See Rosemont's review of Marx's *Ethnological Notebooks*, in "Karl Marx and the Iroquois," 8.
47 Baker, *Critical Memory*.
48 Hogan, *Mean Spirit*, 221.
49 García Márquez, *Crónica de una muerte anunciada*.
50 Hogan, *Osage Indian Murders*.
51 See Wilson, *Underground Reservation*, 145–47. See also Burns, *History of the Osage People*, 440–42.
52 Wilson, *Underground Reservation*, 147.
53 Hogan, *Mean Spirit*, 341.
54 Hogan, *Mean Spirit*, 341.
55 Mathews, *Sundown*; see also Mathews, *The Osages*.
56 Rosemont, "Karl Marx and the Iroquois," 15.
57 Rosemont, "Karl Marx and the Iroquois," 17.
58 Hogan, *Mean Spirit*, 341.
59 McAuliffe, *Bloodland*, 176.
60 McAuliffe, *Bloodland*, 177–78.
61 Wilkins and Lomawaima, *Uneven Ground*, 22.
62 See Deloria, "Promises Made, Promises Broken," 144.
63 Wallace, *Long, Bitter Trail*, 38.
64 Wallace, *Long, Bitter Trail*, 39.
65 Cited in Clark, *Lone Wolf v. Hitchcock*, 2.
66 Debo, *And Still the Waters Run*, 32.
67 The state also voiced reformist and moralist discourses, echoing the white (Christian) man's burden, when it saw fit to do so.
68 Prucha, *American Indian Treaties*, 4, 6.
69 Wallace, *Long, Bitter Trail*, 54.
70 Debo, *And Still the Waters Run*, 4.
71 Wallace, *Long, Bitter Trail*, 75.
72 Hogan, *Mean Spirit*, 4.
73 Debo, *And Still the Waters Run*, xxi.
74 Debo, *And Still the Waters Run*, 14.
75 Debo, *And Still the Waters Run*, 15–16.
76 Miles, *Ties That Bind*.
77 Clark, *Lone Wolf v. Hitchcock*, 104.
78 Clark, *Lone Wolf v. Hitchcock*, 102–5.
79 Cited in Clark, *Lone Wolf v. Hitchcock*, 104.

80 In 1831, John Marshall in *Cherokee Nation v. Georgia* referred to the Cherokee as a distinct nation, and in *Worcester v. Georgia* (1832) he called Indian nations domestic dependent nations under the protection of the United States (Prucha, *American Indian Treaties*, 4, 5).

81 On "domestic dependent nations," see Wilkens and Lomawaima, *Uneven Ground*, 61.

82 See *Lone Wolf v. Hitchcock*, 187 U.S. 553, in appendix 3 of Clark, *Lone Wolf v. Hitchcock*, 133–43.

83 Clark, *Lone Wolf v. Hitchcock*, 2.

84 Dunbar-Ortiz, *Indigenous Peoples' History*, 173.

85 Debo, *And Still the Waters Run*, 32.

86 Banner, *How the Indians Lost Their Land*, 289.

87 Debo, *And Still the Waters Run*, 103.

88 See Dunbar-Ortiz, *Indigenous Peoples' History*, 169, on effects of 1924 Indian Citizenship Act.

89 Hogan, *Mean Spirit*, 221.

90 McCumber quoted in Thorne, *World's Richest Indian*, 39.

91 Thorne, *World's Richest Indian*, 38.

92 Thorne, *World's Richest Indian*, 39–40.

93 Thorne, *World's Richest Indian*, 41.

94 Thorne, *World's Richest Indian*, 40.

95 Oklahoma Closure Act 1908, referenced in Thorne, *World's Richest Indian*, 154.

96 Hogan, *Mean Spirit*, 61.

97 Hogan, *Mean Spirit*, 63.

98 Hogan, *Mean Spirit*, 63.

99 Thorne, *World's Richest Indian*, 44.

100 The intriguing particulars of Barnett's case are amply discussed in Thorne, *World's Richest Indian*.

101 Thorne, *World's Richest Indian*, 218.

102 Debo, *And Still the Waters Run*, 309.

103 As Debo notes, "In this confused atmosphere of guardian frauds, forgery and the great speculative value of uncertain titles, murder became very common" (*And Still the Waters Run*, 200).

104 Debo, *And Still the Waters Run*, 325.

105 Thorne, *World's Richest Indian*, 147, 149.

106 Debo, *And Still the Waters Run*, 357.

107 Thorne, *World's Richest Indian*, 222. In fact, the US government has refused to see Indians as legal landowners since they possess no legally recognized title to the lands they occupy. As late as 1955, in Tee-Hit-Ton, the Supreme Court ruled that occupancy of land by Indian tribes did not give them land rights; "tribal ownership of land was only deemed real if it was 'recognized' by the U.S. government" (Wilkins and Lomawaima, *Uneven Ground*, 23). The

US government is thus seen as holding the ultimate title to Indian lands and allowing the Indians the right of occupancy.

108 Ward Churchill is cited in Thorne, *World's Richest Indian*, 221.
109 See, for example, US Department of the Interior, "Native American Trust Litigation." See also historian Nick Estes's work on tracing the US government's role in the dispossession of Native American land and curtailment of rights, bringing this process to the present-day Dakota pipeline (Estes, *Our History Is the Future*).
110 Thorne, *World's Richest Indian*, 48.
111 Thorne, *World's Richest Indian*, 153.
112 Debo, *And Still the Waters Run*, 92.
113 *The Exiles*, a 1961 film by Kent MacKenzie, is a documentary about displaced Native Americans living in the Bunker Hill district of Los Angeles, rereleased by Milestone in 2008.
114 Dunbar-Ortiz, *Indigenous Peoples' History*, 174.
115 Hogan, *Woman Who Watches Over the World*, 65.
116 Burns, *History of the Osage People*, 206.
117 Burns, *History of the Osage People*, 40.
118 Wilson, *Underground Reservation*, 2.
119 Burns, *History of the Osage People*, 241.
120 Wilson, *Underground Reservation*, 170.
121 Wilson, *Underground Reservation*, 7.
122 Wilson, *Underground Reservation*, 9.
123 Wilson, *Underground Reservation*, 17.
124 Wilson, *Underground Reservation*, 12.
125 Wilson, *Underground Reservation*, 31.
126 Wilson, *Underground Reservation*, 50.
127 Three distribution centers for annuities were set up, but, as indicated by Wilson, "direct cash outlays were replaced by mailed checks" after World War I (*Underground Reservation*, 51). The pattern of delay, deny, defer continued.
128 Wilson, *Underground Reservation*, 34.
129 Wilson, *Underground Reservation*, 36.
130 Wilson, *Underground Reservation*, 63.
131 Wilson, *Underground Reservation*, 92–93.
132 Wilson, *Underground Reservation*, x.
133 Wilson, *Underground Reservation*, xi.
134 Burns, *History of the Osage People*, 417–20.
135 Burns, *History of the Osage People*, 421–22.
136 Wilson, *Underground Reservation*, 138–40.
137 Fairfax attorney D. Lafe Hubler, cited in Wilson, *Underground Reservation*, 140–41.
138 See McAuliffe, *Bloodland*.

139 Wilson, *Underground Reservation*, 151.
140 Wilson, *Underground Reservation*, 158.
141 Wilson, *Underground Reservation*, xii.
142 Callinicos, *Resources of Critique*, 256.
143 Hogan, *Mean Spirit*, 375.
144 Hogan, *Power*, 127.
145 Hogan, *Power*, 158.
146 De Angelis, "Separating the Doing and the Deed," 77–78.
147 See Foley and Hamm, "James Bay Dam, Electricity and Impacts."
148 Discussed in Agreements, Treaties and Negotiated Settlements Project, "James Bay and Northern Quebec Agreement and Complementary Agreements."
149 See Foley and Hamm, "James Bay Dam, Electricity and Impacts," case number 91, p. 4.
150 See Agreements, Treaties and Negotiated Settlement Project, "James Bay and Northern Québec Agreement and Complementary Agreements."
151 Hogan, *Solar Storms*, 281.
152 Hogan, *Solar Storms*, 39.
153 Hogan, *Solar Storms*, 52.
154 Hogan, *Solar Storms*, 283.
155 Hogan, *People of the Whale*.
156 Silko, *Almanac of the Dead*.
157 Silko, *Ceremony*.
158 Silko, *Ceremony*, 127.
159 Silko, *Ceremony*, 261.
160 Silko, *Gardens in the Dunes*.
161 Cuero, *Autobiography of Delfina Cuero*, 23.
162 First displaced by the Spanish Mission of San Diego, for which many of them worked, and later by the white settlers, some of the Kumeyaay Indians ended up on reservations, but not Delfina Cuero's family, who, like other southern Kumeyaay Indians, moved constantly from place to place, seeking work in El Cajon, Jamacha, Jamul, and then Barrett, doing farm labor or ranch work and getting paid in food and old clothing while living in the little houses made of willows, yucca, posts, reeds, and other brush that they built away from the ranch house. As more settlers moved in, the Kumeyaay had to move farther away from their traditional grounds around coastal San Diego, toward the mountains; eventually, in the case of Cuero's family, they moved south near Tecate in Baja California, where other Indians allowed them to stay, unaware that they had crossed into another country. Faced with serial displacements, survival and the need for a place to live have been Delfina Cuero's overriding concerns; when last contacted in 1970, she lived in Jamul, near San Diego, caring for an invalid woman.

163 References to the rebellion in Mexico would place the narrative between 1910 and 1920, but before the construction of the Colorado Aqueduct in 1932.
164 Silko, *Gardens in the Dunes*, 204.
165 Dispossession continues to be protested throughout the world, as evident in recent demonstrations where forceful shouts of "Occupation is a crime, from Standing Rock to Palestine" can be heard.
166 Vaughn, "Natives Struggle to Stay One with the Land."

Chapter Three. Enclosures in New Mexico

1 Weber, *Spanish Frontier in North America*, 107.
2 Jameson, "The Valences of History," in *Valences of the Dialectic*, 549.
3 Rebolledo and Márquez, *Women's Tales from the New Mexico WPA*.
4 Weber, *Spanish Frontier in North America*, 86.
5 Dunbar-Ortiz, *Roots of Resistance*, 25.
6 Schroeder, "Shifting for Survival in the Spanish Southwest," 242.
7 Dunbar-Ortiz, *Roots of Resistance*, 22.
8 Weber's notes to Schroeder, "Shifting for Survival in the Spanish Southwest," 238.
9 Chacón, *Writings of Eusebio Chacón*, 12–166.
10 Hammond, "Search for the Fabulous," 21.
11 Hammond, "Search for the Fabulous," 24.
12 Any colonizer, or adelantado, seeking to gain a contract from the Crown to settle a proposed area had to show proof of personal investment in the project. See Dunbar-Ortiz, *Roots of Resistance*, 27–28.
13 Westphall, *Mercedes Reales*, 4.
14 Westphall, *Mercedes Reales*, 4.
15 Dunbar-Ortiz, *Roots of Resistance*, 29.
16 Brooks, *Captives and Cousins*, 36.
17 Weber, *Spanish Frontier in North America*, 63.
18 Weber, *Spanish Frontier in North America*, 64.
19 Pérez de Villagrá, *History of New Mexico*.
20 Hodge, foreword to Pérez de Villagrá, *History of New Mexico*, 19.
21 Dunbar-Ortiz, *Roots of Resistance*, 29.
22 Weber, *Spanish Frontier in North America*, 65, 67.
23 Dunbar-Ortiz, *Roots of Resistance*, 33.
24 Weber, *Spanish Frontier in North America*, 101.
25 Weber, *What Caused the Pueblo Revolt of 1680?* See also chapter 1, this volume.
26 Maciel and Gonzales-Berry, "Nineteenth Century," 16.
27 Simmons, "Settlement Patterns and Village Plans," 100–101.
28 As Westphall notes, "The right of usufruct is normally perpetual unless the

land is not properly maintained, is used for purposes other than originally granted, or is abandoned" (*Mercedes Reales*, 12–13).

29 Westphall, *Mercedes Reales*, 16–17.
30 Westphall, *Mercedes Reales*, 11.
31 Westphall, *Mercedes Reales*, 45, 50.
32 Westphall, *Mercedes Reales*, 15.
33 Westphall, *Mercedes Reales*, 52.
34 Kiser, "A 'Charming Name for a Species of Slavery.'"
35 Rebolledo and Márquez, *Women's Tales from the New Mexico WPA*, 403.
36 Rebolledo and Márquez, *Women's Tales from the New Mexico WPA*, 395, 359.
37 Rebolledo and Márquez, *Women's Tales from the New Mexico WPA*, 358.
38 Rebolledo and Márquez, *Women's Tales from the New Mexico WPA*, 360.
39 Debt peonage is a kind of indentured servitude, with the difference that indentured servitude was based on a contract with a stipulated number of years. But in the case of debt peonage, servitude lasted as long as the debt, which in many cases never ended and in fact tended to grow due to family needs that required more indebtedness.
40 Rebolledo and Márquez, *Women's Tales from the New Mexico WPA*, 358–64.
41 Gildersleeve, *Reports of Cases Argued and Determined in the Supreme Court*, 190.
42 Gildersleeve, *Reports of Cases Argued and Determined in the Supreme Court*, 191.
43 Rebolledo and Márquez, *Women's Tales from the New Mexico WPA*, 403, 364.
44 Rebolledo and Márquez, *Women's Tales from the New Mexico WPA*, 403.
45 Kiser, "A 'Charming Name for a Species of Slavery,'" 169.
46 Ortiz Vásquez, *Enchanted Temple of Taos*, 15–16.
47 Rebolledo and Márquez, *Women's Tales from the New Mexico WPA*, 396.
48 Chávez, *New Mexico Past and Future*, 90–91.
49 "Unlike the chattel slavery elsewhere in North America, bonded slavery found affinity in the kin-based systems motivated less by demand for units of labor than their desire for prestigious social units." Brooks, *Captives and Cousins*, 34.
50 Westphall, *Mercedes Reales*, 11.
51 Jaramillo, *Romance of a Little Village Girl*.
52 See Weber, *Mexican Frontier*, 211.
53 Weber, *Mexican Frontier*, 211.
54 Weber, *Mexican Frontier*, 214.
55 Weber, *Mexican Frontier*, 261.
56 Weber, *Mexican Frontier*, 215–16.
57 Weber, *Mexican Frontier*, 250.
58 Weber, *Mexican Frontier*, 261.
59 See Maciel and Gonzales-Berry, *Contested Homeland*, 13.
60 Weber, *Mexican Frontier*, 263.

61 Weber, *Mexican Frontier*, 272–75.
62 US historian Fredrick Jackson Turner's assessment of the overall benefits of imperialist expansion here seem to find an echo in Weber, *Mexican Frontier*, 276.
63 Weber, *Mexican Frontier*, 277.
64 Ebright, "New Mexican Land Grants," 26.
65 Westphall, *Mercedes Reales*, 45.
66 Ebright, "New Mexican Land Grants," 26.
67 Weber rightfully recognizes that Armijo was also part owner of the Beaubien-Miranda lands but notes that "there is no reason to suppose that he acted solely out of self-interest as has been suggested" (*Mexican Frontier*, 194).
68 Weber, *Mexican Frontier*, 193.
69 See Chávez, *But Time and Change*, 131.
70 When José Chávez became governor in 1845, he went even further in allowing Beaubien, Bent, and St. Vrain to settle foreigners on the Beaubien-Miranda grant, a practice prohibited under then current policy (Weber, *Mexican Frontier*, 194).
71 Weber, *Mexican Frontier*, 36.
72 Weber, *Mexican Frontier*, 190.
73 Westphall, *Mercedes Reales*, 11.
74 Westphall, *Mercedes Reales*, 15.
75 Dunbar-Ortiz, *Roots of Resistance*, 10.
76 Dunbar-Ortiz, *Roots of Resistance*, 84.
77 Westphall, *Mercedes Reales*, 22.
78 Reséndez, *Changing National Identities at the Frontier*, 249.
79 Herrera, "New Mexico Resistance to U.S. Occupation," 26, 30.
80 Herrera, "New Mexico Resistance to U.S. Occupation," 29.
81 Herrera, "New Mexico Resistance to U.S. Occupation," 30.
82 Garrard, *Wah-to-yah and the Taos Trail*, 189.
83 Garrard, *Wah-to-yah and the Taos Trail*, 172, 173, 189.
84 Herrera, "New Mexico Resistance to U.S. Occupation," 35.
85 Herrera, "New Mexico Resistance to U.S. Occupation," 37.
86 Candelaria, *Not by the Sword*.
87 Westphall, *Mercedes Reales*, 14.
88 Gonzalez and Raleigh, *Caballero*.
89 Candelaria, *Not by the Sword*, 160.
90 Candelaria, *Not by the Sword*, 109–10.
91 Candelaria, *Not by the Sword*, 25.
92 Maciel and Gonzales-Berry, *Contested Homeland*, 12, 13.
93 Quoted in Weber, *Foreigners in Their Native Land*, 161.
94 Anaya, *Shaman Winter*, 170.
95 Candelaria, *Not by the Sword*, 107.

96 Candelaria, *Not by the Sword*, 148.
97 Chávez, *But Time and Change*, 86.
98 Vigil, *Los Patrones*, 9.
99 Chávez, *But Time and Change*, 23, 40–47.
100 See Cather, *Death Comes for the Archbishop*, for a negative portrayal.
101 Herrera, "New Mexico Resistance to U.S. Occupation," 30.
102 Jaramillo, *Romance of a Little Village Girl*, 7.
103 Jaramillo, *Romance of a Little Village Girl*, 7.
104 Jaramillo, *Romance of a Little Village Girl*, 9.
105 Ebright, "New Mexican Land Grants," 49.
106 Jaramillo, *Romance of a Little Village Girl*, 10.
107 Jaramillo, *Romance of a Little Village Girl*, 15.
108 Gómez-Quiñones, *Roots of Chicano Politics*, 236–237.
109 Gómez-Quiñones, *Roots of Chicano Politics*, 237, 240.
110 Nieto-Phillips, *Language of Blood*, 49, 53, 73, 77, also ties New Mexicans' insistence on whiteness to campaigns for statehood.
111 See Meléndrez and Lomelí's edition and translation of Eusebio Chacón, *The Writings of Eusebio Chacón*, 12, 255.
112 Chacón, *Writings of Eusebio Chacón*, 187.
113 Chacón, *Writings of Eusebio Chacón*, 188.
114 Chacón, *Writings of Eusebio Chacón*, 188.
115 Chacón, *Writings of Eusebio Chacón*, 188-189.
116 Chacón, *Writings of Eusebio Chacón*, 191.
117 Ebright, "New Mexican Land Grants," 44.
118 Ebright, "New Mexican Land Grants," 38.
119 Ebright, "New Mexican Land Grants," 39–40.
120 See Rebolledo and Márquez, *Women's Tales from the New Mexico WPA*, 152, 153.
121 Ebright, "New Mexican Land Grants," 46.
122 Ebright, "New Mexican Land Grants," 33.
123 Rodriguez, "Land, Water, and Ethnic Identity," 338.
124 See Ebright for a discussion of the various contingencies regarding validation of titles ("New Mexican Land Grants," 27–28).
125 Ebright, "New Mexican Land Grants," 29.
126 Ebright, "New Mexican Land Grants," 31.
127 Ebright, "New Mexican Land Grants," 32.
128 Ebright, "New Mexican Land Grants," 32.
129 See Ebright, "New Mexican Land Grants," 38. For further updated details of continuing lawsuits on Tierra Amarilla lands, see Ebright, Hughes, and Hendricks, *Four Square Leagues*.
130 Jaramillo, *Romance of a Little Village Girl*, 4.
131 Ebright, "New Mexican Land Grants," 46–47.

132 Ebright, "New Mexican Land Grants," 48–49.
133 Ebright, "New Mexican Land Grants," 41.
134 Ebright, "New Mexican Land Grants," 44, the Hayes case.
135 Ebright, "New Mexican Land Grants," 44, 45.
136 Maciel and Gonzales-Berry, *Contested Homeland*, 17.
137 Maciel and Gonzales-Berry, *Contested Homeland*, 16.
138 Rodriguez, "Land, Water, and Ethnic Identity," 338.
139 Rodriguez, "Land, Water, and Ethnic Identity," 342.
140 See US Census Bureau, Quick Facts: New Mexico, accessed July 27, 2020, https://www.census.gov/quickfacts/fact/table/NM/PSTO45219.
141 Gómez-Quiñones, *Roots of Chicano Politics*, 278.
142 Arellano, "People's Movement," 50, 59.
143 Arellano, "People's Movement," 61.
144 Arellano, "People's Movement," 62–63.
145 Rosenbaum and Larson, "Mexicano Resistance to the Expropriation," 288.
146 Rosenbaum and Larson, "Mexicano Resistance to the Expropriation," 288.
147 Rosenbaum and Larson, "Mexicano Resistance to the Expropriation," 289.
148 Martínez, "Las Gorras Blancas," 234.
149 Weber, *Foreigners in Their Native Land*, 235.
150 Weber, *Foreigners in Their Native Land*, 235–38.
151 Weber, *Foreigners in Their Native Land*, 237.
152 Rosenbaum and Larson, "Mexicano Resistance to the Expropriation," 293.
153 Rosenbaum and Larson, "Mexicano Resistance to the Expropriation," 293.
154 Rosenbaum and Larson, "Mexicano Resistance to the Expropriation," 293.
155 Quoted in Rosenbaum and Larson, "Mexicano Resistance to the Expropriation," 295.
156 Rosenbaum and Larson, "Mexicano Resistance to the Expropriation," 295.
157 Gómez-Quiñones, *Roots of Chicano Politics*, 280.
158 Arellano, "People's Movement," 63.
159 Gómez-Quiñones, *Roots of Chicano Politics*, 281.
160 Rosenbaum and Larson, "Mexicano Resistance to the Expropriation," 290.
161 Arellano, "People's Movement," 71.
162 Arellano, "People's Movement," 72; Vigil, *Los Patrones*, 88–89.
163 Arellano, "People's Movement," 75.
164 Ebright, "New Mexican Land Grants," 42.
165 Ebright, "New Mexican Land Grants," 46.
166 Chacón, *Writings of Eusebio Chacón*, 82.
167 Gómez-Quiñones, *Roots of Chicano Politics*, 282.
168 Vigil, *Los Patrones*, 112–13.
169 Arellano, "People's Movement," 71.
170 Arellano, "People's Movement," 74.
171 Cabeza de Baca, *We Fed Them Cactus*, x.

172 Cabeza de Baca, *We Fed Them Cactus*, 50.
173 Cabeza de Baca, *We Fed Them Cactus*, 89–90.
174 Cabeza de Baca, *We Fed Them Cactus*, 90.
175 Rosenbaum and Larson, "Mexicano Resistance to the Expropriation," 295. Some hold that La Mano Negra was an anarchist-inflected society imported to New Mexico by recent Spanish immigrants who operated a bootlegging ring as well as by a gang that controlled northern New Mexico's criminal activity.
176 Rosenbaum and Larson, "Mexicano Resistance to the Expropriation," 295.
177 Rosales, *Chicano*, 154.
178 Rosenbaum and Larson, "Mexicano Resistance to the Expropriation," 297.
179 Rosenbaum and Larson, "Mexicano Resistance to the Expropriation," 297.
180 Rosales, *Chicano*, 168.
181 Elizondo, *Muerte en una estrella*, 102.
182 Maciel and Gonzales-Berry, *Contested Homeland*, 15.
183 Rosenbaum and Larson, "Mexicano Resistance to the Expropriation," 280.
184 Rosenbaum and Larson, "Mexicano Resistance to the Expropriation," 280.
185 Rosenbaum and Larson, "Mexicano Resistance to the Expropriation," 281.
186 Gómez, *Manifest Destinies*, 98.
187 Vigil, *Los Patrones*, 45.
188 Vigil, *Los Patrones*, 46.
189 Gómez, *Manifest Destinies*, 100–105.
190 Gómez-Quiñones, *Roots of Chicano Politics*, 238.
191 Chávez, *But Time and Change*, 140.
192 Chávez, *But Time and Change*, 144–46.
193 Vigil, *Los Patrones*, 95.
194 Vigil, *Los Patrones*, 101.
195 See Secor-Welsh, introduction to *My Life on the Frontier, 1864–1882*, by Miguel Antonio Otero, xlii.
196 Gómez-Quiñones, *Roots of Chicano Politics*, 259.
197 Secor-Welsh, introduction, xix.
198 Secor-Welsh, introduction, xxx.
199 Gómez-Quiñones, *Roots of Chicano Politics*, 241.
200 Secor-Welsh, introduction, xlii.
201 Otero, *My Life on the Frontier, 1864–1882*, 83.
202 Secor-Welsh, introduction, xxxi.
203 Rivera, introduction to *The Real Billy the Kid*, by Miguel Antonio Otero, xiii.
204 Otero, *Real Billy the Kid*, 73.
205 De Aragón, new foreword to *My Nine Years as Governor*, by Miguel Antonio Otero, iii.
206 Otero, *My Life on the Frontier, 1882–1897*, 98–101.
207 Gómez-Quiñones, *Roots of Chicano Politics*, 241.

208 Ebright, "New Mexican Land Grants," 39–40.
209 Rivera, introduction, xxxiii–xxxiv.
210 Rivera, introduction, xxxiv.
211 Gómez-Quiñones, *Roots of Chicano Politics*, 260.
212 Vigil, *Los Patrones*, 102.
213 Rivera, introduction, xiii.
214 Rivera, introduction, xvi.
215 Gómez-Quiñones, *Roots of Chicano Politics*, 261.
216 Padilla, "Leaving a 'Clean and Honorable Name,'" 161.
217 Otero, *Real Billy the Kid*, 45.
218 Chávez, *New Mexico Past and Future*, 131.
219 Maciel and Gonzales-Berry, *Contested Homeland*, 18.
220 Maciel and Gonzales-Berry, *Contested Homeland*, 21.
221 Nieto-Phillips, "Spanish American Ethnic Identity," 97–142.
222 As noted by Nieto-Phillips, the issue of statehood had the support of a number of Nuevomexicano ricos, Anglos, land speculators, and politicians who were interested in gaining "greater local control over land, resources, and political offices" ("Spanish American Ethnic Identity," 105). For further discussion on this point, see Nieto-Phillips, *Language of Blood*, 106.
223 Padilla, *My History, Not Yours*.
224 Padilla, *My History, Not Yours*, 118.
225 Meléndez, "Nuevo México by Any Other Name," 144.
226 Referenced in Meléndez, "Nuevo México by Any Other Name," 144.
227 Weber, *Spanish Frontier in North America*, 260.
228 Chávez, *Short Stories of Fray Angélico Chávez*.
229 In Chávez's story "A Romeo and Juliet Story in Early New Mexico," on the other hand, a modern perspective is developed, in contrast to other stories. This tale speaks not only to the racism of Nuevomexicanos/as but also to the reality that there was a good bit of racial mixing.
230 Padilla, *My History, Not Yours*, 202–3.
231 Padilla, *My History, Not Yours*, 203.
232 Cabeza de Baca, *We Fed Them Cactus*, 176.
233 Cabeza de Baca, *We Fed Them Cactus*, 6.
234 Cabeza de Baca, *We Fed Them Cactus*, 121.
235 Cabeza de Baca, *We Fed Them Cactus*, 129.
236 Cabeza de Baca, *We Fed Them Cactus*, 81.
237 What did occur is that the grant was patented by Congress to the entire town, but as Rosenbaum and Larson explain, the grant of Las Vegas would be in the hands of land speculators by 1902 ("Mexicano Resistance to the Expropriation," 288–93).
238 Cabeza de Baca, *We Fed Them Cactus*, x.
239 Cabeza de Baca, *We Fed Them Cactus*, 53.

240 Cabeza de Baca, *We Fed Them Cactus*, 178.
241 Cabeza de Baca, *We Fed Them Cactus*, 178.
242 Cabeza de Baca, *We Fed Them Cactus*, 17.
243 Cabeza de Baca, *We Fed Them Cactus*, 31.
244 Cabeza de Baca, *We Fed Them Cactus*, 60.
245 Cabeza de Baca, *We Fed Them Cactus*, 61.
246 Cabeza de Baca, *We Fed Them Cactus*, 73.
247 Cabeza de Baca, *We Fed Them Cactus*, 176.
248 Cabeza de Baca, *We Fed Them Cactus*, 176.
249 Cabeza de Baca, *Good Life*, 14.
250 Padilla, *My History, Not Yours*, 199; Jaramillo, *Shadows of the Past*.
251 Padilla, *My History, Not Yours*, 215.
252 Jaramillo, *Shadows of the Past*, 12.
253 Jaramillo, *Shadows of the Past*, 31.
254 Jaramillo, *Shadows of the Past*, 13–14.
255 Jaramillo, *Shadows of the Past*, 97.
256 Jaramillo, *Shadows of the Past*, 35.
257 Ulibarrí, *Mi abuela fumaba puros*, 159–61.
258 Ulibarrí, *Mi abuela fumaba puros*, 159.
259 Ulibarrí, *Mi abuela fumaba puros*, 159.
260 Jaramillo, *Shadows of the Past*, 187.
261 Jaramillo, *Shadows of the Past*, 187.
262 Herrera, "New Mexico Resistance to U.S. Occupation," 30.
263 Rodriguez, "Land, Water, and Ethnic Identity," 382.
264 De Angelis, "Separating the Doing and the Deed," 77.
265 Rodriguez, "Land, Water, and Ethnic Identity," 313.
266 Since then, Brabeck-Letmathe has backtracked and said that what he meant is that water should be better managed. See "Does Peter Brabeck-Letmathe Believe That Water Is a Human Right?," Nestlé, accessed July 27, 2020, https://www.nestle.com/ask-nestle/human-rights/answers/nestle-chairman-peter-brabeck-letmathe-believes-water-is-a-human-right.
267 Anaya, *Alburquerque*, 120.
268 Anaya, *Jemez Spring*, 111.
269 Anaya, *Jemez Spring*, 252.
270 Anaya, *Jemez Spring*, 252.
271 Shiva, *Water Wars*, ix.
272 "All Issues," Environment New Mexico, accessed July 27, 2020 https://www.environmentnewmexico.org/issues.
273 Like water, salt was also part of the commons in the past. In the WPA testimonies, one of the women, Chana, recalls that until 1904, the salt lakes east of Estancia Valley in New Mexico were communal and salt was free, but after the land was privatized under the Homestead Act and thereafter sold, Nuevo-

mexicanos/as had to pay for access to the salt (Rebolledo and Márquez, *Women's Tales from the New Mexico WPA*, 21).

Chapter Four. Texas Narratives of Dispossession

1. Jameson, *Valences of the Dialectic*, 549.
2. Semo, *Historia Mexicana*.
3. In the south, what Valerio-Jiménez calls "a northern Mexican regional identity" was dominant, as the lower Rio Grande valley residents were closely linked to communities or *villas del norte* on the south side of the Rio Grande. These villas saw themselves as geographically isolated from more southern settlements and towns in New Spain and therefore as a separate regional entity. See Valerio-Jiménez, *River of Hope*, 277. Also see Montejano, *Anglos and Mexicans in the Making of Texas*.
4. Arreola, *Tejano South Texas*, xi.
5. Lefebvre's notion of space as socially constructed is useful here, especially his distinction of perceived space, conceived space, and lived space. See Lefebvre, *Production of Space*.
6. Arreola, *Tejano South Texas*, 6.
7. It was also closely linked to communities south of the Rio Grande; in fact ranchers in South Texas often had their homes or second homes on the south side of the river.
8. This newer generation of historians and geographers is intent on questioning long-standing presuppositions, bringing interdisciplinary lenses to the object of study and fleshing out historical idiosyncrasies. See, for example, Valerio-Jiménez, *River of Hope*; Ramos, *Beyond the Alamo*; Reséndez, *Changing National Identities at the Frontier*.
9. Alonzo, *Tejano Legacy*.
10. Hinojosa, *Claros varones de Belken*, 11.
11. Newcomb, *Indians of Texas*, 29.
12. Those Coahuiltecas who were not decimated or pushed out of the territory would be enslaved and used as forced labor; in time they would undoubtedly mix with mestizos and Spaniards moving north. Our word *mitote*, for example, comes from the Coahuiltecas, who were first described by Cabeza de Vaca in his account of the 1527 Narváez expedition sent by Spain to explore Florida. For more information on Coahuiltecan culture, see Lovett, González, Bacha-Garza, and Skowronek, *Native American Peoples of South Texas*, 17.
13. Newcomb, *Indians of Texas*, 282.
14. Newcomb, *Indians of Texas*, 334.
15. The 1527 Narváez expedition to Florida was a disaster from the beginning. Of the three hundred crew members, four would survive and travel through Coahuilteca and Karankawa territory in 1528–36. Cabeza de Vaca's account of

the voyage would provide detailed ethnographic information on Texas Indians. See Núñez Cabeza de Vaca, *La relación*.
16 Pérez, *Forgetting the Alamo*.
17 See Weber, *Spanish Frontier in North America*, 113.
18 Valerio-Jiménez, *River of Hope*, 27.
19 Valerio-Jiménez, *River of Hope*, 27.
20 Valerio-Jiménez, *River of Hope*, 27.
21 The French established Québec in 1608, and by 1682 La Salle was exploring the Mississippi River valley from Canada to the Gulf of Mexico for France. In 1685 Spain learned of La Salle's expedition from Canada, and from 1686 to 1689 Spanish soldiers searched for his post on the Gulf.
22 Weber, *Spanish Frontier in North America*, 144.
23 González and Raleigh, *Caballero*.
24 Semo, *Historia Mexicana*.
25 Arreola, *Tejano South Texas*, 36.
26 Weber, *Bárbaros*, 105–6.
27 Alonzo, *Tejano Legacy*, 28.
28 Weber, *Bárbaros*, 106.
29 Alonzo, *Tejano Legacy*, 31.
30 Valerio-Jiménez, *River of Hope*, 58.
31 Alonzo, *Tejano Legacy*, 49.
32 Alonzo, *Tejano Legacy*, 34–35.
33 Alonzo, *Tejano Legacy*, 39.
34 Valerio-Jiménez, *River of Hope*, 52.
35 Alonzo, *Tejano Legacy*, 55.
36 Grants consisted of two or more *sitios*. A sitio measured 4,428 acres of land. Haciendas could measure five or more sitios (Alonzo, *Tejano Legacy*, 36, 39).
37 Alonzo, *Tejano Legacy*, 44; see also Montejano, *Anglos and Mexicans in the Making of Texas*; Valerio-Jiménez, *River of Hope*; and Gonzalez, *Dew on the Thorn*.
38 Alonzo cites Paredes in his studies where he notes that "the patriarchs held the reins of power in the ranchos, making decisions concerning planting, rodeos, or roundups as well as decisions affecting family matters" (Alonzo, *Tejano Legacy*, 45).
39 Valerio-Jiménez, *River of Hope*, 28.
40 Alonzo, *Tejano Legacy*, 272.
41 Weber, *Mexican Frontier*, 175.
42 Bancroft, *History of the North Mexican States and Texas*, 52.
43 Arreola, *Tejano South Texas*, 37.
44 See the indispensable work of Paul W. Gates, *History of Public Land Law Development*, for information on land grants in Texas.
45 Chávez Orozco, "Orígenes de la cuestión tejana," 197.

46 Gates, *History of Public Land Law Development*, 81.
47 Mier y Terán, *Crónica de Tejas*. Mier y Terán was an engineer by training and head of Mexico's Escuela de Artillería.
48 Chávez Orozco, "Orígenes de la cuestión tejana," 173.
49 Another empresario who received colonization contracts in Texas was the Mexican Lorenzo de Zavala. Unlike Mier y Terán, who wished to suspend settlement by US colonists, de Zavala, who was a great admirer of the United States, by 1835 had joined the movement for Texas independence from Mexico. See de Zavala, *Journey to the United States of North America*, 2, 202.
50 Alamán cited in Weber, *Mexican Frontier*, 170.
51 In his reports, Mier y Terán suggested suspending additional settlement by Americans and establishing garrisons of troops as colonies. Also coming to Texas were numerous Indian tribes that were being displaced in the southern and midwestern United States, as Indian Country kept being enclosed. Native tribes in Texas were also being dispossessed and were unable to hold on to their lands without proper title (Mier y Terán, *Crónica de Tejas*, 184).
52 Chávez Orozco, "Orígenes de la cuestión tejana," 190.
53 Gómez-Quiñones, *Roots of Chicano Politics*, 144.
54 Gates, *History of Public Land Law Development*, 81.
55 Bancroft, *History of the North Mexican States and Texas*, 148.
56 Gates, *History of Public Land Law Development*, 81.
57 Gates, *History of Public Land Law Development*, 82.
58 Gómez-Quiñones, *Roots of Chicano Politics*, 183.
59 Cited in Gómez-Quiñones, *Roots of Chicano Politics*, 183.
60 Bancroft, *History of the North Mexican States and Texas*, 346.
61 Montejano, *Anglos and Mexicans in the Making of Texas*, 31.
62 Weber, *Spanish Frontier in North America*, 247, 246.
63 Alonzo, *Tejano Legacy*, 97.
64 Valerio-Jiménez, *River of Hope*, 148.
65 Valerio-Jiménez, *River of Hope*, 180. The elite Tejanos/as, those of the large landowning families, would reach accommodation with the Anglos to retain their lands (149). While Alonzo does not see the blatant violence that other historians find in Anglo-Tejano relations, he notes that in south Texas, Tejanos/as lost their lands in a more gradual process of dispossession (Alonzo, *Tejano Legacy*, 280).
66 Montejano, *Anglos and Mexicans in the Making of Texas*, 30.
67 See Graham, *Kings of Texas*, 29.
68 Domenech cited in Graham, *Kings of Texas*, 36.
69 Olmsted, cited in Graham, *Kings of Texas*, 63.
70 The Anglo disdain for Mexican residents and communities is clear in the articles published by Edward King in 1874. See King, *Texas: 1874*, 111.
71 Graham, *Kings of Texas*, 175, 185.

72 The King Ranch is the largest ranch in the United States and, Graham notes, it is composed of four divisions (Santa Gertrudis, Laureles, Norias, and Encino) situated in south Texas (Graham, *Kings of Texas*, 66).
73 Graham, *Kings of Texas*, 76, 80.
74 Graham, *Kings of Texas*, 120.
75 Graham, *Kings of Texas*, 129. Graham cites Hobart Huson, who in his monumental two-volume history of Refugio County, describes "a mass exodus of *Tejanos* following the outbreaks of vigilantism and violence in the wake of the Swift murders: The roads were lined with ox-carts and wagons headed west" (130). In Refugio County, Thad Swift and his wife were found murdered and cut to pieces at their house in June 1874.
76 Gómez-Quiñones, *Roots of Chicano Politics*, 202.
77 Already in 1850 there were separatists interested in forming the Territory of the Río Grande, but these efforts failed to materialize. See Larralde and Esparza, *Chicano Chronicle*.
78 Valerio-Jiménez, *River of Hope*, 224.
79 Graham, *Kings of Texas*, 80.
80 Graham, *Kings of Texas*, 83.
81 Valerio-Jiménez, *River of Hope*, 226.
82 Valerio-Jiménez, *River of Hope*, 222.
83 Valerio-Jiménez, *River of Hope*, 275.
84 Gómez-Quiñones, *Roots of Chicano Politics*, 205.
85 Valerio-Jiménez, *River of Hope*, 271.
86 McNelly's policy was to apply the Spanish *ley de fuga* and kill all prisoners who tried to escape (Graham, *Kings of Texas*, 139). McNelly would even go south of the border in search of raiders and kill the wrong vaqueros (153). King was a strong supporter of McNelly's Rangers, who did his bidding; the state of Texas would ultimately dismiss McNelly from the Rangers in 1877 for his zero-tolerance policy regarding Tejano-Mexicanos.
87 Paredes, *George Washington Gómez*, 12.
88 See Hinojosa, *Klail City Death Trip Series*; Ferber, *Giant*.
89 Montejano, *Anglos and Mexicans in the Making of Texas*, 106.
90 Montejano, *Anglos and Mexicans in the Making of Texas*, 107.
91 Montejano, *Anglos and Mexicans in the Making of Texas*, 109.
92 Montejano, *Anglos and Mexicans in the Making of Texas*, 110.
93 Montejano, *Anglos and Mexicans in the Making of Texas*, 104.
94 Montejano, *Anglos and Mexicans in the Making of Texas*, 105.
95 Foley, *White Scourge*, 45.
96 Cited in Foley, *White Scourge*, 53.
97 Foley, *White Scourge*, 59.
98 Montejano, *Anglos and Mexicans in the Making of Texas*, 114.
99 Montejano, *Anglos and Mexicans in the Making of Texas*, 114.

100 Montejano, *Anglos and Mexicans in the Making of Texas*, 115.
101 Montejano, *Anglos and Mexicans in the Making of Texas*, 116.
102 Montejano, *Anglos and Mexicans in the Making of Texas*, 117.
103 Gómez-Quiñones, *Roots of Chicano Politics*, 349.
104 Graham, *Kings of Texas*, 204.
105 Gómez-Quiñones, *Roots of Chicano Politics*, 351.
106 Behind this irredentist sedicioso movement was much bitter resentment against the Anglo ranchers who had used various means to dispossess Tejanos/as.
107 Montejano, *Anglos and Mexicans in the Making of Texas*, 113.
108 Alonzo, *Tejano Legacy*, 9.
109 Alonzo, *Tejano Legacy*, 11.
110 Alonzo, *Tejano Legacy*, 12.
111 Gómez-Quiñones, *Roots of Chicano Politics*, 307.
112 Alonzo, *Tejano Legacy*, 12.
113 Montejano, *Anglos and Mexicans in the Making of Texas*, 297.
114 Montejano, *Anglos and Mexicans in the Making of Texas*, 298; Gómez-Quiñones, *Roots of Chicano Politics*, 310.
115 Alonzo, *Tejano Legacy*, 8.
116 See Sandra Cisneros's short story "Mericans."
117 History recalls a number of abuses, not only lynchings of Mexicans but also the appropriation of vital goods and services. The El Paso Salt War serves as a telling example. In the end Rangers dispossessed the people of the salt lake held in common, and thereafter all were forced to pay a fee for salt. See Weber, *Foreigners in Their Native Land*, 208.
118 See Valerio-Jiménez's chapter on the matter of contested citizenship (*River of Hope*, 222–74). Questioning of US citizenship would remain an issue for ethnic Mexicans, as the deportation of US citizens of Mexican descent during the 1930s as well as in the current moment under President Trump demonstrate.
119 For further discussion, see Cleary, Esty, and Lye, "Peripheral Realisms," particularly the article by Esty and Lye, "Peripheral Realisms Now."
120 Paredes, "Shadow on the Border," 141.
121 Perales and Ramos, "Building a Project to Expand Texas History," xi.
122 See "Early Life and Education," in González, *Dew on the Thorn*, ix.
123 Jameson, *Antinomies of Realism*, 271.
124 Limón, introduction to González and Raleigh, *Caballero*.
125 Cited in Limón, introduction, xix, from a letter by González.
126 Limón, introduction, xix.
127 Limón, introduction, xix.
128 For Don Santiago, an arranged marriage is a way to ensure the bloodline, a fruitful marriage with many children, and class status.

129 González and Raleigh, *Caballero*, 280.
130 Alonzo, *Tejano Legacy*, 266.
131 Jameson, *Antinomies of Realism*, 289.
132 González, *Woman Who Lost Her Soul*.
133 González, *Dew on the Thorn*, 7.
134 González, *Dew on the Thorn*, 9.
135 Limón, introduction, 8, comment on "bracketed passage" in González.
136 To use Limón's words, introduction, 9.
137 González, *Dew on the Thorn*, 10.
138 González, *Dew on the Thorn*, 11.
139 González, *Dew on the Thorn*, 11.
140 González, *Dew on the Thorn*, 12.
141 González, *Dew on the Thorn*, 14.
142 González, *Dew on the Thorn*, 15.
143 González, *Dew on the Thorn*, 14.
144 González, *Dew on the Thorn*, 144.
145 González, *Dew on the Thorn*, 179.
146 Rivera, *Y no se lo tragó la tierra*.
147 Pérez, *Forgetting the Alamo*, 105.
148 Pérez, *Forgetting the Alamo*, 165.
149 Pérez, *Forgetting the Alamo*, 201.
150 Pérez, *Forgetting the Alamo*, 22.
151 Taibo, *El Álamo*.
152 The story of Texas independence, says Taibo, has been told from the perspective of the white dominant class and not that of the dispossessed Mexicanos, the slaves, the Apaches and Comanches, and all the other Indians who would be forced out of the state (*El Álamo*, 16). We agree with that assessment.
153 Taibo, *El Álamo*, 155.
154 Taibo, *El Álamo*, 223.
155 Treviño, *Seguín*. Interestingly, Treviño filmed *Seguín* on the same sets that John Wayne used for his 1960 film *The Alamo*.
156 Ramos, *Beyond the Alamo*, 159.
157 Flores, *Remembering the Alamo*, 12.
158 See Flores, *Remembering the Alamo*, 160. Like Taibo, Flores recognizes that most of the defenders of the Alamo were not Texans (30).
159 De Zavala, *History and Legends of the Alamo*. Adina de Zavala is the granddaughter of Lorenzo de Zavala and New York–born Emily West; her father was Augustine de Zavala, who married the Irish-born Julia Tyrrell.
160 Montejano, *Anglos and Mexicans in the Making of Texas*, 224.
161 Gómez-Quiñones, *Roots of Chicano Politics*, 136, 270.
162 Tafolla, *Life Crossing Borders*.
163 Valerio-Jiménez, *River of Hope*, 247.

164 Gómez-Quiñones, *Roots of Chicano Politics*, 277.
165 Gómez-Quiñones, *Roots of Chicano Politics*, 307.
166 Saldívar, *Borderlands of Culture*, 37.
167 Paredes, *George Washington Gómez*, 20.
168 Paredes, *George Washington Gómez*, 102–3.
169 Jameson, *Antinomies of Realism*, 146.
170 Montejano, *Anglos and Mexicans in the Making of Texas*, 297.
171 According to Sandos, the armed insurrection that erupted in South Texas needs to be viewed in relation to at least three factors: the internal conflicts resulting from Tejano dispossession, the Mexican Revolution of 1910, and the revolutionary politics of the Flores Magón brothers. See Sandos, *Rebellion in the Borderlands*.
172 Sandos, *Rebellion in the Borderlands*, xvii.
173 Montejano, *Anglos and Mexicans in the Making of Texas*, 117.
174 Montejano, *Anglos and Mexicans in the Making of Texas*, 126.
175 Montejano, *Anglos and Mexicans in the Making of Texas*, 117.
176 Graham, *Kings of Texas*, 204.
177 Paredes, *George Washington Gómez*, 15.
178 Paredes, *George Washington Gómez*, 16.
179 Paredes, *George Washington Gómez*, 148.
180 Paredes, *George Washington Gómez*, 147.
181 Paredes, *George Washington Gómez*, 147.
182 Paredes, *George Washington Gómez*, 148.
183 Paredes, *George Washington Gómez*, 195.
184 Paredes, *George Washington Gómez*, 197.
185 Paredes, *George Washington Gómez*, 294.
186 Paredes, *George Washington Gómez*, 300.
187 Paredes, *George Washington Gómez*, 300.
188 Paredes, *George Washington Gómez*, 300.
189 Montejano, *Anglos and Mexicans in the Making of Texas*, 28.
190 See *Klail City Death Trip Series*, Hinojosa's chronicle/cronicón of the Texas lower Rio Grande valley, that includes fifteen works, among them *Estampas del Valle y otras obras*; *Generaciones y semblanzas*; *Klail City y sus alrededores*; *Korean Love Sons*; *Rites and Witnesses*; *Mi querido Rafa*; *The Valley*; *Dear Rafe*; *Partners in Crime*; *Klail City*; *Claros varones de Belken*; *Becky and Her Friends*; *Ask a Policeman*; *The Useless Servants*; and *We Happy Few*.
191 Hinojosa, *Claros varones de Belken*, 115, 129. See also Hinojosa, *Valley*.
192 Hinojosa, *Claros varones de Belken*, 207.
193 The population of the Rio Grande valley today is close to 1.5 million, a product of mass Mexican migration post-1848.
194 The insinuation in the novel is that the Leguizamón family is Jewish, but of course with names like Jehú and Buenrostro and brothers named Aaron and

Israel the idea is that several of these families, including the Buenrostros and Malacaras, are probably descendants of *conversos*. The Leguizamón family, however, is said not to be *raza*, to be motherless—"*no tener madre*"—an insult in Mexican speech. Hinojosa, *Claros varones de Belken*, 147.
195 Hinojosa, *Valley*, 80.
196 Hinojosa, *Valley*, 80.
197 Hinojosa, *Claros varones de Belken*, 10.
198 Noddy is not a graduate of some fancy business school. He is said to be the son of fruit tramps who arrived in early 1900, before the seditionists; though poor, he had a good head for business; he married Blanche Cook—with the good sense to marry up—and took over managing the bank and other business affairs of the family.
199 Hinojosa, *Claros varones de Belken*, 51.
200 Hinojosa, *Mi querido Rafa*, 25.
201 Hinojosa, *Ask a Policeman*, 60.
202 Descendants of the nephew of Father José Nicolás Ballí, who was granted Padre Island off the Texas coast in 1759, have sued Gilbert Kerlin, a New York lawyer, who in association with his uncle Fredric Gilbert in 1938 bought land on South Padre Island from fifty-four Ballí heirs, paying each no more and often less than $300, with the stipulation that they would retain subsoil mineral rights (Alonzo, *Tejano Legacy*, 156).
203 Cisneros, *Land Grant*.

Conclusion

1 León-Portilla, *Los antiguos mexicanos*, 76, 99. See also León-Portilla, "Los aztecas."
2 Paredes, *With His Pistol in His Hand*, 56.
3 De Angelis, "Separating the Doing and the Deed."
4 See Federici, "Women, Land Struggle, and the Valorization of Labor"; and Federici, "Debt Crisis," 303–16.
5 Caffentzis, "Power of Money."
6 Caffentzis, "Power of Money."
7 See Moore, *Capitalism in the Web of Life*; see also Malm, *Fossil Capital*.
8 De Angelis, "Separating the Doing and the Deed," 79; Federici, "Debt Crisis," 313.
9 Limón, *The River Flows North*.
10 De Angelis, "Separating the Doing and the Deed," 80–81.
11 See, in particular, Rivera, "Salamanders" and "Zoo Island."
12 Rivera, "Salamanders," 225.

Bibliography

Agreements, Treaties and Negotiated Settlements Project. "James Bay and Northern Quebec Agreement and Complementary Agreements." November 11, 1975. http://www.atns.net.au/agreement.asp?EntityiD=2026.
Albó, Xavier. "Del indio negado al permitido y al protagónico en América Latina." In *Atlas Lingüístico de América Latina y el Caribe*, 981–1003. Cochabamba, Bolivia: UNICEF.
Alonzo, Armando. *Tejano Legacy: Rancheros and Settlers in South Texas, 1734–1900*. Albuquerque: University of New Mexico Press, 1998.
Amin, Samir. *Accumulation on a World Scale*. New York: Monthly Review Press, 1974.
Anaya, Rudolfo. *Alburquerque*. Albuquerque: University of New Mexico Press, 1992.
Anaya, Rudolfo. *Jemez Spring*. Albuquerque: University of New Mexico Press, 2005.
Anaya, Rudolfo. *Shaman Winter*. Albuquerque: University of New Mexico Press, 1999.
Arellano, Anselmo. "The People's Movement: Las Gorras Blancas." In *The Contested Homeland: A Chicano History of New Mexico*, edited by David Maciel and Erlinda Gonzales-Berry, 59–82. Albuquerque: University of New Mexico Press, 2000.
Arreola, Daniel D. *Tejano South Texas: A Mexican Cultural Province*. Austin: University of Texas Press, 2002.
Baker, Houston A., Jr. *Critical Memory: Public Spheres, African American Writing, and Black Fathers and Sons in America*. Athens: University of Georgia Press, 2001.
Baker, Houston A., Jr. "Critical Memory and the Black Public Sphere." In *The Black

Public Sphere: A Public Culture Book, edited by the Black Public Sphere Collective, 5–37. Chicago: University of Chicago Press, 1995.

Bancroft, H. H. *History of the North Mexican States and Texas: The Works*. Vol. 16. San Francisco: History Company, 1889.

Banner, Stuart. *How the Indians Lost Their Land: Law and Power on the Frontier*. Cambridge, MA: Harvard University Press, 2005.

Barr, Juliana. *Peace Came in the Form of a Woman: Indians and Spaniards in the Texas Borderlands*. Chapel Hill: University of North Carolina Press, 2007.

Benson, Lee. "The Historian as Myth Maker: Turner and the Closed Frontier." In *The Frontier in American Development: Essays in Honor of Paul W. Gates*, edited by David M. Ellis, 3–19. Ithaca, NY: Cornell University Press, 1969.

Berle, Adolf A. "A Few Questions for the Diplomatic Pouch." *New York Times*, February 15, 1959.

Brenner, Robert. "Agrarian Class Structure and Economic Development in Pre-industrial Europe." In *The Brenner Debate: Agrarian Class Structure and Economic Development in Pre-Industrial Europe*, edited by T. H. Aston and C. H. E. Philpin, 10–63. New York: Cambridge University Press, 1990.

Briggs, Charles L., and John R. Van Ness, eds. *Land, Water, and Culture: New Perspectives on Hispanic Land Grants*. Albuquerque: University of New Mexico Press, 1987.

Brito, Aristeo. *El Diablo en Texas*. Tucson: Editorial Peregrinos, 1976.

Brooks, James F. *Captives and Cousins: Slavery, Kinship, and Community in the Southwest Borderlands*. Chapel Hill: University of North Carolina Press, 2002.

Burns, Louis F. *A History of the Osage People*. Tuscaloosa: University of Alabama Press, 2004.

Byrd, Jodi A. *The Transit of Empire: Indigenous Critiques of Colonialism*. Minneapolis: University of Minnesota Press, 2011.

Cabeza de Baca, Fabiola. *We Fed Them Cactus*. Albuquerque: University of New Mexico Press, 1954.

Cabeza de Baca Gilbert, Fabiola. *The Good Life: New Mexico Traditions and Food*. Santa Fe: Museum of New Mexico Press, 2005.

Cable, George Washington. *The Grandissimes: A Story of Creole Life*. New York: Penguin, 1988.

Caffentzis, George. "On the Notion of a Crisis of Social Reproduction: A Theoretical Review." *Commoner*, no. 5 (autumn 2002): 1–22.

Caffentzis, George. "The Power of Money: Debt and Enclosure." *Commoner*, no. 7 (spring/summer 2003): 1–4.

Caffentzis, George. "A Tale of Two Conferences: Globalization, the Crisis of Neoliberalism, and the Question of the Commons." *Borderlands* 11, no. 2 (September 2012): http://borderlands.net.au/vol11no2_2012/caffentzis_globalization.pdf.

Callinicos, Alex. *The Resources of Critique*. Cambridge: Polity, 2006.

Candelaria, Nash. *Inheritance of Strangers*. Tempe, AZ: Bilingual Review, 1985.

Candelaria, Nash. *Not by the Sword*. Tempe, AZ: Bilingual Review, 1982.

Cather, Willa. *Death Comes for the Archbishop*. New York: Knopf, 1927.

Chacón, Eusebio. *The Writings of Eusebio Chacón*. Edited and translated by A. Gabriel Meléndez and Francisco A. Lomelí. Albuquerque: University of New Mexico Press, 2012.

Chávez, Fray Angélico. *But Time and Change: The Story of Padre Martínez of Taos, 1793–1867*. Santa Fe: Sunstone, 1981.

Chávez, Fray Angélico. "A Romeo and Juliet Story in Early New Mexico." In *The Short Stories of Fray Angélico Chávez*, edited by Genaro Padilla, 37–45. Albuquerque: University of New Mexico Press, 1987.

Chávez, Fray Angélico. *The Short Stories of Fray Angélico Chávez*. Edited by Genaro Padilla. Albuquerque: University of New Mexico Press, 1987.

Chávez, Thomas E. *New Mexico Past and Future*. Albuquerque: University of New Mexico Press, 2006.

Chávez Orozco, Luis. "Apéndice: Orígenes de la cuestión tejana." In *Crónica de Tejas: Diario de viaje de la comisión de límites*, edited by Mauricio Molina, 171–200. Mexico City: Instituto Nacional de Bellas Artes y Gobierno del Estado de Tamaulipas, 1988.

Cisneros, Carlos. *The Land Grant*. Houston: Arte Público, 2012.

Cisneros, Sandra. "Mericans." In *Woman Hollering Creek*, 17–20. New York: Vintage, 1992.

Clark, Blue. *Lone Wolf v. Hitchcock: Treaty Rights and Indian Law at the End of the Nineteenth Century*. Lincoln: University of Nebraska Press, 1994.

Cleary, Joe, Jed Esty, and Colleen Lye, eds. "Peripheral Realisms" (special issue). *Modern Language Quarterly* 73, no. 3 (2012).

Cuello, José. "Beyond the 'Borderlands' Is the North of Colonial Mexico: A Latin Americanist Perspective to the Study of the Mexican North and the United States Southwest." In *Proceedings of the Pacific Coast Council on Latin American Studies* 9 (1982): 1–24.

Cuero, Delfina. *The Autobiography of Delfina Cuero, a Diegueño Indian*, as told to Florence C. Shiek. Interpreter, Rosalie Pinto Robertson. Los Angeles: Dawson Book Shop, 1968.

Culture Clash. *Oh, Wild West! The California Plays*. New York: Theatre Communications Group, 2011.

Dean, Mitchell. *Governmentality: Power and Rule in Modern Society*. London: Sage, 1999.

De Angelis, Massimo. "Separating the Doing and the Deed: Capital and the Continuous Character of Enclosures." *Historical Materialism* 12, no. 2 (2004): 57–87.

De Aragón, Ray John. Foreword to *My Life on the Frontier, 1882–1897*, by Miguel Antonio Otero. Santa Fe: Sunstone, 2007.

De Aragón, Ray John. Foreword to *My Nine Years as Governor of the Territory of New Mexico, 1897–1906*, by Miguel Antonio Otero. Santa Fe: Sunstone, 2007.

Debo, Angie. *And Still the Waters Run: The Betrayal of the Five Civilized Tribes*. Norman: University of Oklahoma Press, 1940.

Decker, Leslie E. "The Great Speculation: An Interpretation of Mid-Century Pioneering." In *The Frontier in American Development. Essays in Honor of Paul W. Gates*, edited by David M. Ellis, 357–80. Ithaca, NY: Cornell University Press, 1969.

Defoe, Daniel. *Moll Flanders*. New York: T. Y. Crowell, 1970.

Deloria, Vine, Jr. "Promises Made, Promises Broken." In *Native Universe: Voices of Indian America*, edited by Gerald McMaster and Clifford E. Trafzer, 143–59. Washington, DC: National Geographic, 2004.

de Zavala, Adina. *History and Legends of the Alamo and Other Missions in and around San Antonio*. Edited by Richard R. Flores. Houston: Arte Público, 1996.

de Zavala, Lorenzo. *Journey to the United States of North America, 1834–1846*. Houston: Arte Público, 2005.

Dunbar-Ortiz, Roxanne. *An Indigenous Peoples' History of the United States*. Boston: Beacon, 2014.

Dunbar-Ortiz, Roxanne. *Roots of Resistance: Land Tenure in New Mexico, 1680–1980*. Los Angeles: Chicano Studies Research Center, 1980.

Dussel, Enrique. "Philosophy of Liberation: The Postmodern Debate and Latin American Studies." In *Coloniality at Large: Latin America and the Postcolonial Debate*, edited by Mabel Moraña, Enrique Dussel, and Carlos A. Jáuregui, 335–49. Durham, NC: Duke University Press, 2008.

Ebright, Malcolm. "New Mexican Land Grants: The Legal Background." In *Land, Water, and Culture: New Perspectives on Hispanic Land Grants*, edited by Charles L. Briggs and John R. Van Ness, 15–66. Albuquerque: University of New Mexico Press, 1987.

Ebright, Malcolm, Rick Hendricks, and Richard W. Hughes. *Four Square Leagues: Pueblo Indian Land in New Mexico*. Albuquerque: University of New Mexico Press, 2015.

Elizondo, Sergio. *Muerte en una estrella*. Mexico: Tinta Negra Editores, 1984.

Elizondo, Sergio. *Shooting Star*. Translated by R. Sánchez and B. Pita. Houston: Arte Público, 2014.

Espinoza, Conrado. *Under the Texas Sun / El Sol de Texas*. Houston: Arte Público, 2007.

Estes, Nick. *Our History Is the Future*. London: Verso, 2019.

Esty, Jed, and Colleen Lye. "Peripheral Realisms Now." *Modern Language Quarterly* 73, no. 3 (2012): 269–88.

Federici, Silvia. "The Debt Crisis, Africa and the New Enclosures." In *Midnight Oil: Work, Energy, War, 1973–1992*, edited by Midnight Notes Collective, 303–16. New York: Autonomedia, 1992.

Federici, Silvia. "Women, Land Struggle, and the Valorization of Labor." *Commoner*, no. 10 (spring/summer 2005), 216–33.

Ferber, Edna. *Giant*. New York: Perennial Classics, 2000.

Flores, Richard R. *Remembering the Alamo: Memory, Modernity, and the Master Symbol*. Austin: University of Texas Press, 2002.

Foley, M. E., and A. Hamm. "James Bay Dam, Electricity and Impacts." *Trade and Environment Case Studies* 2, no. 1 (1992).

Foley, Neil. *The White Scourge: Mexicans, Blacks, and Poor Whites in Texas Cotton Culture*. Berkeley: University of California Press, 1997.

Foucault, Michel. "Governmentality." In *The Foucault Effect: Studies in Governmentality*, edited by Graham Burchell, Colin Gordon, and Peter Miller, 87–104. Chicago: University of Chicago Press, 1991.

García Márquez, Gabriel. *Chronicle of a Death Foretold (Crónica de una muerte anunciada)*. Translated by Gregory Rabasa. New York: Knopf, 1983.

Garrard, Lewis H. *Wah-to-yah and the Taos Trail*. Norman: University of Oklahoma Press, 1955.

Gates, Paul. *History of Public Land Law Development*. Washington, DC: Zenger, 1968.

Gates, Paul W. *Land and Law in California: Essays on Land Policies*. Ames: Iowa State University Press, 1991.

George, Henry. *The Land Question: What It Involves and How Alone It Can Be Settled*. New York: Robert Schalkenbach Foundation, 1953.

Gildersleeve, Charles H. *Reports of Cases Argued and Determined in the Supreme Court*. Chicago: Calleyham and Co., 1911.

Girard, Rene. *The Scapegoat*. Translated by Yvonne Freccero. Baltimore, MD: Johns Hopkins University Press, 1986.

Goeman, Mishuana. *Mark My Words: Native Women Mapping Our Nations*. Minneapolis: University of Minnesota Press, 2013.

Gómez, Laura E. *Manifest Destinies: The Making of the Mexican American Race*. New York: New York University Press, 2007.

Gómez-Quiñones, Juan. *Roots of Chicano Politics, 1600–1940*. Albuquerque: University of New Mexico Press, 1994.

González, Jovita. *Dew on the Thorn*. Edited by José E. Limón. Houston: Arte Público, 1997.

González, Jovita. *The Woman Who Lost Her Soul and Other Stories*. Houston: Arte Público, 2000.

González, Jovita, and Eve Raleigh. *Caballero: A Historical Novel*. College Station: Texas A&M University Press, 1996.

Graham, Don. *Kings of Texas: The 150-Year Saga of an American Ranching Empire*. Hoboken, NJ: Wiley, 2003.

Hämäläinen, Pekke, and Benjamin Johnson. *Major Problems in the History of North American Borderlands: Documents and Essays*. Belmont, CA: Wadsworth, 2012.

Hammond, George P. "The Search for the Fabulous in the Settlement of the Southwest." In *New Spain's Far Northern Frontier: Essays on Spain in the American*

West, 1540–1821, edited by David J. Weber, 17–34. Dallas: Southern Methodist University Press, 1979.

Harootunian, Harry. *Marx after Marx*. New York: Columbia University Press, 2015.

Harootunian, Harry. "Piercing the Present with the Past." *Historical Materialism* 23, no. 4 (2015): 60–74.

Harvey, David. *Cosmopolitanism and the Geographies of Freedom*. New York: Columbia University Press, 2009.

Harvey, David. *Justice, Nature, and the Geography of Difference*. Oxford: Blackwell, 1996.

Harvey, David. *The New Imperialism*. Oxford: Oxford University Press, 2003.

Herrera, Carlos. "New Mexico Resistance to U.S. Occupation during the Mexican-American War of 1846–1848." In *The Contested Homeland: A Chicano History of New Mexico*, edited by David Maciel and Erlinda Gonzales-Berry, 23–42. Albuquerque: University of New Mexico Press, 2000.

Hinojosa, Rolando. *Ask a Policeman*. Houston: Arte Público, 1998.

Hinojosa, Rolando. *Claros varones de Belken*. Tempe, AZ: Bilingual Press, 1986.

Hinojosa, Rolando. *Mi querido Rafa*. Houston: Arte Público, 1981.

Hinojosa, Rolando. *The Klail City Death Trip Series*. Houston: Arte Público, 1973–91.

Hinojosa, Rolando. *The Valley*. Tempe, AZ: Bilingual Press, 1983.

Hodge, F. W. Foreword to *History of New Mexico, 1610*, by Gaspar Pérez de Villagrá. Translated by Gilberto Espinosa, 17–34. Los Angeles: Quivira Society, 1933.

Hogan, Lawrence J. *The Osage Indian Murders: The True Story of a Multiple Murder Plot to Acquire the Estates of Wealthy Osage Tribe Members*. Frederick, MD: Amlex, 1998.

Hogan, Linda. *Mean Spirit*. New York: Ivy, 1990.

Hogan, Linda. *People of the Whale*. New York: Norton, 2008.

Hogan, Linda. *Power*. New York: Norton, 1998.

Hogan, Linda. *Solar Storms*. New York: Simon and Schuster, 1995.

Hogan, Linda. *The Woman Who Watches Over the World*. New York: Norton, 2001.

Jameson, Fredric. *The Antinomies of Realism*. London: Verso, 2013.

Jameson, Fredric. *The Political Unconscious: Narrative as a Socially Symbolic Act*. Ithaca, NY: Cornell University Press, 1981.

Jameson, Fredric. *Postmodernism, or, The Cultural Logic of Late Capitalism*. Durham, NC: Duke University Press, 1991.

Jameson, Fredric. *Valences of the Dialectic*. London: Verso, 2009.

Jaramillo, Cleofas M. *Romance of a Little Village Girl*. Albuquerque: University of New Mexico Press, 2000.

Jaramillo, Cleofas M. *Shadows of the Past (Sombras del Pasado): Santa Fe, 1941*. New York: Arno, 1974.

Kamins, Charles. "Ethnic Cleansing: We Have It Here Too!" *International Journal on World Peace* 9, no. 3 (1992): 111–15.

King, Edward. *Texas: 1874: An Eyewitness Account of Conditions in Post-Reconstruction Texas*. Houston: Cordovan, 1974.
Kiser, William S. "A 'Charming Name for a Species of Slavery': Political Debate on Debt Peonage in the Southwest, 1840s–1860s." *Western Historical Quarterly* 45, no. 2 (2014): 169–89.
Larralde, Carlos, and Carlos Esparza. *A Chicano Chronicle*. San Francisco: R & E Research Associates, 1977.
Lee, Lawrence B. Introduction to *Land and Law in California: Essays on Land Policies*, by Paul W. Gates, ix–xxiv. Ames: Iowa State University Press, 1991.
Lefebvre, Henri. *The Production of Space*. Translated by Donald Nicholson-Smith. Cambridge: Blackwell, 1991.
León-Portilla, Miguel. *Los antiguos mexicanos*. Mexico City: Fondo de Cultura Económica, 1973.
León-Portilla, Miguel. "Los aztecas: Disquisiciones sobre un gentilicio." *Estudios de cultura Náhuatl* 31 (2000): 307–13.
Limón, Graciela. *The River Flows North*. Houston: Arte Público, 2009.
Limón, José E. Introduction to *Caballero: A Historical Novel*, by Jovita González and Eve Raleigh, xii–xxvi. College Station: Texas A&M University Press, 1996.
Lomelí, Francisco A., and A. Gabriel Meléndez, ed. and trans. *Writings of Eusebio Chacón*, by Eusebio Chacón. Albuquerque: University of New Mexico Press, 2012.
Lovett, Bobbie L., Juan L. González, Roseann Bacha-Garza, and Russell K. Skowronek, eds. *Native American Peoples of South Texas*. Edinburg: University of Texas–Pan American, 2014. https://www.utrgv.edu/chaps/_files/documents/native-american-peoples-of-south-texas-pdf.pdf.
Maciel, David, and Erlinda Gonzales-Berry, eds. *The Contested Homeland: A Chicano History of New Mexico*. Albuquerque: University of New Mexico Press, 2000.
Maciel, David, and Erlinda Gonzales-Berry. "The Nineteenth Century: Overview." In *The Contested Homeland: A Chicano History of New Mexico*, edited by David Maciel and Erlinda Gonzales-Berry, 12–22. Albuquerque: University of New Mexico Press, 2000.
MacKenzie, Kent, dir. *The Exiles*. 1961. New York: Milestone Films, 2008.
Magdoff, Fred. "Twenty-First-Century Land Grabs: Accumulation by Agricultural Dispossession." *Monthly Review* 65, no. 6 (2013): 1–18.
Malm, Andreas. *Fossil Capital: The Rise of Steam Power and the Roots of Global Warming*. London: Verso, 2016.
Martínez, Felix. "Las Gorras Blancas: Nuestra Plataforma, 1890." In *Foreigners in Their Native Land: Historical Roots of the Mexican Americans*, edited by David J. Weber, 234–38. Albuquerque: University of New Mexico Press, 1973.
Marx, Karl. *Capital*. Vol. 1. New York: International, 1967.
Marx, Karl. *Gundrisse*. New York: Vintage/Random House, 1973.
Marx, Karl, and Frederick Engels. *Ireland and the Irish Question*. Moscow: Progress, 1978.

Mathews, John Joseph. *The Osages: Children of the Middle Waters*. Norman: University of Oklahoma Press, 1961.
Mathews, John Joseph. *Sundown*. Norman: University of Oklahoma Press, 1934.
McAuliffe, Dennis. *Bloodland: A Family Story of Oil, Greed and Murder on the Osage Reservation*. San Francisco: Council Oak, 1999.
Meléndez, A. Gabriel. "Nuevo Mexico by Any Other Name." In *The Contested Homeland: A Chicano History of New Mexico*, edited by David Maciel and Erlinda Gonzales-Berry, 143–68. Albuquerque: University of New Mexico Press, 2000.
Midnight Notes Collective, ed. *Midnight Oil: Work, Energy, War, 1973–1992*. New York: Autonomedia, 1992.
Mier y Terán, Manuel. *Crónica de Tejas: Diario de viaje de la comisión de límites*. Selección y prólogo de Mauricio Molina. Mexico City: Instituto Nacional de Bellas Artes y Gobierno del Estado de Tamaulipas, 1988.
Mignolo, Walter D. "The Geopolitics of Knowledge and the Colonial Difference." In *Coloniality at Large: Latin America and the Postcolonial Debate*, edited by Mabel Moraña, Enrique Dussel, and Carlos A. Jáuregui, 225–58. Durham, NC: Duke University Press, 2008.
Mikesell, Marvin, and Alexander Murphy. "A Framework for a Comparative Study of Minority-Group Aspirations." *Annals of the Association of American Geographers* 81, no. 4 (1991): 581–604.
Miles, Tiya. *Ties That Bind: The Story of an Afro-Cherokee Family in Slavery and Freedom*. Berkeley: University of California Press, 2015.
Montejano, David. *Anglos and Mexicans in the Making of Texas, 1836–1986*. Austin: University of Texas Press, 1987.
Moore, Jason W. *Capitalism in the Web of Life: Ecology and the Accumulation of Capital*. London: Verso, 2015.
Morales, Alejandro. *Reto en el Paraíso*. Ypsilanti, MI: Bilingual Editorial Press, 1983.
Newcomb, W. W. *The Indians of Texas from Prehistoric to Modern Times*. Austin: University of Texas Press, 2002.
Newkirk, Vann R., II. "The Great Land Robbery: The Shameful Story of How 1 Million Black Families Have Been Ripped from Their Farms." *Atlantic*, September 2019.
Nieto-Phillips, John. *The Language of Blood: The Making of Spanish-American Identity in New Mexico, 1880s–1930s*. Albuquerque: University of New Mexico Press, 2004.
Nieto-Phillips, John. "Spanish American Ethnic Identity and New Mexico's Statehood Struggle." In *The Contested Homeland: A Chicano History of New Mexico*, edited by David Maciel and Erlinda Gonzales-Berry, 97–142. Albuquerque: University of New Mexico Press, 2000.
Núñez Cabeza de Vaca, Álvar. *La relación 1542*. Houston: Arte Público, 1993.
Olivera, Oscar, and Tom Lewis. *Cochabamba! Water War in Bolivia*. Cambridge, MA: South End Press, 2004.

Ortiz Vásquez, Dora. *Enchanted Temple of Taos: My Story of Rosario*. Santa Fe: Rydel, 1975.

Otero, Miguel Antonio. *My Life on the Frontier, 1864–1882*. Albuquerque: University of New Mexico Press, 1987.

Otero, Miguel Antonio. *My Life on the Frontier, 1882–1897*. Santa Fe: Sunstone, 2007.

Otero, Miguel Antonio. *My Nine Years as Governor of the Territory of New Mexico, 1897–1906*. Santa Fe: Sunstone, 2007.

Otero, Miguel Antonio. *The Real Billy the Kid*. Houston: Arte Público, 1998.

Padilla, Genaro M. "Leaving a 'Clean and Honorable Name': Rafael Chacón's 'Memorias.'" In *My History, Not Yours: The Formation of Mexican American Autobiography*, 153–95. Madison: University of Wisconsin Press, 1993.

Padilla, Genaro M. *My History, Not Yours: The Formation of Mexican American Autobiography*. Madison: University of Wisconsin Press, 1993.

Paredes, Américo. *George Washington Gómez*. Houston: Arte Público, 1990.

Paredes, Américo. "A Shadow on the Border." In *The Borderlands of Culture: Américo Paredes and the Transnational Imaginary*, edited by Ramón Saldívar, 139–42. Durham, NC: Duke University Press, 2006.

Paredes, Américo. *With His Pistol in His Hand*. Austin: University of Texas Press, 1958.

Park, Joseph F. "Spanish Indian Policy in Northern Mexico, 1765–1810." In *New Spain's Far Northern Frontier: Essays on Spain in the American West, 1540–1821*, edited by David J. Weber, 217–34. Dallas: Southern Methodist University Press, 1979.

Perales, Monica, and Raúl A. Ramos. "Building a Project to Expand Texas History." In *Recovering the Hispanic History of Texas*, edited by Monica Perales, vii–xv. Houston: Arte Público, 1997.

Perelman, Michael. *The Invention of Capitalism: Classical Political Economy and the Secret History of Primitive Accumulation*. Durham, NC: Duke University Press, 2000.

Pérez, Emma. *Forgetting the Alamo, or, Blood Memory: A Novel*. Austin: University of Texas Press, 2009.

Pérez de Villagrá, Gaspar. *History of New Mexico, 1610*. Translated by Gilberto Espinosa. Los Angeles: Quivira Society, 1933.

Poyo, Gerald E., and Gilberto M. Hinojosa. "Spanish Texas and Borderlands Historiography in Transition: Implications for United States History." *Journal of American History* 75, no. 2 (1988): 393–416.

Prucha, Francis Paul. *American Indian Treaties: The History of a Political Anomaly*. Berkeley: University of California Press, 1994.

Quijano, Aníbal. "Coloniality of Power, Eurocentrism, and Social Classification." In *Coloniality at Large: Latin America and the Postcolonial Debate*, edited by Mabel Moraña, Enrique Dussel, and Carlos A. Jáuregui, 181–224. Durham, NC: Duke University Press, 2008.

Quiñonez, Ernesto. *Chango's Fire*. New York: Harper Perennial, 2005.
Ramos, Raul. *Beyond the Alamo: Forging Mexican Ethnicity in San Antonio, 1821–1861*. Chapel Hill: University of North Carolina Press, 2008.
Rana, Aziz. *The Two Faces of American Freedom*. Cambridge, MA: Harvard University Press, 2010.
Rebolledo, Tey Diana, and María Teresa Márquez, eds. *Women's Tales from the New Mexico WPA: La Diabla a Pie*. Houston: Arte Público, 2000.
Reséndez, Andrés. *Changing National Identities at the Frontier: Texas and New Mexico, 1800–1850*. Cambridge: Cambridge University Press, 2004.
Ricoeur, Paul. *Memory, History, Forgetting*. Translated by Kathleen Blamey and David Perllauer. Chicago: University of Chicago Press, 2004.
Rivera, John Michael. Introduction to *The Real Billy the Kid*, by Miguel Antonio Otero, xi–xlv. Houston: Arte Público, 1998.
Rivera, Tomás. "The Salamanders." In *Tomás Rivera: The Complete Works*, edited by Julián Olivares, 12–123. Houston: Arte Público, 1992.
Rivera, Tomás. *Y no se lo tragó la tierra*. Berkeley: Quinto Sol, 1971.
Rivera, Tomás. "Zoo Island." In *Tomás Rivera: The Complete Works*, edited by Julián Olivares, 138–42. Houston: Arte Público, 1992.
Rodriguez, Sylvia. "Land, Water, and Ethnic Identity." In *Land, Water, and Culture: New Perspectives on Hispanic Land Grants*, edited by Charles L. Briggs and John R. Van Ness, 313–403. Albuquerque: University of New Mexico Press, 1987.
Rosales, F. Arturo. *Chicano: The History of the Mexican American Civil Rights Movement*. Houston: Arte Público, 1996.
Rosenbaum, Robert J., and Robert W. Larson. "Mexicano Resistance to the Expropriation of Grant Lands in New Mexico." In *Land, Water, and Culture: New Perspectives on Hispanic Land Grants*, edited by Charles L. Briggs and John R. Van Ness, 269–310. Albuquerque: University of New Mexico Press, 1987.
Rosemont, Franklin. "Karl Marx and the Iroquois." Posted on Libcom.org, July 7, 2009. http://libcom.org/library/karl-marx-iroquois-franklin-rosemont.
Saldívar, Ramón. *The Borderlands of Culture: Américo Paredes and the Transnational Imaginary*. Durham, NC: Duke University Press, 2006.
Sánchez, Rosaura. *Telling Identitie: The Californio testimonios*. Minneapolis: University of Minnesota Press, 1995.
Sandos, James A. *Rebellion in the Borderlands: Anarchism and the Plan of San Diego, 1904–1923*. Norman: University of Oklahoma Press, 1992.
Schroeder, Albert H. "Shifting for Survival in the Spanish Southwest." In *New Spain's Far Northern Frontier: Essays on Spain in the American West, 1540–1821*, edited by David J. Weber, 237–56. Dallas: Southern Methodist University Press, 1979.
Secor-Welsh, Cynthia. Introduction to *My Life on the Frontier, 1882–1897*, by Miguel Antonio Otero, vii–lxxix. Albuquerque: University of New Mexico Press, 1987.

Semo, Enrique. *Historia mexicana: Economía y lucha de clases.* Mexico City: Facultad de Economía, UNAM, Serie Popular Era, 1988.

Shiva, Vandana. *Water Wars: Privatization, Pollution, and Profit.* Cambridge, MA: South End Press, 2002.

Silko, Leslie Marmon. *Almanac of the Dead.* New York: Penguin, 1991.

Silko, Leslie Marmon. *Ceremony.* New York: Viking, 1977.

Silko, Leslie Marmon. *Gardens in the Dunes.* New York: Simon and Schuster, 1999.

Simmons, Marc. "Settlement Patterns and Village Plans in Colonial New Mexico." In *New Spain's Far Northern Frontier: Essays on Spain in the American West, 1540–1821,* edited by David J. Weber, 97–116. Dallas: Southern Methodist University Press, 1979.

Smith, Neil. *Uneven Development: Nature, Capital, and the Production of Space.* Athens: University of Georgia Press, 2008.

Stedman Jones, Gareth. "The History of U.S. Imperialism." In *Ideology in Social Science: Readings in Critical Social Theory,* edited by Robin Blackburn, 96–118. New York: Pantheon, 1972.

Sturken, Marita. *Tangled Memories: The Vietnam War, the AIDS Epidemic and the Politics of Remembering.* Berkeley: University of California Press, 1997.

Tafolla, Santiago. *A Life Crossing Borders: Memoir of a Mexican American Confederate.* Edited by Carmen Tafolla and Laura Tafolla. Houston: Arte Público, 2010.

Taibo, Paco Ignacio, II. *El Álamo: Una historia no apta para Hollywood.* Mexico City: Editorial Planeta Mexicana, 2011.

Thorne, Tanis C. *The World's Richest Indian: The Scandal over Jackson Barnett's Oil Fortune.* Oxford: Oxford University Press, 2005.

Tomba, Massimiliano. "Marx's Temporal Bridges and Other Pathways." *Historical Materialism* 23, no. 4 (2015): 75–91.

Treviño, Jesús Salvador, dir. *Seguín.* KPBS/KCET American Playhouse Series, 1982.

Truett, Samuel, and Elliott Young. "Borderlands Unbound." In *Continental Crossroads: Remapping U.S.–Mexico Borderlands History,* edited by Samuel Truett and Elliott Young, 325–28. Durham, NC: Duke University Press, 2004.

Turner, Fredrick Jackson. "The Significance of the Frontier in American History." In *The Frontier in American History,* 1–38. New York: Dover, 1996.

Ulibarrí, Sabine R. *Mi abuela fumaba puros: My Grandmother Smoked Cigars.* Berkeley: Quinto Sol, 1977.

US Department of the Interior. "Native American Trust Litigation." March 10, 2010. https://www.doi.gov/ocl/hearings/111/CobellvsSalazar_031010.

Valerio-Jiménez, Omar S. *River of Hope: Forging Identity and Nation in the Rio Grande Borderlands.* Durham, NC: Duke University Press, 2013.

Vaughn, Carson. "Natives Struggle to Stay One with the Land." *Native Daughters,* n.d. Accessed July 27, 2020, http://cojmc.unl.edu/nativedaughters/environmentalists/natives-struggle-to-stay-one-with-the-land.

Venegas, Daniel. *Las aventuras de Don Chipote o cuando los pericos mamen.* Houston: Arte Público, 1999.

Veracini, Lorenzo. *Settler Colonialism: A Theoretical Overview*. New York: Palgrave Macmillan, 2010.

Vicens Vives, Jaime. *An Economic History of Spain*. Translated by Frances M. López-Morillas. Princeton, NJ: Princeton University Press, 1969.

Vigil, Maurilio. *Los Patrones: Profiles of Hispanic Political Leaders in New Mexico History*. Washington, DC: University Press of America, 1980.

Viñas, David. *Indios, ejército y frontera*. Buenos Aires: Siglo XXI Editores, 1982.

Viramontes, Helena María. *Their Dogs Came with Them*. New York: Atria, 2007.

Wallace, Anthony F. C. *The Long, Bitter Trail*. New York: Hill and Wang, 1993.

Weber, David J. *Bárbaros: Spaniards and Their Savages in the Age of Enlightenment*. New Haven, CT: Yale University Press, 2005.

Weber, David J., ed. *Foreigners in Their Native Land: Historical Roots of the Mexican Americans*. Albuquerque: University of New Mexico Press, 1973.

Weber, David J. "John Francis Bannon and the Historiography of the Spanish Borderlands: Retrospect and Prospect." *Journal of the Southwest* 29, no. 4 (1987): 331–63.

Weber, David J. *The Mexican Frontier, 1821–1846*. Albuquerque: University of New Mexico Press, 1982.

Weber, David J., ed. *New Spain's Far Northern Frontier: Essays on Spain in the American West, 1540–1821*. Dallas: Southern Methodist University Press, 1979.

Weber, David J. *The Spanish Frontier in North America*. New Haven, CT: Yale University Press, 2009.

Weber, David J., ed. *What Caused the Pueblo Revolt of 1680?* Boston: Bedford St. Martin's, 1999.

Westphall, Victor. *Mercedes Reales: Hispanic Land Grants of the Upper Rio Grande Region*. Albuquerque: University of New Mexico Press, 1983.

Wilkins, David E., and K. Tsianina Lomawaima. *Uneven Ground: American Indian Sovereignty and Federal Law*. Norman: University of Oklahoma Press, 1994.

Wilson, Terry P. *The Underground Reservation: Osage Oil*. Lincoln: University of Nebraska Press, 1985.

Wolfe, Patrick. *Settler Colonialism and the Transformation of Anthropology: The Politics and Poetics of an Ethnographic Event*. London: Cassell, 1999.

Wood, Ellen Meiksins. "Logics of Power: A Conversation with David Harvey." *Historical Materialism* 14, no. 4 (2006): 9–34.

Index

accumulation by dispossession, 2, 15, 48
Acoma massacre of 1599, 96–97; narrated by Perez de Villagrá, as, 97. *See also* New Mexico: decimation of Indigenous population
Adams-Onís Treaty (1819), 158
Alamán, Lucas, 158
Alamo, the, 154; representations of, 176, 180–83; siege of, 159, 181. *See also* Texas
Álamo: Una historia no apta para Hollywood, El (Taibo) 181–82, 238n152
Albó, Xavier, 34
Alburquerque (Anaya), 145–46
allotment of Indigenous land. *See* Dawes Act; Curtis Act
Almanac of the Dead (Silko), 87
Alonzo, Armando C., 152–56, 161, 166–67
Amir, Samir, 6
Anaya, Rudolfo, 23, 116, 145–47. *See also individual works*
Apache Nation, 22, 32, 63–65, 97–98, 111, 153, 180, 238n152. *See also* Indigenous nations
Arellano, Anselmo, 119, 121
Arreola, Daniel D., 151
Ask a Policeman (Hinojosa), 198
Austin, Moses, 157
Aventuras de Don Chipote, Las (Venegas), 184, 186

Baker, Houston A., Jr., 21, 51
Bancroft, Hubert H., 160
Banner, Stuart, 65
Barceló, Gertrudis, 104
Barnett, Jackson, 69–70, 73
Barr, Juliana, 31
Benson, Lee, 11
Bent, Charles, 106, 108, 112
Berle, Adolf A., 27
Béxar, San Antonio de. *See* Texas
Big Tree, Treaty of (1797), 46. *See also* Seneca Nation
Bolton, Herbert E., 18–19, 136
Brenner, Robert, 28

Briggs, Charles L., 18
British colonialism, 3, 10, 19, 27–30, 44, 47, 84; colonies, types of, 29, 32–37, 60, 63
Brito, Aristeo, 185
Brooks, James, 96
Buffalo Creek, Treaty of (1838), 47. *See also* Seneca Nation
Bureau of Indian Affairs (BIA), 5; containment and surveillance, role in, 47, 50, 61; representation in *Mean Spirit*, 66–72, 75–76, 78. *See also* Oklahoma
Burke Act and Oklahoma Enabling Act of 1906 (Forced Fee Patenting Act), 47–49, 51, 61, 64–65, 67–69, 75. *See also* Oklahoma
Burns, Louis F., 72–73
Byrd, Jodi A., 35

Caballero: A Historical Novel (González and Raleigh), 109, 156, 170–78
Cabeza de Baca, Ezekiel, 123
Cabeza de Baca, Fabiola, 114, 123–25, 137–42, 194. *See also individual works*
Cabeza de Baca, Manuel, 123, 125
Cabeza de Vaca, Álvar Núñez, 95, 153, 185
Cable, George Washington, 40
Caffentzis, George, 2–3
Callinicos, Alex, 80
Canary Islanders, 154–55
Candelaria, Nash, 109–12, 123–24, 126. *See also individual works*
Capitalocene epoch, 206
Cass, Lewis, 44
Catron, Thomas Benton, 116, 129–32. *See also* Santa Fe Ring
Ceremony (Silko), 88
Chacón, Eusebio, 95, 114, 122, 134–35
Chacón, Rafael. *See* Padilla, Genaro M.
Chango's Fire (Quiñónez), 17
Chávez, Fray Angélico, 112, 128, 136

Chávez, Thomas E., 102, 133
Chavez Ravine (Culture Clash), 17, 207
Cherokee Nation v. Georgia (1830), 64
Chimayó Rebellion of 1837, 104, 111
Churchill, Ward, 71
Cibola: mythical city of, 95
Cisneros, Carlos, 199–201
citizenship: of Indigenous populations, 7, 48, 63, 65, 67; of Mexicans, 113, 163, 168, 218n51, 237n118
Civil War. *See* US Civil War
Claros varones de Belken County (Hinojosa), 195–96
Coahuilteca Indians, 153, 233n12
Collier, John, 49
colonialism. *See* British colonialism; French colonialism; Mexican colonialism; Spanish colonialism; US colonialism
coloniality of power, 14
commodification of land, 27, 36, 99, 107, 156, 179, 198, 203–8
Coronado, Francisco Vásquez de, 94
Cortina, Juan Nepomuceno, 163, 177
Court of Private Land Claims, 99–106, 113–15, 117, 122, 131
Crazy Horse, 56, 65–66
Cree Nation, 66, 82–84. *See also* Indigenous nations
Crime of 1908, 68–69. *See* Oklahoma Closure Act
critical memory, 21–23, 51, 54, 59, 90, 143, 203–4, 208–11
Crónica de una muerte anunciada (García Márquez), 52
Cuello, José, 19
Cuero, Delfina, 88–89, 224n162
Culture Clash, 17, 207. *See also individual works*
Curtis Act of 1898, 47–49, 61, 65, 67

Dakota Access Pipeline, 90, 206
Dawes Act, 47–49, 51, 61, 64–65, 69, 75–76, 220n32

De Angelis, Massimo, 3, 6, 7, 50, 82–85, 145, 205–07, 213n3
De Aragón, Ray John, 131
Debo, Angie, 50, 63, 72
debt peonage, 33; in New Mexico, 1, 100–03, 113, 138, 141, 143, 178, 226n39; in Nuevo Santander/Texas, 20, 150, 154–56, 170–71
Decker, Leslie E., 11
Deloria, Vine, 60
Dew on the Thorn (González), 156, 170–71, 175–78
de Zavala, Adina, 183
Diablo en Texas, El (Brito), 185
dispossession, 11–12, 202, 204; of Indigenous nations in Oklahoma, 47–50, 52–55, 68, 73, 79; of Indigenous in New Mexico, 95–96, 103, 139, 152, 172; of Nuevomexicanos/as, 103–05, 110–15, 119–24, 132–37, 141–43; of Tejanos/as, 149–51, 160–73, 181–87, 191–99, 201
Domenech, Abbé Emmanuel H.D., 161
Dunbar-Ortiz, Roxanne, 12, 44, 90, 94, 107

Ebright, Malcolm, 106, 115–17, 122, 132
Eimer, Margaret. *See* Eve Raleigh
Enchanted Temple of Taos (Ortiz Vásquez), 101–2
enclosure: history of, 1–5, 9, 13–16, 28–42, 71–77, 93–103, 120–21, 150, 206–8, 213n5, 216n11; discursive legitimations of, 7–8, 16–17, 23–27, 43, 50–51, 61; literary representations of, 55–62, 72, 79, 81–91, 125–37, 145–47, 173–205
encomiendas, 4, 15, 23, 30–32, 98–99. *See also* Spanish colonialism
Escandón, José de, 32–33, 155–56, 178, 195
Estes, Nick, 90
Esty, Jed, 23–24

Espinoza, Conrado, 184
Exiles, The (MacKenzie), 72

Federal Bureau of Investigation (FBI), 53–58, 61, 71, 80, 193
Federal Land Grant Alliance, 125. *See also* Nuevomexicanos/as; Tijerina, Reies López
Federici, Silvia, 205–6
Five Civilized Tribes, 45–50, 62, 65, 67, 71, 73–75. *See also* Indigenous nations
Flores, Richard R., 181–83
Foley, Neil, 165
Fontainebleau Treaty of 1762, 38, 155
Forget the Alamo (Pérez), 23, 179–82, 204
Foucault, Michel, 5
French colonialism, 5, 35, 38–40, 155. *See also* Louisiana Purchase

Gadsden Purchase of 1853, 109, 118, 160
García Márquez, Gabriel, 52
Gardens in the Dunes (Silko), 88–89
Garrard, Lewis H., 108
Gates, Paul, 9, 27, 35–38, 40, 220n28, 220n32
gender: dispossession and, 8, 18, 68, 78, 86–90, 104, 168, 174, 207–9. *See also* marriage
George, Henry, 37
George Washington Gómez (Paredes), 187–93, 199
Gildersleeve, Charles, H., 101
Goeman, Mishuana, 12, 48, 90
Gómez, Laura E., 127
Gómez-Quiñones, Juan, 113, 119, 129, 131–33, 160–63, 168, 183
Gonzales-Berry, Erlinda, 99, 111, 118, 126, 133
González, Jovita, 109, 152, 155–56, 161–64, 166, 169. *See also individual works*

Good Life, The (Cabeza de Baca), 141
Gorras Blancas, Las, 119–25, 128–29, 140–43
governmentality, 5, 24, 36, 43, 47–50, 61
Graham, Don, 161–62, 190
Greenville, Treaty of (1795), 44. *See also* US treaties
Guadalupe Hidalgo, Treaty of (1848), 109, 113–16, 160. *See also* US-Mexican War
guardianship system: abuse of Indians, 5, 43–47; in Oklahoma, 49–50, 54, 57, 64–65, 70; regarding "blanket Indians" 68–71, 76, 78–79. *See also Lone Wolf v. Hitchcock*
Gutiérrez, Ramón, 135

Hämäläinen, Pekke, 18
Harootunian, Harry, 13–14
Harvey, David, 3, 6, 21–22, 34
Herrera, Carlos, 107–8, 112
Hinojosa, Gilberto M., 18
Hinojosa, Rolando, 152, 161–64, 186–87, 194–99, 204. *See also* individual works
History and Legends of the Alamo (de Zavala), 183, 238n159. *See also* Alamo, the
History of New Mexico (Pérez de Villagrá), 97
Hogan, Linda, 49–91. *See also individual works*
Homestead Act of 1862, 37–38, 140
homesteads. *See* land tenancy: homesteading; United States: homesteading vs. land speculation

imperialism. *See* British colonialism; French colonialism; Mexican colonialism; Spanish colonialism; US colonialism
Indian Appropriation Act of 1904, 67
Indian Citizenship Act of 1924, 65

Indian Claims Commission of 1955, 64–65
Indian Removal Act of 1830, 5, 45, 62, 64
Indian Reorganization Act of 1934, 49, 65, 71, 220n28
Indian Self Determination Act of 1975, 60
Indigenous commons, 2–4, 6–8, 34, 47, 217n21; in Hogan, 51, 55–59, 77, 87, 99; in New Mexico, 118–19, 140; in Texas, 149, 152, 232n273
Indigenous devastation and genocide, 4, 5, 11, 33–34, 44–49, 52, 86, 90–97, 153–56, 180
Indigenous dispossession, 2–7, 10–14, 27, 29–42; in Oklahoma, 45–92; in New Mexico, 107, 125, 134, 140–47; in Texas, 149–204
Indigenous lands: privatization of, 45–48, 51, 55, 58–64, 75–77
Indigenous nations. *See* Apache Nation; Coahuiltecas; Cree Nation; Inuit Nation; Five Civilized Tribes; Osage Nation; Seneca Nation; Sioux Nation
Indigenous peoples: massacres of, 15, 35, 60–67, 109. *See also* Acoma; Sand Creek; Wounded Knee
Indigenous removal and relocation, 5, 27, 34–36, 44–51, 56–67, 73–77, 84, 150
Indigenous resistance, 1, 56, 65–66, 73–74, 89–90. *See also* Pueblo Revolt; Wevokah and the Ghost Dance
Inheritance of Strangers (Candelaria), 123
Inuit Nation, 66, 82–84
Ireland: British invasion of, 28, 63
Israeli settler colonialism, 27, 160

Jackson, Andrew, 5, 38–39, 44–47, 62, 219n7

James Bay Hydroelectric Project (Hydro-Quebec), 82–84
Jameson, Fredric, 21, 93, 170
Jaramillo, Cleofas M., 102–3, 114, 137–38. *See also individual works*
Jefferson, Thomas, 60–62, 218n48
Jemez Spring (Anaya), 146
Johnson, Benjamin H., 18
Johnson, Walter, 46

Kearny, Stephen W., 105–8, 111–12
King Ranch, 162–65, 188, 190–91; *kineños*, 189–90.
Kiser, William S., 101
Klail City Death Trip Series, The (Hinojosa), 164, 186, 194–98, 204
Knights of Labor, 121–22, 124. *See also* Las Gorras Blancas; Partido del Pueblo Unido; *La voz del pueblo*
Kumeyaay people, 88–89, 224n162. *See also* Cuero, Delfina

land dispossession. *See* dispossession
Land Grant, The (Cisneros), 199–201
land tenancy: agribusiness, 151, 164; homesteading, 34–40, 79, 107, 120, 128, 137–39, 143; *latifundia*, 29–31; mission system, 4–11, 19, 30–33, 93–99, 110, 135, 150–56, 183, 203, 217n27, 224n162. *See also* allotment of Indigenous land; *encomiendas*; Indigenous commons; Indigenous lands: privatization of; *partidarios*
Laredo, 152, 156–58
Larson, Robert W., 119, 124–26
Lee, Lawrence, 36
Lefebvre, Henri, 48
León Portilla, Miguel, 203
Life Crossing Borders, A (Tafolla), 184
Limón, Graciela, 207
Limón, José E., 176
Lincoln County War, 126–27, 130, 132
Lodge, Henry Cabot, 63
Lomawaima, K. Tsianana, 60

Lone Wolf v. Hitchcock (1903), 64
Louisiana Purchase of 1803, 35–41, 74, 116, 160
Lye, Colleen, 23–24

Maciel, David, 99, 111, 118, 126, 133
MacKenzie, Kent, 72
Mano Negra, La, 125, 230n175
marriage: as access to Indigenous headrights, 53, 68–70, 78–79; as mechanism for accommodation and merger, 18–20, 68–79, 104, 112, 143, 150, 169–74, 197, 237n128
Martínez, Félix, 120
Martínez, Padre José Antonio, 101–06, 112, 123, 128
Marx, Karl, 4, 27–28, 51, 58, 213n5, 216n11, 220n45
Mathews, John Joseph, 54–55, 76
Mean Spirit (Hogan), 49–56, 58–61, 65–69, 73, 75–81, 85–87
Meriam Report of 1928, 49, 71
McAuliffe, Dennis, 59, 71, 79
McCumber, Porter, 67
McNelly, Leander, 236n86. *See also* Texas Rangers
Meléndez, Gabriel, A., 135
Mexican colonialism: in New Mexico, 1, 10–15, 19, 27, 30, 42, 92–98, 104–12, 134; in Texas, 151, 157–59, 181
Mi abuela fumaba puros (Ulibarrí), 144
Mier y Terán, Manuel, 158–59
Mignolo, Walter D., 14
Mikesell, Marvin, 18
Miles, Tiya, 63
Montejano, David, 156, 161, 164–66, 183, 189, 194
Morales, Alejandro, 24. *See also individual works*
Murphy, Alexander, 18
My Life on the Frontier, 1864–82 (Otero), 128
My Life on the Frontier, 1882–97 (Otero), 129, 131

Index 257

My Years as Governor of the Territory of New Mexico (Otero), 131

Native American. *See* Indigenous commons; Indigenous devastation and genocide; Indigenous dispossession; Indigenous lands; Indigenous Nations; Indigenous peoples; Indigenous removal and relocation; Indigenous resistance
Newcomb, W. W., 153
New Deal policies: on Indians, 49
New Mexico: communal land grants, 99–102, 106, 115–19, 127, 137, 140, 198; Coronado invasion of, 94–95; decimation of Indigenous population in, 30, 97; enslavement of Indigenous population of, 96, 100–103, 138, 141, 157; federalists vs. centralists in, 104, 159; rebellions of Indigenous people in, 22–23, 93, 98–103, 108, 112; land speculation post-1848 in, 107, 120, 132; social stratification in, 104, 134, 137, 145, 150; statehood struggles and congressional rejection of statehood, 113, 134; US invasion, 105–18, 137–39, 141; US territory and later statehood in 1912, 93, 107, 113, 121–28, 133–35. *See also* Acoma massacre; Chimayó Rebellion of 1837; debt peonage; Lincoln County War; Mexican colonialism; *partidarios*; Pueblo Revolt of 1680; Santa Fe Ring; Spanish colonialism; Taos Rebellion of 1847; US colonialism
Nieto-Phillips, John, 134
nostalgia, 21, 113, 124, 137, 141–45
Not by the Sword (Candelaria), 109–10, 123
Nuevomexicanos/as: accommodation vs. armed resistance, 94, 107–13, 145; Anglo racism against, 113, 134; collusion with Indigenous dispossession, 10–15, 20, 42, 92–94, 103–17, 125, 133–43; genízaros, 100, 107, 139; identity as White Hispanos/as or Spanoamericans, 16, 20, 104–6 113–14, 128, 134–38, 143; loss of land grants, 30, 42, 103–5, 110–15, 119–24, 132–43. *See also* Court of Private Land Claims; dispossession: of Nuevomexicanos/as; Federal Land Grant Alliance; *La voz del pueblo*; Las Gorras Blancas; Tijerina, Reies López; Martínez, Padre José Antonio; Partido del Pueblo Unido; Penitentes; Tierra Amarilla land claims; Tierra Amarilla courthouse raid
Nuevo Santander settlement. *See* Escandón, José de; Spanish colonialism; Texas

Oklahoma: "blanket Indians," 68; restricted and nonrestricted Indians, 49–50, 67–68, 71, 78; statehood, 65, 68; as a territory, 65. *See also* BIA; guardianship system; Indigenous commons: in Hogan; Indigenous dispossession: in Oklahoma; Indigenous removal and relocation; Osage Nation
Oklahoma Closure Act (Crime of 1908), 68–69
Oklahoma Indian Welfare Act of 1936, 49
Olmsted, Frederick Law, 161
Osage Nation: culture and history, 47–50, 52–56, 59–60, 71–76, 79; National Council, 74–75; Reign of Terror, 52–53, 67, 79; "underground reservation," 76–77, 79. *See also* Barnett, Jackson; Indigenous dispossession; Osage Removal Act of 1870
Osage Removal Act of 1870, 74
Oñate, Juan de, 96–98, 114
Ortiz Vásquez, Dora, 101–02. *See also individual works*
Otero, Miguel, Sr., 115, 127–28, 132

Otero, Miguel Antonio, Jr., 127–133. See also *individual works*

Padilla, Genaro M., 135–37, 142; on Rafael Chacón, 133
Palestinians, dispossession of, 27, 160, 208, 225n165
Paredes, Américo, 152, 163–69, 177, 186–93, 199. See also *individual works*
partidarios, 100, 140
Partido del Pueblo Unido, El, 122–25
Penitentes, Los, 112, 129, 142–44
People of the Whale (Hogan), 87
Perales, Mónica, 169
Pérez, Emma, 23, 179–82, 204. See also *individual works*
Pérez de Villagrá, Gaspar, 97. See also *individual works*
peripheral realism, 23, 168
Philippines, 35
Pinckney Treaty of 1795, 38
Plan de San Diego Uprising of 1915, 165–66, 187–90
Power (Hogan), 81–82
Poyo, Gerald E., 18
Preemption Act of 1841, 37–38, 218n51, 220n28
Presidio, Texas. See Brito
Prucha, Francis Paul, 46
Public Law 949, 72. See Relocation Act of 1956
Pueblo Revolt of 1680, 22–23, 98, 103, 112

Quebec. See James Bay Hydroelectric Project
Quijano, Aníbal, 14
Quiñónez, Ernesto, 17. See also *individual works*
Quivira, mythical city of, 95

Raleigh, Eve (pseud. of Margaret Eimer), 109, 170. See also *individual works*

Ramos, Raúl, 19, 152, 169, 182
Rana, Aziz, 10
Real Billy the Kid, The (Otero), 127, 130, 132
Rebolledo, Tey Diana, and María Teresa Márquez, on WPA project, 94, 101–02, 109, 118
Relocation Act of 1956, 72
Remembering the Alamo (Flores), 181–83
Reséndez, Andrés, 107, 152
Reto en el Paraíso (Morales), 24
rinches. See Texas Rangers
Rivera, John Michael, 130; on Otero's *The Real Billy the Kid*, 127, 130–32
Rivera, Tomás, 179, 204, 209–10. See also *individual works*
River Flows North, The (Limón), 207
Romance of a Little Village Girl (Jaramillo), 103, 112–16, 136–37, 143–44
Rodríguez, Sylvia, 118, 145
Rosenbaum, Robert J., 119, 124–26

"Salamanders, The" (Rivera), 209–10
Sand Creek, massacre at, 65
Santa Fe Ring, 116, 122, 129, 132. See also Catron, Thomas Benton
Secor-Welsh, Cynthia, 128–29
sediciosos. See Tejanos/as: *sedicioso* movement
Semo, Enrique, 151, 155
Seneca Nation, 46–48, 219n26, 221n46
settler colonialism: modalities of, 1, 10–13, 15, 216n1; relation to dispossession, 26–27; Mexican period of, 106, 158, 181; Spanish period of, 30–35, 42; US period of, 63, 90–95, 98
Shadows of the Past (Jaramillo), 142–45
Shaman Winter (Anaya), 23, 111
Shiva, Vandana, 147
Silko, Leslie Marmon, 87–91. See also *individual works*
Simmons, Marc, 99

Sioux Nation, 41, 52–57, 66, 73, 77, 90–91
slavery: of Indigenous peoples, 11, 20, 29–30, 63, 92–98; relation to debt peonage, 100–103, 138–39, 156; Black slavery in Texas, 46, 62–63, 151–60, 164, 180–182, 205. *See also* debt peonage; New Mexico: enslavement of Indigenous population of
Smith, Neil, 13, 17
Solar Storms (Hogan), 82–86
Southwest regions of the United States: traits of, 11–12, 21, 150–51, 205
Spanish Borderlands: Bolton's notion of, 18–30, 35, 136
Spanish colonialism, 1, 3, 10–15; mixed colonial models, 26–35, 42, 92–98, 106–110, 141, 181; of New Mexico: 11, 15, 19, 28–30, 93, 96–157; of Nuevo Santander/Texas: 11, 31–182. See also *encomiendas;* land tenancy
Stedman Jones, Gareth, 10, 34–35

Tafolla, Santiago, 184
Taibo, Paco Ignacio, II, on events at the Alamo, 181–82
Taos Rebellion of 1847, 108–9, 111–12. *See also* Nuevomexicanos/as: accommodation vs. armed resistance
Tejanos/as: armed resistance of, 163–67, 173–74, 177, 199; class and racial divisions in, 16, 20, 42, 150, 164–67, 175–78, 183–95; conscription into Confederate Army, 183–84; Cortinista uprisings, 163, 176–77, 184; economic transformations, 149, 163–71, 179, 184–85, 195; elites support of Confederacy and Klu Klux Klan, 183–84, 205; identity, fluidity of, 151, 162–70, 181–83, 190, 193; increased Mexican immigration, effects of, 164–70, 174, 186, 188, 192; influx of Anglo Midwest farmers, impact of, 164–65, 171, 175, 179; landless wage workers, 165–67, 204; landlords as slaveholders, 183; legal struggles of, 161–62, 167, 174–77, 197–201, 240n202; Mexican and Black cotton fieldworkers, 149, 164–67, 184; outnumbered and dispossessed, 12, 30, 62, 160–64, 174, 180–86, 194; *sedicioso* movement, 165–66, 187–90, 237n106; victims of violence, racism and lynchings, 41, 160–67, 180, 186–87, 236n75. *See also* dispossession: Tejanos/as; Plan de San Diego Uprising
terra nullius, notion of, 27, 216n16
Texas: Mexican independence in 1821, 12, 33, 103–4, 110, 157–59; Mexican centralists vs. federalists conflicts, 159; Nuevo Santander settlements, 33, 150–57, 169, 195; San Antonio de Béxar, presidio and villa of, 19–20, 32, 154, 158, 182; semifeudal *rancho* system, 31, 33, 149–50, 155–56, 168–75; Texas independence in 1836, 12, 151, 159, 182–83, 238n152; US annexation of Texas Republic in 1845, 12, 151, 159, 161. *See also* Alamo, the; debt peonage in Nuevo Santander/Texas; Guadalupe-Hidalgo, Treaty of; Indigenous dispossession: in Texas; Mexican colonialism; Spanish colonialism; US-Mexican War
Texas Rangers: McNelly and, 163, 236n86; *rinche* violence against Tejanos/as, 5, 160–69, 177, 185, 189–98, 201, 237n117
Their Dogs Came with Them (Viramontes), 17, 207
Thorne, Tanis C., 70–72
Tierra Amarilla courthouse raid, 125–26. *See also* Federal Land Grant Alliance; Tijerina, Reies López
Tierra Amarilla land claims, 116, 126, 143, 228n129

Tijerina, Reies López, 125–126. *See also* Federal Land Grant Alliance
Tomba, Massimiliano, 93
Trail of Tears, 46, 56, 62, 73. *See also* Indigenous removal and relocation
Truett, Samuel, 18
Turner, Fredrick Jackson, 10, 41, 105
Twitchell, Ralph E., 132

Ulibarrí, Sabine R., 144. *See also individual works*
Under the Texas Sun (Espinoza), 184
United States: Civil War, 24, 63, 163, 183–84, 205; democracy and equality, myths of, 11–12, 36; homesteading vs. land speculation, 34–40, 64, 79, 107, 120, 128–43; land policies, 5, 11, 26, 34–41, 47, 49, 61–67; narrative of free vacant land, 10, 12, 27, 35–43, 59, 99–100, 167; preemptions acts, 37–38, 120, 218n51, 220n28; public land, 35–39, 42–43, 106–07, 115–21, 137, 157; westward movement, 10, 41. *See also* Gadsden Purchase; Indigenous dispossession; Louisiana Purchase; US colonialism; US-Mexican War
US acts. *See* Burke Act and Oklahoma Enabling Act of 1906 (Forced Fee Patenting Act); Curtis Act of 1898; Dawes Act of 1887; Homestead Act of 1862; Indian Appropriation Act of 1904; Indian Citizenship Act of 1924; Indian Removal Act of 1830; Indian Reorganization Act of 1934 (Wheeler-Howard Act); Indian Self Determination and Education and Assistance Act of 1975; Oklahoma Closure Act (Crime of 1908); Oklahoma Enabling Act of 1906; Oklahoma Indian Welfare Act of 1936; Osage Removal Act of 1870; Preemption Act of 1841; Relocation Act of 1956 (Public Law 949)

US agencies, commissions, policies, and reports. *See* Bureau of Indian Affairs (BIA); Federal Bureau of Investigation (FBI); Indian Claims Commission of 1955; Meriam Report of 1928; New Deal policies
US colonialism, 3, 10–18, 20, 34–35, 40–42, 63, 87–91; replacing Mexican/Spanish colonialism, 105, 112–20, 131–34, 145–67, 181. *See also* Indigenous dispossession
US court decisions: *See Cherokee Nation v. Georgia* (1830); Court of Private Land Claims; *Lone Wolf v. Hitchcock* (1903)
US-Mexican War of 1846–48, 30, 35, 39, 95, 100; invasion of New Mexico, 105–14, 118, 131, 134, 137; invasion of Mexico, 149, 151, 154, 159–62, 168–74, 185–89. *See also* Guadalupe-Hidalgo Treaty of 1848
US treaties: *See* Adams-Onís (1819); Big Tree (1797); Buffalo Creek (1838); Greenville (1795); Guadalupe-Hidalgo (1848); Pinckney (1795)

Valerio-Jiménez, Omar S., 19, 152–56, 161, 184, 197
Van Ness, John, 18
Venegas, Daniel, 184, 186. *See also individual works*
Veracini, Lorenzo, 27
Vigil, Maurilio, 112, 127
Viñas, David, 4, 33
Viramontes, Helena María, 17, 207. *See also individual works*
Voz del pueblo, La (newspaper), 120–23

Wallace, Anthony F. C., 44, 46
Weber, David J., 18–22, 30–31, 93–98, 103–5, 120, 156–60, 167
We Fed Them Cactus (Cabeza de Baca) 124, 137–41

Westphall, Victor, 96, 99, 102, 106, 109
Wevokah and the Ghost Dance, 56, 66, 73, 89–90
Wheeler-Howard Act. *See* Indian Appropriation Act
Wilkins, David E., 60
Wilson, Terry P., 53, 73, 76, 79

Wounded Knee Massacre, 52, 56, 63, 66

Y no se lo tragó la tierra (Rivera), 179, 204, 209–10
Young, Elliott, 18

"Zoo Island" (Rivera), 209–10

www.ingramcontent.com/pod-product-compliance
Lightning Source LLC
Chambersburg PA
CBHW050213240426
43671CB00013B/2321